COMMENTARIES

ON THE

CONFLICT OF LAWS,

FOREIGN AND DOMESTIC,

IN REGARD TO

CONTRACTS, RIGHTS, AND REMEDIES,

AND ESPECIALLY IN REGARD TO

MARRIAGES, DIVORCES, WILLS, SUCCESSIONS, AND JUDGMENTS.

BY

JOSEPH STORY, LL.D.

EIGHTH EDITION.

BY

MELVILLE M. BIGELOW.

BOSTON:

LITTLE, BROWN, AND COMPANY.

1883.

CHAPTER IX.

PERSONAL PROPERTY.

374. *Subjects to be considered.* — We next come to the consideration of the operation of foreign law in relation to personal, real, and mixed property, according to the known divisions of the common law, or to movable and immovable property, according to the known divisions of the civil law and continental jurisprudence. For all the purposes of the present commentaries it will be sufficient to treat the subject under the heads of personal or movable property, and real or immovable property, (*a*) since the class of mixed property appertains to the latter.[1]

375. *Terms of Foreign Law.* — We have already had occasion to state that in the civil law the term 'bona' includes all sorts of property, movable and immovable; as the corresponding word 'biens,' in French, also does.[2] But there are many cases in which a broad distinction is taken by foreign jurists between movable property and immovable property, as to the operation of foreign law. We have also had occasion to explain the general distinction between personal and real laws respectively, and mixed laws, in the sense in which the terms are used in continental jurisprudence; personal being those which have principally persons for their objects, and only treating of property incidentally; real, being those which have principally property for their object, and speaking of persons only in relation to pro-

---

[1] See on the subject of this chapter, 3 Burge, Col. & For. Law, pt. 2, c. 20, p. 749-780.

[2] See Livermore, Dissert. p. 81, s. 106; 1 Boullenois, obs. 2, p. 28; Id. obs. 6, p. 127; Rodenburg, de Divers. Stat. tit. 1, c. 2; 2 Boullenois, Appx. p. 6; Merlin, Répert. Biens, s. 1.

(*a*) Leasehold or chattel interests in land are classed as immovables. Freke *v.* Carbery, L. R. 16 Eq. 461; In bonis Gentili, Ir. R. 9 Eq. 541. But see Despard *v.* Churchill, 53 N. Y. 192.

perty; and mixed, being those which concern both persons and property.[1]

376. *Doctrine concerning Movables.* — According to this distribution all laws respecting property, whether it be movable or immovable, would fall under the denomination of real laws; and of course, upon the principles of the leading foreign jurists, would seem to be limited in their operation to the territory where the property is situate.[2] This however is a conclusion which upon a larger examination will be found to be erroneous, the general doctrine held by nearly all foreign jurists being that the right and disposition of movables is to be governed by the law of the domicil of the owner, and not by the law of their local situation.[3]

377. *Grounds of the Doctrine.* — The grounds upon which this doctrine as to movables is supported, are differently stated by different jurists; but the differences are more nominal than real. Some of them are of opinion that all laws which regard movables are real; but at the same time they maintain that, by a fiction of law, all movables are supposed to be in the place of the domicil of the owner, a quo legem situmque accipiunt. Others are of opinion that such laws are personal, because movables have in contemplation of law no situs, and are attached to the person of the owner, wherever he is; and being so adherent to his person, they are governed by the same laws which govern his person, that is, by the law of the place of his domicil.[4] The former

---

[1] Ante, s. 12–16; 1 Boullenois, Princ. Gén. p. 4–9; Id. obs. 2, p. 29; Id. obs. 6, p. 122–127; P. Voet, de Statut. s. 4, c. 2, n. 2, p. 117, ed. 1715; Id. p. 130, 131, ed. 1661.

[2] Thus Muhlenbruch (Doctrina Pandectarum, vol. 1, lib. 1, s. 72, p. 167) lays down the following rule: Jura, quæ proxime rebus sunt scripta, velut quæ ad dominii causam spectant, vel ad vectigalium tributorumque onus, vel ad pignorum in judicati executionem et capiendorum et distrahendorum, tum etiam rerum apud judicem petendarum persequendarumve rationem, et quæ sunt reliqua ex hoc genere, æstimantur ex legibus ejus civitatis, ubi sitæ sunt res, de quibus agitur, atque collocatæ, nullo rerum immobilium atque mobilium habito discrimine.

[3] See ante, s. 362; post, s. 377–380. See Foelix, Conflit des Lois, Revue Étrang. et Franç. tom. 7, 1840, p. 216–218, 221–227. See Cockerell *v.* Dickens, 3 Moore P. C. 98, 132; Thomson *v.* Advocate-General, 13 Sim. 153, 160; 12 Cl. & F. 1; In re Bruce, 2 C. & J. 436.

[4] 'Mobilia,' says John Voet, 'vero ex lege domicilii ipsius defuncti, vel quia semper domino præsentia esse finguntur, vel ex comitate passim usu inter gentes recepta.' J. Voet, ad Pand. 38, 17, 34, p. 596. And in another place

opinion is maintained by Paul Voet, Rodenburg, and Boullenois ; and the latter by D'Argentré, Burgundus, Hertius, and Bouhier.[1] Paul Voet says : ' Verum mobilia ibi censeantur esse, secundum juris intellectum, ubi is, cujus ea sunt, sedem atque larem suarum fortunarum collocavit.'[2] So Rodenburg: 'Mobilia quippe illa non ideo subjacent statuto (reali), quod personale illud sit ; sed quod mobilia, certo ac fixo situ carentia, ibi quemque situm velle habere, ac existere intelligimus, ubi larem ac fortunarum fixit summam, etc. In domicilii loco mobilia intelligantur existere.'[3] Again, in another place he says : ' Et quidem, de mobilibus si quæratur, cum semper ibi esse existimentur, ubi creditor foret domicilium, cujus ossibus vagæ hæ res intelliguntur adhærere.'[4] Boullenois affirms the same doctrine, and gives this reason for it, that, as movables have no such fixed and perpetual situs as lands have, it is necessary that their situs should depend upon the pleasure of the owner, and that they have the very situs which he wishes, when they have that of his own domicil.[5]

378. *D'Argentré.* — On the other hand, D'Argentré says : ' De mobilibus alia censura est ; quoniam per omnia ex conditione personarum legem accipiunt, et situm habere negantur, nisi affixa et cohærentia, nec loco contineri dicuntur propter habilitatem motionis et translationis. Quare statutum de bonis mobilibus vere personale est, et loco domicilii judicium sumit ; et quod-

he adds: ' Sed considerandum, quadam fictione juris, seu malis, præsumptione, hanc de mobilibus determinationem conceptam niti ; cum enim certo stabilique hæc (mobilia) situ careant, nec certo sint alligata loco ; sed ad arbitrium domini undiquaque in domicilii locum revocari facile ac reduci possint, et maximum domino plerumque commodum adferre soleant, cum ei sunt præsentia ; visum fuit hanc inde conjecturam surgere, quod dominus velle censeatur, ut illuc omnia sua sint mobilia, aut saltem esse intelligantur, ubi fortunarum suarum larem summamque constituit ; id est, in loco domicilii.' J. Voet, ad Pand. 1, 4, 2, s. 11, p. 44. Hertius says : ' Nam mobiles ex conditione personæ legem accipiunt, nec loco continentur.' 1 Hertii Opera, de Collis. Leg. s. 4, n. 6, p. 122, 123, ed. 1737 ; Id. p. 174, ed. 1716 ; Foelix, Conflit des Lois, Revue Étrang. et Franç. 1840, tom. 7, p. 221, 222 ; ante, s. 362.

[1] Livermore, Dissert. p. 128, 129 ; 1 Boullenois, obs. 19, p. 338–340 ; 1 Hertii Opera, de Collis. Leg. s. 4, c. 2, n. 6, p. 122, 123, ed. 1737 ; Id. p. 174, ed. 1716.

[2] P. Voet, de Stat. s. 4, c. 2, n. 2, p. 118, ed. 1715 ; Id. s. 9, c. 1, s. 8, p. 255 ; Id. p. 132, 309, ed. 1661.

[3] Rodenburg, de Divers. Stat. tit. 1, c. 2, sub finem ; 2 Boullenois, Appx. p. 6 ; 1 Boullenois, obs. 2, p. 25, 28 ; Id. obs. 6, p. 140.

[4] Rodenburg, de Divers. Stat. tit. 2, c. 5, s. 16 ; 2 Boullenois, Appx. 48.

[5] Boullenois, obs. 16, p. 223, 224 ; Id. obs. 19, p. 338 ; Id. Prin. Gén. 33, p. 8 ; 3 Burge, Col. & For. Law, pt. 1, c. 20, p. 750, 751.

cunque judex domicilii de eo statuit, ubique locum obtinet. Observatio indubita est, mobilia personam sequi, nec situ judicari, aut a locis judicium accipere.'[1] Bouhier is quite as explicit. As movables, says he, have no fixed situs, and are easily transported from one place to another, according to the pleasure of the owner, therefore it is supposed, by a sort of fiction, that they adhere to his person; and from hence comes the maxim in our customary law, that movables follow the body or person of the owner; meubles suivent le corps, ou la personne, mobilia sequuntur personam.[2]

878 a. *Burgundus.* — *Hertius.* — Burgundus puts the doctrine in the strongest form. 'Puto equidem,' says he, 'mobilia sequi conditionem personæ, id est, si persona fuerit servituti obnoxia bona quoque ejus mobilia libera esse desinere, cum apud nos servitus magis sit bonorum, quam personæ. Ut puta, si quis natus in simili regione territorii Alostensis, inde postea alio migraverit, atque decesserit, bona ejus mobilia quocunque loco reperta, cedunt natalis soli dominio. Quia perinde haberi debent, ac si per eventum nativitatis, alienæ se potestati, ac dominio defunctus subjecisset. Non aliter quam mobilia clerici, quæ et conditionem ejus sequuntur. Sed tamen, ut existimem, bona moventia, et mobilia ita comitari personam, ut extra domicilium ejus censeantur existere, adduci sane non possum. Quod neque rationi, neque juri scripto congruat, sicuti nec doctorum opinionibus, aut forensi usu firmatur. Credo ego, mobilia comitari personam quamdiu domicilium non habet. Quod utique procedere poterit, si quis domicilio relicto naviget, vel iter faciat, quærens quo se conferat, atque ubi domicilium constituat.'[3] Hertius says: 'Nam mobiles ex conditione personæ legem accipiunt, nec loco continentur.'[4]

879. *Probable Origin of the Doctrine.* — But, whether the one

---

[1] D'Argentré, de Leg. Brit. tom. 1, des Donations, art. 218, gloss. 6, n. 30, p. 654; Livermore, Dissert. s. 213, p. 128–130; 1 Boullenois, obs. 19, p. 339.

[2] Bouhier, Cout. de Bourg. c. 25, s. 2, p. 490; 1 Boullenois, obs. 19, p. 338. 'Les meubles,' says Cochin, 'quelque sorte qu'ils soient, suivent le domicile.' Cochin, Œuvres, tom. 5, p. 85, 4to ed.; 2 Henry, Œuvres, lib. 4, c. 6, quest. 105, p. 612; Id. 720; ante, s. 362; 3 Burge, Col. & For. Law, pt. 2, c. 20, p. 750, 751; Foelix, Conflit des Lois, Revue Étrang. et Franç. tom. 7, s. 32, p. 221, 222.

[3] Burgundus, tract. 2, n. 20, p. 71, 72.

[4] 1 Hertii Opera, de Collis. Leg. s. 4, n. 6, p. 122, 123, ed. 1737; Id. p. 174, ed. 1716; ante, s. 362. See J. Voet, Comm. ad Pand. 2, 38, 17, n. 34, p. 596.

opinion or the other is adopted, it has been truly remarked by Boullenois that the same conclusion is equally true, that movables follow the person.[1] The probability is, that the doctrine itself had not its origin in any distinction between real laws or personal laws, or in any fictitious annexation of them to the person of the owner, or in their incapacity to have a fixed situs; but in an enlarged policy, growing out of their transitory nature and the general convenience of nations. If the law rei sitæ were generally to prevail in regard to movables, it would be utterly impossible for the owner in many cases to know in what manner to dispose of them during his life, or to distribute them at his death, not only from the uncertainty of their situation in the transit to and from different places, but from the impracticability of knowing, with minute accuracy, the law of transfers inter vivos, or of testamentary dispositions and successions in the different countries in which they might happen to be. Any change of place at a future time might defeat the best-considered will; and any sale or donation might be rendered inoperative from the ignorance of the parties of the law of the actual situs at the time of their acts. These would be serious evils, pervading the whole community, and equally affecting the subjects and the interests of all civilized nations. But in maritime nations, depending upon commerce for their revenues, their power, and their glory, the mischief would be incalculable. (a) A sense of general utility therefore must have first suggested the doctrine; and as soon as it was promulgated, it could not fail to recommend itself to all nations by its simplicity, its convenience, and its enlarged policy.[2]

---

[1] 1 Boullenois, obs. 19, p. 339. See also J. Voet, ad Pand. 38, 17, s. 34, p. 596; Holmes *v.* Remsen, 4 Johns. Ch. (N.Y.) 487; 1 Burge, Col. & For. Law, pt. 1, c. 1, p. 28, 29; Foelix, Conflit des Lois, Revue Étrang. et Franç. tom. 7, 1840, p. 204–206.

[2] See Harvey *v.* Richards, 1 Mason, 412; ante, s. 372 a. Mr. Justice Bayley, in delivering his opinion in the case of In re Ewin, 1 C. & J. 156, said: ' Now what is the rule with respect to it? It is clear from the authority of Bruce *v.* Bruce, — and the case of Somerville *v.* Somerville, — that the rule is that personal property follows the person, and it is not in any respect to be regulated by the situs; and if in any instance the situs has been adopted as the rule by which the property is to be governed, and the lex loci rei sitæ resorted to, it has been improperly done. Wherever the domicil of the proprietor is,

(a) See Swearingen *v.* Morris, 14 Ohio St. 428.

380. *Its General Recognition.* — But be the origin of the doctrine what it may, it has so general a sanction among all civilized nations that it may now be treated as a part of the jus gentium. (*a*) Lord Loughborough has stated it with great clearness and force in one of his most elaborate judgments. 'It is a clear proposition,' said he, 'not only of the law of England, but of every country in the world where law has the semblance of science, that personal property (*b*) has no locality; The meaning of that is, not that personal property has no visible locality, but that it is subject to that law which governs the person of the owner. With respect to the disposition of it, with respect to the transmission of it, either by succession, or by the act of the party, it follows the law of the person. The owner in any country may dispose of his personal property. If he dies, it is not the law of the country in which the property is, but the law

there the property is to be considered as situate; and in the case of Somerville *v.* Somerville, which was a case in which there was stock in the funds of this country, which were at least as far local as any of the stocks mentioned in this case are local, there was a question whether the succession to that property should be regulated by the English or by the Scotch rules of succession. The Master of the Rolls was of opinion that the proper domicil of the party was in Scotland. And having ascertained that, the conclusion which he drew was, that the property in the English funds was to be regulated by the Scotch mode of succession; and if the executor had, as he no doubt would have, the power of reducing the property into his own possession, and putting the amount into his own pocket, it would be distributed by the law of the country in which the party was domiciled. Personal property is always liable to be transferred, wherever it may happen to be, by the act of the party to whom that property belongs; and there are authorities that ascertain this point, which bears by analogy on this case, namely, that if a trader in England becomes bankrupt, having that which is personal property, debts, or other personal property, due to him abroad, the assignment under the commission of bankruptcy operates upon the property and effectually transfers it, at least against all those persons who owe obedience to these bankrupt laws, the subjects of this country.'

(*a*) Bremer *v.* Freeman, 10 Moore, P. C. 358.

(*b*) Referring to this passage, Lord Selborne said, in Freke *v.* Carbery, L. R. 16 Eq. 466, ' The passage . . . from Story, in which the words of Lord Loughborough were cited with approbation, is simply a translation into the phraseology of the English law of the maxim of the general law, mobilia sequuntur personam, and is certainly not meant to apply arbitrarily in a new sense, because Lord Loughborough used the word " personal " instead of " movable." The doctrine depends upon a principle which is expressed in the Latin words; and that is the only principle of the whole of our law, as to domicil when applicable to the succession of what we call personal estate.' He referred also to s. 447, post.

of the country of which he was a subject, that will regulate the succession.'[1] (a)   The same doctrine was recognized by Lord Chief Justice Abbott on another important occasion. 'Personal property,' said he, 'has no locality, and even with respect to that, it is not correct to say that the law of England gives way to the law of a foreign country, but that it is part of the law of England that personal property should be distributed according to the jus domicilii.'[2]   The same doctrine has been constantly maintained both in England and America, with unbroken confidence and general unanimity.[3] (b)

381. *Foreign Jurists.* — Foreign jurists are not less expressive in its favor. 'Constat inter omnes,' says Bretonnier, 'que les meubles suivent les personnes, et se réglent suivant la coutume du domicile.'[4]   And he speaks but the common language of the continental jurists.[5]   Pothier, after remarking that movables have no locality, adds: 'All things which have no locality follow the person of the owner, and are consequently governed by the law or the custom which governs his person, that is to say, by that of

---

[1] Sill *v.* Worswick, 1 H. Bl. 690; Hoffman *v.* Carow, 22 Wend. (N.Y.) 285, 323.

[2] Birtwhistle *v.* Vardill, 5 B. & C. 438, 451, s. c. 6 Bligh, 32–88; 2 Cl. & F. 571.

[3] The authorities on this point are very numerous. See Henry on Foreign Law, p. 13–15; 4 Cowen (N. Y.) 517, note; 2 Kent Com. 428, 405; Kames Eq. b. 3, c. 8, s. 3, 4; Ersk. Inst. b. 3, tit. 2, s. 40, p. 515; Dwarris on Statutes, 649, 650; In re Ewing, 1 Tyrw. 91; 1 Rose, 478; 5 B. & C. 451, 452; 2 Bell Com. p. 2-10, 4th & 5th ed.; Pipon *v.* Pipon, Ambler, 25; Potter *v.* Brown, 5 East, 130; Holmes *v.* Remsen, 4 Johns. Ch. (N. Y.) 460; Guier *v.* O'Daniel, 1 Binn. (Pa.) 349, note; Bruce *v.* Bruce, 2 B. & P. 229, note; Livermore, Diss. p. 128–132; De Sobrey *v.* De Laistre, 2 Harr. & J. (Md.) 191, 224; Hunter *v.* Potts, 4 T. R. 182, 192; Phillips *v.* Hunter, 2 H. Bl. 402, 405; Goodwin *v.* Jones, 3 Mass. 514, 517; Blake *v.* Williams, 6 Pick. (Mass.) 286, 314; 3 Burge, Col. & For. Law, pt. 2, c. 20, p. 749–753; French *v.* Hall, 9 N. H. 137; Cockerell *v.* Dickens, 3 Moore P. C. 98, 131, 132.

[4] 2 Henrys, Œuvres, lib. 4, quest. 127, p. 720.

[5] See 1 Boullenois, obs. 18, p. 328; obs. 19, p. 339, 340; Bouhier, c. 22, p. 429, s. 79, c. 25, p. 490, s. 2; 5 Cochin, Œuvres, 85; Livermore, Dissert. s. 212–216, p. 129, 130; Huberus, de Confl. Leg. lib. 1, tit. 3, s. 15.   See Foelix, Conflit des Lois, Revue Étrang. et Franç. tom. 7, 1840, s. 32–35, p. 221-229.

(a) See Thomson *v.* Advocate-General, 12 Clark & F. 1.

(b) See note to s. 383, post. But the laws of one state cannot regulate the transfer, by operation of law, of property located in another. Receiver *v.* First National Bank, 34 N. J. Eq. 450.

the place of his domicil.'[1]   Merlin adopts language equally general and exact. 'Movables,' says he, 'are governed by the law of the domicil of the owner, wherever they may be situate; and this law of course changes with his change of domicil.'[2] Bynkershoek asserts the principle to be so well established that no one has dared to question it: 'Adeo recepta hodie sententia est, ut nemo ausit contra hiscere.'[3] Huberus says: 'Verum in mobilibus nihil esse causæ, cur aliud, quam jus domicilii sequamur; quia res mobiles non habent affectionem versus territorium, sed ad personam patrisfamilias duntaxat, qui aliud, quam quod in loco domicilii obtinebat, voluisse obtinere non potest.'[4] So that there seems a general although not an entire harmony on this point between foreign jurists and domestic jurists.[5]

[1] Póthier, Coutume d'Orléans, c. 1, s. 2, tom. 10, p. 7, 4to ed.; Id. Traité des Choses, s. 3, tom. 8, p. 109, 4to ed.

[2] Merlin, Répert. Biens,'s. 1, n. 12; Id. Meubles, s. 1; Id. Loi, s. 6, n. 3.

[3] 2 Kent Com. 429; Bynkershoek, Quest. Priv. Juris. lib. 1, c. 16, p. 179, 180, ed. 1744. Bynkershoek, in the passage here referred to, is speaking of the right of succession; but his language has been thought susceptible of a broader interpretation. See post, s. 483.

[4] Huberus, ps. 1, lib. 3, tom. 1, de Success. ab Intest. n. 21 (s).

[5] See Foelix, Conflit des Lois, Revue Étrang. et Franç. tom. 7, 1840, s. 82-85, p. 221-229. See also Muhlenbruch, Doctr. Pand. 1, 1, s. 72, 73, p. 166-170, who seems to make the law rei situs govern in many cases, as well with respect to movables as immovables. Jura, quæ proxime rebus sunt scripta, vel quæ ad dominii causam spectant, etc., æstimantur ex legibus ejus civitatis, ubi sitæ res, de quibus agitur, atque collocatæ, nullo rerum immobilium atque mobilium habito discrimine. Id. s. 72. Mr. Foelix says on this subject: 'Par la nature des choses, les meubles, soit corporels, soit incorporels, n'ont pas, à l'égal des immeubles, une assiette fixe dans l'endroit où ils se trouvent de fait: ils dépendent nécessairement de la personne de l'individu à qui ils appartiennent, et ils subissent la destination qu'il leur donne. Chaque individu étant légalement censé avoir réuni sa fortune au lieu de son domicile, c'est-à-dire au siège principal de ses affaires, on a toujours regardé en droit les meubles comme se trouvant au lieu du domicile de celui à qui ils appartiennent; peu importe si, de fait, ils se trouvent ou non au dit lieu. Par une fiction légale, on les considère comme suivant la personne, et comme étant soumis à la même loi qui régit l'état et la capacité de cette personne; et nous avons vu (supra, n°. 21) que cette loi est celle du domicile (mobilia sequuntur personam; mobilia ossibus inhærent). En d'autres termes, le statut personnel gouverne les meubles corporels ou incorporels. Ce statut est à leur égard réel, par suite de la fiction qui les répute se trouver au lieu régi par ce même statut. Tel a toujours été le sentiment presque unanime des auteurs et des cours de justice. Témoins Dumoulin, Chopin, Bretonnier, d'Argentré, Brodeau, Lebrun, Poullain du Parc, Burgundus, Rodenburg, Abraham à Wesel, Paul Voet, Jean Voet, Sande, Christin, Gail, Carpzov, Wernher, Mevius, Franzké, Boullenois, Pothier, Struve, Leyser, Huber, Hert, Hommel, Danz, Glück, Thibaut, Merlin, MM.

382. *Movables annexed to Immovables.* — When however we speak of movables as following the person of the owner, and as governed by the law of his domicil, we are to limit the doctrine to the cases in which they may be properly said to retain their original and natural character. For movables may become annexed to immovables, either by incorporation or as incidents; and then they take the character of the latter.[1] Thus in the language of the common law, movables annexed to the freehold are deemed a part of the latter. Such are the common cases of fixtures of personal property in houses, in mills, and in other hereditaments, whether for use or for ornament. In the law of foreign countries a similar distinction is recognized; and wherever movables become thus fixed by operation of law, or by the express determination of the owner, they are deemed a part of the immovable property.[2] John Voet ranks them among immovables. 'Idemque statuendum in mobilibus, per patrisfamilias destinationem perpetui usus gratia ad certum locum, domum puta, vel

Mittermaier, Hauss, Meier, Favard, Duranton, Story, Wheaton, Rocco, et Burge. Trois auteurs seulement ne sont pas entièrement d'accord, en cette matière, avec ceux que nous venons de citer: ce sont Tittman, M. Mühlenbruch, et M. Eichhorn. Le premier, en soumettant les meubles à la même loi qui régit les immeubles, ne s'attache qu'à l'un des cas exceptionnels, dont nous parlerons au n° 33 ci-après, sans examiner la règle elle-même. M. Mühlenbruch repousse toute distinction entre les meubles et les immeubles par rapport à la loi qui les régit, par le seul motif, que l'opinion contraire établirait une différence entre la succession dans les immeubles et celle dans les meubles du même individu; nous démontrerons ci-après la nécessité de reconnaître cette différence. M. Eichhorn, en rejetant l'application de la loi de la situation des meubles, n'admet cependant la règle qu'avec la modification que, selon les circonstances, il faudra appliquer la loi du lieu où la cause se plaidera: il cite comme exemple le cas où le défendeur en revendication invoque la maxime, qu'en fait de meubles possession vaut titre.' Foelix, Conflit des Lois, Revue Étrang. et Franç. 1840, tom. 7, s. 32, p. 221-224. (a)

[1] Ante, s. 371; post, s. 447.
[2] Pothier, Traité des Choses, s. 1; Id. Coutume d'Orléans, c. 3, art. 46-48; Merlin, Répert. Biens, s. 1, n. 18, s. 2, n. 1; Id. Meubles, s. 2, 3; 1 Bell Com. s. 660, p. 648-652, 4th ed.; 2 Bell Com. p. 2-4, 4th ed.; 1 Bell Com. p. 752-755, and 2 Bell Com. p. 1-10; 1 Boullenois, obs. 19, p. 340, 841; 1 Kames on Equity, b. 3, c. 8, s. 3; Ersk. Inst. b. 3, tit. 9, s. 4.

(a) In the section following that from which the above-quoted extract is made, Foelix mentions the cases in which the rule mobilia sequuntur personam is applicable, and those in which it has no application, and he gives examples of both classes of cases. This section is quoted at length, ante s. 322 *b*, in the author's note; and is translated by Westlake in his second edition, p. 158.

fundum, delatis, it aut perpetuo illic istius usus causa mansura sint, etiamsi vel nunquam immobilibus naturaliter jungenda sint, vel ex destinatione jungenda, necdum tamen inceperint immobilibus juncta esse, modo ad ipsas ædes fundosve, quibus jungenda sunt, delata fuerint.'[1] Among the class of immovables are also ranked, as we have seen, heritable bonds by the Scottish law, and ground rents, and other rents charged on lands.[2]

883. *Transfer of Movables by the Lex Domicilii.* — It follows as a natural consequence of the rule which we have been considering (that personal property has no locality) that the laws of the owner's domicil should in all cases determine the validity of every transfer, alienation, or disposition made by the owner, whether it be inter vivos, or be post mortem.[3] And this is regularly true, unless there is some positive or customary law of the country where they are situate, providing for special cases (as is sometimes done), or, from the nature of the particular property, it has a necessarily implied locality.[4] Lord Mansfield has mentioned, as among the latter class, contracts respecting the public funds or stocks, the local nature of which requires them to be carried into execution according to the local law.[5] The same rule may properly apply to all other local stock or funds, although of a personal nature, or so made by the local law, such as bank stock, insurance stock, turnpike, canal, and bridge shares, and other incorporeal property owing its existence to, or regulated by,

[1] J. Voet, ad Pand. 1, 8, 14, p. 67.

[2] 1 Bell Com. s. 660, p. 648–652; 2 Bell Com. p. 2–4, 4th ed.; Ersk. Inst. b. 2, c. 2, s. 9–20; Pothier, Traité des Choses, s. 8; ante, s. 366, 367, and note; post, s. 447.

[3] Livermore, Dissert. s. 215–220, p. 130–137; French v. Hall, 9 N. H. 137; Sessions v. Little, 9 N. H. 271.

[4] Mr. Chief Justice Tilghman on one occasion said: ' The proposition' (that personal property has no locality, but is transferred according to the law of the country in which the owner is domiciled) ' is true in general, but not to its utmost extent, nor without several exceptions. In one sense personal property has locality, that is to say, if tangible, it has a place in which it is situated, and if invisible (consisting of debts), it may be said to be in the place where the debtor resides; and of these circumstances the most liberal nations have taken advantage, by making such property subject to regulations which suit their own convenience.' ' Every country has a right of regulating the transfer of all personal property within its territory; but when no positive regulation exists, the owner transfers it at his pleasure.' Milne r. Moreton, 6 Binn. (Penn.) 361; 3 Burge, Col. & For. Law, pt. 2, c. 20, p. 751, 752; ante, s. 364 and note.

[5] Robinson v. Bland, 2 Burr. 1079; 1 W. Bl. 247; ante, s. 364.

peculiar local laws.[1] No positive transfer can be made of such property except in the manner prescribed by the local regulations.[2] But nevertheless contracts to transfer such property would be valid if made according to the lex domicilii of the owner, or the lex loci contractus, unless such contracts were specially prohibited by the lex rei sitæ; and the property would be treated as personal, or as real, in the course of administration, according to the local law.[3] (a)

[1] 2 Bell Com. p. 4, 5, 4th ed.; Id. p. 1-10, 5th ed.; 1 Id. p. 65, 67, 68, 4th ed.; Id. p. 105-108, 5th ed.; 3 Burge, Col. & For. Law, pt. 2, c. 20, p. 750-752. Mr. Burge says that, although stocks of this nature can only be transferred according to the forms of the lex rei sitæ, so as to confer a legal title on the purchaser, yet it will give the purchaser a right of action to compel the vendor to make a transfer in the manner required by the local law. Ibid.; ante, s. 364, note. Erskine, in his Institutes (b. 3, tit. 9, s. 4), puts the like exceptions. 'We must except,' says he, 'from this general rule, as civilians have done, certain movables, which by the destination of the deceased are considered as immovables. Among these may be reckoned the shares of the trading companies, or of the public stocks of any country, for example, the Banks of Scotland, England, and Holland, the South Sea Company, &c., which are, without doubt, descendible, according to the law of the state where such stocks are fixed. But the bonds or notes of such companies make no exception from the general rule. They are accounted part of the movable estate of the deceased.' Ante, s. 364, 365; post, s. 398; Robertson on Successions, p. 94, 95. See Attorney-General v. Dimond, 1 C. & J. 356, 370, 371; Attorney-General v. Hope, 1 C. M. & R. 538; 8 Bligh, 44; 2 Cl. & F. 84; Attorney-General v. Bouwens, 4 M. & W. 171, 191-193; post, s. 432.

[2] Though stock abroad may be, as to its transfer, affected by the local laws, it is not to be treated, as of course, as partaking of the character of real estate, and descendible as such. On the contrary, if it be by the local law personal estate, it may be disposed of by an administration as such; and the title passes, if it be made in the forms prescribed by the foreign law. See Attorney-General v. Dimond, 1 Tyrw. 243; In re Ewing, 1 Tyrw. 91; Ersk. Inst. b. 3, tit. 9, s. 4; 1 Bell Com. p. 65; 2 Bell Com. p. 4, 5, 4th & 5th ed.; ante, s. 364, 365.

[3] Abbott on Shipping, pt. 1, c. 2, s. 10; 1 Chitty on Comm. & Manuf. 556, 558, 569, &c.; 2 Kent Com. 145, 146.

(a) *Mobilia sequuntur Personam.* — The exceptions to the maxim mobilia sequuntur personam have become so numerous that it cannot be safely invoked for the decision of any but the simplest cases at the present day; if indeed a case can ever be safely decided upon a maxim. The exceptions would probably be less frequent if the maxim were lex *situs* mobilia regit. But no maxim is needed; any would be apt to mislead. The question is, how far will a state permit a non-resident having personalty within its limits, or the creditors resident or non-resident of such a person, or the course of the foreign law under which the non-resident owner is domiciled, to control that property; and this question should be decided upon its merits, uninfluenced by maxim. The answer to the question will depend partly on the nature of the property and partly upon the mode of disposing of it or affecting it.

The author has in s. 383 referred to certain cases in which, from ' the local nature' of the property, the mode of disposition must be controlled by the law of the situs. These are contracts relating to the public funds or stocks, and to private funds or stocks whose existence arises under or is regulated by peculiar local laws, such as bank, insurance, turnpike, canal, bridge, and the like stocks. The transfer of ships and of goods in the warehouses or in the docks of the government is also mentioned in s. 384.

The mode of disposition is a more common factor in the question of the law to be applied; and the answer will be more or less varied according as the disposition is by will, intestacy, gift, sale, mortgage, assignment, or contract, or by proceedings in bankruptcy or insolvency.

To dispose of personalty within a particular state or country by will, it is only necessary that the execution and terms of the will should conform to the law of the foreign testator's domicil at the time of his death. Moultrie v. Hunt, 23 N. Y. 394; Parsons v. Lyman, 20 N. Y. 103; Knox v. Jones, 47 N. Y. 389; Lawrence v. Kitteridge, 21 Conn. 577; Swearingen v. Morris, 14 Ohio St. 424; Fellows v. Miner, 119 Mass. 541; Gilman v. Gilman, 52 Me. 165; post, s. 465. The law of the domicil governs also the capacity of the testator at the time of making the will. Lawrence v. Kitteridge, supra. But with regard to probate jurisdiction, it is held that a bond left by a testator has its situs where it was left, and is assets there. Beers v. Shannon, 73 N. Y. 292.

It is held also that in the matter of the execution of a power of appointment of personalty conferred by a testator upon a donee, the law of the domicil of the donor and owner of the property, not that of the donee of the power, will govern, especially when the property is held and controlled in the domicil of the donor. Sewall v. Wilmer, 132 Mass. 131; Bingham's Appeal, 64 Penn. St. 345.

The distribution of the estate of an intestate domiciled in another state at the time of his death will also be controlled by the law of the decedent's domicil. Thorne v. Watkins, 2 Ves. 35; Bempde v. Johnstone, 3 Ves. 196; Moye v. May, 8 Ired. Eq. (N.C.) 131; Noonan v. Kemp, 34 Md. 73; Wilkins v. Ellett, 9 Wall. 740; Parsons v. Lyman, 20 N. Y. 103. And in the case of a married woman's personalty, in the absence of a matrimonial contract the matrimonial domicil governs. Noonan v. Kemp, supra; Newcomer v. Orem, 2 Md. 297. This however supposes that the interests of creditors in the state of the situs are not involved; when such interests are interposed, the estate will first be distributed among them to the amount of the debts due. ' After the death of the owner the property has a situs, and then the disposition of the property among the creditors is to be regulated by the lex rei sitæ.' Moore v. Bonnell, 2 Vroom (N. J.) 90; Moye v. May, supra.

In the case of disposition by gift, sale, mortgage, or assignment of property located in the domicil of the parties, the law of the place of the transaction will govern the validity and force of the same, at least where citizens of the state of the forum are not concerned by having a lien on or right to the property. Some question of this proposition has been made, and domestic creditors have sometimes been

ble transfer of ships and of goods in the warehouses or in the docks of a government, which would fall within the same predi-

allowed to seize property of the debtor brought within their state, which he had legally conveyed by the law of his domicil, but not by that of the forum. Skiff v. Solace, 23 Vt. 279. But this case was overruled in Jones v. Taylor, 30 Vt. 42. See also Mead v. Dayton, 28 Conn. 33; Bush v. Edgerly, 81 N.Y. 199. In the last cited case it was doubted whether, after a title to pro- perty had been acquired by the law of a vendor's domicil, and of the situs and forum, such title could be treated as divested, in a contest between citi- zens of that forum, by the surrepti- tious removal of the property into another state and sale of it there under different laws. It was thought that the decisions were opposed to such a result. The following cases were cited as authority: Taylor v. Boardman, 25 Vt. 581; Martin v. Hill, 12 Barb. (N. Y.) 631; French v. Hall, 9 N. H. 137; Langworthy v. Little, 12 Cush. (Mass.) 109.

It is apprehended that the law to be applied in these cases, unless the situ- ation is very peculiar, is that of the situs. It has often been declared in England that if personalty is disposed of in a way binding where it is situ- ated, that disposition is binding every- where. Cammell v. Sewell, 3 Hurl. & N. 617, 638, Pollock, C. B.; 5 Hurl. & N. 728, 744; Castrique v. Imrie, L.R. 4 H.L. 414. 429, intimating the exist- ence of limitations to the rule. And see Pond v. Cooke, 45 Conn. 126; Bal- lard v. Winter, 39 Conn. 179; Jones v. Taylor, 30 Vt. 42; Comer v. Cun- ningham, 77 N. Y. 397. So it has been held in this country that a mortgage of personalty made at its situs, and valid there, will be good on the remo- val of the property to another state. Smith v. McLean, 24 Iowa, 322; Fer- guson v. Clifford, 37 N. H. 86 ; Jones v. Taylor, 30 Vt. 42; Barker v. Stacy,

25 Miss. 471; Blystone v. Burgett, 10 Ind. 28. And this even though the property was but temporarily at the place of the mortgage. Langworthy v. Little, 12 Cush. (Mass.) 100. And if the mortgage is invalid at the situs. it will be invalid on the removal of the property to another jurisdiction. Blystone v. Burgett, supra.

But it has been held that liens given by statute in one state upon movables have no priority over liens afterwards acquired in another state (to which they have been removed) by citizens thereof proceeding in the latter state. Donald v. Hewitt, 33 Ala. 534, 546; Marsh v. Elsworth, 37 Ala. 85; Mer- rick v. Avery, 14 Ark. 370; Wood- ward v. Roane, 23 Ark. 523. How far this view is consistent with sound principle, even if with the fundamen- tal law against impairing the obliga- tion of contracts, deserves to be con- sidered. Cases of this sort carry the consequences of situs to an extreme; the only ground of decision apparently being found in the interests of domes- tic creditors.

On the other hand it has been held that the transfer of a judgment debt according to the lex domicilii of the judgment creditor, though not by the lex situs, should be respected every- where. Clark v. Connecticut Peat Co., 35 Conn. 303. So of an assignment of a claim under an insurance policy. Ib.; Vanbuskirk v. Hartford Ins. Co., 14 Conn. 583. And this even against an attaching creditor in the state of the forum. Clark v. Connecticut Peat Co., supra, denying Worden v. Nourse, 36 Vt. 756. See also Martin v. Potter, 34 Vt. 87, to the same effect as Wor- den v. Nourse. And a mortgage of personalty located in another state will be valid between the parties unless it is shown that a delivery was necessary by the lex loci contractus. Rhode Is-

cament), the general rule is, that a transfer of personal property, good by the law of the owner's domicil, is valid wherever else

land Bank *v.* Danforth, 14 Gray (Mass.) 123. So also an assignment of a vessel at sea in favor of creditors, made in a state in which all the parties reside, will prevail on the arrival of the vessel in another state, if the assignment was valid where made. Southern Bank *v.* Wood, 14 La. An. 554; Thuret *v.* Jenkins, 7 Mart. (La.) 853 ; Crapo *v.* Kelly, 16 Wall. 610, reversing 45 N. Y. 86; post, s. 391. See Fell *v.* Darden, 17 La. An. 236.

A different question arises where the interests of creditors are involved; though some dispute has arisen among the authorities with regard to the effect of voluntary assignments and dispositions made abroad as opposed to transfers by virtue of bankruptcy and insolvency laws. The distinction taken in the text has often been repeated, and in some cases the law of the place of the sale or contract has been applied to voluntary dispositions. Caskie *v.* Webster, 2 Wall. jr. 131; Dundas *v.* Bowler, 3 McLean, 397 (these two cases are overruled by Green *v.* Van Buskirk, infra); Hanford *v.* Paine, 32 Vt. 442; Law *v.* Mills, 18 Penn. St. 185.

But while there may be a distinction for some purposes between voluntary and involuntary assignments, the better opinion is that the distinction should not apply to the cases under consideration, but that the lex situs should govern both. Green *v.* Van Buskirk, 5 Wall. 307; 7 Wall. 139; Hervey *v.* Rhode Island Loc. Works, 93 U. S. 664; Moore *v.* Bonnell, 2 Vroom (N. J.) 90, 94; Varnum *v.* Camp, 1 Green (N. J.) 326; Bentley *v.* Whittemore, 19 N. J. Eq. 462; Ingraham *v.* Geyer, 13 Mass. 146; Fall River Iron Works *v.* Croade, 15 Pick. (Mass.) 11; Zipcey *v.* Thompson, 1 Gray (Mass.) 243; Pierce *v.* O'Brien, 129 Mass. 314; Fox *v.* Adams, 5 Greenl.

(Me.) 245; Richmondville Manuf. Co. *v.* Prall, 9 Conn. 489; Maberry *v.* Shisler, 1 Har. (Del.) 349; Edgerly *v.* Bush, 81 N. Y. 199, 208; Guillander *v.* Howell, 35 N. Y. 657. Of course if the assignment is good both by the lex situs and by the lex domicilii, it will be enforced everywhere. Ockerman *v.* Cross, 54 N. Y. 29.

The doctrine that the lex situs must govern in a question of the rights of creditors was, at the first stage of progress from the application of the lex domicilii, applied only in favor of domestic creditors. See Bentley *v.* Whittemore, 19 N. J. Eq. 462, reversing 18 N. J. Eq. 366. And in this connection may be noticed the discrimination against foreign creditors in cases of contract merely, irrespective of the existence of property; a discrimination which went so far as to declare that a discharge in insolvency of a debtor in the state of the forum upon a contract payable there barred the claims of foreign creditors, whether parties or not to the proceedings. Scribner *v.* Fisher, 2 Gray (Mass.) 43; ante, s. 341, note.

But this doctrine was overruled by the Supreme Court of the United States in Baldwin *v.* Hale, 1 Wall. 223, and the overruling authority has been accepted as final. Stoddard *v.* Harrington, 100 Mass. 88; Kelley *v.* Drury, 9 Allen (Mass.) 28; Pratt *v.* Chase, 44 N. Y. 597; Newmarket Bank *v.* Butler, 45 N. H. 236 (overruling other cases of that state); Felch *v.* Bugbee, 48 Me. 9; Gilman *v.* Lockwood, 4 Wall. 409.

Indeed the progress has been firm in the Supreme Court of the United States; and the just principle has there been reached and applied that no discrimination should be made against foreign creditors; they as well as the domestic creditors being entitled to

the property may be situate.[1] But it does not follow that a transfer made by the owner according to the law of the place of its actual situs would not as completely divest his title, nor even that transfer by him in any other foreign country, which would be good according to the law of that country, would not be equally effectual, although he might not have his domicil there. For purposes of this sort, his personal property may in many cases be deemed subject to his disposal, wherever he may happen to be at

[1] 1 Kames Eq. b. 3, c. 8, s. 3. In the case of a movable subject lying in Scotland, says Erskine, the deed of transmission, if perfected according to the lex domicilii, is effectual to carry the property; for movables have no permanent situation. Ersk, Inst. b. 3, tit. 2, s. 40, p. 515; 3 Burge, Col. & For. Law, pt. 2, c. 20, p. 750–752; ante, s. 364, note.

the benefit of the lex situs in questions of movables. Green v. Van Buskirk, 5 Wall. 307; 7 Wall. 139. See also Paine v. Lester, 44 Conn. 196. But the courts have not all reached this high position, and the law is still in a state of transition (see Bentley v. Whittemore, 19 N. J. Eq. 462, reversing 18 N. J. Eq. 366; ante, s. 325 g), unless the authority of the Supreme Court of the United States is final.

It is agreed however that the law of the situs will govern in favor of creditors domiciled in the state in which the property lies, especially when that is also the state of the forum. Rice v. Courtis, 32 Vt. 460; Clark v. Tarbell, 58 N. H. 88; Osgood v. Maguire, 61 N. Y. 524. The last case cited decides that the claim of a domestic receiver over property of the debtor located within the State will prevail over a subsequent attachment made in another state; casting some doubt upon Taylor v. Columbian Ins. Co., 14 Allen (Mass.) 353.

That the lex situs applies to cases arising under foreign insolvency laws see Baldwin v. Hale, 1 Wall. 223; Dunlap v. Rogers, 47 N. H. 281, 287 (overruling Hall r. Boardman, 14 N. H. 38; Hoag v. Hunt, 21 N. H. 106; Brown v. Collins, 41 N. H. 405; Whitney v. Whiting, 35 N. H. 471); Felch v. Bugbee, 48 Me. 9; Johnson v. Parker, 4 Bush (Ky.) 149; Einer v. Beste, 32 Mo. 240, 251. See Paine v. Lester, 44 Conn. 196. But a legal discharge in insolvency between citizens of the state in which it is granted will be valid everywhere as between *them*. Felch v. Bugbee, 48 Me. 9, 11; Stevens v. Norris, 10 Fost. (N. H.) 466; Brigham v. Henderson, 1 Cush. (Mass.) 430. Comp. Rhode Island Bank v. Danforth, 14 Gray (Mass.) 123. And this even of contracts made and to be performed in another state. Marsh v. Putnam, 3 Gray (Mass.) 551. But concerning the effect in the United States of a discharge granted in a foreign country, see Very v. McHenry, 29 Me. 214; Peck v. Hibbard, 26 Vt. 704; ante, s. 341.

Of course for the purpose of taxation the lex situs will prevail. Graham v. First National Bank, 84 N. Y. 398, 401.

Upon this whole subject of the maxim mobilia sequuntur personam the reader is also referred to Mr. Westlake's chapter 6 in his work on Private International Law (ed. 1880), where the foundation of that maxim is examined and its insufficiency pointed out. And see Wharton, Confl. of Laws, s. 297 et seq., 334 et seq. (2d ed.); Dicey on Domicil, 262; Bar, International Law, s. 59, 60 (trans. by Gillespie); Savigny, s. 366 (Guthrie); ante, s. 322 b, note, quoting Foelix.

the time of the alienation. Thus a merchant domiciled in America may doubtless transfer his personal property according to the law of his domicil, wherever the property may be. But if he should direct a sale of it or make a sale of it in a foreign country, where it is situate at the time, according to the laws thereof, either in person or by an agent, the validity of such a sale would scarcely be doubted. If a merchant is temporarily abroad, he is understood to possess a general authority to transfer such personal property as accompanies his person, wherever he may be; so always that he does not violate the law of the country where the act is done.[1] The general convenience and freedom of commerce require this enlargement of the rule; for otherwise the sale of personal property actually situate in a foreign country, made according to the forms prescribed by its laws, might be declared null and void in the country of the domicil of the owner. In the ordinary course of trade with foreign countries, no one thinks of transferring personal property according to the forms of his own domicil; but it is transferred according to the forms prescribed by the law of the place where the sale takes place.

385. *Conflict between Lex Situs and Lex Domicilii.* — A question involving other considerations may be presented; and that is, whether a transfer of personal property is good, which is made according to the law of the owner's domicil, but not in conformity to the law of the place where it is situate? And whether there is any difference in such a case between the transfer being made by the owner in his place of domicil, or its being made in the place rei sitæ? For instance, let us suppose that, by the law of the domicil of the owner, a sale of goods is complete and perfect to pass the title without any delivery; and that, by the law of the place of their situs, the sale is not complete until delivery. In such a case, if the transfer of the goods is made in the domicil of the owner, would it be valid without any delivery thereof, so as to pass the title against third persons? If it would, in such a case, what would be the effect if the transfer was made in the place where the goods were situate, without any such delivery?

386. *Doctrine in Louisiana.* — The former question has been much discussed in the courts of Louisiana, from a supposed difference between the rule of the common law, and that of the civil law on this subject. By the common law a sale of goods is, or

---

[1] See 1 Kames Eq. b. 3, c. 8, s. 3.

may be, complete without delivery.[1] But by the law of Louisiana delivery is necessary to complete the transfer, according to the well-known rule of the civil law : ' Traditionibus et usucapionibus dominia rerum, non nudis pactis, transferuntur.'[2] Upon the fullest examination, and after repeated arguments, the Supreme Court of Louisiana have held the doctrine that the transfer of personal property in that state is not complete, so as to pass the title against creditors, unless a delivery is made in conformity to the laws of that state, although the transfer is made by the owner in his foreign domicil, and would be good without delivery by the laws of that domicil.[3]

387. *Olivier* v. *Townes.* — The reasoning by which this doctrine is maintained is most fully developed in a case in which a transfer of a part of a ship was made in Virginia, the ship at the time of the sale being locally at New Orleans ; and, before any delivery thereof, she was attached by the creditors of the vendor.[4] It was therefore a case of conflict of rights between the creditor and the purchaser. The learned judge,[5] who delivered the opinion of the court on that occasion, said : ' The position assumed in the present case is, that, by the laws of all civilized countries, the alienation of movable property must be determined according to the laws, rules, and regulations in force where the owner's domicil is situated. Hence it is insisted that, as by the law existing

[1] The common law deems a sale, as between the parties, complete without delivery, but not as to third persons. If therefore a sale is made, the purchaser, in order to complete his title against creditors and other purchasers, must take possession within a reasonable time. Where the property is at sea at the time, and is incapable of delivery, there the title is complete without delivery. But it may be lost by an omission to take possession within a reasonable time after its arrival in port. See Meeker v. Wilson, 1 Gall. 419; 1 Black. Com. 446, 448; 2 Kent Com. 492, 493, 498, 515-522; Bholen v. Cleveland, 5 Mason, 174; 3 Chitty on Comm. & Manuf. c. 5, s. 2, p. 272, &c.; Lanfear v. Sumner, 17 Mass. 110; Bigelow's Digest, Sale, A. B.; post, s. 389. See also Long on Sales, by Rand, ed. 1839, c. 7, p. 259-307.

[2] Cod. 2, 3, 20; Olivier v. Townes, 2 Mart. N.S. (La.) 93, 102; Norris v. Mumford, 4 Mart. (La.) 20; Durnford v. Brooks, 3 Mart. (La.) 222, 225.

[3] The point appears to have been first decided in Norris v. Mumford, 4 Mart. (La.) 20; and it has been repeatedly since adjudged in other cases, and particularly in Ramsey v. Stevenson, 5 Mart. (La.) 23; Fisk v. Chandler, 7 Mart. (La.) 24; and Olivier v. Townes, 2 Mart. N.S. (La.) 93. Mr. Livermore has contested the doctrine asserted in these decisions with great earnestness and ability. Livermore, Dissert. s. 220-223, p. 137-140.

[4] Olivier v. Townes, 2 Mart. N.S. (La.) 93, 102.

[5] Mr. Justice Porter.

in the state where the vendor lived no delivery was necessary to complete the sale, it must be considered as complete here ; and, that it is a violation of the principle just referred to, to apply to the contract rules which are peculiar to our jurisprudence, and different from those contemplated by the parties to the contract.'

888. *Same continued.* — ' We readily yield an assent to the general doctrine for which the appellee contends. He has supported it by a variety of authorities drawn from different systems of jurisprudence. But some of those very books furnish also the exception on which we think this case must be decided, namely, that " when those laws clash with and interfere with the rights of the citizens of the countries where the parties to the contract seek to enforce it, as one or other of them must give way, those prevailing where the relief is sought must have the preference." Such is the language of the English books to which we have been referred ; and Huberus, whose authority is more frequently resorted to on this subject than that of any other writer, because he has treated it more extensively and with greater ability, in his treatise *De Conflictu Legum* (n. 11), tells us, " Effecta contractuum, certo loco initorum, pro jure loci illius alibi quoque observantur, si nullum inde civibus alienis creetur prejudicium, in jure sibi quæsito." The effects of a contract entered into at any place will be allowed, according to the law of that place, in other countries, if no inconvenience will result therefrom to the citizens of that other country, with respect to the right which they demand. This distinction appears to us founded on the soundest reasons. The municipal laws of a country have no force beyond its territorial limits ; and when another government permits these to be carried into effect within her jurisdiction, she does so upon a principle of comity. In doing so, care must be taken that no injury is inflicted on her own citizens ; otherwise justice would be sacrificed to courtesy. Nor can the foreigner or stranger complain of this. If he sends his property within a jurisdiction different from that where he resides, he impliedly submits it to the rules and regulations in force in the country where he places it. What the law protects, it has a right to regulate. A strong evidence of this is furnished by the doctrine in regard to successions. The general principle is, that the personal property must be distributed according to the law of the state where the testator dies ; but, so far as it concerns creditors, it is governed by the law of

the country where the property is situated. If an Englishman or a Frenchman dies abroad and leaves effects here, we regulate the order in which his debts are paid by our jurisprudence, not by that of his domicil,'[1]

389. *Same continued.* — 'We proceed to examine whether giving effect to the law of Virginia, on the contract now set up, would be working an injury to this state or its citizens. In doing this we must look to the general doctrine and the effect it would have on our ordinary transactions, as well as its operation in this particular case. If we held here that this sale can defeat the attachment, we should, on the same principle, be obliged to decide that the claimant would hold the object sold in preference to a second purchaser, to whom it was delivered; the rule being that, when the debtor can sell and give to the buyer a good title, the creditor can seize; or, in other words, where the first sale is not complete as to third persons, the creditor may attach and acquire a lien.[2] In relation to movable property, our law has provided that delivery is essential to complete the contract of sale as to third parties. This valuable provision, by which all our citizens are bound in their dealings, protects them from the frauds to which they would be daily subjects, were they liable to be affected by previous contracts not followed by the giving of possession. The exemption contended for here, in behalf of the residents of another state, would deprive them of that protection, wherever their rights, as purchasers, came in contact with strangers; a protection which, it may be remarked, it is of the utmost importance, owing to our peculiar position, that we should carefully maintain. This city is becoming a vast storehouse for merchandise sent from abroad, owned by non-residents and deposited here for sale; and our most important commercial transactions are in relation to property so situated. If the purchasers of it should be affected by all the previous contracts made at the owner's domicil, although unaccompanied by delivery, it is easy to see to what impositions such a doctrine would lead; to what inconvenience it would expose us; and how severely it would check and embarrass our dealings. However anxious we may be to extend courtesy and afford protection to the people of other countries, who come themselves or send their property within our jurisdiction, we can-

---

[1] Post, s. 524.   [2] M'Neill *v.* Glass, 1 Mart. N.S. (La.) 261.

not indulge our feelings so far as to give a decision that would let in such consequences as we have just spoken of. It would be giving to the foreign purchaser an advantage which the resident has not; and that, frequently, at the expense of the latter. This, in the language of the law, we think, would be a great inconvenience to the citizens of this state; and therefore we cannot sanction it.' [1]

390. *Remarks upon this Reasoning.* — There is certainly great force in this reasoning upon general principles. And no one can seriously doubt that it is competent for any state to adopt such a rule in its own legislation, since it has perfect jurisdiction over all property, personal as well as real, within its own territorial limits.[2] Nor can such a rule, made for the benefit of innocent purchasers and creditors, be deemed justly open to the reproach of being founded in a narrow or a selfish policy. But how far any court of justice ought, upon its own general authority, to interpose such a limitation, independently of positive legislation, has been thought to admit of more serious question; since the doctrine which it unfolds aims a direct blow at the soundness of

[1] Olivier v. Townes, 2 Mart. N.S. (La.) 97–103. But see 1 Kames Eq. b. 3, c. 8, s. 3. The doctrine of this case seems supported by that of Lanfear v. Sumner, 17 Mass. 110, although in the latter case the court do not found their judgment upon any supposed conflict between foreign and domestic laws. There can be little doubt that the sale and assignment in Philadelphia in that case was a complete transfer by the lex loci contractus; and there was certainly legal diligence in endeavoring to obtain possession after the sale. The court however thought that delivery was essential to perfect the transfer by the law of Massachusetts; and as there had been no delivery until the property was attached by the attaching creditor in Massachusetts, they decided in favor of the title of the latter against the vendee. The court also said that where each of the parties claimed the same goods by a legal title, he who first obtained possession would hold against the other; and for this principle they relied on Lamb v. Durant, 12 Mass. 54, and Caldwell v. Ball, 1 T. R. 205. The former case is certainly in point. But in the latter the decision was in favor of the party who first had acquired a legal title by the prior indorsement of the bills of lading to him. 'Whoever,' said Ashhurst, J., ' was first in possession, not of the goods, but of either of these bills of lading, had the legal title vested in him.' Buller, J., said: ' Both parties claim under T.; but F. & Co. have the first legal right, for two bills of lading were first indorsed to them.' But see Conard v. Atlantic Insurance Co., 1 Pet. 386, 445; Nathan v. Giles, 5 Taunt. 558; Bholen v. Cleveland, 5 Mason, 174.

[2] See Livermore, Dissert. s. 221, p. 137, 138; Id. s. 249, p. 159–162; Campbell v. Hall, Cowp. 208; Hunter v. Potts, 4 T. R. 182, 192; Phillips v. Hunter, 2 H. Bl. 402, 405; Sill v. Worswick, 1 H. Bl. 673, 690, 691; Davis v. Jacquin, 5 Harr. & J. (Md.) 100.

the policy on which the general rule, that personal property has no locality, is itself founded.[1] It is not indeed very easy to reconcile it with the doctrine maintained by Lord Loughborough (which has been already cited [2]), or with other cases to the same effect. Nor is it easy to say to what extent it may be pressed in subversion of the general rule; since every country has so many minute regulations in regard to the transfers of personal property incorporated into its municipal code, each of which may be properly deemed beneficial to its own government, or to the interests of its citizens.[3]

391. *Case illustrating the Doctrine.* — Another case illustrative of the doctrine may be stated. A ship belonging to New York, and owned there, was transferred, while at sea, according to the law of the owner's domicil; and the ship subsequently arrived at New Orleans, and was attached by creditors, before any delivery thereof to the vendee. The question was whether the attachment overreached the title by the transfer. The Supreme Court of Louisiana held that it did not; and that the transfer was valid to all intents and purposes. The court took the distinction that the transfer was complete before the Louisiana laws could locally attach upon it. 'In the present case' said the court, 'the ship, the subject of the sale, was a New York ship, and the vendor and vendee resident in New York. If therefore, according to the lex loci contractus, that of the domicil of both parties, the sale transfers the property without a delivery, it did eo instanti, or not at all. In transferring it, it did not work any injury to the rights of the people of another country; it did not transfer the property of a thing within the jurisdiction of another government. If two persons in any country choose to bargain as to the property which one of them has in a chattel not within the jurisdiction of the place, they cannot expect that the rights of persons in the country in which the chattel is will be permitted to be affected by their contract. But, if the chattel be at sea, or in any other place, if any there be, in which the law of no

[1] See, Livermore Dissert. s. 221–223, p. 137–140.

[2] Ante, s. 380; Sill v. Worswick, 1 H. Bl. 690. See also 1 Kames Eq. b. 3, c. 8, s. 3; Ersk. Inst. b. 3, tit. 2, s. 40; Bruce v. Bruce, 2 B. & P. 229, note 231; Hunter v. Potts, 4 T. R. 182, 192; Phillips v. Hunter, 2 H. Bl. 402, 405.

[3] Mr. Burge manifestly deems the decision untenable. 3 Burge, Col. & For. Law, pt. 2, c. 20, p. 763, 764.

particular country prevails, the bargain will have its full effect, eo instanti, as to the whole world. And the circumstance of the chattel being afterwards brought into a country, according to the laws of which the sale would be invalid, would not affect it.'[1] (a) But if the ship had been, at the time of the sale, in New Orleans, and she had been attached before an actual delivery to the vendee, the title of the attaching creditor would have prevailed.[2]

392. *Decisions in Massachusetts.* — But let us suppose two persons, each claiming as purchaser under different transfers of the same personal property, one by a transfer from a partner in the place where the property is locally situate, and another by a transfer made by the other partner in the domicil of the firm; and by the law of the latter place, delivery is not essential to complete the transfer, but by the law of the former it is; which title is to prevail? According to the doctrine held in Louisiana, the title of the purchaser in the place rei sitæ ought to prevail.[3] And that doctrine seems confirmed by the reasoning in certain decisions of the Supreme Court of Massachusetts, although the precise point as to the conflict of laws was not litigated, and the law of Massachusetts was supposed to require a delivery to complete the title.[4]

393. *Remarks upon a Supposed Case.* — A case somewhat different has been put by the Supreme Court of Louisiana. 'If,' say the court, 'A. and B. be partners in New Orleans, and C. purchases from A. a quantity of cotton in the warehouse of the firm; will his right thereto, if he take instant possession of it, be affected by a sale made a few days before by B. in Natchez or Mobile? Will not C. be listened to in his own state, when he shows that by the lex fori, by the lex loci contractus, by that of the domicil of his vendors and of his own, the sale and delivery vested the property?'[5] The case is certainly very strongly put.

---

[1] Thuret v. Jenkins, 7 Mart. (La.) 318, 353, 354.

[2] Price v. Morgan, 7 Mart. (La.) 707; ante, s. 325 s, 386–389.

[3] Ramsey v. Stevenson, 5 Mart. (La.) 23, 77, 78; Thuret v. Jenkins, 7 Mart. (La.) 353.

[4] See Lamb v. Durant, 12 Mass. 54; Lanfear v. Sumner, 17 Mass. 110; ante, s. 386, 389, note.

[5] Thuret v. Jenkins, 7 Mart. (La.) 353.

(a) See ante, s. 384, note.

But after all it must entirely depend upon the point whether the prior transfer at Natchez or Mobile conveyed a perfect title by the law of those places without delivery; and if so, whether the lex rei sitæ ought to prevail against it? If no delivery were required by the law of Louisiana to perfect the title, the Natchez or Mobile purchaser would prevail even in the courts of Louisiana, against the purchaser in New Orleans, whatever might be the apparent hardship of the case under all the circumstances.

394. On the other hand, let us take the case of a shipment of goods from England to New Orleans, on account and risk of a merchant domiciled in England, who owes debts in New Orleans; and a subsequent transfer of the bill of lading in England to a purchaser after their arrival at New Orleans, but before the unlading thereof. Could a creditor of the shipper at New Orleans in such a case, by an attachment, oust the title of the purchaser because there had been no delivery to the purchaser under the bill of lading? By the law of England,[1] and indeed by that of many other commercial states, the legal title of the goods passes by the mere indorsement and delivery of the bill of lading, without any actual possession of the goods by the purchaser.[2] Would such a title so acquired be devested by the want of a delivery according to the laws of Louisiana? If so, it would most materially impair the confidence which the commercial world have hitherto reposed in the universal validity of the title acquired under a bill of lading. No opinion is intended to be here expressed on the point by the author; but it is presented in order to show that the doctrine is not without its embarrassments.

395. *Transfer of Choses in Action.* — If however the doctrine of the law rei sitæ is to prevail over that of the law of the place of the transfer in some cases, even in respect to movables, what is to be said in relation to assignments of choses in action or debts due by debtors resident in a foreign country? Would an attachment before notice defeat such assignments in favor of the

---

[1] Lickbarrow v. Mason, 2 T. R. 63; Abbott on Shipping, pt. 3, c. 9, s. 16.

[2] By the old French law, bills of lading were not negotiable, so as to pass a title in the property to the assignee, but only gave him a right of action subordinate to the rights of third persons. 1 Emérig. Assur. c. 11, s. 3. By the Code of Commerce (art. 281), bills of lading are now negotiable so as to pass the property to the indorsee. See 3 Pardessus, pt. 3, tit. 4, c. 3, art. 727.

attaching creditor, although notice of the assignment should be afterwards given to him within a reasonable time ?.[1] By the law of some countries an assignment of a debt is good without any notice to the debtor, and takes effect instanter; by the law of other countries notice is necessary to perfect the title.[2] Would an assignment of a debt in the creditor's domicil, where it would be good without any such notice, be ineffectual, if the debtor resided in a country where such notice would be necessary ? (a) Suppose an attachment made by a creditor in the intervening period between the time of the assignment and the notice; would the assignment or the attachment be entitled to a preference?[3] By the Scottish law a creditor may assign his debt to another person ; but the transfer is not complete, so as to vest the title absolutely in the assignee, until notice of the assignment, or, as the Scotch phrase is, until an intimation of the assignment is given to the debtor.[4] If therefore an assignment is made, a

[1] See Sill v. Worswick, 1 H. Bl. 691, 692; Bholen v. Cleveland, 5 Mason, 174. See Holmes v. Remsen, 4 Johns. Ch. (N. Y.) 460; Lewis v. Wallis, Sir T. Jones, 223; 1 Kames Eq. b. 3, c. 8, s. 3, p. 844.

[2] 3 Burge, Col. & For. Law, pt. 2, c. 20, p. 777, 778.

[3] See In re Wilson, cited 1 H. Bl. 691, 692; post, s. 399 a.

[4] See Ibid.; Selkrig v. Davis, 2 Rose, 315; Stein's Case, 1 Rose, 481; 2 Bell Com. p. 21–23, 4th ed. ; Id. p. 16–23, 5th ed. ; 3 Burge, Col. & For. Law, pt. 2, c. 20, p. 777, 778. But see In re Wilson, cited 1 H. Bl. 691, 692. I have stated the law of Scotland as I understand it to be stated in the opinion of Lord Eldon, in Selkrig v. Davis (2 Rose, 315; 2 Dow. 230, 250), though it would seem to be exactly like the Massachusetts law stated in the next section (s. 396). And so it was understood by Lord Hardwicke and Lord Loughborough. The following passage from the judgment of the latter in Sill v. Worswick, 1 H. Bl. 691, 692, gives a very exact view of their opinions. 'A question of this nature came before Lord Hardwicke very largely in the bankruptcy of Captain Wilson. With the little explanation I am enabled to give of that case, in which the Court of Sessions entirely concurred with Lord Hardwicke, the distinctions will be apparent. There were three different sets of creditors, who claimed, subject to the determination of the court, on the ground that Wilson had considerable debts due to him in Scotland. By the law of Scotland debts are assignable, and an assignment of a debt notified to the debtor, which is technically called an intimation, makes a specific lien quoad that debt. An assignment of a debt not intimated to the debtor gives a right to the assignee to demand that debt; but it is a right inferior to that of the creditor who has obtained his assignment and intimated it. By the law of Scotland also there is a process for the recovery of debts which is called an arrestment. Some of Wilson's creditors had assignments of specific debts intimated to the debtors, and completed by that intimation, prior to the act of bankruptcy. Others

(a) See Clark v. Connecticut Peat Co., 35 Conn. 303.

creditor of the original creditor may, before such intimation, arrest or attach the debt in the hands of the debtor, and will thereby acquire a preference over the assignee. That doctrine, it would seem, has been actually applied in Scotland to debts due by Scottish debtors to foreign creditors, and assigned in the domicil of the latter.[1]

396. *Effect of Assignment of Debt without Notice.* — According to our law a different doctrine would prevail; for an assignment operates, per se, as an equitable transfer of the debt.[2] Notice is indeed indispensable to charge the debtor with the duty of payment to the assignee ; so that, if without notice he pays the debt to the assignor, or it is recovered by process against him, he will be discharged from the debt.[3] But an arrest or attachment of

had assignments of debts not intimated before the bankruptcy. Others had arrested the debts due to him subsequent to the bankruptcy, and were proceeding under those arrestments to recover payment of those debts. The determination of Lord Hardwicke and that of the Court of Sessions entirely concurred. The first class I have mentioned, namely, the creditors who had specific assignments of specific debts, intimated to the debtors prior to the bankruptcy, were holden by Lord Hardwicke to stand in the same situation as creditors claiming by mortgage antecedent to the bankruptcy. All, therefore, he would do with respect to them was that, if they recovered under that decree, they could not come in under the commission without accounting to the other creditors for what they had taken under their specific security. With respect to the next class of creditors, Lord Hardwicke was of opinion, and the Court of Sessions were of the same opinion, that their title, being a title by assignment, was preferable to the title by arrestment; and they likewise held that the arrestments being subsequent to the bankruptcy were of no avail, the property being by assignment vested in the assignees under the commission. It is in this sense that an expression has been used by Lord Mansfield, in one or two cases, in which his language rather than his decision has been quoted with respect to the law of Scotland, namely, that the effect of the assignment under a commission of bankruptcy was the same as a voluntary assignment. For so the law of Scotland treats it, in contradistinction to the assignment perfected by intimation, and to an assignment which the party might be compelled to make. But it does not follow that it is an assignment without consideration. On the contrary, it is for a just consideration; not indeed for money actually paid, nor for a consideration immediately preceding the assignment. In that respect therefore it is a voluntary assignment. But taking it to be so, it excludes and is preferable to all others attaching; it is preferable to all the arresters; it is preferable to all creditors who stand under the same class, and to all who have not taken the steps to acquire a specific lien till after the act of bankruptcy committed.'

[1] Sill *v.* Worswick, 1 H. Bl. 691, 692.

[2] See ante, s. 395 and note; 3 Burge, Col. & For. Law, pt. 2, c. 20, p. 777, 778.

[3] Foster *v.* Sinkler, 4 Mass. 450; Blake *v.* Williams, 6 Pick. (Mass.) 286,

the debt in his hands by any creditor of the assignor will not entitle such creditor to a priority of right, if the debtor receives notice of the assignment pendente lite, and in time to avail himself of it in discharge of the suit against him.[1]

397. *Principle applicable in Case of Conflict.* — In such case of conflict of laws, the difficulty of applying any other than the general principle, that movables are transferable according to the law of the domicil of the owner, is apparent. Let us take the case of a Massachusetts creditor, assigning in that state a debt contracted there, and due to him by a person then domiciled in Scotland. The transfer is in equity complete in the place where it is made without notice; but in the place where the debt is due it is not complete without notice. To give effect in such a case to the law of Scotland, in opposition to that of Massachusetts, would be to give a locality to the debt, and to subject it to the exclusive operation of the law of the debtor's domicil. And it might involve this most serious difficulty, that if the debtor were afterwards found in Massachusetts, or in any other country than Scotland, he might be compelled to pay the debt to the assignee, although it might have been recovered from him in Scotland by a creditor in a proceeding by attachment of the debt in his hands, he having had notice of the assignment pendente lite.

398. *Language of Lord Kenyon.* — The reasoning of Lord Kenyon, in a celebrated case,[2] would certainly lead to the conclusion that an assignment of personal property, whether it were of goods or debts, according to the law of the owner's domicil, would pass the title in whatever country it might be, unless there were some prohibitory law in that country. His language is: 'Every person having property in a foreign country may dispose of it in this; though indeed if there be a law in that country directing a particular mode of conveyance, that ought to be adopted. But in this case no law of that kind is stated; and we cannot conjecture that it is not competent to the bankrupt himself, prior to his bankruptcy, to have disposed of his property as he pleased.'

307, 308, 314; Wood v. Partridge, 11 Mass. 488; Dix v. Cobb, 4 Mass. 508; Bholen v. Cleveland, 5 Mason, 174; Holmes v. Remsen, 4 Johns. Ch. (N. Y.) 460, 486. See 3 Burge, Col. & For. Law, pt. 2, c. 20, p. 777, 778; Muir v. Schenck, 3 Hill (N. Y.) 228. But see Story Eq. Jur. s. 421 a, s. 1035 a.

[1] Ibid.

[2] Hunter v. Potts, 4 T. R. 182, 192. See Livermore, Dissert. p. 140-159; Id. p. 159, s. 249. See ante, s. 383.

The same doctrine is maintained by Lord Hardwicke and Lord Loughborough. And all these learned judges apply it equally to the cases of assignments of goods and debts, to voluntary assignments by the party, and also, as we shall more fully see hereafter, to assignments by operation of law, as in cases of bankruptcy. The question of prior notice or intimation does not seem to have been thought by them material, for they treat the transfer as complete from the time of the assignment; and if that has priority in point of time, over an arrest or attachment of the property, it is to prevail. The law of England would certainly give effect to such an assignment of any goods or debts in England which were assigned by the owner in a foreign country.[1]

899. *Situs of Debts.* — Lord Kames, in commenting on the subject says : ' That considering a debt as a subject belonging to the creditor, the natural fiction would be, if any were admissible, to place it with the creditor, as in his possession, upon the maxim mobilia non habent sequelam. Others are more disposed to place it with the debtor.'[2] But in fact a debt is not a corpus capable of local position, but purely a jus incorporale.[3] And therefore where the debtor and creditor live in different countries, and are subjected to different laws, Lord Kames thinks the law of the domicil of the creditor ought to prevail.[4] He then adds: ' When

---

[1] See Solomons *v.* Ross, and other cases cited, 1 H. Bl. 131, 132, note; Sill *v.* Worswick, 1 H. Bl. 665, 690, 691; In re Wilson, cited id. p. 691–693; Lewis *v.* Wallis, T. Jones, 223. See also Selkrig *v.* Davis, 2 Rose, 97, 291, 315–317; Kames Eq. b. 3, c. 8, s. 4; Scott *v.* Allnutt, 2 Dow. & Cl. 404, 412; Livermore, Dissert. p. 159; Ogden *v.* Saunders, 12 Wheat. 364, 365. See also Merlin, Répert. Faillité, p. 412, 414, 415.

[2] Kames Eq. b. 3, c. 8, s. 4. See Morrison's Case, 4 T. R. 185; 1 H. Bl. 677; ante, s. 362; Rodenburg, de Divers. Stat. tit. 2, c. 5, s. 16; 2 Boullenois, Appx. p. 47–49;' ante, s. 377.

[3] See ante, s. 362, 376, 384; 3 Burge, Col. & For. Law, pt. 2, c. 20, p. 777–779.

[4] On this point I cannot do better than insert a passage from Mr. Livermore's Dissertations, p. 162, s. 251, illustrative of the same principles. ' It was formerly doubted by some whether personal actions should be considered as movables, and whether they should not be considered to have a location in the domicil of the debtor. But the common opinion seems to be well settled that, considered actively, and with respect to the interest of the creditor and his representatives, they must be considered as attached to the person of the creditor; and this, although the payment of the debt is secured by an hypothecation upon an immovable property. Such is the doctrine of Dumoulin. Nomina et jura, et quæcumque incorporalia, non circumscribantur loco, et sic non opus est accedere ad certum locum. Tum si hæc jura alicubi esse censerentur, non reputarentur esse in re pro illis hypothecata,

the creditor makes a voluntary conveyance, it is to be expected that he should speak in the style and form of his own country; and consequently that the rule of his own country should be the rule here. In a word, the will of a proprietor, or of a creditor, is good title jure gentium, that ought to be effectual everywhere. Thus an assignment made by a creditor in Scotland, according to our forms, of a debt due to him by a person in a foreign country, ought to be sustained in that country as a good title for demanding payment; and a foreign assignment of a debt due here, regular according to the law of the country, ought to be sustained by our judges.'[1] In another place he adds: ' An equitable title, in opposition to one that is legal, can never found a real action, actio in rem. It cannot have a stronger effect than to found an action against the proprietor to grant a more formal right, or in his default, that the court shall grant it. But in the case of a debt, where the question is not about property, but payment, an equitable title coincides, in a good measure, with a legal title. An assignment made by a foreign creditor according to the formalities of his country will be sustained here as a good title for demanding payment from the debtor; and it will be sustained, though informal, provided it be good jure gentium; that is, provided that the creditor really granted the assignment. Such effect hath an equitable title; and a legal title can have no stronger effect.'[2] This is in perfect coincidence with the law of England and America.[3]

nec in debitoris persona, sed magis in persona creditoris, in quo active residient, et ejus ossibus inhærent. Molin. Oper. Comm. ad Consuet. Paris, tit. 1, de Fiefs, s. 1, n. 9, p. 56, 57. So also Casaregis, after saying that movables are attached to the person of the owner, and at his death will be distributed according to the laws of his domicil, proceeds to consider what will be the rule with respect to debts, and determines that they follow the person of the creditor. An ita dicendum de nominibus debitorum, actionibus, ac juribus, quæ bona neque dicuntur mobilia neque immobilia, sed tertiam speciem bonorum componunt, et dicuntur incorporalia? Et respondeo affirmative; nam statutum bene comprehendit nomina debitorum, licet forensium, quia eorum obligationes non circumscribuntur locis, ideoque attenditur statutum, cui subjectus est testator. Et hæc verior est sententia; nam debitorum nomina, tanquam personæ cohærentia, debent regulari secundum statuta loci cui creditor est subjectus.' Casaregis, In Rubr. Stat. Civ. Genuæ de Success. ab Intest. n. 64, 65, tom. 4, p. 42, 43.

[1] Kames Eq. b. 3, c. 8, s. 4.

[2] Kames Eq. b. 3, c. 8, s. 4, sub finem. See also Huberus, de Confl. Leg. lib. 1, tit. 3, s. 9.

[3] See Holmes v. Remsen, 4 Johns. Ch. (N. Y.) 460, 486; 20 Johns. (N. Y.)

399 a. Priority between Assignment or Attachment. — Questions may arise upon the conflict of laws, where an assignment is validly made of personal property in one country by the owner thereof, and the property is at the time of the assignment locally in another country, by whose laws it is liable to be attached by a trustee process or garnishment; and an attachment is actually made by a creditor of the assignor before notice of the assignment. In such a case, as we have seen,[1] if notice thereof is given before judgment in the suit, the assignee will be entitled to maintain his priority of title. But suppose the lex fori enforces a different rule, and will in no such case entitle the creditor to a priority of right and a judgment against the property; will that judgment conclude the assignee, if the property is afterwards found in the country where the assignment is made, by whose laws the maxim prevails, qui prior est in tempore, potior est in jure? Suppose the property to be found in a different foreign country, and the assignee should sue for the same in the courts thereof; what law ought to be regarded in ascertaining the title; the law of the place of the assignment, or that of the judgment? Will it make any difference whether the assignee might or might not have intervened for his right in the first suit before judgment? or, that he happened to be in the country where the judgment was rendered at the time of the rendition thereof? These are questions more easily put than answered; and will well deserve the attention of courts of justice, when they are called upon to enforce the rights of creditors in the local tribunals, against the prior claims of title of assignees under assignments of debts or other personal property, made in a foreign country.[2]

400. But where an attachment or garnishment has been made by a creditor according to the local law rei sitæ, before any assignment by the party, or by operation of law in invitum, there is room for a distinction; and it may well be held that in such a

---

229, 267; Milne *v.* Moreton, 6 Binn. (Pa.) 353, 361, 369; Blake *v.* Williams, 6 Pick. (Mass.) 286, 307, 314. It is a very different question when an assignment of a debt is lawfully made, whether the assignee can sue the debtor in his own name, or must sue in the name of the assignor. That point has been sometimes thought to belong to the mode of remedy rather than the right, and of course is to be governed by the lex fori. See 3 Burge, Col. & For. Law, pt. 2, c. 20, p. 777, 778. And see also Wolff *v.* Oxholm, 6 M. & S. 92, 93. But see Alivon *v.* Furnival, 1 C. M. & R. 277, 296; post, s. 420, 566.

[1] Ante, s. 396.   [2] Ante, s. 395, 396.

case, the attaching creditor is entitled to a priority over the assignee. For in such case the rule may justly prevail, 'qui prior est in tempore potior est in jure;' and the creditor is equitably entitled to the benefits of his diligence. A case to this effect is reported by Casaregis, and reasoned out with great force upon general principles. The doctrine does not indeed seem in its nature susceptible of any well-founded doubt; and it is in entire conformity to the principles on the same subject recognized both in England and in America.[1] (a)

401. *Stoppage in Transitu.* — *Revendication.* — *Liens.* — There are some other matters connected with this subject which deserve attention. Upon the sale of goods on credit, by the law of some commercial countries, a right is reserved to the vendor to retake them, or he has a lien upon them for the price, if unpaid; and in other countries he possesses a right of stoppage in transitu only in cases of insolvency of the vendee.[2] The Roman law did

---

[1] Mr. Livermore, in his Dissertations (p. 159-162), has given the case and the reasoning of Casaregis at large. See Selkrig v. Davis, 2 Rose, 291, 310; Casaregis, Il Cambista Instruito, c. 7, tom. 3, p. 64.

[2] Abbott on Shipp. pt. 1, c. 1, s. 6; Id. pt. 3, c. 9, s. 2; 1 Domat, Civil Law, b. 1, tit. 2, s. 3, n. 1, 2; Id. s. 12, n. 13; Id. b. 3, tit. 1, s. 5, n. 3, 4, note; Merlin, Répert. Revendication, s. 1, n. 8; Code Civil, art. 2102; 4 Pardessus, Droit Com. art. 939, 940, 1204; 2 Kent Com. 540; ante, s. 322-328; 3 Burge, Col. & For. Law, pt. 2, c. 20, p. 770.

(a) See ante, s. 183. note. If by the law of the place of the domicil of the payee of a chose in action, where the same is payable, the chose is not subject to attachment by process of foreign attachment; or if by such law the same has been duly assigned, and such assignment perfected by notice, in conformity to the law of the place of the domicil of the payor, such chose in action cannot be held upon the debt of the payee under process of foreign attachment. Baylies v. Houghton, 15 Vt. 626. But an assignment of such chose in action, good by the law of the place of the domicil of the payee, but not perfected according to the law of the place of the domicil of the payor by notice to him of such assignment, will not defeat a valid attachment of the same by such process. Emerson v. Partridge, 27 Vt. 8; Ward v. Morrison, 25 Vt. 593. And the same is true when a chose in action is made payable in the state of the domicil of the debtor, although not subject to attachment by the law of the state where the payee resides. Ib. And in regard to the transfer of negotiable securities in payment of or as collateral security for an existing debt of the assignor, where the law of the place of the domicil of the assignor saves all equities to the real owner of such securities, but the law of the place of the assignment gives the assignee perfect title under such assignment, it is held that the effect of the assignment, and the title acquired under it, must be determined by the law of the place where the same was made. Culver v. Benedict, 13 Gray (Mass.) 7.

not generally consider the transfer of property to be complete by sale and delivery alone, without payment or security given for the price, unless the vendor agreed to give a general credit to the purchaser; but it allowed the vendor to reclaim the goods out of the possession of the purchaser, as being still his own property. ‘Quod vendidi,’ say the Pandects, ‘non aliter fit accipientis, quam si aut pretium nobis solutum sit, aut satis eo nomine datum, vel etiam fidem habuerimus emptori sine ulla satisfactione.’[1] The present code of France gives a privilege or right of revendication against the purchaser for the price of goods sold, so long as they remain in the possession of the debtor.[2] In respect to ships, a privilege is given by the same code to certain classes of creditors (such as vendors, builders, repairers, mariners, &c.) upon the ship, which takes effect even against subsequent purchasers until the ship has made a voyage after the purchase.[3] And by the general maritime law, acknowledged in most, if not in all commercial countries, hypothecations and liens are recognized to exist for seamen's wages, and for repairs of foreign ships, and for salvage.[4]

402. *Recognition of these Rights in Foreign Countries.* — The question then naturally arises, whether if such privileges, hypothecations, or liens are recognized in the country where the contracts, or acts which give rise to them are made, they are to be deemed obligatory in every other place where the property may be found, even against innocent purchasers, or against creditors who would otherwise, by the law rei sitæ, have a preference of right? Would an attachment, for instance, of foreign creditors prevail against them in the tribunals of the domicil of such creditors? Upon the general principles already stated as to the operation of contracts, and the rule that movables have no locality, it would seem that these privileges, hypothecations, and liens ought to prevail over the rights of subsequent purchasers and creditors in every other country. That having once attached rightfully in rem, they ought not to be displaced by the mere

[1] Digest, 18, 1, 19; Id. 14, 4, 5, 18. As to liens for unpaid purchase-money on lands, see ante, s. 322 b, and Gilman v. Brown, 1 Mason, 219–221.

[2] Code Civil, art. 2102, n. 4.

[3] Code of Commerce, art. 192, 193; 3 Pardessus, Droit. Com. art. 942, 950. See also 1 Valin Com. 340; Abbott on Shipp. pt. 1, c. 1, s. 6.

[4] See ante, s. 322 a, 323; Conflit des Lois, Revue Étrang. et Franç. tom. 6, 1840, s. 33, p. 227, 228.

change of local situatredion of the property.[1] (a) This doctrine was in some measure recogcamized in an important case in England, where the right of stoppage in transitu was supposed to depend upon doctrines of foreign law, materially different from the law of England. The right conferred by the foreign law was upheld against the claims of English creditors, under the circumstances of that case, which were somewhat peculiar, the lien having been given by the foreign law, and enforced in the foreign country, so far as to compel the master, who was in possession of the goods, to recognize it, and to agree to hold the property subject to it.[2]

402 a. Nevertheless, as we have already seen, there is no inconsiderable conflict of opinion among foreign jurists, and even among domestic jurists, as to the extent to which the right of

[1] See Livermore, Dissert. p. 159, s. 249; ante, s. 322.

[2] Inglis v. Usherwood, 1 East, 515; Abbott on Shipp. pt. 3, c. 9, s. 3. On that occasion Lord Kenyon said: 'The decision in this case will not at all trench upon the general rule of law respecting the right of stopping goods in transitu; but, giving the plaintiffs the full benefit of the argument that the delivery of the goods on board a chartered ship was a delivery to the bankrupt, still the circumstance of the Russian ordinance set forth in the case varies it very importantly, and takes it out of the general rule. By that law, the consignors, under the circumstances stated, had a right to repossess themselves of their goods, and they did so in effect; not indeed by actually taking them out of the ship on board of which they were laden, or by instituting legal process for the recovery of them; but having a right so to do, which it became unnecessary to exert, because it was in the first instance acknowledged and submitted to by the captain, in whose possession the property was, they imposed terms upon him that he should sign bills of lading to their order, upon his compliance with which, they suffered the cargo to proceed to the place of its destination, disposable there as events might turn out. The goods are therefore sent with the condition attached to them. The law of Russia in this respect is a very equitable law; and I have often lamented that our own code was defective in the same particular. For every man contracting to supply another with goods acts on the presumption that that other is in a condition to pay for them; and therefore, when the condition of the consignee is altered at the time of the delivery, and he is insolvent, and no longer capable of performing his part of the contract, honesty and good faith require that the contract should be rescinded. However the contrary has been settled to be law, unless the consignor stop the goods in transitu before they get into the consignee's possession. But this being a transaction into a foreign country, where a more equitable law in this respect prevails, I am far from being desirous of limiting its operation; and, for the reasons before given, I think that the consignors have substantially availed themselves of it; and that the defendant, by delivering the goods to their order, has done no more than he was bound to do.'

(a) See Harmer v. Bell, 7 Moore, P. C. 267; Marsh v. Elsworth, 37 Ala. 85.

privilege or priority ought to be allowed in cases where such privilege or priority has arisen under foreign laws against subsequent purchasers, (a) or against creditors in the country where the property is subsequently found. Whether an exception would be allowed generally in favor of maritime liens and privileges and priorities, founded upon the public policy of giving them full effect as matters of public convenience and interest, founded upon the necessities and exigencies of commerce and naval intercourse, may admit of question. It is highly probable however that most, if not all, commercial nations will adopt such an exception upon the principle of comity sub mutuæ vicissitudinis obtentu. Indeed upon any other system, bottomry bonds, respondentia bonds, and other maritime hypothecations, would constitute so unsafe a security that no merchant abroad would venture tó lend his money upon so fragile a title, which might be undermined or destroyed by a local law, wholly unknown and unsuspected by him.

403. *Operation of Assignment in Bankruptcy.* — Hitherto we have been considering cases of voluntary transfers inter vivos, and we are now naturally led to the consideration of involuntary transfers by operation of law in the domicil of the owner, such as are statutable transfers under the bankrupt or insolvent laws of the country of his domicil. The great question here is, whether an assignment under such laws has a universal operation, so as to transfer the movable property of the bankrupt or insolvent in all other countries to the same extent as a voluntary transfer made by him would, and thus to withdraw it from the process of the local foreign laws by way of arrest, attachment, or otherwise, issued in favor of the foreign creditors in the country where the movable property is situate. This question has been very gravely discussed both at home and abroad ; and the courts of England and the courts of America have arrived at opposite conclusions respecting it. The courts of the former country uniformly maintain the doctrine of the universal operation of such an assignment upon all movable property wherever it may be locally situate at the time of the assignment. Many (but not all) of the courts of the latter country confine the operation of such an assignment to the territory where the party is declared bankrupt

(a) Ante, s. 322-328; post, s. 424-528.

or insolvent. The question is worthy of a very full examination, and a summary of the reasoning on each side of the question will therefore be here brought under review.

404. Those who maintain that assignments under bankrupt or insolvent laws are, and ought to be, of universal operation to transfer movable property, in whatever country it may be locally situate, adopt reasoning to this effect.[1] (a) The general principle certainly is, that personal property has no locality, but that, as to its disposition, it is subject to the law which governs the person of the owner, that is to say, it is subject to the law of his domicil.[2] There can be no doubt that the owner may, by a voluntary assignment or sale, made according to the law of his domicil, transfer the title to any person, wherever the property may be locally situate.[3] Now an assignment under the bankrupt laws of his domicil is, by operation of law, a valid transfer of all the bankrupt's property, as valid as if made personally by him.[4] The

[1] Mr. Bell has examined this subject with his usual ability and accuracy, and vindicated at large the propriety of the rule giving universal effect to assignments in bankruptcy. See 2 Bell Com. b. 8, c. 2, s. 1266, p. 684-690, 4th ed.; Id. p. 680-691, 5th ed.

[2] Sill v. Worswick, 1 H. Bl. 690, 691; Hunter v. Potts, 4 T. R. 182.

[3] In re Wilson, cited 1 H. Bl. 691, 692.

[4] Sill v. Worswick, 1 H. Bl. 691, 692; Hunter v. Potts, 4 T. R. 182, 192; Phillips v. Hunter, 2 H. Bl. 402, 405; Goodwin v. Jones, 3 Mass. 517. 'It is a proposition,' said the court, in Phillips v. Hunter, 2 H. Bl. 402, 403, 'not to be disputed, that previous to the bankruptcy the bankrupts themselves might have transferred or assigned this property, though abroad, as absolutely as if it had been in their own tangible possession in this country; and it seems that the assignees under their commission were entitled by operation of law to do with it, after the bankruptcy, what the bankrupts themselves might have done.' In Potts v. Hunter, 4 T. R. 182, 192, the court said: ' The only question here is whether or not the property in that island (Rhode Island) passed by the assignment in the same manner as if the owner (the bankrupt) had assigned it by his voluntary act. And that it does so pass cannot be doubted, unless there were some positive law of that country to prevent it.' ' On the general reason of the thing, if there be no positive decision to the contrary, no doubt could be entertained but that by the laws of this country, uncontradicted by the laws of any other country where personal property may happen to be, the commissioners of a bankrupt may dispose of the personal property of a bankrupt here, though such property be in a foreign country.' In Goodwin v. Jones, 3 Mass. 517, Mr. Chief Justice Parsons said: ' The

(a) It has been held that a general assignment is not invalid because some of the assigned property is land situated in another state, by whose laws the assignment was ineffectual to pass land. Watkins v. Wallace, 19 Mich. 57.

law upon his bankruptcy transfers his whole property to the assignees, who thus become lege loci the lawful owners of it, and entitled to administer it for the benefit of all his creditors. The mode of transfer is wholly immaterial. The only proper question is, whether it is good according to the law of his domicil.[1] This rule is admitted and applied in all cases of the succession to movable property in cases of intestacy, where the property passes by mere operation of law, in the same manner, and to the same extent, as where it passes by the voluntary act or transfer inter vivos of the owner, or where it passes by his last will or testament.[2]

405. The same principle applies with equal force and general convenience to the disposition of the effects of bankrupts ; for the just and equal distribution of all the funds of that class of debtors becomes the common concern of the whole commercial world. In cases of intestacy, it is presumed to be the intent of the intestate that his movables, which by fiction of law have no locality independent of his person, should be brought home, and distributed according to the law of his domicil. It is equally to be presumed, as the understanding of the commercial world, that the bankrupt's effects should follow his person, and be distributed in the place of his domicil, where the credit was bestowed, or the payment expected according to the laws thereof.[3] An assignment under the bankrupt laws ought to be deemed in all respects of equal force and validity with a voluntary assignment of the party ; for by implication of law he consents to all transfers made of his property according to the law of his domicil. Great inconveniences would follow from a different proceeding. Different commissions might issue in different countries, and have concurrent operation simul et semel in different countries. And thus it would be in the power of the bankrupt to throw his pro-

assignment of a bankrupt's effects may be considered as his own act, as it is in the execution of laws by which he is bound, he himself being competent to make such an assignment, and voluntarily committing the act which authorized the making of it.' See also Livermore's Dissert. p. 159, s. 249, 250. The same doctrine was affirmed by Lord Mansfield in Wadham v. Marlow, cited 1 H. Bl. 437–439, note; s. s. and s. p. 8 East, 314, 316, note z.

[1] Ante, s. 399; post, s. 420, 566.
[2] Sill v. Worswick, 1 H. Bl. 690, 691.
[3] Holmes v. Remsen, 4 Johns. Ch. (N. Y.) 460, 470; Hunter v. Potts, 4 T. R. 182, 192.

perty under either commission at pleasure, and to give local preferences to different creditors, according to his own partialities or prejudices. Such a state of things, and such conflicting systems, would lead to great public inconvenience and confusion, and be the source of much fraud and injustice, and disturb the equality and equity of any bankrupt system in any country.[1]

406. There is great wisdom therefore in adopting the rule that an assignment in bankruptcy shall operate as a complete and valid transfer of all his movable property abroad, as well as at home; and it has accordingly received a very general sanction. It is true that any nation may adopt, if it pleases, a different system, and prefer an attaching domestic creditor to a foreign assignee or to foreign creditors. But such a course of legislation can hardly be deemed consistent with the general comity of nations, and could scarcely fail to bring on a retaliatory system of preferences in every other nation injured thereby. But until such a legislation is positively made and interposes a direct obstruction, the true rule is to follow out the lead of the general principle, that makes the law of the owner's domicil conclusive upon the disposition of his personal property.[2] This reasoning

[1] Holmes v. Remsen, 4 Johns. Ch. (N. Y.) 471; Phillips v. Hunter, 2 H. Bl. 402. In Phillips v. Hunter, 2 H. Bl. 402, 403, the court said: 'The great principle of the bankrupt laws is justice founded on equality. This being the principle of those laws, it seems to follow that the whole property of the bankrupt must be under their (the assignees') control, without regard to the locality of that property, except in cases which directly militate against the particular laws of the country in which it happens to be situated.' 'If the bankrupt laws were circumscribed by the local situation of the property, a door would be open to all the partiality and undue preferences which they were framed to prevent; it being easy to foresee how frequently property would be sent abroad with that unjust view, immediately previous to and in contemplation of bankruptcy.'

[2] Holmes v. Remsen, 4 Johns. (N. Y.) 471, 472; Hunter v. Potts, 4 T. R. 182, 192; Sill v. Worswick, 1 H. Bl. 691, 693. In Phillips v. Hunter, 2 H. Bl. 402, 405, the court said: 'It is true that the laws of the country where the property is situated have the immediate control over it, in respect to its locality and the immediate protection afforded to it, yet the country where the proprietor resides, in respect to another species of protection afforded to him and his property, has a right to regulate his contract relating to that property.' And in Hunter v. Potts, 4 T. R. 182, the court said: 'Every person having property in a foreign country may dispose of it in this; though indeed if there be a law in that country directing a particular mode of conveyance, that must be adopted.' 'If,' said Lord Loughborough, 'the bankrupt happens to have property which lies out of the jurisdiction of the law of England, if the country in which it lies proceeds according to the principles of well-regulated

applies in an especial manner to contracts made in the very country where the party is declared bankrupt.[1]

407. There are many authorities in favor of this doctrine. As early as 1728, Lord Talbot, then at the bar, gave an opinion that the statutes of bankruptcy of England did not extend to the plantations; yet that the personal property of an English bankrupt in the plantations passed to the assignees.[2] Lord Hardwicke, in a case in judgment before him, adopted and acted upon the doctrine that an assignment in bankruptcy in England conveyed the personal property of the bankrupt in foreign countries; and that their title would overreach that of an attaching creditor after the assignment, although at that time it was not made known to the debtor.[3] In another case in the Court of Chancery, in England, in 1704, where the property of the owner, who was domiciled in Holland, was taken under a commission of bankruptcy, and, according to the laws of Holland, the administration thereof given to and vested in persons who are called curators of desolate estates, it was decided that the curators had, immediately upon their appointment, a title to recover the debts due to the bankrupt in England, in preference to the diligence of particular creditors seeking to attach those debts.[4] In another case, in 1769, the same point was decided.[5] These are cases in which the rule was asserted in favor of foreign assignees.[6] A like decision in favor of English assignees was made in the Court of Chancery in Ireland in 1763.[7] Lord Thurlow gave it the sanction of his own great name in a case decided by him in 1787.[8]

justice, there is no doubt that it will give effect to the title of the assignees.' ' But if the law of that country preferred him (a creditor) to the assignees, though I must suppose that determination wrong, yet I do not think that my holding a contrary opinion would revoke the determination of that country, however I might disapprove of the principle on which that law so decided.' Sill v. Worswick, 1 H. Bl. 691, 698.

[1] Sill v. Worswick, 1 H. Bl. 691, 693, 694; Phillips v. Hunter, 2 H. Bl. 404, 405; Hunter v. Potts, 4 T. R. 182.

[2] Livermore, Dissert. 140; Beames, Lex Mercatoria, p. 5, 6, 6th ed.

[3] In Wilson's Case, cited in 1 H. Bl. 691, 692, and probably decided between 1752 and 1756. See also s. c. cited in Hunter v. Potts, 4 T. R. 186, 187.

[4] Solomons v. Ross, 1 H. Bl. 131, note; Id. 691; s. c. Cooke's Bank. Laws, 306, 4th ed.

[5] Jollett v. Deponthieu, 1 H. Bl. 132, note, Id. 691.   [6] Ibid.

[7] Neale v. Cottingham, 1 H. Bl. 132, note; s. c. cited in Hunter v. Potts, 4 T. R. 194, and Cooke's Bank. Laws, p. 303, 4th ed. 1799. See also Quelin v. Moisson, 1 Knapp, 265, note.

[8] Ex parte Blakes, 1 Cox, Cases in Equity, 398.

408. The question was most elaborately considered in England in two cases decided in 1791, in which it was solemnly held that the operation of the bankrupt laws is to vest in the assignees all the personal property of the bankrupt, wherever it may be situate; and that whenever that property shall be brought into England by any person who has obtained it, the assignees will have a right to recover it of him, for the benefit of all the creditors; and consequently that an attachment and recovery of such property, made by a creditor in a foreign country after such assignment, will be held inoperative; upon the principle that the title which is prior in point of time ought to obtain preference in point of right and law.[1] Upon a writ of error, the general doctrine maintained in these cases was affirmed; but in its actual application it was restricted to attachments made by British creditors against British debtors. In this state the doctrine remained until a very recent period, when, in the case of the bankruptcy of an English partner in a Scotch partnership, it was discussed anew. A commission of bankruptcy was issued in England; and subsequently an arrest, attachment, or sequestration was made by a creditor, of debts due to the bankrupt in Scotland. The question then arose, whether the assignees, or the attaching creditor, was entitled to priority; and this depended on the question whether an English commission of bankruptcy passed to the assignees the title to property, or debts locally situate, or due, in Scotland. The Court of Session in Scotland held that it did;[2] and, upon appeal, this judgment was affirmed by the House of Lords. 'One thing,' said Lord Eldon, 'is quite clear, that there is not in any book any dictum or authority that would authorize me to deny, at least in this place, that an English commission passes, as with respect to the bankrupt and his creditors in England, the personal property he has in Scotland or in any foreign county.'[3]

[1] Sill v. Worswick, 1 H. Bl. 665, 690, 691, 694; Hunter v. Potts, 4 T. R. 192; s. c. in Err. 2 H. Bl. 402.

[2] The Court of Sessions in Scotland gave very elaborate opinions on this subject, in the Royal Bank of Scotland v. Cuthbert, commonly cited as Stein's Case, 1 Rose, Appx. 472; 2 Rose, 78, 91. See also Smith v. Buchanan, 1 East, 6; 2 Bell Com. 684–687, 4th ed.; Id. p. 680–691, 5th ed.

[3] Selkrig v. Davis, 2 Rose, 291, 314; 2 Dow, 230, 250; 2 Rose, 97. See also Ex parte D'Obree, 8 Ves. 82; 2 Bell Com. 684–687, 4th ed.; Holmes r Remsen, 4 Johns. (N. Y.) Ch. 460; 20 Johns. (N. Y.) 229. The judgment of

409. *Propositions established in England.* — This is now accordingly the settled law of England, (*a*) in which the following

Lord Eldon, which was affirmed apparently with entire unanimity, contains many striking remarks upon the difficulties attendant upon any other system of international jurisprudence. The following extracts are particularly valuable to be submitted to the consideration of the American courts: ' In whatever way a Scottish sequestration may be enforced, the distribution of a bankrupt's effects under it is perfectly different from what it is under an English commission of bankruptcy. The Scottish law cuts down all securities that have been made or given within a certain number of days prior to the issuing of the sequestration, whether they have been given bona fide, or given, as we should say, in contemplation of bankruptcy. On the other hand, in our law, though the approximation of the security to the date of the commission may be evidence that it was given in contemplation of bankruptcy, yet it is but evidence, and the security may be perfectly good. Again, in England, a man cannot become a bankrupt without committing an act of bankruptcy. The commission must be founded on that act of bankruptcy; and there are various other differences applying to the property of a bankrupt, as administered under an English commission, or vice versa, as distributed by the rules and according to the forms of a Scottish sequestration. If, my lords, you attempt to obviate these inconveniences by a coexisting sequestration and commission, the difficulty is tenfold greater, unless the one should be used merely as the means of assisting the distribution of the funds on the other. What personal property shall belong to the one proceeding, and what to the other proceeding, is no ordinary difficulty. The counsel for the appellant say there is no difficulty. That a debt owing to the house in Scotland, wherever the debtor lives, ought to go to the Scotch sequestration; and in like manner that the debt owing to the house in England, wherever the debtor lives, should go to the commission. But the house may be constituted of persons of whom it may be difficult to say whether a man is a Scotchman or an Englishman. It may happen that a house is composed of persons, some of whom reside in Scotland and some in England. I should wish to know, not only how the joint debts due to one firm, and the joint debts due to the other, are to be distributed; but where separate debts are due to each, whether the separate debts are to be a fund of distribution under the English commission, or under the Scottish sequestration, or what is to become of them. All these difficulties certainly belong to this case. But notwithstanding that, one thing is quite clear, there is not in any book any dictum or authority that would authorize me to deny, at least in this place, that an English commission passes, as with respect to the bankrupt and his creditors in England, the personal property he has in Scotland, or in any foreign country. It is admitted that the assignment under the English commission, as between the bankrupt and the English and Scotch proprietors, passes the Scotch property, and vests in the assignees, when the Scotch creditors have not used legal diligence. I think the case was put at the bar thus: That the commission of bankruptcy operated so as to bring into the fund the Scotch personal property, provided that such personal property was not arrested by legal diligence in Scotland, prior to the intimation of the assignment in Scotland. It was therefore argued that this was to be put on the same

(*a*) See In re Blithman, 35 Beav. 219.

propositions are firmly established ; *first*, that an assignment under the bankrupt law of a foreign country passes all the personal property of the bankrupt locally situate, and debts owing in England ; *secondly*, that an attachment of such property by an English creditor, after such bankruptcy, with or without notice to him, is invalid to overreach the assignment ; *thirdly*, that in England the same doctrine holds under assignments by her own bankrupt laws, as to personal property and debts of the bankrupt in foreign countries ; *fourthly*, that, upon principle, all attachments made by foreign creditors, after such assignment in a foreign country, ought to be held invalid ; *fifthly*, that at all events a British creditor will not be permitted to hold the property acquired by a judgment under any attachment made in a foreign country after such assignment ; and, *sixthly*, that a foreign creditor, not subjected to British laws, will be permitted to retain any such property acquired under any such judgment, if the local laws (however incorrectly upon principle) confer on him an absolute title.[1] There is no inconsiderable weight of American authority on the same side ; but it must be admitted that the preponderating authority is certainly now the other way.[2]

footing as the case of the assignation of a particular debt to a particular individual. Now, your lordships need not be told that, by the law of Scotland, if B. assign a debt which is due from C. to B., a creditor of B. may arrest that debt in the hands of the debtor, notwithstanding the assignment, unless the assignee has given an intimation formally to the person by whom the debt is owing. That must be admitted. Upon that it has been insisted here that no intimation has been given, and that this subsequent arrestment in 1798 ought to have the preference of the title of the assignees under the commission. that was sued out in the year 1782.' 2 Rose, 314–316. He afterwards proceeded to decide that no intimation was necessary ; and, if necessary, it was given. Id. 318, 319. See Quelin *v.* Moisson, 1 Knapp, 265.

[1] 2 Bell Com. s. 1266, p. 687-690, 4th ed. ; Id. p. 680-690, 5th ed. ; Holmes *v.* Remsen, 4 Johns. Ch. (N. Y.) 460 ; 20 Johns. (N. Y.) 229 ; Dwarris on Statutes, 650, 651.

[2] Mr. Chief Justice Parsons certainly held this opinion in Goodwin *v.* Jones, 3 Mass. 517. And Mr. Chancellor Kent has sustained it in one of his most elaborate judgments, which will well reward a diligent perusal. Holmes *v.* Remsen, 4 Johns. Ch. (N. Y.) 460. This is also, as we shall see, the law in France and Holland. Post, s. 417. See Parish *v.* Seton, Cooper's Bank. Law, 27 ; Holmes *v.* Remsen. 4 Johns. Ch. (N. Y.) 484 ; 20 Johns. (N. Y.) 258 ; Blake *v.* Williams, 6 Pick. (Mass.) 312, 313 ; Merlin, Répertoire, Faillité et Banqueroute, Art. 10. Mr. Chancellor Kent, in his Commentaries, 2 Kent Com. 404–408, has with great candor admitted that the American doctrine is now established the other way by a preponderance of authority ; although he has an undisguised distrust of the validity of its foundation. There are not

410. *The American Doctrine.* — *Reasons in its Support.* — The reasoning which is urged in support of what may be deemed the American doctrine is to the following effect. (a) It is admitted that the general rule is, that personal property, including debts, has no locality, but follows, as to its disposition and transfer, the law of the domicil of the owner. But every country may by positive law regulate as it pleases the disposition of personal property found within it, and may prefer its own attaching creditors to any foreign assignee ; and no other country has any right to question the determination. When there is no positive law, the general rule is to govern, with the exception of such cases as fall within the known principle of Huberus, that it is not prejudicial to the state, or to the just rights of its citizens. And this exception is the very ground upon which the objection to the ubiquity of operation of the bankrupt laws of a country, as respects the personal estate of the bankrupt, is to be rested.[1] (b)

411. There is a marked distinction between a voluntary conveyance of property by the owner, and a conveyance by mere operation of law in cases of bankruptcy in invitum. Laws cannot force the will, nor compel any man to make a conveyance. In place of a voluntary conveyance of the owner, all that the legislature of a country can do, when justice requires it, is to assume the disposition of his property in invitum. But a statutable conveyance, made under the authority of any legislature, cannot operate upon any property, except that which is within its own territory. This makes a solid distinction between a voluntary conveyance of the owner and an involuntary legal conveyance by the mere authority of law. The former has no relation to place ; the latter, on the contrary, has the strictest relation

a few jurists in America, each of whom may be disposed to use on this occasion the language of a great orator of antiquity, ' Ego assentior Scævolæ.' See Livermore, Dissert. s. 223-248, p. 140-158. There are in Mr. Henry's Appendix to his work on Foreign Law, p. 251-258, some curious opinions given by counsel in 1715, as to the effect of an attachment after a foreign bankruptcy. See also Devisme v. Martin, Wythe (Va.) 133.

[1] Blake v. Williams, 6 Pick. (Mass.) 286; Olivier v. Townes, 14 Mart. (La.) 93, 97-100; Milne v. Moreton, 6 Binn. (Pa.) 353.

(a) See Betton v. Valentine, 1 Curtis, C. C. 168; Booth r. Clark, 17 How. 322; Tully v. Herrin, 44 Miss. 626.

(b) See Very v. McHenry, 29 Me. 208; Frazier v. Fredericks, 4 Zab. (N. J.) 166.

to place. This distinction is insisted on with great force by Lord Kames.[1] (*a*) It is therefore admitted that a voluntary assignment by a party, according to the law of his domicil, will pass his personal estate, whatever may be its locality, abroad as well as at home. (*b*) But it by no means follows that the same rule should govern in cases of assignments by operation of law. (*c*)

412. The true rule in such cases is to hold that the assignees are in the same situation as the bankrupt himself in regard to foreign debt. They take the property under the assignment, subject to every equity belonging to foreign creditors, and subject to the remedies provided by the laws of the foreign country where the debt is due; and when they are permitted to sue in a foreign country, it is not as assignees having an interest, but as the representatives of the bankrupt. They stand upon the footing of administrators only, with a right to sue for the benefit of all the creditors. But our local law will not regard the choses in action of the debtor as exclusively appropriated to the use of such assignees; and a preference can be gained by them only by pursuing the remedies which our local laws afford. This was formerly the rule in England.[2]

413. Nor can it be truly said that an assignment by the bankrupt laws is with the consent of the bankrupt, because he assents by implication to such laws. This is a very unsafe and dangerous principle on which to risk the doctrine; for in the same way it may be said that a man committing a crime for which his estate is forfeited, voluntarily consents to its transfer. But the principle, whether correct or not, can only apply to cases where the debtor and creditor belong to the same country. It is wholly inapplicable to foreign creditors.

---

[1] Kames Eq. b. 3, c. 8, s. 6; Remsen *v.* Holmes, 20 Johns. (N. Y.) 258, 259; Milne *v.* Moreton, 6 Binn. (Penn.) 353, 369; ante, s. 351 *b.*

[2] See Mawdesley *v.* Parke, cited 1 H. Bl. 680.

(*a*) Woodward *v.* Roane, 23 Ark. 526; Thurman *v.* Stockwell, cited in 35 N. Y. 661; Frazier *v.* Fredericks, 4 Zab. (N. J.) 162.

(*b*) See Speed *v.* May, 17 Penn. St. 91; Law *v.* Mills, 18 Penn. St. 185.

(*c*) It is well settled that a general assignment by an insolvent debtor, under and by force of the insolvent law of his domicil, cannot pass real estate situated in another state. See Hutcheson *v.* Peshine, 1 Green (N. J. Eq.) 167; Rodgers *v.* Allen, 3 Ham. (Oh.) 488; McCullough *v.* Rodrick, 2 id. 234; Osborn *v.* Adams, 18 Pick. (Mass.) 247.

414. Besides, national comity requires us to give effect to such assignments only so far as may be done without impairing the remedies, or lessening the securities, which our laws have provided for our own citizens. The rule is: 'Quatenus sine prejudicio indulgentium fieri potest.'[1] And after all this is mere comity, and not international law. All comity of this sort must be built up, in a great measure, upon the doctrine of reciprocity; and this is extremely difficult from the known diversities in the jurisprudence of different nations.[2] It would prejudice the rights and remedies of our citizens in our own courts to suffer the assignments under foreign bankrupt laws to prevail over their own diligence in seeking remedies against their debtors in our own courts. If there is in such cases a conflict between our own laws and foreign laws as to the rights of our citizens, and one of them must give way, our own laws ought to prevail.[3] The most convenient and practical rule is, that statutable assignments, as to creditors, shall operate intra-territorially only. If our citizens conduct themselves according to our laws in regard to the property of their debtors found within our jurisdiction, it is reasonable that they should reap the fruits of their diligence, and not be sent to a foreign country to receive such a dividend of their debtors' effects, as the foreign laws allow. If each government in cases of insolvency should sequester and distribute the funds within its own jurisdiction, the general result will be favorable to the interest of creditors, and to the harmony of nations. This is the rule adopted in all cases of administration of the property of deceased persons; and there is no real difference between the principle of those cases and of cases of bankruptcy.[4] (a)

415. *Change of the English Doctrine.* — Down to the time of the American Revolution, this may be fairly deemed to have been the English doctrine. It has since been changed. Even in

[1] Huberus, lib. 1, tit. 3, De Confl. Leg. s. 2.

[2] Blake v. Williams, 6 Pick. (Mass.) 286, 313–315; Milne v. Moreton, 6 Binn. (Penn.) 353, 375; Remsen v. Holmes, 20 Johns. (N. Y.) 229, 263, 264.

[3] Potter v. Brown, 5 East, 124; ante, s. 326.

[4] Remsen v. Holmes, 20 Johns. (N. Y.) 229, 265; Milne v. Moreton, 6 Binn. (Penn.) 353, 361; Blake v. Williams, 6 Pick. (Mass.) 286.

(a) See Booth v. Clark, 17 How. 336; May v. Breed, 7 Cush. (Mass.) 41; Taylor v. Columbian Ins. Co., 14 Allen (Mass.) 355; Pingree v. Hudson River Ins. Co., 10 Gray (Mass.) 170; Chafee v. Fourth National Bank, 71 Me. 514.

England the principle has not as yet been applied in favor of any foreign countries, except such as have bankrupt laws in form or substance; and we have none in our country.[1] It can make no difference in the case whether the debt of the attaching creditor accrued here or in foreign countries; for in either case the question is not as to the validity of the contract, but as to a collateral matter, that is to say, the effect to be given to it in a conflict between rights growing out of our own laws and those of a foreign country.[2] (a)

416. *Validity of Voluntary Assignments.* — Neither is it true that even the voluntary conveyances of parties in all cases are to be held valid where they are prejudicial to the rights and remedies of our own citizens. In Massachusetts, for instance, it has been held that a voluntary assignment by a debtor of all his property, made in Pennsylvania for the benefit of creditors generally, shall not prevail over a subsequent attachment of the funds of the debtor made after the assignment; because such an assignment would be void by the laws of Massachusetts, if made in that state, as being in fraud of creditors; and it is unjust and unequal in its effects, and prejudicial to the citizens of the State. In such a case therefore the party who shall by process first attach the debt or seize the property ought to prevail, whether creditor or assignee.[3] (b)

417. *Old Law of France and Holland.* — It is admitted in the reasoning in the American cases, that the old law of France and

[1] Remsen v. Holmes, 20 Johns. (N.Y.) 229; Blake v. Williams, 6 Pick. (Mass.) 286; Milne v. Moreton, 6 Binn. (Penn.) 353; Wallace v. Patterson, 2 Harr. & McH. (Md.) 463; Abraham v. Plestoro, 3 Wend. (N. Y.) 538, 549, 550.

[2] Milne v. Moreton, 6 Binn. (Penn.) 360.

[3] Ingraham v. Geyer, 13 Mass. 146, cited 6 Pick. (Mass.) 307. See also Olivier v. Townes, 14 Martin (La.) 93, 97-100. This summary of the American reasoning is principally extracted from the three leading cases of Milne v. Moreton, 6 Binn. (Penn.) 353, Remsen v. Holmes, 20 Johns. (N. Y.) 229, and Blake v. Williams, 6 Pick. (Mass.) 286, where the subject is very elaborately discussed. The same doctrine will be found supported in other American cases, cited in 2 Kent Com. 406-408. See also Olivier v. Townes, 2 Mart. N.S. (La.) 93, 99; Harrison v. Sterry, 5 Cranch, 289; Ogden v. Saunders, 12 Wheat. 213, 360-369; Saunders v. Williams, 5 N. H. 213; Plestoro v. Abraham, 1 Paige (N. Y.) 237; 3 Wend. (N. Y.) 538; Fox v. Adams, 5 Greenl. (Me.) 245; Wallace v. Patterson, 2 Harr. & McH. (Md.) 463; Ogden v. Saunders, 12 Wheat. 213, 359-362; ante, s. 399-401.

(a) See Einer v. Beste, 32 Mo. 240.
(b) See Lehmer v. Herr, 1 Duv. (Ky.) 360.

Holland is in coincidence with the British doctrine.[1] The modern law of those countries is equally decisive in its support, and very recent cases have given it a complete confirmation in their tribunals. The principal grounds of their decisions may be summed up in the following propositions. (1) That the law of the domicil may rightfully devest the debtor of the administration of his property, and place it under the administration of assignees or syndics. (2) That laws whose effects are to regulate the capacity and incapacity of persons, their personal actions, and their movables, everywhere belong to the category of personal statutes. (3) That it is a matter of universal jurisprudence, and especially of that of France and the Netherlands, that the debts, actively considered, of an inhabitant against a foreigner, are deemed a part of his movable property, and have their locality in the place of domicil of the creditor.[2] At the same time, it is admitted that a purchaser from the bankrupt, in a foreign country, of property there locally situate, would be entitled to hold it against the assignees, if, at the time, he had no knowledge of any bankruptcy, or of any intent to defraud creditors.[3]

418. *Confirmatory Assignment by the Bankrupt.* — The American doctrine has been followed out to another result. Suppose (as was the fact in one case), after a commission and assignment in bankruptcy in England, the bankrupt should voluntarily make a confirmatory conveyance in aid of the commission; the question is, whether it will have the effect of a voluntary assignment, so as to defeat a subsequent attachment in America. It has been held by a learned judge in New York that it will not; because, by the law of England, the commission devests the title of the bankrupt in all his property throughout the world, and he no longer has any capacity to convey it; but, in regard to that property, he is to be treated as civiliter mortuus.[4] There is great difficulty in maintaining this doctrine. For if the statutable assignment does, per se, transfer the personal property of the bankrupt in foreign countries to the assignees, and devest all his

[1] Holmes v. Remsen, 4 Johns. Ch. (N. Y.) 484; 20 Johns. (N. Y.) 258; Blake v. Williams, 6 Pick. (Mass.) 312, 313; ante, s. 409, note; Henry on For. Law, p. 127–135, 153–160, 248–250.

[2] Merlin, Répertoire, Faillité and Banqueroute, s. 2, 3, art. 10, p. 412; Henry on Foreign Law, p. 127–135, 175.

[3] Merlin, id. p. 415, 416.

[4] Mr. Justice Platt, in Remsen v. Holmes, 20 Johns. (N. Y.) 267.

title to it, then it would seem to follow that a subsequent attachment of it must be wholly inoperative, because he has no longer any attachable interest in it. We are not at liberty to treat the property as still in him for one purpose, and out of him for another. The doctrine of Mr. Chancellor Kent is certainly here far more satisfactory, giving to such a voluntary assignment a full confirmatory effect.[1]

419. *Other Questions concerning Assignment in Bankruptcy.* — There are some other questions arising from the operation of foreign bankrupt laws, and other analogous systems of proceeding for the benefit of creditors generally, in invitum, which have come under judicial cognizance, and deserve attention. In the first place, suppose a British subject is declared bankrupt, while he is on a voyage in transitu from England to America; and he has a large shipment of property with him; is he entitled to hold it when it arrives in America? Or can his assignees maintain a suit against him, or against other persons, holding it for his use, not being creditors? It has been held, by a learned Chancellor of New York (Walworth), that the assignees are entitled to recover, upon the ground that the assignment operates as a good conveyance to them against the bankrupt, and those holding for his use. On that occasion the learned judge stated the distinction between that case and the preceding cases. 'In those cases,' said he, 'the contest was between foreign assignees and domestic creditors claiming under the laws of the country where the property was situate, and where the suits were brought. The question in those cases was, whether the personal property of the debtor was to be considered as having locality, for the purpose of giving a remedy to the creditors residing in the country where the property was in fact situated at the time of the foreign attachment. In this case the controversy is between the bankrupt and his assignees and creditors, all residing in the country under whose laws the assignment was made. Even the property itself at the time of assignment was constructively within the jurisdiction of that country, being on the high seas, in the actual possession of a British subject. Under such circumstances the assignment had the effect to change the property, and devest the title of the bankrupt, as if the

---

[1] Holmes *v.* Remsen, 4 Johns. Ch. (N. Y.) 489.

same had been sold in England under an execution against him, or he had voluntarily conveyed the same to the assignees for the benefit of his creditors.'[1] Upon an appeal however this doctrine was not in terms confirmed by the appellate court; and some of the judges dissented from the doctrine of the chancellor. But the case was ultimately reversed on another point.[2]

420. *Remarks on the American Doctrine.* — It is obvious that the great question involved in this case was, whether an assignment under a foreign bankrupt law operates as a transfer of personal property in this country. It matters not, in respect to the bankrupt himself, or others claiming under him, not being creditors or purchasers, whether it operates as a legal or as an equitable transfer. In either way it will devest him of his beneficial interest. Upon this point, it is impossible not to feel that the general current of American authority is in perfect coincidence with that of England, in favor of the title of the assignees.[3] In most of the cases in which assignments under foreign bankrupt laws have been denied to give a title against attaching creditors, it has been distinctly admitted that the assignees might maintain suits in our courts under such assignments for the property of the bankrupt.[4] This is avowed in the most unequivocal manner

[1] Plestoro *v.* Abraham, 1 Paige (N. Y.) 236; 3 Wend. (N. Y.) 538.

[2] Abraham *v.* Plestoro, 3 Wend. (N. Y.) 538. It is difficult to perceive how the doctrine of the chancellor, as to the operation of the British bankrupt laws upon British subjects and their property in transitu can be answered. The transfer must be admitted to be operative to devest the bankrupt's title to the extent of an estoppel as to his own personal claim in opposition to it; for the law of America, be it what it may, had not then operated upon it. It was not locally within our jurisdiction. No one could doubt the right of the assignee to personal property locally in England at the time of the assignment. In what respect does such a case differ from a case where it has not passed into another jurisdiction? Is there any substantial difference between its being on board of a British vessel and its being on board of an American vessel on the high seas? See ante, s. 391.

[3] See 1 H. Bl. 691; 6 M. & S. 126; 1 East, 6; Cooke's Bank. Laws, (4th ed.) 304; Doug. 161, 170; ante, s. 408-410.

[4] In Alivon *v.* Furnival, 1 C. M. & R. 296, it was held that, if by the law of the foreign country the assignees or syndics of a foreign bankrupt may sue there, the same right to sue in England will be allowed by the comity of nations; and that if there are three assignees or syndics appointed under the foreign law, and two may by that law sue without joining the third, the same right to sue by two will be acknowledged and enforced by the same comity in England. Upon that occasion Mr. Baron Parke, in delivering the opinion of the court, said: ' This is a peculiar right of action created by the law of the

in the leading cases in Pennsylvania and New York, already cited, and it is silently admitted in those in Massachusetts.[1] And unless the admission can be overthrown, it surrenders the principle; for no one will contend that the assignees can sue either in law or in equity in our courts, unless they possess some title under the assignment. The point has hitherto been a struggle for priority and preference between parties claiming against the bankrupt under opposing titles; the assignees claiming for the general creditors, and the attaching creditors for their separate rights.

421. *Language of Marshall, C. J.* — It is true that Mr. Chief Justice Marshall, in delivering the opinion of the court in Harrison v. Sterry,[2] used the following language: 'As the bankrupt law of a foreign country is incapable of operating a legal transfer of property in the United States, the remaining two thirds of the funds are liable to the attaching creditors, according to the legal preference obtained by their attachments.' But the very terms of this statement show that the court were examining the point only as between the conflicting rights of the assignees and those of the attaching creditors, and not in relation to the bankrupt himself. And this is manifestly the light in which the doctrine was contemplated by the majority of the court in a subsequent case.[3]

422. *Bankruptcy of one Partner.* — In cases of partnership, where there are different firms in different countries, or some of the partners reside in one, and some in another country, there are still more embarrassing difficulties attendant upon questions of foreign bankrupt assignments. If one partner is declared a bankrupt under a foreign commission, his share and interest only in the funds there can pass to his assignees, as against the part-

country, and we think it may by the comity of nations be enforced in this, as much as the right of foreign assignees or curators, or foreign corporations appointed or created in a different way from that which the law of this country requires.' See ante, s. 355, 399, 400; post, s. 565, 566.

[1] Holmes v. Remsen, 4 Johns. Ch. (N. Y.) 485; 20 Johns. (N. Y.) 262, 263; Milne v. Moreton, 6 Binn. (Penn.) 363, 374; Livermore, Dissert. 142, 152; Blake v. Williams, 6 Pick. (Mass.) 305; Ingraham v. Geyer, 13 Mass. 146, 147; Goodwin v. Jones, 3 Mass. 517. But see contra, Orr v. Amory, 11 Mass. 25. See ante, s. 399, note; post, s. 566.

[2] 5 Cranch, 289, 302. See also Ogden v. Saunders, 12 Wheat. 361, 362-364.

[3] Ogden v. Saunders, 12 Wheat. 359-365.

ners in another country. And of course they must take subject
to an account between all the partners, and stand precisely as the
bankrupt does, on a settlement of all claims as between debtor and
creditor.[1] Let us suppose the case of a partnership in the British
West Indies and in England; and one of the partners resides in
England and becomes bankrupt, and an assignment is made ; and
afterwards a British West India creditor of the firm attaches a
debt due to the firm in the West Indies, and procures a judgment
and satisfaction there. Can he be compelled to refund the same
upon a suit brought by the assignees against him in England ?
Sir William Grant, in a case of this sort, decided in the negative ;
and on that occasion seemed to have great difficulty in reconciling his mind to the decisions upon the more general questions
of satisfaction obtained abroad by a creditor in case of a sole
bankruptcy. He held that the bankruptcy of the partner resident in England could not affect the partners remaining in the
West Indies, in a country not subject to the bankrupt law, so as
to divest them of the management of the partnership concerns, or
of the disposition of the partnership property. If they applied
the partnership assets in the payment of the partnership debts ;
or if, in a legal course of proceedings against them, the debts were
recovered according to the law of the country, no jurisdiction
could exist in England to force the partnership, or the creditor,
to refund what he had so received or so recovered. Under such
circumstances the foreign partners and foreign creditors must be
left to their general rights and remedies.[2] The same doctrine
seems to be acknowledged in other nations where there are part-
nerships and partners resident in different countries.[3]

423. *Transfer by Marriage.* — But whatever may be the rule in
relation to foreign voluntary assignments or foreign bankrupt assignments for the benefit of creditors generally, there is no doubt
that there are some assignments which take effect by mere operation of law in foreign countries, and are admitted to have universal validity and effect upon personal property, without respect
to its locality.[4] Such is the case of a transfer of personal property arising from marriage. Thus a marriage contracted by

[1] Harrison v. Sterry, 5 Cranch, 289, 302.
[2] Brickwood v. Miller, 3 Meriv. 279.
[3] See Merlin, Répertoire, Faillité et Banqueroute, s. 2, art. 10, p. 414.
[4] See ante, s. 398.

citizens of Massachusetts is a gift in law to the husband of all the personal tangible property of the wife, and operates as a transfer of it to him, wherever it may be situate, at home or abroad. And the right thus acquired by the law of the matrimonial domicil will be held of perfect force and validity in every other country, notwithstanding the like rule would not arise in regard to domestic marriages by its own municipal code. This doctrine was adverted to by Lord Meadowbank, in a very important case already referred to, as perfectly clear and established. 'In the ordinary case,' says he, 'of a transference by contract of marriage, when a lady of fortune, having a great deal of money in Scotland, or stock in the banks or public companies there, marries in London, the whole property is, ipso jure, her husband's. It is assigned to him. The legal assignment of a marriage operates without regard to territory, all the world over.'[1] Lord Eldon, on several occasions, has given this doctrine the fullest sanction of his own judgment, averring that notice was not even necessary to give full effect to such a title.[2] The same doctrine was fully admitted in Remsen v. Holmes;[3] and it is treated by elementary writers as beyond controversy.[4] We have already seen that foreign jurists press the doctrine to its fullest extent.[5]

423 a. *Conflicting Claims to Debtor's Property.* — It is principally in cases of voluntary assignments, made by a debtor for the benefit of creditors, or of involuntary assignments under the bankrupt laws of a State against a debtor in invitum, that questions arise respecting the conflicting rights of creditors (concursus creditorum) as to the priorities and privileges in the distribution and marshalling of the assets, when they are insufficient to pay all the debts of the party. We have already had occasion to take notice that generally in cases of movable property, the priorities and privileges are to be adjusted, and the distribution is to be made, according to the law of the domicil of the debtor,[6] founded upon the notion that there all his movable property is in contemplation of law concentrated, although a part of it may

[1] Ante, s. 59, note; Royal Bank of Scotland v. Cuthbert, 1 Rose Appx. 481. See ante, s. 396–398.

[2] Selkrig v. Davis, 2 Rose, 97, 99, 291, 317.

[3] 20 Johns. (N. Y.) 267.

[4] 2 Bell Com. s. 1266, p. 696, 697, 4th ed.; Id. p. 680, 685, 686, 5th ed.; Livermore, Dissert. 140, s. 223.

[5] Ante, s. 145–147.

[6] Ante, s. 323–328.

be locally situated elsewhere, according to the maxim: 'Mobilia non habent sequelam ; mobilia tanquam ossibus affixa personæ.'[1] And in relation to immovable property the distribution is to be made according to the lex rei sitæ.[2] Exceptions may doubtless exist, where the law of the country in which either movable or immovable property is situate, prescribes a different rule, which must then be obeyed.[3] Similar rules will govern in cases of voluntary assignments by debtors, and of involuntary assignments under the bankrupt laws of a state. In each case the lex loci of the assignment or the bankruptcy will ordinarily form the basis of the priorities and privileges attaching to his movable property, and will regulate the distribution thereof among his creditors, at least if that is the place of his domicil, and of the situs of the property. If the property is immovable, or is situate elsewhere, the lex loci rei sitæ will, or at least may, govern the same.[4]

423 b. *Law governing Priorities.* — Priorities and privileges are indeed generally treated as belonging to the form and order of proceedings, and are therefore properly governed by the lex fori ; and they are not treated as belonging to the merits and matters of the decision. Rodenburg says: 'Primum utamur vulgata DD. distinctione, qua separantur ea, quæ litis formam concernunt ac ordinationem, separantur ab iis, quæ decisionem aut materiam. Lis ordinanda secundum morem loci, in quo ventilatur. Ut si judicati exequendi causa bona debitoris distrahantur, qui solvendo sit, executio peragatur eo loci ubi bona sita sunt, aut in causam judicati capiuntur. Sin cesserit foro debitor, aut propalam desierit esse solvendo, ut isti mobilium capioni, aut ulli omnino executioni non sit ultra locus, facta jam omnium creditorum conditione pari, disputatio de privilegiis, aut concursu creditorum, veniat instituenda, ubi debitor habuerit domicilium.'[5]

423 c. *Foreign Jurists.* — Matthæus (whose opinions have been already in part cited in another place [6]) holds that hypothecations of movables are to be governed by the law of the domicil of the debtor ; and hypothecations of immovables by the lex loci rei

[1] Ante, s. 362, 377, 378.   [2] Ante, s. 322-328; post, s. 428.
[3] See Rodenburg, de Divers. Statut. tit. 2, c. 5, s. 5, 6; 2 Boullenois, p. 87, 88; post, s. 550.
[4] Ante, s. 322, 328, 385-400, 402-422.
[5] Rodenburg, de Divers. Statut. tit. 2, c. 5, s. 16; 2 Boullenois, Appx. p. 46, 47; ante, s. 325 c-325 f, and note.
[6] Ante, s. 825 i, 325 k.

sitæ. In respect to priorities and privileges between hypothe-cary creditors upon movables, the law of the domicil of the debtor is to govern; and in respect to such priorities and privi-leges between hypothecary creditors upon immovables, the law of the situs rei, unless indeed the contest solely concerns their rights in the domicil of the debtor. 'Quantum ad leges, secundum quas in disputatione de protopraxia judicandum, distinctio adhi-benda est. Si bona mobilia debitoris in diversis provinciis sint, spectandæ sunt leges ejus loci, ubi debitor domicilium habet. Est enim vulgatum apud doctores, mobilia sequi personam, et id-circo censeri eo jure, quod obtinet, ubi domicilium persona ha-bet. Itaque si in loco domicilii valet pignus rei mobilis nudo pacto constitutum, manente possessione penes debitorem, potior erit in pignore is, cui ante res obligata est, licet non sit translata in eum possessio. Et si creditor aliquis in loco domicilii debitoris privilegium inter personales habeat, gaudebit eodem privilegio in ea civitate, in qua debitor tabernam habuit et merces. Contra, si in loco domicilii mobilia non habeant sequelam, nec creditor privilegium, frustra volet uti jure alterius civitatis, in qua utrum-que contrario modo se habere perspicit.' Quantum vero ad præ-dia attinet, separanda videtur hypotheca ab eo privilegio, quod quis inter hypothecarios exercet. In æstimanda hypotheca spec-tanda sunt ejus territorii jura, ubi prædium situm est. Itaque si in loco domicilii debitoris prædia obligari possint citra judicis auctoritatem, prædia vero sita sint in ea provincia, ubi, oppigne-ratio judicialis desideratur, frustra obtendes locum domicilii, ad excludendum secundum creditorem, cui coram judice loci præ-dium pignori nexum est. Quod, si utrique fundus rite oppigne-ratus sit, disputetur autem solummodo de privilegio, quod alter inter hypothecarios in loco domicilii debitoris habere se dicit, tum locus domicilii spectandus videtur: quia privilegium illud per-sonam concernit, fundum autem pigneratum non afficit.' [1]

423 d. Mr. Burge maintains a similar opinion, taking a distinc-tion between ordinary liens and the priorities between creditors. 'The vendor's lien,' says he, 'on the movables sold, and the right to stop them in transitu for the payment of the price, are privi-leges which attach to the subject sold, and are governed by the lex loci contractus. They are distinguished from the preferences

[1] Matthæus, de Actionibus, lib. 1, c. 21, s. 10, n. 35, p. 294, 295; Id. n. 41, p. 298, 299.

which a creditor may claim on the estate of a debtor, when it is distributed under an execution sale, or general concursus of his creditors. The latter depend not on the lex loci contractus, but on that of the place where the movable estate is fictione juris considered to be situated; namely, in the domicil of its owner. The lex loci contractus, although it is properly invoked as between the parties to the contract, yet it is considered unjust to give it effect against third parties, the creditors.'[1]

423 *e*. Mr. Bell adopts the doctrine in its fullest extent, that an assignment in bankruptcy conveys all the movable property of the bankrupt, wherever it may be, and it is to be distributed according to the law of the place where the debtor has his domicil, and the proceedings in bankruptcy are had. But in relation to immovable property, that it is to be distributed and administered according to the territorial law, his language is: ' The great rule on which the whole of the doctrine relative to the international effect of bankruptcy depends, has been completely fixed in all the three kingdoms upon a general principle of the law of nations, namely, that the personal estate is held as situate in that country where the bankrupt has his domicil, and that it is to be administered in bankruptcy according to the rules of the law of that country, just as if locally placed within it. The consequence of fixing this rule is, that a commission of bankruptcy in England or in Ireland, and the assignment following on it, or a sequestration in Scotland, and the conveyance to the trustee, have the effect of transferring to the trustee or assignees the whole personal estate of the bankrupt; that this transference defeats all preferences attempted to be obtained by the diligence of the law of the country where such estate happens to be placed, or by any voluntary conveyance of the bankrupt, after the period when the effect of the proceedings under the bankruptcy attaches to the funds.'[2] And again: ' Another great point in this doctrine is, what effect shall be allowed in Scotland to a different decision in any foreign country from that which has been adopted in these islands? Let it be supposed, for example, that effects of the bankrupt are in a country in which the sequestration and the conveyance to the trustee are held to be of no force, and where preference is given

---

[1] 3 Burge, Col. & For. Law, pt. 2, c. 20, p. 770; Id. p. 778, 779; ante, s. 327, note.
[2] 2 Bell Com. s. 1266, p. 684, 685, 4th ed.; Id. p. 681, 682, 5th ed.

to the diligence of the country in which the effects are situated; is the creditor who recovers payment under such local rule obliged to pay over to the trustee in this country, for general distribution, the money he has received? And this again resolves into two questions: (1) Whether the creditor can claim for any balance without having communicated what he has received? and, (2) Whether he is liable to an action for restitution? In England, where there is no provision by statute for regulating this matter, it is held, (1) That an English creditor, who, having notice of the bankruptcy, makes affidavit in England, in order to proceed abroad, cannot retain against the assignees what he recovers; (2) That a creditor in the foreign country would not, if preferred by the laws of that country, be obliged to refund in England; and, (3) That, at all events, such a creditor cannot take advantage of the bankrupt laws in England, without communicating the benefit of his foreign proceedings. In Scotland, there is an express provision in the statute relative to payments and preferences abroad, the policy of which it is proper to explain. As the jurisdiction of the Court of Session does not reach foreign countries, wherever the principle of the law of nations does not operate, or has been evaded, it is provided: (1) That the creditor who, after the first deliverance on the petition for sequestration, shall obtain payment or preference abroad, shall be obliged to communicate and assign the same to the trustee for behoof of the creditors, before he can draw any dividend out of the funds in the hands of the trustee; and, (2) That, in all events, whether he claims under the sequestration or not, he shall be liable to an action before the Court of Session, at the instance of the trustee, to communicate the said security or payment, in so far as the jurisdiction of the court can reach him. It may however, as already observed, be doubted whether this enactment, in so far as it exposes a creditor to a challenge, even where he does not claim under the sequestration, might be held to include foreign creditors not apprised of the bankruptcy and proceedings in this country, but who, having recovered in the usual way the property of their debtor abroad, should have come afterwards to Scotland. Recently the question occurred under these enactments, whether a local statute in one of our colonies abroad, which was said to proceed on views of local utility, did not so far qualify the sequestration statute of this country that the foreign creditors should be entitled to retain the preference they had obtained. But the court held that the preference could not be supported. As to real estate, the estate in land or connected with land, there is a difference of principle very remarkable. The real estate is not, like the personal, regulated by the law of the domicil, but by the territorial law. A real estate in England is not held to be under the disposition of the bankrupt laws of Scotland, if the proprietor be a trader there. Nor is an heritable estate in Scotland affected by the commission of the English law. And yet the spirit and policy of the laws, considered internationally, should open to the creditors of a bankrupt in either country the power of attaching his real estates.' [1]

423 f. *Preferences by the Debtor.* — In regard to voluntary assignments for the benefit of creditors with certain preferences, they must, as has been already stated,[2] as to their validity and operation, be governed by the lex loci contractus. (a) If they are valid there, full operation will ordinarily be given to them in every other country where the matter may come into litigation and discussion. But it is a very different question, whether they shall be permitted to operate upon property locally situated in another country, whether movable or immovable, by whose laws such a conveyance would be treated as a fraud upon the unpreferred creditors. That question was discussed in the case already alluded to, where an assignment, made in Alabama, giving preferences to certain creditors, came collaterally under discussion in Louisiana, by whose laws such an assignment would be treated as a fraud. On that occasion the court said: 'We find no difficulty in assenting to the proposition, that contracts entered into in other states, as it relates to their validity and the capacity of the contracting parties, are to be tested here by the lex loci celebrati contractus. This court has often recognized that doctrine as well settled. When a contract is entered into in Alabama, in conformity to the local law, to have its effects and execution there, it is clear the courts of this state cannot declare its nullity on the ground that such a contract would not be valid according to our system of jurisprudence. Such would be the case, even if

[1] 2 Bell Com. s. 1266, p. 689, 690, 4th ed.; Id. p. 685, 686, 5th ed. See Lord Eldon's remarks in Selkrig v. Davis, 2 Rose, 311.

[2] Ante, s. 259 a.

(a) See United States v. Bank of United States, 8 Rob. (La.) 262.

one of the contracting parties, or both, were not citizens of Alabama. If Andrews, for example, had been a citizen of Louisiana, having creditors and effects both here and in Alabama, had gone over to that state, and transferred a portion of his property there to certain preferred creditors, such a transaction, as to its legality, would depend upon the law of Alabama. But if such a citizen of Louisiana should immediately afterwards seek to avail himself of the benefit of our insolvent laws, a different question would present itself. Although our courts might not be authorized to annul such contracts, as to their effects between the parties ; yet they might well inquire whether it was not the intention of the legislature to afford the protection of the insolvent laws to such only as shall have abstained from giving an undue preference to certain creditors, in derogation of that vital principle of our system, that the property of the debtor forms the common pledge of his creditors, and although such preferences may be tolerated by the lex loci. If the legislature has thought proper to declare such a condition as one upon which shall depend the right to claim the benefit of the insolvent laws, which it is not denied they had an unquestionable right to do, then there is an end to the argument, unless it can be shown that the mere residence of the party in another state dispenses him from a compliance with the creditor.' [1]

423 g. *Collisions at Sea.* — These are by no means the only cases of a conflict of laws, or of rights growing thereout, touching personal or movable property ; and which ought to admonish us of the danger and difficulty of attempting to lay down universal rules on such complicated subjects. By the laws of many of the nations of continental Europe, in cases of collision of ships by accident, without any fault on either side, the loss is to be sustained by a contribution by both ships.[2] By the law of England in such a case there is no contribution whatsoever; but each party is to bear his own loss. Res perit domino.[3] Now let us suppose that such a collision takes place upon the high seas, beyond any territorial jurisdiction, between an English ship and a foreign continental ship, whose laws divide the loss, and

---

[1] Andrews v. His Creditors, 11 La. 476, 477. See also 2 Bell Com. s. 1266, p. 684–686, 4th ed.; Id. p. 681–683, 5th ed.

[2] Story on Bailm. s. 608; Peters v. Warren Ins. Co., 14 Pet. 99.

[3] Story on Bailm. s. 608, 610.

both or either of the ships is injured thereby. How is the loss to be borne? Will it make any difference whether the proceeding against the ship or owners for redress is in England, or in the proper continental court? (a) If the right depends upon the law of the place where the proceedings are had against the ship or the owner, then there will be no reciprocity in the operation of the rule. In a case so confessedly novel in its presentation, it will be found very difficult to affirm any ground of principle upon which the law of the one country, rather than that of the other, ought to prevail.[1] (b)

423 h. *Torts committed on the Seas.* — Considerations of an analogous nature may be presented in cases of torts committed on the high seas, and in other extra-territorial places, by the subjects of one nation upon vessels or other movable property belonging to the subjects of another nation, where the laws of these nations are different, touching either the nature and character and consequences of the tort, or the rule of damages applicable thereto. It is not easy to say, in such cases, what laws ought to govern.

---

[1] The very question was recently presented at Havre, in France, in the case of the steamship James Watt, an English ship, which was seized in France for having by collision run down a French ship at sea. The court of Rouen, it is said, decided against the right to seize and detain her. But the ground of the decision is not stated. See also Abbott on Shipp. by Shee, p. 184, note z, the case of the Maria, there stated. See also 3 Hagg. Adm. 169, 184, 244. See also General Steam Nav. Co. v. Guillou, 11 M. & W. 877.

(a) See The Leon, 6 P. D. 148.

(b) This subject received great consideration in a recent case before the Privy Council. A British steamer collided with a Norwegian bark in Belgian waters, through the alleged negligence of those employed on the steamer, which was however in charge of a pilot whom by the Belgian law the steamer was obliged to employ. By that law the owners are responsible for damages done by collision, although the vessel is in charge of a compulsory pilot, which is contrary to the law of England (see the Merchant Shipping Act, 1854, 17 & 18 Vict. c. 114, s. 388); and the question was whether the Belgian or the English law as to the foundation of the liability was to be adopted in the English courts; and it was held that the foreign law did not supersede the English law, and consequently that the owners of the steamer were not liable in an English court, whether they were so or not in a Belgian tribunal. The Halley, Law Rep. 2 P. C. 193. In the earlier case of Smith v. Condry, 1 How. 28, it was held by the Supreme Court of the United States that the liability for a collision between two American vessels in an English port must be determined by the law of England; and if by the English law the owner is not responsible for the negligence of a licensed pilot, he will not be so held in America, but apparently the question was not much discussed. See The Scotland, 105 U. S. 24.

The most that can with any probability be stated is, that, in the absence of any general doctrine to the contrary, either each nation would, in respect to the case when pending in its own tribunals, follow its own laws; [1] or would apply the rule of reciprocity, granting or refusing damages, according as the law of the foreign country to which the injured ship belonged would grant or withhold them in the case of an injured ship belonging to the other nation.[2] The rule of reciprocity is often applied in cases of the recapture of ships from the hands of a public enemy.[3]

[1] See Percival v. Hickey, 18 Johns. (N. Y.) 257.
[2] The Girolamo, 3 Hagg. Adm. 169.
[3] The Santa Cruz, 1 Rob. 50; 2 Wheat. Appx. 44, 45; The Adeline, 9 Cranch, 244. In the case of The Vernon, 1 W. Rob. 316, which was a case of collision between a British ship, having on board a licensed pilot, and a foreign ship, the British ship's pilot being in fault, Dr. Lushington held the owners of the British ship not responsible for the damage, upon the ground that the foreign ship seeking the remedy must take it according to the law of the country where the suit is brought. Quære, if this was a case within the meaning of the rule, did the statute apply to foreign ships or only to British ships ?

CHAPTER X.

REAL PROPERTY.

424. *The Law governing Immovables.* — Having disposed of the more important questions which have arisen respecting personal property, we are next led to the consideration of the operation of foreign law in regard to real or immovable property. (*a*) And here the general principle of the common law is, that the laws of the place where such property is situate, exclusively govern in respect to the rights of the parties, the modes of transfer, and the solemnities which should accompany them.[1] (*b*) The title therefore to real property can be acquired, passed, and lost only according to the lex rei sitæ. This is generally, although (as we shall presently see) not universally, admitted by courts and by jurists, foreign as well as domestic. Paul Voet states the rule in a brief but clear manner: 'Ut immobilia statutis loci regantur, ubi sita.'[2] He adds in another place, 'Quid si itaque contentio de aliquo jure in re, seu ex ipsa re descendente, vel ex contractu, vel actione personali, sed in rem scripta? An spectabitur loci statutum, ubi dominus habet domicilium, an statutum rei sitæ? Respondeo: Statutum rei sitæ.'[3] Sir William Grant lays down

[1] See on the subject of this chapter, 2 Burge, Col. & For. Law, pt. 2, c. 9, p. 840–870; 4 Id. pt. 2, c. 4, s. 5, p. 150, &c.; Id. c. 5, n. 11, p. 171, 217; Id. c. 12, p. 576; Foelix, Conflit des Lois, Revue Étrang. et Franç. tom. 7, 1740, s. 27–37, p. 216–230; Id. p. 307–312.

[2] P. Voet, de Stat. s. 9, c. 1, n. 3, p. 253, ed. 1715; Id. p. 307, ed. 1661. Yet we shall see that Paul Voet adopts some strange notions as to the forms and solemnities of instruments of transfer of real estate, whether inter vivos or testamentary, holding that the lex loci actus, and not the lex loci rei sitæ, ought to govern. Post, s. 442.

[3] P. Voet, de Statut. s. 9, c. 1, n. 2, p. 253, ed. 1715; Id. p. 305, ed. 1661.

(*a*) Leasehold or chattel interests in land are classed as immovables. Freke *v.* Carbery, L. R. 16 Eq. 461; In bonis Gentili, Ir. R. 9 Eq. 541. But see Despard *v.* Churchill, 53 N. Y. 192. See also s. 447, post.

(*b*) See however, for a qualification of this rule, Watkins *v.* Wallace, 19 Mich. 57.

the rule in very expressive terms. ' The validity of every disposition of real estate,' says he, ' must depend upon the law of the country in which that estate is situated.' [1] The same rule would also seem equally to apply to express liens and to implied liens upon immovable estate.[2]

425. *Personal and Real Laws.* — And here it may be proper to advert a little more particularly to some of the definitions of foreign jurists in regard to personal laws and to real laws. We have already seen that laws purely personal are those which solely affect the person, without any reference to property.[3] Laws purely real, directly and indirectly regulate property and the rights of property, without intermeddling with or changing the state of the person.[4] There are other laws again which are deemed both personal and real, containing a mixed operation upon persons and property, and which are therefore called mixed.[5] Thus a particular law which shall authorize a minor or other person, ordinarily incapacitated, to dispose of property under particular circumstances, would be deemed a mixed law; because so far as it affects the particular capacity of a person it is personal; and so far as it enables him to do a particular act respecting property it is real.[6] In illustration of these distinctions, Boullenois considers the law known as the Senatus-consultum Velleianum, prohibiting married women from making contracts, as purely personal; a law declaring that no person of full age shall devise more than a third or fourth part of his property, as purely real; and a law allowing a minor (otherwise incapacitated), when married, to make a testament or donation in favor of his wife, as mixed.[7] These distinctions are very

[1] Curtis v. Hutton, 14 Ves. 537, 541; Chapman v. Robertson, 6 Paige (N. Y.) 627, 630; Elliott v. Lord Minto, 6 Madd. 16; Birtwhistle v. Vardill, 5 B. & C. 438; 9 Bligh, 32-88; post, s. 428-444.

[2] See 1 Boullenois, p. 683 et seq., 689, 818; Rodenburg, de Divers. Stat. tit. 2. c. 3. s. 16; 2 Boullenois, Appx. 47; 1 Hertii Opera, de Collis. Leg. s. 4, n. 64, p. 150; P. Voet, de Stat. s. 9, c. 1, n. 2, p. 253, ed. 1715; Id. p. 307, ed. 1661; ante s. 322-328; Id. s. 363-374; 1 Burge, Col. & For. Law, pt 1, c. 1, p. 23, 26; Curtis v. Hutton, 14 Ves. 537, 541; Elliott v. Lord Minto, 6 Madd. 16.

[3] 1 Boullenois, Prin. Gén. 10, p. 4.

[4] 1 Boullenois, Prin. Gén. 22, p. 6; Id. Prin. Gén. 21, p. 7. See P. Voet, de Stat. s. 4, c. 2, n. 4, p. 134, 135, ed. 1661.

[5] 1 Boullenois, Prin. Gén. 15, 16, p. 5.   [6] Ibid.

[7] 1 Boullenois, Prin. Gén. 14, 15, 16, p. 5-7; Id. obs. 2, p. 25-28; Id. obs.

important in examining the doctrines of foreign jurists, as they often enter very deeply into the elements of their particular opinions.[1]

426. *Foreign Jurists.* — Now in regard to laws purely real, Boullenois lays down the rule in the broadest terms, that they govern all real property within the territory, but have no extension beyond it. 'Les lois réelles n'ont point d'extension directe ni indirecte hors la jurisdiction et la domination du législateur.'[2] In regard to mixed laws he lays down the rule expressly, that of right they act only upon real property within the territory to which the persons are subject; but that sometimes they act upon real property situate elsewhere; and then it is only because the laws are conformable to each other, and by a sort of kindred title only (à titre de paternité seulement).[3] Rodenburg lays down a like rule in regard to real laws, dismissing as unnecessary the class of mixed laws: 'Statuta realia inter et personalia hoc interest, quod illa, in re scripta, territorii sui concludantur metis, hæc extra eas vim et effectum protendant.'[4] Paul Voet contends that no personal laws can regularly extend to immovable property situate in a foreign country; 'Non tamen statutum personale sese regulariter extendet ad bona immobilia alibi sita;'[5] and he treats it as utterly unimportant whether it assume to do so directly or indirectly, openly or consequentially. 'Neque hic distinguam, cum lex non distinguat, an sese extendat statutum

16, p. 206; obs. 23, p. 456, 457, 477, 488; 2 Boullenois, obs. 32, p. 11. This definition of mixed laws is given by Boullenois, who has drawn it from Rodenburg. But it is very different, as he informs us, from the sense in which D'Argentré, Burgundus, and Voet use the same phrase. 1 Boullenois, Prin. Gén. 16, p. 5; Id. obs. 5, p. 122–140; Rodenburg, de Div. Stat. tit. 1, c. 2; 1 Boullenois, obs. 2, p. 25–29; Id. obs. 3, p. 29–48. See also 1 Froland, Mém. c. 6, p. 114.

[1] J. Voet has devoted a whole title to the subject of personal, real, and mixed laws, which will reward the diligence of the student in a thorough perusal. J. Voet, ad Pand. 1, 1, 4, p. 2, 38 et seq. The same subject is elaborately discussed by Froland. 1 Froland, Mém. c. 4, p. 49, c. 5, p. 31, c. 6, p. 114.

[2] 1 Boullenois, Prin. Gén. 27, p. 7; Id. 280. Froland lays down the rule in even more brief terms. Le statut réel ne sort point de son territoire. 1 Froland, Mém. 156. And he applies the same rule to mixed statutes. Id. 157.

[3] 1 Boullenois, Prin. Gén. 20, 21, p. 6; 1 Boullenois, obs. 16, p. 223, 224.

[4] Rodenburg, de Div. Statut. tit. 1, c. 3; 2 Boullenois, Appx. p. 7; 1 Boullenois, 145; Id. obs. 9, p. 152; Id. 230.

[5] P. Voet, ad Stat. s. 4, c. 2, n. 6, p. 123, ed. 1715; Id. p. 138, ed. 1661.

directe ad bona extra territorium statuentium sita, an indirecte, an propalam, an per consequentiam. Cum non sint indirecte, in fraudem legis aut statuti permittenda, quæ directe sunt prohibita.'[1]

426 a. John Voet resolutely maintains the same opinion.[2] D'Argentré holds the following language: 'Quæ realia aut mixta sunt, haud dubie locorum et rerum situm sic spectant, ut aliis legibus, quam territorii, judicari non possint.'[3] Huberus, after remarking that the foundation of the general doctrine is the subjection of every man to the laws of a country, so long as he continues to act there, which makes his act there valid or invalid, according as those declare it, proceeds to say that this reasoning does not apply to immovable property, which does not depend upon the mere will of the owner; but, so far as certain characters are impressed upon it by the law of the country where it is situate, these characters remain indelible in that country, whatever dispositions the laws of other countries or the acts of private persons may ordain otherwise or contrary thereto. Nor would it be without great confusion and prejudice to the country where the immovable property is situate, that its own laws respecting it should be changed by such dispositions. 'Fundamentum universæ hujus doctrinæ diximus esse, et tenemus, subjectionem hominum infra leges cujusque territorii, quamdiu illic agunt, quæ facit, ut actus ab initio validus aut nullus, alibi quoque valere aut non valere non nequeat. Sed hæc ratio non convenit rebus immobilibus, quando illæ spectantur, non ut dependentes a libera dispositione cujusque patrisfamilias, verum quatenus certæ notæ lege cujusque reip., ubi sita sunt, illis impressæ reperiuntur; hæ notæ manent indelibiles in ista republica, quicquid aliarum civitatum leges, aut privatorum dispositiones, secus aut contra statuant; nec enim sine magna confusione præjudicioque reip., ubi sitæ sunt res soli, leges, de illis latæ, dispositionibus istis mutari possent.'[4] He adds in another place: 'Communis et recta sententia est, in rebus immobilibus servandum est jus loci, in quo bona sunt sita.'[5]

[1] P. Voet, de Stat. s. 4, c. 2, 6, 7, p. 123, 124, ed. 1715; post, s. 442.
[2] J. Voet, ad Pand. 1, 1, 4, s. 7, p. 40; ante, s. 54 a; post, s. 433 a.
[3] D'Argentr. de Briton. Leg. art. 218, gloss. 6, n. 8, p. 650; post, s. 439; Livermore, Dissert. s. 97, p. 77.
[4] Huberus, de Conflict. Leg. lib. 1, tit. 3, s. 15; post, s. 413.
[5] Huberus, tom. 1, pt. 1, lib. 3, tit. 13, s. 21. De Success. ab Intes. p. 278. See post, s. 443, 443 a, 476.

426 *b*. Christinæus takes the common distinction in various places between movable property and immovable property, alleging that it is observed, as a general rule, that movable property is governed by the law of the domicil, and real property by the law of the situs rei. 'Ubi pro regula generali servatum fuit, quod bona mobilia sequi et regulari debent secundum statuta loci domicilii ejus, ad quem pertinent vel spectant, immobilia vero juxta statuta locorum, ubi illa sunt sita, ut communiter tenent interpretes, licet dicta regula non semper locum habeat.' [1]

427. But it is wholly unnecessary to repeat at length the opinions of foreign jurists, since in the main proposition they generally, although not universally, concur (for some of them insist upon certain exceptions, to which we may hereafter allude) that the law of the situs exclusively governs as to immovable property.[2] Pothier has laid down the rule in the most general form,

[1] Christinæus, tom. 2, decis. 5, n. 1–4, p. 7. Mr. Foelix on this subject says: 'Cette loi réelle régit les biens situés dans l'étendue du territoire, pour lequel elle a été rendue, en excluant l'application de la loi personelle du propriétaire, ou de celle du lieu où l'acte a été passé ; (nous parlerons plus bas de l'application de cette dernière loi); mais aussi les effets de cette loi ne s'étendent jamais au-delà des limites du territoire. Telle est la règle reconnue par toutes les nations et professée par les auteurs. Nous citerons Burgundus (tract. 1, nos. 4, 11, 12, et 14), Rodenburg (tit. 1, c. 2), Paul Voet (de statutis, s. 4, c. 2, nos. 4, et 6), Jean Voet (ad ff. tit. de Stat. no. 3), Abraham à Wessel (art. 16, no. 19), Christin. (Decisiones, vol. 2, tit. 1, dec. 3, no. 2), Boullenois (aux endroits cités au no. 24 ci-dessus, et t. 1, p. 107), Hert. (sect. 4, s. 9), Huber. (no. 15), Cramer (Observationes Juris Universi, tom. 5, obs. 1462), Pothier (sur la coutume d'Orléans, c. 1, s. 2, nos. 22, 23, et 24; c. 3, no. 51), Vattel (liv. 2, c. 8, s. 103 et 110), Gluck (Commentaire, s. 76, Droit Privé, s. 17 et 18,) Danz (Manuel, t. 1, s. 53, no. 1), Portalis, père (Exposé de motifs du Code Civil, Locré, t. 1, p 581; v. aussi le discours du tribun Faure, ibid, p. 613), Meier (pt. 17), MM. Mittermaier (s. 32), Eichhorn (s. 36), Tittman (ch. 5), Muhlenbruch (s. 72, no. 2), Brinkmann (p. 10 et 11), Story (s. 374, 424, et suiv., et surtout s. 428), Wheaton (c. 2, s. 5, t. 1, p. 136), Rocca (pt. 104, 110, 118 et 122), et Burge (Règle 6, t. 1, p. 25; t. 2, p. 14, 26, 78, et 840).' Foelix (Conflit des Lois, Revue Étrang. et Franç. tom. 7, s. 27, p. 217, 218).

[2] The learned reader may consult Livermore's Dissert. s. 9–162, p. 28–106; Hertii Opera, tom. 1, de Collis. Leg. s. 4, n. 9, p. 125, ed. 1737 ; Id. p. 177, ed. 1716; Ersk. Inst. b. 3, tit. 2, s. 40, p. 515; Bouhier, Cout. de Bourg. c. 23, s. 36, 37–63, p. 456, 457 ; 2 Bell Com. s. 1266, p. 690, 4th ed.; Id. p. 687, 688, 5th ed.; Fergusson on Marr. and Div. 395; Le Brun, de la Communauté, lib. 1, c. 5, p. 9, 10; D'Aguesseau, Œuvres, tom. 4, p 660, 4to ed.; Cochin, Œuvres, tom. 1, p. 545, 4to ed.; Id. p. 555; Henry on Foreign Law, p. 12, 14, 15; Id. App. p. 196; J. Voet, ad Pand. 1, 4, 2, s. 3, 5, 6, p. 39, 40; 1 Froland, Mém. c. 4, p. 49, c. 7, p. 155; 2 Kames Eq. b. 3, c. 8, s. 2. Mr. Burge on this subject says: 'The summary given in the preceding chapters exhibits a great

declaring that real laws have an exclusive dominion over all
things submitted to their authority, whether the persons owning

diversity amongst the laws which regulate the modification and creation of
estates and interests in real property, and the transfer and acquisition of it.
The law of the place, where the act making the modification or alienation is
passed, frequently differs either from that of the place in which the party to
the act was domiciled, or from that of the place in which the property is situated. It becomes necessary to inquire which of these conflicting laws is
selected, and what are the principles on which the selection is made. There
exists a difference of opinion amongst jurists, as to the law which ought to
govern the decisions of some of the subjects comprehended under the titles
which have been just mentioned, when one of the conflicting laws affects persons as well as things, or where it applies to the form and solemnity of the *acte*
by which the modification or alienation of property is passed, as well as to
things. The primary or principal object of the law, or the comparative degree
in which, in the one case, it affects persons or things, and in the other, the
form of the act or thing, affords the ground on which some jurists consider the
law as real or personal, and accordingly adopt the lex loci rei sitæ, or the law
of the domicil, or that of the place in which the act is passed. In the opinion
of other jurists, if the law of the situs be prohibitive, it must be preferred to
the personal law of the domicil, without regard to the object of that law, or
its immediate effect upon the status of the person. There is however no difference of opinion among them in adopting the lex loci rei sitæ in all questions
regarding the modification or creation of estates or interests in immovable property. This subject does not involve any of the considerations which, in
other cases, produced that difference of opinion. The law primarily and principally affects things. It is wholly independent of the status of persons, and
is strictly a real law. There is the concurrence therefore not only of those
jurists who give the greatest effect to the lex loci rei sitæ; but even of those
who are disposed to give such an effect to laws affecting the general status of
persons as would greatly control the operation of the lex loci rei sitæ. Thus,
according to the definition of Rodenburg, " In solas nudasque res statuti dispositio dirigitur, ut nullum intervenire necesse sit actum hominis aut aliquam
concurrere personæ operam." It is comprised in the rule laid down by Burgundus: " Statuta realia sunt, quæ de jure, et conditione, seu qualitate rei disponunt. Statuto reali propositum est dirigere res ipsas, certisque qualitatibus
dominia afficere." The doctrine of D'Argentré is to the same effect: " Realia
sunt, ut quæ de modo dividendarum hereditatum constituuntur, in capita, in
stirpes, aut talia. Item de modo rerum donandarum, et quota donationum."
" Item illud, ne in testamento legari posset viro ab uxore, quod quidem de
immobilibus constituit et rebus soli, etsi mixtam habeat de personis conside-
tionem, quando impotentia agnatis applicatur rei soli : Nam si de mobilibus
solum quæreretur, posset videri in totum esse personale." The doctrine of
Dumoulin is: " In his quæ concernunt rem, vel onus rei, debet inspici consuetudo loci ubi sita res est." Boullenois also concurs in treating that law as real:
" Qui affecte directement les biens en fixant leur sort, et leur destination par
une disposition particulière et indépendante de l'état personnel dont l'homme
est affecté pour les actes du commerce civil, encore que quelquefois ce statut
ait égard à l'état personnel que nous avons ci-devant appellé par politique et
distinctif." Merlin maintains the same doctrine : " Si l'objet principal, direct,

them live within the territory or without the territory.[1] And
Vattel has laid it down as a principle of international law, that ✓

immédiat de la loi, est de régler la qualité, la nature des biens, la manière d'en
disposer," it is a real law, and that, "les effets par rapport aux personnes ne
sont plus, que des conséquences éloignées de la réalité." The estate or interest
which the law permits or prohibits to be created in immovable property, whether
it be by substitution, entail, executory devise, condition, or any other species
of limitation, may be considered as a quality impressed on and inherent in the
property. So also are the rules and limits under which the permission is
given. According to the doctrine of those jurists who are the most disposed
to allow personal laws affecting the general status to control those of the situs,
the law which confers on immovable property its qualities, is strictly real, and
prevails over the personal law. Thus Hertius defines the law to be real when
it impresses any certain quality on immovable property: "Rebus fertur lex,
cum certam iisdem qualitatem imprimit, vel in alienando, e. g. ut ne bona
avita possint alienari, vel in acquirendo, e. g. ut dominium rei immobilium venditæ non aliter acquiratur, nisi facta fuerit judicialis resignatio." The same
rule is laid down by Mestertius and Burgundus, and is followed by Boullenois.
These jurists, in treating of the solemnities which the law requires should accompany certain acts, distinguish those which are "tanquam qualitates rebus
impressæ." The existence and nature of those qualities must be determined by
the law of the situs. It is conceived therefore to be indisputable that the law
of the situs must be adopted in all questions respecting the power of alienating
immovable property, or the restrictions under which that power may be exercised. Hence also it follows that the law of the situs must prevail when the
question regards the existence or validity of any substitution, the degrees to
which it may be limited, the manner of computing those degrees, or the extent
to which the power of alienation may be restrained, and generally the condition to which the persons substituted may be subjected. Upon the same principles it will decide if the question regard the acts which are essential to
render the substitution or entail valid, or the respective rights and liabilities
of the fiduciary, fidei commissary, or tenant in tail.' 2 Burge, Col. & For. Law,
pt. 2, c. 9, p. 840–844. Again, alluding to the same subject in another place,
he says: ' In treating of the alienations of real property by act inter vivos, it
has been stated as a conclusion, sanctioned by the authority of jurists and of
judicial decisions, and most consistent with admitted principles, that the capacity to make and to take under the alienation was governed by the law of the
actual situs of the property if it were immovable, and by that of the domicil
if it were movable. It is admitted by all jurists that the transfer of and title
to real property must be regulated by the lex loci rei sitæ; that a law which
prohibits its alienation is a real law, and must, in whatever place the alienation is attempted, prevent the acquisition of any title. It necessarily follows
from that admission, that the character and effect of the law must be the same,
whether its prohibition has relation to the quality of the property itself, or to
the person of the owner; or whether the prohibition be general and absolute,
or partial and qualified, or existing only sub modo. It is a quality impressed
on the property no less when the property is prohibited to be alienated under

---

[1] Pothier, Coutume d'Orléans, c. 1, s. 2, n. 22-24, c. 3, n. 51.

immovables are to be disposed of according to the laws of the country where they are situate.[1]

428. *Uniformity of Doctrine in England and America.* — The consent of the tribunals, acting under the common law, both in England and America, is in a practical sense absolutely uniform on the same subject. All the authorities in both countries, so far as they go, recognize the principle in its fullest import, that real estate, or immovable property, is exclusively subject to the laws of the government within whose territory it is situate.[2] (*a*)

particular circumstances, than when it is prohibited to be alienated under any circumstances, or when it is prohibited to be alienated by and to persons standing in certain relations to each other, or by persons who are under a certain age, or who are in any situation which by the law precludes them from making or taking under the alienation.' 4 Burge, Col. & For. Law, pt. 2, c. 12, p. 577; Id. p. 550-596.

[1] Vattel, b. 2, c. 8, s. 110; Id. s. 103; Chapman *v.* Robertson, 6 Paige (N. Y.) 627.

[2] The authorities are very numerous in which it has been decided or taken for granted; and among them in England are, Sill *v.* Worswick, 1 H. Bl. 665; Hunter *v.* Potts, 4 T. R. 182; Phillips *v.* Hunter, 2 H. Bl. 402; Selkrig *v.* Davis, 2 Rose, 291; 2 Dow, 230; Coppin *v.* Coppin, 2 P. Wms. 290, 293; Brodie *v.* Barry, 2 V. & B., 130; Birtwhistle *v.* Vardill, 5 B. & C. 438; 2 Bell Com. 690, 4th ed.; Id. p. 687, 5th ed.; and in America are, United States *v.* Crosby, 7 Cranch, 115; Clark *v.* Graham, 6 Wheat. 577; Kerr *v.* Moon, 9 Wheat. 566; Harper *v.* Hampton, 1 Harr. & J. (Md.) 687; Goodwin *v.* Jones, 3 Mass. 514, 518; Cutter *v.* Davenport, 1 Pick. (Mass.) 81, 86; Holmes *v.* Remsen, 4 Johns. Ch. (N. Y.) 460; 20 Johns. (N. Y.) 254; Hosford *v.* Nichols, 1 Paige (N. Y.) 220; Blake *v.* Williams, 6 Pick. (Mass.) 286; Milne *v.* Moreton, 6 Binn. (Penn.) 359. See also 4 Cowen, 510, 527, note; Dwarris on Stat. 620, 649; Wills *v.* Cowper, 2 Ham. Ohio, 124; Henry on Foreign Law, 8, 9; McCormick *v.* Sullivant, 10 Wheat. 192; Darby *v.* Mayer, 10 Wheat. 465; Curtis *v.* Hutton, 14 Ves. 537, 541; Elliott *v.* Lord Minto, 6 Madd. 16; Chapman *v.* Robertson, 6 Paige (N. Y.) 627, 630; Cockerell *v.* Dickens, 3 Moore P. C. 98, 131, 132; Tulloch *v.* Hartley, 1 Y. & C. C. C. 114; post, s. 434; ante, s. 424.

(*a*) See Potter *v.* Titcomb, 22 Me. 300; McGoon *v.* Scales, 9 Wall. 23; Oakey *v.* Bennett, 11 How. 33; Knox *v.* Jones, 47 N. Y. 389; White *v.* Howard, 46 N. Y. 144; Monroe *v.* Douglass, 5 N. Y. 447; Wheeler *v.* Walker, 64 Ala. 560; Goodman *v.* Winter, Id. 410; Brock *v.* Frank, 51 Ala. 85; Pope *v.* Pickett, 51 Ala. 584; Lingen *v.* Lingen, 45 Ala. 410; Apperson *v.* Bolton, 29 Ark. 418; Gardner *v.* Commercial Bank, 95 Ill. 298; Besse *v.* Pellochoux, 73 Ill. 285; Bissell *v.* Terry, 69 Ill. 184; City Ins. Co. *v.* Commercial Bank, 68 Ill. 348; Cooley *v.* Scarlett, 38 Ill. 316; Hutcheson *v.* Peshine, 16 N. J. Eq. 167; Beall *v.* Lowndes, 4 S. C. 258; Chamberlain *v.* Napier, 15 Ch. D. 614; Brine *v.* Insurance Co., 96 U. S. 627; Collier *v.* Blake, 14 Kans. 250; Sell *v.* Miller, 11 Ohio St. 331; Nicholson *v.* Leavitt, 4 Sandf. 276; Augusta Ins. Co. *v.* Morton, 3 La. An. 418. But see Watkins *v.* Wallace, 19 Mich. 57.

So that we may here fully adopt the language of John Voet: 'De realibus quidem, cum plerorumque consensus sit, id pluribus docere supervacuum fuerit.'[1] Indeed so firmly is this principle established, that in cases of bankruptcy the real estate of the bankrupt, situate in foreign countries, is universally admitted not to pass under the assignment, although, as we have seen, there are great diversities of opinion as to movables.[2] And Lord Eldon has gone so far as to declare that there exists no legal or equitable obligation (although there is a moral obligation) in the bankrupt to make a conveyance thereof to his assignees; and that the creditors are without redress, unless by way of remedy in rem where the real estate is situate, or by withholding a certificate of discharge until the bankrupt executes such a conveyance.[3]

429. *Application of the Rule.* — Considering however the diversity of opinion on this subject among foreign jurists, it may be of some utility to examine into the application of the general rule in some of its more important aspects. We shall therefore consider it, first, in relation to the capacity of persons to take or to transfer real estate; secondly, in relation to the forms and solemnities necessary to transfer it; thirdly, in relation to the extent of interest to be taken or transferred in it; and fourthly, in relation to the subject-matter itself, or what are properly to be deemed immovables.

430. *Capacity to take.* — First, in relation to the capacity of persons to take or transfer real estate. It may be laid down as a general principle of the common law, that a party must have a capacity to take according to the law of the situs, otherwise he will be excluded from all ownership. Thus if the laws of a country exclude aliens from holding lands, either by succession, or by purchase, or by devise, such a title becomes wholly inoperative as to them, whatever may be the law of the place of their domicil.[4] On the other hand, if by the local law aliens may take and hold lands, it is wholly immaterial

[1] J. Voet, ad Pand. 1, 5, 2, s. 6, p. 40.

[2] Selkrig v. Davis, 2 Rose, 97, 191; 2 Dow, 230, 250; 2 Bell Com. 690, 4th ed.; Id. p. 687, 5th ed.; ante, s. 403–422, 423 a.

[3] Selkrig v. Davis, 2 Rose, 97, 281; 2 Dow, 230, 250. But see Stein's Case, 1 Rose. 462; ante, s. 423 a.

[4] See Buchanan v. Deshon, 1 Har. & G. (Md.) 280; Sewall v. Lee, 9 Mass. 363.

what may be the law of their own domicil either of origin or of choice. (a)

431. *Capacity to transfer.* — So if a person is incapable from any other circumstance of transferring his immovable property by the law of the situs, his transfer will be held invalid, although by the law of his domicil no such personal incapacity exists. On the other hand, if he has capacity to transfer by the law of the situs, he may make a valid title, notwithstanding an incapacity may attach to him by the law of his domicil. (b) This is the silent but irresistible result of the principle adopted by the common law, which has no admitted exception. We may illustrate the principle by an application to cases of common occurrence under the dominion of the common law. By that law a person is deemed a minor, and is incapable of conveying real estate, until he has arrived at twenty-one years of age. But by the law of some foreign countries minority continues until twenty-five or even until thirty years of age. Let us then suppose a foreigner owning lands in England or America (where the common law prevails), who is by the law of his domicil in his minority, but who is over twenty-one years of age. It is clear that he may convey his real estate in England or America, notwithstanding such domestic incapacity ; for he is of the age required by the local law.[1] On the other hand, let us suppose a married woman, who is domiciled in a foreign country, and by the law of that country is capable of alienating her real estate without the consent of her husband, owning real estate in England or in America, where she is incapable of alienating it without such consent; she cannot alienate it without the consent of her husband ; and her separate act will be held ipso facto void by the law of the situs.(c)

432. *Foreign Jurists.* — But however clear this may seem according to the principles of the common law on this subject, a very different doctrine is, as we have already seen, maintained by many foreign jurists on this very point.[2] They contend that

[1] See Saul v. His Creditors, 5 Mart. N.S. (La.) 569, 597.
[2] Ante, s. 51, 52-61, 65; 1 Burge, Col. & For. Law, pt. 1, c. 1, p. 21-23.

(a) This subject of the capacity to take is more fully considered in c. 4, ante, and in the notes. The effect of legitimation and of adoption is considered in s. 93 s, and note at the end of the section.

(b) See Sell v. Miller, 11 Ohio St. 331; O'Dell v. Rogers, 44 Wis. 136.

(c) See Doyle v. McGuire, 38 Iowa, 410; Frierson v. Williams, 57 Miss. 451; Shacklett v. Polk, 51 Miss. 378; Thurston v. Rosenfield, 42 Mo. 474.

the capacity or incapacity of persons to transfer property, or
to do any other act, depends altogether upon the law of the
place of their domicil. If they have a capacity or incapacity
there, it governs all their property elsewhere, whether movable
or immovable. Thus Boullenois maintains that if a man has
immovable property in a place where majority is attained at
twenty-five, and by the law of his domicil he is of age at twenty, he may at twenty sell or alienate such immovable property.
And on the other hand, if by the law of the situs of the immovable property he is of age at twenty, but by the law of his
domicil not until twenty-five, he cannot sell or alienate such
property until the age of twenty-five.[1] Rodenburg adopts the
same doctrine, and maintains it with abundance of zeal.[2] After having remarked that among personal statutes are to be
reckoned all laws which affect the state or condition of the
person, such as laws respecting majority, the paternal power
over children, the marital power over the wife, and cases of
prodigals, he adds : ' De quibus et similibus id juris est, ut quo-
cumque transtulerit persona statuto loci domicilii ita affecta, habilitatem aut inhabilitatem ademptam domi, circumferat ubique,
ut in universa territoria suum statutum exerceat effectum.'[3]

[1] Ante, s. 52, 71. There is a curious distinction maintained by many
jurists on this subject, which deserves notice. They say that if the local law
fixes the age of majority at a particular period, and declares that until the
party has arrived at that period he shall not alienate immovable property, in
that case the local law governs; for it does not turn upon the mere fact of being
a major or not. But if the local law only says that no person who is not a
major shall alienate, then, if the party is a major by the law of his domicil,
though not by that of the rei sitæ, he may alienate the property, because the
only point is majority or not, and that must be ascertained by the lex domicilii; for the state or capacity of a person by the law of his domicil extends
everywhere. Boullenois dwells much on this distinction, and it has received
the support of Merlin. 1 Boullenois, obs. 4, p. 57; Id. obs. 5, p. 102; Id. obs.
12. p. 175; Id. obs. 13, p. 183; Id. obs. 23, p. 499; Id. obs. 28, p. 700, 705,
720; Boullenois, Quest. Mixt. p 19; 2 Merlin, Répertoire, Testament, s. 1, 6,
art. 3, p. 318, art. 2, p. 317, 318; Id. art. 3; 2 Froland, Mém. des Stat.
p. 824, 825; Livermore, Dissert. s. 44, p. 48; Id. s. 47, 48, p. 50; Id. s. 59–62,
p. 58–60.

[2] Rodenburg, de Div. Stat. tit. 2, c. 1; 2 Boullenois, Appx. p. 10; 1 Boullenois, 77, 79, 154, 155, 194, 295; 1 Hertii Opera, de Collis. Leg. s. 4, n. 23,
p. 133, ed. 1737; Id. p. 175, ed. 1716; Livermore, Dissert. s. 31, p. 40; Id.
s. 44, p. 48; Id. s. 45, 46, p. 49; Bouhier, Cout. de Bourg. c. 24, s. 91–108,
p. 476–478; ante, s. 51, 51 a, 52, 52 a, 53.

[3] Rodenburg, de Divers. Stat. tit. 2, c. 1; 2 Boullenois, Appx. p. 11;
ante, s. 51.

Yet Rodenburg himself deserts this doctrine in regard to the capacity and incapacity to make a will or testament, which he holds must be according to the lex rei sitæ.[1] There are many others who adhere to the same opinion.[2] The ground-

[1] Rodenburg, de Divers. Stat. tit. 2, c. 5, n. 7; 2 Boullenois, Appx. p. 38, 39. His language is: Sed, ut id, quod instat, agamus: quid si nostras testetur anno ætatis decimo quarto, sortieturne effectum dispositio in rebus, quæ alterius regionis solo inhæreant, in qua major ad testandum desideratur ætas? Sit dubitanda ratio, quod de personarum ætate ac capacitate lata lex in personam concepta esse videatur, adeoque ad quæcunque producenda territoria. Verum contra reale statutum esse inde dixeris, quod in statutum ac conditionem personæ non sit scriptum, sed expressim directum in rerum alienationes aut alterationes, et quidem per solam testamenti speciem, adeoque circumscriptive ad istum alienationis actum; cujusmodi statuta realia esse traditum sæpius; et vel inde in proposito conspicere est, quod immoto personæ statu, quæ nulla ex parte tutelæ subducitur, auctoritate tutoris non spectante minoris testationes, tribuatur nostratibus hæc testamenti factio, adeoque cum status non turbetur, lex personalis dici nequeat. See also 4 Burge, Col. & For. Law, pt. 2, c. 12, p. 578, 579. On this subject Mr. Burge has well remarked: ' The difficulty of adopting such a distinction arises from the consequences to which it leads, for it seems to import that if the law of the situs prohibits the alienation by a minor, the question whether he is a minor, or, in other words, whether he is competent to make a testament, is to be determined, not by that law, but by the law of his domicil. But if the law had prohibited an alienation by a person who had not attained the age of twenty-one or twenty-five years, or any other age which was prescribed by the law as the age of majority, the law of the situs would prevail, and the competence of the person would depend on his having attained that age. But without further pursuing the inquiry, which has already been made in the former volume, it may be considered, that the opinions of Dumoulin, Burgundus, Peckius, John and Paul Voet, and the decision reported by Stockmans, afford authority sufficient to justify the conclusion that the capacity to alienate by testament is that which is established by the law of the country in which the immovable property is situated, and by that of the domicil, when the testamentary disposition regards movable property.' Ibid. See also 1 Burge, Col. & For. Law, pt. 1, c. 1, p. 21-23; post, s. 433 a.

[2] Ante, s. 51-54, 60; 1 Froland, Mém. des Statuts, 65, 66; Livermore, Dissert. s. 47, p. 54, s. 55, p. 56; 2 Froland Mém. des Stat. p. 1576-1594; Merlin, Répertoire, Testament, s. 1, 5, art. 2, p. 517, 518; 1 Boullenois, obs. 6, p. 127-140; Id. obs. 28, p. 705-731. This is manifestly the opinion of Mr. Livermore (Diss. p. 40-42; 48-57). So of Merlin (Répertoire, Majorité, s. 5; Autorisation Maritale, s. 10, art. 2; Id. Puissance Paternelle, s. 7, p. 142-146); of Froland (1 Froland, Mém. des Stat. p. 156, 171; 2 Id. p. 1595); of Bouhier (Bouhier, Cout. de Bourg. c. 23, s. 90-96, p. 461; Id. c. 24, s. 91, &c. p. 476; 1 Boullenois, obs. 28, p. 724); of Pothier (Pothier, Cout. d'Orléans, c. 1, s. 1, n. 7, p. 2); of Huberus (Huberus, lib. 1, tit. 3, s. 12; ante, s. 60); and of Hertius (Hertii Opera, tom. 1, de Collis. s. 4, n. 8, p. 123, 124, ed. 1737; Id. p. 175, ed. 1716). Merlin in another place admits that a law which prohibits a prodigal from making a testament is personal; but at the same time it will not prevent

work of their argument is, that the capacity and incapacity of the person must be uniformly the same everywhere; that the law of the domicil ought to regulate it; and that it would be utterly incongruous to make a minor in one place a major in another, thus investing him with opposite personal qualities.[1]

433. This notion is combated with great vigor and ability by other foreign jurists, whose opinions have been already alluded to.[2] Burgundus admits that personal laws, as to capacity, or incapacity govern all personal acts, such as personal contracts. 'Nam (ut Imola et Castrensis scripsere), qui inhabilis est in uno loco, etiam in alio censetur inhabilis ; quod utique accipiendum est de habilitate, vel inhabilitate, quæ a statuto personali procedit, et ad actus personales dirigitur.'[3] But in regard to immovable property

the prodigal from making a valid will of immovable property in a foreign country which allows it (as in Bourbourg); for which he gives two reasons: first, that a law is real which permits one act to be done by a person who is otherwise incapable; and, secondly, because a real law always prevails when it comes in conflict with a personal law. He applies the same rule to an unemancipated son who cannot by the law of his domicil make a testament, but yet may alienate any of his property acquired in Hainault; for its laws form an exception to the general incapacity of the son, and therefore they are real. Merlin Répertoire, Testament, s. 1, n. 5, art. 1, p. 310. This opinion seems to coincide with that of Hertius (1 Hertii Opera, de Collis. Leg. 4, n. 22, p. 133, ed. 1787; Id. p. 188, ed. 1716). It seems also supported by Rodenburg (Rodenburg, de Div. Stat. pt. 1, tit. 1, c. 2; 2 Boullenois, Appx. p. 4–6, cited by Merlin, ubi supra). But Merlin says that if, by the laws of the country of his domicil, an unemancipated son cannot make a testament, and by the laws of another country he has a general capacity; in such a case such laws are personal and in conflict, and therefore the law of the domicil is to govern. Merlin, ibid. p. 311. See also 1 Boullenois, obs. 5, p. 77, 78. Boullenois lays down some rules upon this subject, which seem also to have received the approbation of Bouhier. (1) When the personal statute of the domicil is in conflict with the personal statute of another place, the law of the domicil is to prevail. (2) When the personal statute of the domicil is in conflict with the real statute of the same or another place, it yields to the real statute. (3) When the real statute of the domicil is in conflict with the real statute of the situs of the property, each one has its own authority in its own territory. 1 Boullenois, Pr. Gén. 29–31; Id. obs. 5, p. 181, 182; Bouhier, Cout. de Bourg. c. 23, s. 90, 96, p. 461; Id. c. 24. s. 91, &c., p. 476; Livermore, Dissert. s. 59, p. 58, 59. See the opinion of Grotius, cited post, s. 479.

[1] Mr. Henry says that the personal statutes of one place may act indirectly and by comity on immovable property situate in another; as a decree of lunacy may by its effects deprive a party of a power to alienate his foreign property, and so of the disability created by bankruptcy. Henry on Foreign Law, 15. This seems inadmissible as a doctrine of the common law.

[2] Ante, s. 52–54 a.

[3] Burgundus, tract. 1, n. 7, 8, p. 19. See also Rodenburg, de Div. Stat.

he says that it is sufficient that a person be of the age required by the law of the situs, to authorize him to make a valid transfer, although he may be incapable by the law of his domicil. His language is: ' Quippe (sicut Bartolus existimat) habilitas personæ ad actus personales non trahit effectum ad res sitas extra territorium. Proinde, si peragendum est aliquid circa rem, jam non respiciemus personæ statum, quem foris assumpsit; sed an mancipans in ea sit conditione quam bonorum situs ipse requirit.' [1] And again : ' Et quidem eodem modo, quoties de jure, vel servitute, aut libertate personæ quæritur, item de facultate ad res personales constituta, respondendum erit secundum conditionem personæ, quam induit in loco domicilii. Et contra, ergo si de jure ac facultate, quæ a re ipsa proficiscitur, item de ejus servitute, atque libertate, plane ad leges situs spectare oportet. Cum enim unicuique provinciæ suæ propriæ sint leges, possessionibus injunctæ atque indictæ, sane incapacitas foris adepta in considerationem venire non potest; sed omnis, sive qualitas, sive personæ habilitas, quoad eadem bona pertinet, a loco situs proficiscitur.' [2] Bartolus affirms the same doctrine. ' Cum est, quod de aliquo jure descendente ex re ipsa servari consuetudo vel statutum loci, ubi est res.' [3] Boullenois, after some fluctuations of opinion, comes to the result that the capacity to make a testament, so far as it regards the person, is personal; but so far as it regards immovables is real, and governed by the law of the situs of the property.[4]

433 a. Stockmans, Dumoulin, Bouhier, Paul Voet, and John Voet maintain the same opinion.[5] Dumoulin says : ' Aut statutum agit in rem, et quacumque verborum formula utatur, semper

tit. 2, c. 1; 2 Boullenois, Appx. p. 11, 12; 1 Boullenois, obs. 6, p. 127–131; Id. p. 199, 201, 202; Livermore, Dissert. s. 47–49, p. 50–52; Bouhier, Cout. de Bourg. c. 24, s. 91, 94–107, p. 476–478.

[1] Burgundus, tract. 1, n. 8, p. 19; ante, s. 54; Livermore, Dissert. s. 47, 48, p. 51, 52.

[2] Burgundus, tract. 1, n. 8, p. 19, 20. See also 1 Boullenois, obs. 6, p. 129, 130; Id. obs. 9, p. 150; ante, s. 372.

[3] Bartol. ad Cod. 1, 1, n. 27; Bartol. Oper. tom. 7, p. 5.

[4] 1 Boullenois, obs. 28, p. 718–720. See Id. obs. 5, p. 81–84, 101, 102. See also Merlin Répert. Testament, s. 1, n. 8, art. 1, p. 310; Cochin, Œuvres, tom. 4, p. 555, 4to ed.

[5] Livermore, Dissert. s. 49–52, p. 52–54; 1 Froland, Mém. des Stat. p. 65, 66; 2 Id. p. 819–823; 4 Burge, Col. & For. Law, pt. 2, c. 12, p. 579; ante, s. 432, note.

inspicitur locus ubi res est.[1] Si statutum dicat, quod minor 25 annis non possit testari de immobilibus, tunc enim non respicit personam, nec agit in personam principaliter, nec in solemnitatem actus, sed agit in certas res, ad finem conservandi patrimonii, et sic est reale. Quia idem est, ac si dictum esset, immobilia non possint alienari in testamento per minores. Unde statutum loci inspicietur, sive persona subdita sit, sive non.'[2] Stockmans says: 'Jampridem pragmaticorum consensa et usu fori invaluit, ut ubicumque agitur de rerum soli alienatione, mancipatione, investura, successione, aliisque translationis et acquisitionis modis, inspiciuntur leges loci, ubi res sitæ sunt, sive quæstio sit de ætate, vel alia qualitate, habilitate, vel inhabilitate personæ sive agatur de statuto verbis in rem, sive in personam, directe concepto; cum effectus ipse, potius quam verba, attendendus sit, qui prorsus realis est, quoties de rebus soli transferendis et mancipandis quæritur; atque proinde ab hoc effectu statutum omne, quod huc respicit, vel eo rem deducit, pro reali habendum judicandumque sit.'[3] Paul Voet adds that personal laws do not regularly extend, so as to affect immovable property in a foreign country, either directly or consequentially.[4] John Voet has gone into an elaborate consideration of the subject, and positively denies that personal laws can operate out of the territory. 'Nulla tamen ratione,' says he, 'sufficiente, cum hæc nitantur, nec a legibus Romanis huic sententiæ patrocinium accedere possit; verius est personalia, non magis quam realia, territorium statuentis posse

---

[1] Molin. Com. ad Cod. 1, 1, 1, Conclus. de Statut. tom. 3, p. 556; Livermore, Dissert. s. 81, p. 69.

[2] Molin. Com. ad Cod. 1, 1, 1, Conclus. de Statut. tom. 3, p. 556; post, s. 475; Bouhier, Cout. de Bourg. c. 24, s. 91–102, p. 476–478; 1 Froland, Mém. des Stat. p. 65.

[3] Stockmans, decis. 125, n. 9, p. 263; ante, s. 54; Livermore, Dissert. s. 50, p. 52, 53; 2 Burge, Col. & For. Law, pt. 2, c. 9, p. 863, 864.

[4] P. Voet, de Stat. s. 4, c. 2, n. 6, p. 124, ed. 1715; Id. p. 138, ed. 1661; ante, s. 54, note. Paul Voet admits that personal laws accompany the person everywhere, as to property within the territory of the government of which he is a subject; but not as to any property elsewhere. Statutum personale ubique locorum personam comitatur, in ordine ad bona infra territorium statuentis, ubi persona affecta domicilium habet. Non tamen statutum personale sese extendit ad bona immobilia alibi sita. P. Voet, de Stat. s. 4, c. 2, n. 6, p. 123, ed. 1715; Id. p. 138, ed. 1661. In another place he says: Immobilia statutis loci reguntur, ubi sita. P. Voet, de Stat. s. 9, c. 1, n. 4, p. 252, 253, ed. 1715; Id. p. 306, 307, ed. 1661; ante, s. 54, note; post, s. 475, 488 b; ante, s. 52, 52 a; J. Voet, ad Pand. 1, 4, s. 2, 9, p. 43.

excedere, sive directo, sive per consequentiam.' And he proceeds to put very pointed inquiries whether any foreign country will permit its own territorial laws to be overthrown by the laws of another country, on the subject of prodigals, infamous persons, minors, illegitimacy, or legitimacy and heirship.[1]

433 *b*. Christinæus adopts the same opinion. ' Quod cum de rebus soli, hoc est immobilibus, agitur, et diversa diversarum possessionum loca, et situs proponuntur, in acquirendis transferendis, et asserendis, dominiis, et in controversia quo jure reguntur, certissimam in usu observationem esse noti satis juris, est, id jus de pluribus spectari, quod loci est vel situs, et suas quoque leges, statuta et consuetudines servandos fore ; sic quod de talibus nulla cujusquam potestas sit præter territorii legem.'[2] Peckius is equally direct. ' Etenim natura statuti est, ut non extendatur ad bona in alio territorio sita, ubi contraria stat juris dispositio.[3] Bona autem dicuntur esse in ejus jurisdictione, in cujus territorio sunt.'[4] And again : ' Quod sive statutum loquatur in rem sive in personam, habeat locum in bonis positis in territorium statuentium, et non in aliis.'[5]

434. *Common Law.* — The opinion of these latter jurists is in coincidence with that of the common law, as already stated ; and it has been fully recognized in England in a recent case, of which we have had occasion to take notice in another place.[6] Upon that occasion Lord Chief Justice Abbott said : ' The rule as to the law of domicil has never been extended to real property ; nor have I found, in the decisions of Westminster Hall, any doctrine giving a countenance to the idea that it ought to be so extended. There being no authority for saying that the right of inheritance follows the law of the domicil of the parties, I think it must fol-

---

[1] J. Voet, ad Pand. 1, 4, s. 7, pars 2, de Stat. p. 40, cited at large, ante, s. 54 *a*. There are some jurists who adopt an intermediate opinion, holding that in order to transfer real property the party must have capacity according to the lex domicilii and the lex rei sitæ. Thus, if in the country rei sitæ the age to convey is twenty-one years, and in the country of the domicil the age is twenty-five years, a party cannot convey, although he is twenty-one years of age, nor unless he is twenty-five. Ante, s. 432, note, s. 388.

[2] Christin. decis. 3. vol. 2, p. 4 ; 1 Boullenois, obs. 6, p. 127-140.

[3] Peck. Oper. de Testam. Conjug. lib. 4, c. 8, n. 5, p. 619, ed. 1666.

[4] Ibid.

[5] Ibid. n. 6, 7, p. 620.

[6] Ante, s. 87.

low that of the country where the land lies.' The same doctrine was concurred in by the other judges.[1]

435. *Forms and Solemnities of Transfer.* — Secondly, in relation to the forms and solemnities of passing the title to real estate.[2] We have already had occasion to examine the point, whether executory contracts respecting real estate must not be in the form prescribed by the local law, in order to have validity; as, for instance, a contract for the sale of land in England to be in writing according to the statute of frauds.[3] The result of that examination was, that in countries acting under the common law the affirmative is admitted; (a) although foreign jurists are divided on the point.[4] It would seem clear also, according to

[1] Birtwhistle v. Vardill, 5 B. & C. 438. But see S.C. 2 Cl. & F. 571; 9 Bligh, 32-88.

[2] See 2 Burge, Col. & For. Law, pt. 2, c. 9, p. 840-870; 1 Id. pt. 1, c. 1, p. 21-23.

[3] Ante, s. 263-373. See also 2 Burge, Col. & For. Law, pt. 2, c. 9, p. 867-869.

[4] Ante, s. 337, 363-373. M. Foelix, speaking on this subject, says: 'Un principe aujourd'hui généralement adopté par l'usage des nations, c'est que "la forme des actes est réglée par les lois du lieu dans lequel ils sont faits ou passés." C'est-à-dire que, pour la validité te tout acte, il suffit d'observer les formalités prescrites par la loi du lieu où cet acte a été dressé ou rédigé: l'acte ainsi passé exerce ses effets sur les biens meubles et immeubles situés dans un autre territoire, dont les lois établissent des formalités différentes et plus étendues (locus regit actum). En d'autres termes, les lois qui réglent la forme des actes étendent leur autorité tant sur les nationaux que sur les étrangers, qui contractent ou disposent dans le pays, et elles participent ainsi de la nature des lois réelles.' Foelix, Conflit des Lois, Revue Étrang. et Franç. 1840, tom. 7, s. 40, p. 346, 347. And again: ' Parmi les écrivains modernes, nous en comptons trois qui n'adoptent point la maxime que la forme des actes est réglée par la loi du lieu dans lequel ils sont faits ou passés. Suivant M. Eichhorn, les actes d'une personne qui affectent sa fortune, doivent, en règle générale, être conformés aux lois de son domicile, quant à la forme et quant à leur substance, lorsqu'on se propose de les mettre à exécution dans ce domicile: la raison en est, dit l'auteur, dans le principe de la souveraineté des nations et dans la loi 21 ff. de obl. et act. (Contraxisse unusquisque in eo loco intelligitur, in quo ut solveret, se obligavit.) Cette règle, continue l'auteur, admet des exceptions: 1°, lorsque l'acte a été fait sans fraude dans un pays étranger où il y a eu impossibilité de remplir les formes prescrites au lieu du domicile de la personne, qui contracte ou qui dispose; 2°, lorsque l'acte a été fait dans un pays étranger dont les lois ne protégent les actes et contrats qu'autant qu'on y a suivi une certaine forme; 3°, lorsque le statut réel exige, pour l'acquisition ou l'aliénation d'un immeuble, un acte qui précède, la forme et le contenu de cet acte doivent se régler par ce statut réel. — Par application de la règle professée par

(a) See Siegel v. Robinson, 56 Penn. St. 19.

the common law, that no conveyance or transfer of land can be
made, either testamentary or inter vivos, except according to the

M. Eichhorn, cet auteur soutient que le testament fait en pays étranger, d'après
les formes qui y sont établies, n'aura ses effets dans la patrie du testateur,
quant à la forme, qu'autant que les lois de cette patrie reconnaissent la
même forme, à moins que le testateur ne soit également décédé dans le pays
de la confection du testament: dans ce dernier cas seulement, ledit testament
sortirait ses effets dans sa patrie.   La proposition enseignée par Eichhorn peut
être vraie en droit étroit; mais elle est contraire à l'usage des nations, attesté
par le sentiment général des auteurs cités plus haut: on ne doit donc pas
s'arrêter à l'opinion isolée de M. Eichhorn.   D'ailleurs, les exceptions admises
par cet auteur, sur tout la première, remènent son système à celui que nous
avons exposé au n° 41: en effet, notre système a précisément sa base principale
dans l'impossibilité ou du moins dans la difficulté de remplir à l'étranger les
formalités prescrites au lieu du domicile de l'individu.   Du reste, notre système admet aussi les deux exceptions énoncées par M. Eichhorn sous les n° 2
et 3, ainsi que nous l'expliquerons au n° suivant.   M. Mühlenbruch, en parlant
des testaments, revient sur l'opinion par lui émise dans sa doctrina pandectarum; il se range de l'avis de M. Eichhorn.   Le troisième auteur qui repousse
l'application de la règle, locus regit actum, en ce qui concerne la forme des
actes, c'est Hauss.   Il regarde cette règle comme vague et inutile, et il n'en
admet l'application que dans deux cas: le premier, lorsqu'il s'agit d'actes de
procédure (si de processu ordinando quæritur); le second, lorsque les parties
en vertu du leur autonomie, se sont soumises aux lois du pays dans lequel elles
ont passé un acte.   L'opinion de cet auteur a sa base dans une confusion
d'idées: il a cherché à appliquer la règle, locus regit actum, non seulement à
la forme des actes, mais encore à leur substance; n'ayant pu parvenir à justifier
cette opinion, il a rejeté entièrement ladite règle, et il a cru trouver uniquement
dans la volonté expresse ou tacite des parties, la base de l'application des lois
du lieu, quant à la forme et quant à la matière de l'acte.   L'acte fait d'après
les formes prescrites par la loi du lieu de sa rédaction est valable, non seulement par rapport aux biens meubles appartenant à l'individu et qui se trouvent
au lieu de son domicile, mais encore par rapport aux immeubles, en quelqu'endroit qu'ils fussent situés.   Cette dernière proposition, selon la nature des
choses, admet une exception, dans le cas où la loi du lieu de la situation prescrit,
à l'égard des actes translatifs de la propriété des immeubles ou qui y affectent
des charges réelles, des formes particulières qui ne peuvent être remplies ailleurs
que dans ce même lieu: telles sont la rédaction des actes par un notaire du
même territoire, la transcription ou l'inscription aux registres tenus dans ce
territoire, des actes d'aliénation, d'hypothèque, etc.   L'acte fait dans un pays
étranger suivant les formes qui y sont prescrites, ne perd pas sa force, quant à sa
forme, par le retour de l'individu au lieu de son domicile: aucune raison de droit
ne milite en faveur de l'opinion contraire.   La règle, locus regit actum, ne doit
pas être étendue au delà des limites que nous lui avons tracées au n° 40, ne
s'applique qu'à la forme extérieure, et non pas à la matière ou substance des
actes, ainsi que nous l'expliquerons encore au s. suivant.   Ainsi, dans un testament, la capacité de la personne et la disponibilité des biens ne se règlent point
par la loi du lieu de la rédaction.   Dans les dispositions entre-vifs, soit à titre
onéreux, soit à titre gratuit, la loi du lieu de la rédaction peut avoir influé, soit
sur l'ensemble de l'acte, soit sur les termes employés par les parties; et, sous

formalities prescribed by the local law. Thus, in England, no instrument not under seal can operate as a conveyance of land, so as to give a perfect title thereto. An instrument, therefore, not under seal, executed in a foreign country where no seal is required to pass the title to lands, would be held invalid to pass land in England.[1] The same rule is established in America, where it is held (as we have seen), that the title to land can be acquired and lost only in the manner prescribed by the law of the place where the property is situate.[2] (a)

436. *Scotch Law.* — Erskine, in his Institutes, states this to be the law of Scotland. 'In the conveyance,' says he, 'of an immovable subject, or of any right affecting heritage, the grantor must follow the solemnities established by the law, not of the country where he signs the deed, but of the state in which the heritage lies, and from which it is impossible to remove it. For though he be sub-

ce double titre, cette loi peut être consultée par les juges comme moyen d'interprétation; mais elle ne forme pas la loi décisive, à moins que les parties ne s'y soient soumises expressément. La règle indiquée au n° 40 ne s'applique pas seulement aux actes publics ou solennels, mais aussi aux actes sous signature privée, comme, par exemple, les testaments olographes. Feu M. Merlin fait remarquer que "la règle, locus regit actum, est générale, et il faudrait, pour la restreindre aux testaments reçus par personnes publiques, une exception autorisée par une loi expresse." Nous ajouterons que les raisons exposées au n° 41 s'appliquent aux actes sous seing-privé comme aux actes publics. Nous regardons comme une erreur l'opinion contraire professée par M. Duranton. Nous empruntons à M. Pardessus une observation importante. C'est que, dans tous les cas où l'une des parties invoque un acte passé hors du royaume, il faut avant tout s'assurer que l'acte a été passé dans le lieu régi par les lois auxquelles on veut le soumettre.' Id. s. 42–47, p. 350–354.

[1] Ante, s. 363, 364. See Dundas v. Dundas, 2 Dow & Cl. 349; Abell v. Douglass, 4 Denio, 305; Coppin v. Coppin, 2 P. Wms. 291, 293; 2 Fonbl. Equity, b. 5, c. 1, s. 6, note, p. 444, 445.

[2] Ante, s. 427, 428; United States v. Crosby, 7 Cranch, 115; Cutter v. Davenport, 1 Pick. (Mass.) 81, 86; Hosford v. Nichols, 1 Paige (N. Y.) 220; Wills v. Cowper, 2 Hamm. (Ohio) 124; Wilcox, 278; Kerr v. Moon, 9 Wheat. 566; McCormick v. Sullivant, 10 Wheat. 192; Darby v. Mayer, 10 Wheat. 465.

(a) See Goddard v. Sawyer, 9 Allen, (Mass.) 78; Houston v. Nowland, 7 Gill & J. (Md.) 480; Osborn v. Adams, 18 Pick. (Mass.) 245; Rabun v. Rabun, 15 La. An. 471. But see Watkins v. Wallace, 19 Mich. 57. The validity of a mortgage of land situated in one state is to be governed by the law of that state, although both parties reside in another state and the mortgage is executed there. Goddard v. Sawyer, 9 Allen, (Mass.) 78. But the *assignment* of a mortgage of real estate, which is mere personalty, is to be governed by the law of the state where made, and not of the state where the land is. Dundas v. Bowler, 3 McLean, 397.

ject with respect to his person to the lex domicilii, that law can have no authority over property which hath its fixed domicil in another territory, and which cannot be tried but before the courts and according to the laws of that state where it is situated. And this rule is so strictly adhered to in practice, that a disposition of an heritable jurisdiction in Scotland, executed in England after the English form, was not sustained, even as an obligation to compel the grantor to execute a more formal conveyance.'[1] He is well borne out in his doctrine by other authorities.[2]

437. *Foreign Jurists.* — Boullenois admits that, when an incapacity to do an act, or to make a conveyance of a thing except by certain formalities, if created by the lex rei sitæ, that law must be observed in regard to that thing, although the party be otherwise capable by the law of his domicil.[3] He adds, in an-

[1] Ersk. Inst. b. 3, tit. 3, s. 40, p. 515; Id. s. 41; 2 Kames Eq. b. 3, c. 8, s. 2, p. 328. But Erskine, in the same section, makes a distinction between contracts to convey real estate situate in Scotland and actual transfers, holding that, if the contract to convey is good by the lex loci contractus, it will be enforced in Scotland; but an actual transfer will not. ' But,' says he, ' though obligations to convey, if they be perfected secundum legem domicilii, are binding here; yet conveyances themselves, if of subjects within Scotland, are not always effectual if they are not executed according to the solemnities of our law.' The other part of the section has been already cited in a note, ante. s. 365. The common law, as we have seen, with masculine vigor and upon principle, rejects such niceties; and indeed it seems repudiated by many of the learned judges of Scotland. Ante, s. 365. See Lang v. Whitlaw, 2 Shaw, App. Cas. p. 13; 5 Wils. & Shaw, p. 66, 67, note; Brack v. Johnston, 5 Wils. & Shaw, p. 61.

[2] Ante, s. 365–367; Jerningham v. Herbert, 1 Tamlyn, 103; Fergusson on Marr. & Div. p. 395, 397. Mr. Burge, speaking on this subject, says: 'There is a perfect uniformity in all systems of jurisprudence in the adoption of this rule. Thus a contract in England for the sale to A. of immovable property situated in England, or in those colonies which are governed by the law of England, would transfer the dominion in equity, and A. would become the owner; but if the property were situated in British Guiana, it would not transfer the dominion. On the other hand, a contract in British Guiana for the sale of immovable property situated in England, or in those colonies, would transfer the dominion on that property; but it would not transfer the dominion of property situated in British Guiana.' 2 Burge, Col. & For. Law, pt. 2, c. 9, p. 865.

[3] 1 Boullenois, obs. 23, p. 476, 477, 488, 492, 498–500; ante, s. 240. Boullenois, speaking on this subject, says: ' Ces formes distinctives des contrats sont, pour la plupart, dictées par le droit commun; mais comme M⁺. Ch. Du Molin observe que chacune des villes ayant jurisdiction, peut prescrire une forme particulière à chaque espèce de contrat, il pourroit arriver que ces formes, ou formalités varieroient à l'infini; que dans le lieu du contrat, il y en auroit

other place, that if these formalities are attached to things and not to persons, then the laws which prescribe them are real ; and consequently the law of the place of their situation must govern.[1] Accordingly he lays it down as a fundamental rule ; ' Quand la loi exige certaines formalités, lesquelles sont attachées

une; que dans le lieu du domicile, il y en auroit une autre; et que dans le lieu de la situation, il y en auroit encore une autre. Dans ces cas, si ceux qui contractent, sont domiciliés dans un lieu, qu'ils contractent dans un autre, et que la chose dont ils contractent, soit encore dans un autre quelle forme les contractants donneront-ils à l'acte, en égard à toutes ces formalités variées et multipliées ? S'il étoit clair que ces formes appartenoient à la solemnité, il n'y auroit pas de difficulté qu'il faudroit suivre ce que la loi du lieu où l'acte se passeroit, prescriroit à cet égard. Si ces formalités étoient habilitantes la personne, il faudroit suivre la loi du domicile de la personne habilitée. Si au contraire elles appartenoient, sive ad substantialia contractus, sive ad naturalia, sive ad accidentalia aut complimentaria, c'est là où se rencontreroit la véritable difficulté; et si vous donnez pour principe général et indéfini, qu'il faut toujours suivre la loi du lieu où se passe le contrat, ou bien qu'il faut toujours suivre la loi de la situation, ou bien qu'il faut toujours suivre la loi du domicile des contractants, il est certain que vous donnerez un faux principe; parce que, comme on le verra ci-après, tantot ces formalités appartiennent au contrat, tantot elles appartiennent et dépendent de la qualité de la personne.' 1 Boullenois, obs. 23, p. 465. Boullenois, in another place, says: ' Quelque variété qu'il y ait dans ce nombre considéré de différentes formalités ou solemnités, quelque différence qu'il y ait même dans nos auteurs pour le langage, ils conviennent unanimement, que pour qu'un acte soit parfait, ex omni parte, il y a des choses requises, pour habiliter et rendre capables les personnes qui contractent, et elles sont attachées à la personne, et dépendent du domicile; qu'il y en a de requises pour la preuve et l'authenticité, et elles dépendent du lieu où se passe le contrat; qu'il y en a attaché aux choses, et elles dépendent de la loi de la situation; qu'il y en a qui sont de l'essence et de la substance intérieure et viscérale des actes, et ces choses sont, selon la nature de chaque acte, communément et assez universellement les mêmes partout; qu'il y en a qui fluent de la nature et espèce dont sont les contrats, soit qu'elles proviennent de la propre nature de ces contrats, soit qu'elles y soient liées et attachées par un usage bien constant, et une coutume invétérée, et ce sont ces choses qui peuvent faire naître le plus de contestation; qu'il y en a qui ne servent que de complément aux actes déjà formés, et elles dépendent des différentes loix ; et qu'il y en a encore qui ne sont que de pure discipline, et d'autres dont l'accomplissement plus ou moins prompt dépend de la volonté des parties, et celles-ci n'entraînent pas de grandes difficultés. Mais la véritable difficulté en cette matière, est de savoir bien discerner toutes ces formalités, et les ranger chacune dans la classe qui leur appartient, afin de ne pas appliquer à une formalité d'une certaine classe, des principes et des décisions qui ne conviennent qu'à une formalité d'une autre classe. Plusieurs exemples vont faire sentir cette difficulté.' 1 Boullenois, obs. 23, p. 456, 457, 488, 492, 498, 499. See Merlin, Répert. Testament, s. 1, 5, art. 1-3.

[1] 1 Boullenois, obs. 23, p. 467, 499, 500. See Livermore, Dissert. p. 58-60; Henry on Foreign Law, p. 50.

aux choses mêmes, il faut suivre la loi de la situation.'[1] Yet, strangely enough, he departs from this general doctrine in relation to testaments, upon some subtile distinctions which he takes between extrinsic and intrinsic forms, between the solemnities required to the perfection and authenticity of an act, and those which relate to the capacity to do it, or to dispose of the thing which is the subject of it.[2]

437 *a*. Sandius (John à Sandé) has given us some quite as subtile distinctions, insisting that there is a wide distinction between the solemnities of an alienation and the thing of which the alienation is the subject: 'Quod multum intersit inter solennitates dispositionis et rem, de qua sit dispositio.' The solemnities respect but the form of the disposition or alienation, and the things disposed of or alienated constitute the substantial matter thereof; so that what respects the solemnities affects only the form of the act, and not the things. 'Solennitates sunt forma; res est subjectum dispositionis; quare tale statutum magis efficere videtur dispositionem ipsam, quam rem.'[3] Accordingly Sandius holds that, if a foreigner makes his will according to the forms and solemnities of the law of the place where it is made, it will be valid even as to immovables in another country, where different forms and solemnities are required. He assigns the following reason: 'Ratio hujus sententiæ est, quod statutum vel consuetudo, præscribens solennitates testamenti, non afficiat res testatoris, neque ejus personam, sed ipsam dispositionem, quæ fit in loco statuti vel consuetudinis. At in cujusvis actus solennitate inspicitur consuetudo loci, ubi is celebratur, eoque in iis quæ spectant ad formam et solennitates testamenti, inspicitur consuetudo loci, ubi illud factum est, licet testator ibi larem fixum non habeat.'[4] And again: 'Deinde hæc sententia non facile ad praxin transferri potest, uti incommoda testari volentibus, qui si habeant bona sita in diversis regionibus, quæ, quod ad testamenti solennitates attinet, diversis moribus reguntur, non possunt secundum hanc sententiam uno testamento defungi, sed si nolint pro parte intestati decedere, coguntur contra juris rationem plura testamenta exarare;

[1] 2 Boullenois, obs. 46, p. 467, rule 4; ante, s. 240. See 1 Boullenois, obs. 9, p. 151.

[2] 1 Boullenois, obs. 21, p. 422–426.

[3] 1 Boullenois, obs. 21, p. 422, 423; Sand. Decis. Frisic. lib. 4, tit. 1, defin. 14, p. 142, 143.

[4] Sand. Decis. lib. 4, tit. 1, defin. 14, p. 142, 143.

singula scilicet juxta consuetudinem cujusque regionis, vel in uno testamento sequi consuetudines plurium locorum, et actum per se individuum huic, et illi loco diversimode impartiri.'[1]

438. D'Argentré and Burgundus maintain with great clearness the general doctrine that the law rei sitæ must govern as to the solemnities of alienation, inter vivos and testamentary.[2] D'Argentré's opinion has been already in part stated.[3] He adds, in another place : ' Cum de rebus soli, id est immobilibus, agitur (qu'ils appellent d'héritage), et diversa diversarum possessionum loca, et situs proponuntur in acquirendis, transferendis, aut asserendis dominiis, et in controversia est, quo jure regantur, certissima usu observatio est, id jus de pluribus spectari, quod loci est, et suos cuique loco, leges, statuta, et consuetudines servandos ; et qui cui mores de rebus, territorio, et potestatibus finibus sint recepti, sic ut de talibus nulla cujusquam potestas sit præter territorii legem. Sic in contractibus, sic in testamentis, sic in commercii omnibus, et locis conveniendi constitutum ; ne contra situs legem in immobilibus quidquam decerni possit privato consensu ; et par est sic judicari.'[4] Burgundus, in addition to what has been already cited,[5] says in another place : ' Siquidem solemnitates testamenti ad jura personalia non pertinent; quia sunt quædam qualitas bonis ipsis impressa, ad quam tenetur respicere quisquis in bonis aliquid alterat. Nam, ut jura realia non porrigunt effectum extra territorium; ita et hanc præ se virtutem ferunt, quod nec alieni territorii leges in se recipiant.'[6] This is also the opinion of other distinguished jurists.[7]

439. Froland treats as clearly real all laws which respect the alienation of immovable property, and consequently that it is go-

---

[1] Id. p. 123.

[2] 1 Boullenois, obs. 6, p. 129; Id. obs. 9, p. 151; Id. obs. 22, p. 422, 425; Cujaccii Opera, tom. 3, lib. 14, c. 12, p. 399, ed. 1758; 2 Burge, Col. & For. Law, pt. 2, c. 9, p. 866.

[3] Ante, s. 426.

[4] D'Argent. de Briton. Leg. art. 218, n. 2, p. 647; ante, s. 371 a.

[5] Ante, s. 872, 433, 438; post. s. 477.

[6] Burgundus, tract. 6, n. 2, 3, p. 128, 129; post, s. 477 ; Rodenburg, de Divers. Stat. tit. 2, c. 3, s. 1, 2; 2 Boullenois, Appx. p. 19–21; 1 Boullenois, obs. 6, p. 129, 130; Id. obs. 9, p. 151; Id. obs. 21, p. 422, 423, 425; ante, s. 433 a ; 4 Burge, Col. & For. Law, pt. 2, c. 12, p. 581–585; post, s. 477.

[7] Ante, s. 363–373. See 2 Burge, Col. & For. Law, pt. 2, c. 9, p. 865, 866; 1 Boullenois, obs. 21, p. 423, 424 ; Sand. Decis. Frisic. lib. 4, tit. 1, defin. 14, p. 142, where many opinions of jurists are cited.

verned by the lex rei sitæ. He lays down, as a fundamental rule : 'La première (chose) que le statut réel ne sort point de son territoire. Et de là vient, que dans le cas, où il s'agit de successions, &c., d'aliénation d'immeubles, &c., il faut s'attacher aux coutumes des lieux, où les fonds sont situés.'[1] Cochin lays down the rule, that, though the formalities of an instrument (acte) may be, and indeed ought to be, according to the law of the place of the instrument; yet, when the clauses or contents of such an instrument are to be applied to property in another country, the law rei sitæ must govern. 'Les formalités dont un acte doit être revêtu se réglent par la loi, qui exerce son empire dans le lieu où l'acte a été passé ; mais quand il s'agit d'appliquer les clauses qu'il renferme, aux biens des parties contractantes, c'est la loi de la situation de ces biens, qui doit seule être consultée.'[2]

440. But there are many other jurists who maintain the same opinion as Cochin, holding that, if the act or instrument have the formalities which are prescribed by the law of the place where it is made, it ought to have a universal operation ;[3] and they apply it especially to the case of testamentary dispositions of real property.[4] They found themselves upon the extreme inconvenience which would otherwise result from requiring parties to make different testaments for their property lying in different countries, and the almost utter impossibility, in many cases, of ascertaining at a critical moment what are the peculiar solemnities prescribed

[1] 1 Froland, Mém. 156; Id. 65.

[2] Cochin, Œuvres, tom. 5, p. 697, 4to ed. There is some difficulty in reconciling this passage with another cited in the note to s. 440. Perhaps Cochin only means here to say that the solemnities of the place where the act is done are to be observed; but that the interpretation of the clauses or provisions of the instrument are to be according to the law of the situs. See also 2 Burge, Col. & For. Law, pt. 2, c. 9, p. 866.

[3] P. Voet, de Statut. s. 4, c. 2, s. 6, p. 123, s. 7, p. 124, ed. 1715; Id. p. 137, ed. 1661; J. Voet, ad Pand. 1, 4, 2, s. 5, 6, p. 39, s. 10, p. 43, 44; 1 Boullenois, obs. 21, p. 426–433. Mr. Livermore, in his Dissertations, sums up the opinions of different jurists. Livermore, Dissert. s. 78–214, p. 69–130. So does Mr. Burge. 4 Burge, pt. 2, c. 12, p. 581–585. Sandius, or Sandé, has also brought together the opinions of different jurists on this subject. Sand. Decis. Frisic. lib. 4, tit. 1, defin. 14, p. 142, 143.

[4] See Rodenburg, de Div. Stat. tit. 2, c. 3; 2 Boullenois, Appx. p. 19; 1 Boullenois, p. 414–421; Id. obs. 21, p. 422–433; 1 Hertii Opera, s. 4, n. 10, p. 125, ed. 1737; Id. p. 179, ed. 1716; J. Voet, ad Pand. 1, 4, 2, 13, p. 43; Bouhier, Cout. de Bourg. c. 23, s. 81–89, p. 460; Vinnius, ad Instit. lib. 2, tit. 10, s. 14, n. 5; 1 Boullenois, obs. 21, p. 426, 427; Merlin, Répert. Loi, s. 6, art. 6, 7.

by the laws of each of these countries.[1] They seem wholly to have overlooked, on the other side, the inconvenience of any nation suffering property, locally and permanently situate within its own territory, to be subject to be transferred by any other laws than its own; and thus introducing into the bosom of its own jurisprudence all the innumerable diversities of foreign laws, to regulate its own titles to such property, many of which laws can be but imperfectly ascertained, and many of which may become matters of subtile controversy.[2] Some of these jurists press their doctrine so far as to doubt whether a transfer, made according to the solemnities of the place where the property is locally situate, would be good, if not also executed according to the law of the place where the act is done.[3]

441. The opinion of these jurists is supported by Dumoulin. His language is : 'Et est omnium doctorum sententia, ubicunque consuetudo, vel statutum locale disponit de solemnitate, vel forma actus, ligari etiam exteros, ibi actum illum gerentes, et gestum esse validum, et efficacem ubique, etiam super bonis solis extra territorium consuetudinis vel statuti.'[4] In another place

[1] Rodenburg, de Div. Stat. tit. 2, c. 3; 2 Boullenois, Appx. p. 19; 1 Boullenois, p. 414–417; Vinnius, ad Instit. lib. 2, tit. 10, s. 14, n. 5; 1 Boullenois, obs. 21, p. 426, 427; Hertii Opera,de Collis. Leg. s. 4, n. 10, p. 126, ed. 1737; Id. p. 179, ed. 1716; Id. n. 23, p. 133, ed. 1737; Id. p. 189, ed. 1716; Foelix, Conflit des Lois, Revue Étrang. et Franç. tom. 7, 1840, s. 41, p. 347, 348. John Voet has given the reasoning on this side of the question. J. Voet, ad Pand. 1, 1, 4, ps. 2, s. 13, 15, p. 45, 46. See also 4 Burge, Col. & For. Law, p. 2, c. 12, p. 590; post, 444 a.

[2] Cochin says it is one of the most uniform principles, that the form of acts depends upon the law of the place where they are passed; so that, if a man is domiciled at Paris, and there has all his property (biens), but he makes his testament in another province under a different law, the law of the latter is alone to be regarded in its form, though the succession to the testator, either of heirship or testamentary, may be regulated by the law of Paris. Cochin, Œuvres, tom. 2, p. 72, 4to ed. See ante, s. 439. D'Aguesseau treats with some sarcasm those who venture to suggest a doubt on the point. ' We leave such discussions,' says he, ' to the ultramontane doctors. We say, with D'Argentré, that these questions are not worthy to occupy a moment's attention. No one can doubt that the formalities of a testament ought to be governed by the law of the place where the act is done.' D'Aguesseau, Œuvres, tom. 1, p. 637, 4to ed.

[3] Rodenburg, de Div. Stat. tit. 2, c. 3; 2 Boullenois, Appx. p. 21; 1 Boullenois, 417; Id. obs. 21, p. 428–430. Grotius appears to have held the same opinion, and to have applied it to the case of wills and testaments. See post, s. 479, where his opinion is cited.

[4] Molin. Opera, tom. 2, ed. 1681, consil. 53, s. 9, p. 965; ante, s. 260, note,

he says : ' Aut statutum loquitur de his, quæ concernunt nudam ordinationem vel solemnitatem actus, et semper inspicitur statutum vel consuetudo loci, ubi actus celebratur, sive in contractibus, sive in judiciis, sive in testamentis, sive in instrumentis, aut aliis conficiendis. Ita quod testamentum, factum coram duobus testibus in locis, ubi non requiritur major solemnitas, valet ubique. Idem in omni alio actu.' [1] And yet Dumoulin, in another place, uses language not very consistent with the foregoing, unless, indeed, he is there to be understood as speaking, not of the forms and solemnities of testaments, but of the operation and interpretation thereof. ' Sed emerget incidens quæstio, cujus loci inspiciatur, an loci testamenti, contractus, vel loci dominantis, an vero loci servientis? Et omnino dicendum inspiciendam consuetudinem loci servientis, seu rei, quæ conceditur.' [2]

441 a. Bouhier maintains that in general the forms and solemnities of all acts done (which of course include testaments) should be according to the law of the place where the acts are done, even when the property is situated elsewhere ; at least if

s. 274 a, 372 a ; 1 Boullenois, obs. 21, p. 423, 429. Mr. Livermore manifestly entertained the opinion that it was sufficient for a testament of immovable property to have the formalities prescribed by the law of the testator's domicil. After adverting to Dumoulin's division of statutes into those which relate to the solemnities and forms of acts (nudam ordinationem vel solemnitatem actus), and those which concern the merits and decisions of causes (quæ meritum causæ vel decisionem concernunt), he added: ' The statutes of the first class I do not consider to be either personal, real, or mixed. They do not act directly upon persons nor upon property, but upon the act for the purpose of determining its authenticity. The laws of some countries require that a testament shall be made in presence of seven witnesses. In other countries the law requires only the presence of a notary and two witnesses. These laws dispose of the solemnities of all testaments made within their jurisdiction ; but they neither affect the capacity of the testator. nor do they dispose of his property. The law of the testator's domicil determines his capacity to make a testament ; the law of the place where his immovable property is situated determines whether it may be disposed of by testament or not ; the will of the testator disposes of his property ; and the sole purpose and effect of the statute, which requires a certain number of witnesses to a testament, is to show whether that will has been expressed or not.'

[1] Molin. Opera, tom. 3, ad Cod. 1, 1, 1, Conclus. de Statutis, p. 554, ed. 1681 ; ante, s. 260 ; post, s. 479 k ; 4 Burge, Col. & For. Law, pt. 2, c. 12, p. 583 ; 1 Boullenois, obs. 21, p. 423, 424 ; ante, 365 a.

[2] Molin. Opera, tom. 1, de Fiefs, s. 33, n. 86, tom. 1, p. 410, ed. 1681 : 1 Boullenois, obs. 21, p. 423–425 ; Burgundus, tract. 6, n. 2, p. 128 ; Bouhier, Cout. de Bourg. c. 23, s. 39–44, p. 454, 455.

the custom of the situs is not in opposition to it.[1] He lays it down in another place among his general rules. ' Tout statut, qui concerne les formalités extrinsèques des actes et leur authenticité, est personnel; en sorte que, quand l'acte est passé dans les formes usitées au lieu, où il est rédigé, il a partout son exécution; ' and he then applies the rule expressly to testaments.[2]

442. Paul Voet holds the opinion that the solemnities of contracts and other instruments respecting the transfer of immovable property are to be according to the laws of the place where the act is done, and not of the rei sitæ; for he holds laws respecting solemnities not to be either real or personal, but of a mixed nature. 'Statutum quippe circa solemnia, nec est in rem, nec in personam, sed mixti generis.'[3] He therefore insists that, if a testament is made according to the solemnities of the place rei sitæ, but not according to that of the testator's domicil, it will not be valid as to property situate elsewhere. ' Verum,' says he, 'quid de solemnibus, in negotiis adhibendis, statuendum erit, si locorum statuta discrepent? Finge, quempiam testari in loco domicilii, adhibitis solemnibus rei sitæ, non sui domicilii; valebitne testamentum ratione bonorum alibi sitorum? Respondeo, quod non. Neque enim aliter testamentum valere potest, quam si ea servetur solemnitas, quam requirit locus gestionis.'[4] He further holds that, if a testament is made by a person in his own country (sui loci) according to the forms and solemnities required by the laws thereof, it will be valid in respect to his immovable property in other countries where different forms and solemnities are required. And this without any distinction, whether such person has retained his original domicil, or whether he is settled in another country. ' Quid, si quispiam testetur secundum solemnia sui loci, puta coram notario et duobus testibus, an vires capiet testamentum ratione bonorum extra territorium statuentis jacentium, puta in Frisia, ubi plures solemnitates requiriuntur? Aff. (affirmo.) Idque procedit, sive testator domicilium prius retinuerit, sive alio transtulerit.'[5] And he adds

[1] Bouhier, Cout. de Bourg. c. 28, s. 10, p. 550.

[2] Bouhier, Cout. de Bourg. c. 23, s. 81, 82, p. 460; Id. c. 28, s. 10–20, p. 550, 551; Id. c. 21, s. 219, p. 417.

[3] P. Voet, de Statut. s. 9, c. 2, n. 3, p. 263, ed. 1715; Id. p. 318, 319, ed. 1661.

[4] P. Voet, de Statut. s. 2, c. 2, n. 1, p. 262, ed. 1715; Id. p. 317, ed. 1661.

[5] P. Voet, de Statut. s. 2, c. 2, n. 2, p. 262, ed. 1715; Id. p. 317, 318, ed. 1661.

that if a foreigner makes his testament according to the law of the place where he is only temporarily abiding, it will still be valid as to his immovable property elsewhere, even in his domicil. 'Quid, si Florensis secundum loci statutum testamentum condat, ubi tantum hospitatur, an valebit alibi, ubi vel immobilia, vel domicilium habet? Respondeo, quod ita. Cum enim agatur de actus solemnitate quæ quoscunque obligat, in loco negotium aliquod gerentes, etiam obligat forensem ibi disponentem, si suam dispositionem vel suum actum velit utilem, licet non præcise liget eundem.'[1] He makes an exception, indeed, of a party's making a testament in a foreign country, with a view to a fraudulent evasion of the law of his own country. 'Si tamen quispiam, ut evitaret solemnitatem loci sui domicilii, in fraudem talis statuti, extra territorium se conferat, ejus testamentum non valere existumarem.'[2]

443. Huberus supports the same opinion. 'In Holland,' says he, 'a testament may be made before a notary and two witnesses. In Friesland it is not valid unless established by seven witnesses. A Batavian made a testament in Holland according to the local law, under which property situate in Friesland is demanded. The question is, whether the judges in Friesland ought to sustain the demand under that testament. The laws of Holland cannot bind the Frisians; and, therefore, by the first axiom, the testament would not be valid in Friesland; but by the third axiom it would be valid; and, according to that, judgment should be pronounced in favor of the testament. But a Frisian goes into Holland, and there makes a testament according to the local law (more loci), contrary to the Frisian law, and returns into Friesland, and dies there. Is the testament valid? It is valid by the second axiom; because while he was in Holland, although temporarily, he was bound by the local law; and an act valid in its

---

[1] P. Voet, de Statut. s. 9, c. 2, n. 3, s. 262, 263, ed. 1715; Id. p. 318, 319, ed. 1661; post, s. 475.

[2] P. Voet, de Statut. s. 9, c. 2, n. 4, p. 264, ed. 1715; Id. p. 318, 319, ed. 1661. In 4 Burge, Col. & For. Law, pt. 2, c. 12, p. 590, Mr. Burge supposes that Paul Voet holds a somewhat differently modified opinion, like that of Rodenburg, that the testament will be good if made either according to the law of the place where it is made, or according to that where he has his domicil. Post, s. 444. See also ante, s. 365 a. I do not see anything in the passage of Paul Voet, referred to by Mr. Burge, that leads to such a conclusion. The text contains all the cases put by Paul Voet on this point, in his work De Statut. s. 9, c. 2.

origin ought to be valid everywhere by the third axiom; and this without any discrimination of movable or of immovable property. So the law is, and is practised.[1] On the other hand, a Frisian makes his will in his own country before a notary and two witnesses; and it is carried into Holland, and property situate there is demanded. It will not be allowed; because the testament was from the beginning a nullity, it being made contrary to the local law. The same law will govern, if a Batavian should make a testament in Friesland, although it would be valid if made in Holland; for, in truth, such an instrument would from the beginning be a nullity for the reasons just stated.'[2]

448 a. What Huberus here says may seem not very consistent with what he has said in another passage already cited;[3] but he has endeavored to reconcile the passages by the following remarks. 'But it may be asked,' says he, 'whether what we have already said does not give rise to an objection, that if a testament is made which is valid by the law of the place, it ought to have the same effect even in respect to property situate elsewhere, where it is lawful to dispose thereof by will. There is no such objection; because the diversity of laws of that sort does not affect immovable property, neither does it speak concerning the same, but only directs the act of making a testament; which, when rightly executed, the law of the country does not prohibit that act from being valid in respect to immovable property, so far as no character impressed upon that property by the law of the place is injured or diminished. This observation has a place also in contracts. Thus, if certain things or rights of the soil of Friesland are sold to persons in Holland, in a mode prohibited in Friesland, though valid where the sale takes place, the things are understood to be well sold. The same is true as to things not indeed immovable, but annexed to the soil. But if corn growing on the soil of Friesland should be sold in Holland, according to the lasts, as it is called, the sale is void, although the law of Holland does not speak on the point, because it is prohibited in Friesland, and it adheres to the soil and is part thereof.' 'Sed an hoc non obstat ei, quod antea diximus, si factum sit testamentum jure loci validum, id effectum habere etiam in bonis

[1] The axioms here referred to by Huberus are those already stated in s. 29.

[2] Huberus, lib. 1, tit. 3, s. 4, 15.   [3] Ante, s. 426.

alibi sitis, ubi de illis testari licet ? Non obstat; quia legum diversitas in alia specie non afficit res soli, neque de illis loquitur, sed ordinat actum testandi; quo recte celebrato, lex reipubl. non vetat illum actum valere in immobilibus, quatenus nullus character illis ipsis a lege loci impressus læditur aut imminuitur. ' Hæc observatio locum etiam in contractibus habet; quibus in Hollandia venditæ res soli Frisici, modo in Frisia prohibito, licet, ubi gestus est, valido, recte venditæ intelliguntur; idemque in rebus non quidem immobilibus, aut solo cohærentibus; uti si frumentum soli Frisci in Hollandia secundum lastas, ita dictas, sit venditum, non valet venditio, nec quidem in Hollandia secundum eam jus dicetur, etsi tale frumentum ibi non sit vendi prohibitum; quia in Frisia interdictum est : et solo cohæret ejusque pars est.'[1]

444. Rodenburg seems at first to consider that laws which regulate the forms and solemnities of acts touching property are neither strictly personal laws nor real laws, but a third sort. 'Subsequitur tertium et ultimum genus, eorum nimirum statutorum, quibus lex præfigitur actui qui a persona peragendus, eundem actum vel vetando, vel certo etiam modo circumscribendo.'[2] He afterwards proceeds to state that the opinion· commonly entertained by jurists is that, as to such acts, the law of the place where the act is done is alone to be regarded, although it respects immovable property. 'Si de solemnibus quæratur, ea jampridem in foro ac pulpito prævaluit opinio, ut spectandæ sint loci cujusque leges, ubi actus conficitur.[3] Quare sicubi ex more loci solemnitate, ordinatum fuerit testamentum, valiturum illud, ubincunque oportuerit exequi.'[4] He then remarks that Cujaccius and Burgundus had attacked this doctrine; holding that testators are bound to observe the forms and solemnities of the lex rei sitæ. He distinguishes cases of this sort from cases of contract which bind only the person : 'Cujus ossibus ubique inhæret, semel ex forma loci contractæ obligationis, nexus. De re vero alibi constituta disponendi, aut ejus in aliam transcribendæ formam hæc non concernunt. Realium namque jurium eorumve actuum, quibus fit mancipatio, aut dominium transfertur, aliam esse rationem, vel

[1] Huberus, de Conflict. Leg. lib. 1, tit. 3, s. 15. Whether this distinction is satisfactory or not, will be for the learned reader to decide. See post, s. 476.

[2] Rodenburg, de Divers. Stat. tit. 2, c. 3, s. 1; 2 Boullenois, Appx. p. 19.

[3] Ibid.　　　　　　　　　　　　　　　[4] Ibid.

quotidiana praxis edocet et recte disputat Burgundus. Jus in re, ut nascatur quod hic ex causa testamenti contingit, non posse id præstare alterius regionis consuetudinem, ut forma illa ac solemnibus circumdaret alienorum fundorum alterationes, adeoque omnino jus diceret extra territorium.'[1] He then proceeds to examine the reasoning upon which the opinion is maintained that the law of the place of the making a testament should govern as to the forms and solemnities thereof, and not the law rei sitæ. He admits his own view to be, that a testament made according to the forms and solemnities of the place where it is made ought to be held valid; and also that a testament made in such place, according to the forms of the law rei sitæ, ought equally to be held valid. The former he treats as an indulgence, founded in general convenience; the latter, as correct in point of strict right. ' Ego potius utrobique pro testamento respondendum duxerim, quippe personæ qualitas ad summam rei non facit, tum factura, si statuta illa, in solemnitates scripta, personalia forent, ut subditus iis gauderet, non gauderet exterus: sed contra constat ea mere realia esse. Quicunque enim fuerit, sive incola, sive exterus, qui rem alienare intendit, necesse habet respicere ad solemnitatem territorii, cui bona sunt obnoxia. Quare dicendum est decidendæ quæstionis rationem in modo prolatis positam esse: necessitatis nimirum rationem, summumque favorem, qui pro testamentis facit, impetrasse, ut, quamvis illa mancipent æque atque alienationes inter vivos, ideoque consimiliter componenda forent ad normam loci, ubi res sitæ sunt, suffecerit tamen ordinasse, secundum leges loci, ubi actus conficitur. Proinde si quis eo, quod ad testandum expeditius sua causa comparatum est, noluerit uti, quod ei forte promptius sit componere suprema ad loci leges, cui bona subjaceant, quo minus testamentum ejus valiturum sit, non video: nulla enim juris ratio, aut æquitatis benignitas patitur, ut quæ salubriter pro utilitate hominum introducuntur, ea nos duriore interpretatione contra ipsorum commodum producamus ad severitatem; nec cum superaddatur alia testandi forma, adimitur prior, quod novæ solemnitatis adjectionem potius dedisse DD. quam priorem ac ordinarium permutasse videantur. Unde consequens est dicere, ne disputem sine speciei oppositione, Amersfurti, ubi coram trinis testibus una cum notario ultima conduntur elogia, viribus subsistere celebrati, coram binis testibus supra no-

[1] Ibid.

tarium, de bonis in Hollandia, aut in alia Provinciæ nostræ parte sitis.'[1] It is hardly possible to conceive a stronger illustration of

[1] Rodenburg, de Div. Stat. tit. 2, c. 3, n. 1, 2; 2 Boullenois, Appx. p. 21, 22; 1 Boullenois, p. 414–418; Id. obs. 21, p. 422, 423. See also 2 Burge, Col. & For. Law, pt. 2, c. 9, p. 865–868. Mr. Burge says: ' In selecting the law by which it is to be determined whether the acts or instruments of alienation have been made with the necessary solemnities to render the alienation valid, the distinction must be made between those which are required for the proof or authentication of the act, and those which are required to be observed as the condition on which alone the law either authorizes the alienation, or gives to it an effect which it withholds if they are not observed. The former are called sometimes solemnia probantia, and the latter solemnia habilitantia. Thus, with respect to the former, if the lex loci contractus treats as null and void every contract, the subject-matter of which exceeds in value a certain sum, if it be not reduced to writing and proved before notaries, &c., when the notarial proof is not that which is prescribed, the contract will be void in whatever place it is enforced. So if those solemnities which the lex loci contractus requires have been observed, and the contract according to that law is valid and obligatory, it will be valid everywhere else. But the latter proposition is subject to the qualification that it does not affect immovable property subject to a law in the country of its situs, which annuls a contract because it has not been entered into with the solemnities which it requires. If the disposition of the law does not annul the contract on account of its non-observance of the solemnities which are prescribed, but gives to it a degree of authenticity or credit which it will want if they are not observed, or if, in other words, its effect is either to dispense with a more formal proof of the instrument, if it bears on it evidence of their observance, or if in consequence of the non-observance it attaches a presumption against the execution of the instrument, and therefore requires from the parties a greater burden of proof, such solemnities are to be classed amongst the proofs in the cause which are governed neither by the lex loci contractus, nor by that of the situs, but by that of the forum. This question, in the opinion of Paul Voet, regards " Non tam de solemnibus, quam probandi efficacia; quæ licet in uno loco sufficiens, non tamen ubique locorum; quod judex unius territorii nequeat vires tribuere instrumento, ut alibi quid operetur." The solemnities which are called habilitantia, and constitute the mode by which alone the alienation of immovable property is permitted to be made, or by which alone that alienation can give to the grantee or purchaser certain rights, are those which are prescribed by the lex loci rei sitæ. As that law may impose restrictions which may wholly or partially withhold the power of alienating immovable property situated within its territory, to which all persons owning that property are subject, it may prescribe the conditions on which such alienation may be made. Thus the law of Scotland does not permit a destination of heritage by a testamentary disposition, neither does it permit certain deeds to be made in lecto. One of the conditions may be the form or manner in which it shall be made. This solemnitas dispositionis is tanquam quædam qualitas rebus impressa, and the validity of the alienation must depend on its compliance with the prescribed solemnity. Amongst the instances illustrating the species of solemnities prescribed by the lex loci rei sitæ. and to which effect must be given in all questions respecting the validity of the alienation, may be mentioned the statute of frauds in England. Unless there

the difficulty of undertaking to build up systems of jurisprudence upon mere theory and private notions of general convenience.

be such an agreement in writing as is required by it, or as is sanctioned by the judicial constructions which it has received, no estate or interest in immovable property situated in England will pass, although, according to the law of the place where the agreement was made, it might be sufficient if it were by parol. The lex rei sitæ must be invoked if the question regard the insinuation or registration of donations or other instruments, or the effects which are induced by the neglect of it. Dumoulin seems to treat it as a solemnity which is of the substance of the contract, and to be governed by the lex loci rei sitæ. "Insinuatio et transcriptio in registris ordinariæ curiæ loci semper omnibus his casibus est de forma et substantia: quemadmodum insinuatio donationis apud magistrum census erat de substantia, si excedebat quingentos aureos." Boullenois considers that, if the registration does not take place when it is prescribed by the lex loci rei sitæ, the alienation is void: "Que si le donateur est domicilié dans un royaume, et les biens situés dans un autre, et que ces deux endroits requièrent une insinuation, je dis dans ce cas contre Thésaurus, que si elle n'est pas insinuée dans les deux endroits, mais dans le seul domicile, donatio insinuatur virtute legis municipalis, non porrigit effectum suum ad bona sita extra territorium, parce que si la donation n'est pas insinuée dans le lieu de la situation, elle n'est pas revêtue de la formalité réelle qu'exige la loi de la situation." ' Vattel affirms ' that the validity of a testament as to its form can only be decided by the domestic judge, whose sentence, delivered in form, ought to be everywhere acknowledged.' But at the same time he admits that the validity of the bequests may be disputed as not being according to the lex rei sitæ. Vattel, b. 2, c. 7, s! 85; Id. s. 111. M. Foelix seems to hold a similar opinion. He says: ' Une autre question est celle de savoir, si le contractant ou disposant qui se trouve en pays étranger, peut se borner à employer les formes prescrites par la loi du lieu de la situation de ses immeubles, au lieu de suivre celle du lieu de la rédaction? Nous tenons pour l'affirmative, par une raison analogue à celle donnée sur la question précédente. Le statut réel régit les immeubles ; c'est un principe résultant de la nature des choses; la permission d'user des formes établies par la loi du lieu de la rédaction de l'acte n'est qu'une exception introduite en faveur du propriétaire, et à laquelle il lui est loisible de renoncer. Tel est aussi le sentiment de Rodenburg, de Jean Voet, et de Vander Kessel; Cocceji soutient même, que la forme des actes entre vifs ou testamentaires est réglé exclusivement par la loi de la situation des biens. Fachinée et Burgundus (v. supra n° 41) partageaient cet avis, mais par rapport aux testaments seulement. En Belgique, l'édit perpétuel de 1611, art. 13, ordonnait qu'en cas de diversité de coutumes au lieu de la résidence du testateur et au lieu de la situation de ses biens on suivrait, par rapport à la forme et à la solennité, la coutume de la situation. Paul Voet, Huber, Hert, Hommel, et l'auteur de l'ancien Répertoire de jurisprudence, se prononcent pour la nullité. Ce dernier invoque l'autorité de Paul de Castres, au passage rapporté au n° précédent, et le principe que la loi lie tous les individus qui vivent dans son ressort, ne fût-ce que momentanément. Nous renvoyons à ce sujet aux observations présentées sur la question précédente. Mevius distingue entre le citoyen faisant partie de la nation dans le territoire de laquelle les biens sont situés, et l'étranger; il n'accorde qu'au premier la faculté de tester ou de contracter partout d'après les formes pre-

The common law has wisely adhered to the doctrine that the title to real property can pass only in the manner, and by the forms, and to the extent allowed by the local law. It has thus cut off innumerable disputes, and given simplicity, as well as uniformity, to its operations.

444 *a*. John Voet maintains in substance the same opinion as Rodenburg; and insists that it is sufficient, for the validity of testaments of immovable property, that the forms and solemnities thereof should be either according to the law of the place where the testament is made, or according to the law of the place rei sitæ. His language is: 'Neque minus de statutis mixtis, actus cujusque solennia respicientibus, percrebuit, insuper habitis de summo cujusque jure ac potestate ratiociniis, ad validitatem actus cujusque sufficere adhibitionem solennitatum, quas lex loci, in quo actus geritur, præscripserit observandas; sic, et quod ita gestum fuerit, sese porrigat ad bona mobilia et immobilia ubicunque sita aliis in territoriis, quorum leges longe alium, longeque pleniorem requirunt solennium interventum; quod ita placuisse videtur, tum, ne in infinitum prope multiplicarentur et testamenta et contractus, pro numero regionum, diverso jure circa solennia utentium; atque ita summis implicarentur molestiis, ambagibus, ac difficultatibus; quotquot actum, res plures pluribus in locis sitas concernentem, expedire voluerint: tum etiam, ne plurima bona fide gesta nimis facile ac propre sine culpa gerentis conturbarentur.' He afterwards adds: 'Posito vero hoc generali circa solennium adhibitionem jure, executiendum superest, quid statuendum sit, si quis, in loco aliquo actum gerens, neglectis loci istius solennibus, adhibuerit ea, quæ vel domicilii vel rei sitæ statuta requirunt, sive diversa illa sint, sive pauciora? Mynsingerus quidem et Michael Grassus actus ita gestus nullius fore momenti pronunciant, sive actum gerens extra domicilii locum servaverit solennia domicilii, sive ea, quæ requirebantur in loco rei immobilis sitæ. Cum enim ante dictum sit, aliquem et ratione domicilii, et ratione bonorum immobilium, subditum esse magistratibus locorum, in quibus vel domicilium fixit, vel bona immobilia possidet; ac quisque magistratus secundum jus summum (de quo superius

scrites au lieu de la situation. L'auteur ne donne pas de motif de cette distinction, et nous ne pouvons la trouver fondée.' Foelix, Conflit des Lois, Revue Étrang. et Franç. 1840, tom. 7, s. 50, p. 359, 360. See also 4 Burge, Col. & For. Law, pt. 2, c. 12, p. 581–587; Id. p. 590.

disputatum, quodque hic usum invenit) sui statuti vires non male tueatur, quo usque potest, iniquus sane esset in sibi subjectum ratione domicilii aut bonorum, si non respectu bonorum in suo territorio jacentium, ratam haberet ultimam voluntatem aut contractum ejus, a quo sua statuta solennium intuitu servanda videt; maxime, cum hac ratione defendens sui statuti potestatem non conturbet aut subvertat alibi bene gesta, atque adeo nequaquam alterius territorii magistratibus ullam videri possit injuriam facere.' [1]

444 *b.* Cujaccius seems to hold that the law of the place of the domicil of the testator ought to be regarded as to the forms and solemnities of making wills and testaments, without reference to the place where the will is made, or the property is situated. ' Quæri hodie sæpenumero solet, cujus regionis aut civitatis leges moresve serviri oporteat in ordinando testamento ; nam quot sunt civitates, tot fere sunt ordinandi testamenti leges et mores ; et soleo dicere, patriam testatoris solam spectari oportere, etc. Jus igitur patriæ spectatur, potius quam jus commune populi Romani, etc. Suæ igitur patriæ et civitatis legibus aut moribus quisquis testari debet, etc. Denique non spectari locum volo, in quo bona sunt, sed patriam testatoris, etc. Et domicilii potius quam originis spectari patriam. Possit autem quis quo loco habet bona, ejus neque originalis esse, neque incola.[2] Nec ejus loci ulla habebitur ratio in faciendo testamento.' This might seem sufficiently explicit. On another occasion, he says : ' Intelligimus, inquam, in faciendo testamento, privilegium et morem patriæ testatoris, spectari oportere, non situm bonorum. Nam sola possessio bonorum non creat mihi patriam. Si possideo prædium in hac urbe, hæc urbs non est ideo mea, nisi in ea posui domicilium. Solam possessionem nec civem facere, nec incolam. Ergo in servandis solemnibus testamenti non spectabo situm bonorum, ut pro vario situ bonorum etiam varia solemnia observentur, variique mores in exequenda defuncti voluntate ; sed spectabo tantum morem et privilegium patriæ testatoris.' [3]

[1] J. Voet, ad Pand. 1, 4, ps. 2, s. 13, 15, p. 45, 46; 4 Burge, Col. & For. Law, pt. 2, c. 12, p. 590; ante, s. 440–443.

[2] Cujac. Opera, tom. 3, Obs. lib. 14, cap. 12, p. 399, ed. 1758; 4 Burge, Col. & For. Law, pt. 2, c. 12, p. 582.

[3] Cujac. Opera, tom. 9, Com. ad Cod. lib. 6, tit. 23, p. 709, ed. 1768; Bouhier, Cout. de Bourg. c. 28, s. 8, p. 549; 1 Boullenois, obs. 21, p. 423; 2 Burge, Col. & For. Law, pt. 2, c. 9, p. 866; 4 Id. pt. 2, c. 12, p. 582; Sand. Decis.

445. *Extent of Interest transferred.* — Thirdly, in relation to the extent of the interest to be taken or transferred. And here there seems a perfect coincidence between the doctrine of the common law and that maintained by foreign jurists. It is universally agreed that the law rei sitæ is to prevail in relation to all dispositions of immovable property, and the nature and extent of the interest to be alienated. If the local law therefore

Frisic. lib. 4, tit. 8, defin. 7, p. 194. Vinnius holds a similar opinion. He says: Quæsitum est, an testamentum juxta alicujus loci consuetudinem, aut statutum factum, etiam vim habet extra illum locum; exempli gratia testator ibi testamentum fecit, ubi coram duobus testibus et notario testari licet, ut in hac nostra Batavia; quæritur, an valeat etiam in iis locis, ubi septem testes requiruntur, uti in Frisia, ubi sequuntur jus civile. Affirmant comm. DD. in L. 1, C. C. de summ. Trinit. et secundum hanc sententiam sæpissime judicatum. Sunt tamen qui in contrarium eant, et in quæstione proposita sic distinguendum arbitrantur, ut circa res quidem mobiles, et nomina, admittenda sit communis interpret. sententia. At circa res soli, spectandum jus ejus loci in quo sitæ sunt, &c. Mihi prior sententia videtur probabilior, multumque referre utrum statutum disponat circa solemnitatem alicujus actus, an circa rem, puta fundum, locumve; quæ statuta in rem concipiuntur. Qualia sunt, quæ de successione ab intestato disponunt, rem ipsam haud dubie afficiunt, ut ubicumque sit, ejus loci ubi est, legibus obstringatur. Idemque habendum de statutis, quæ circa habilitatem personarum, dispensando aliquid, disponunt. Gaill, Coras. Gomes. Quæ autem statuta disponunt circa actus solemnitatem duntaxat, cum neque rem afficiant, neque personam actum celebrantis, sed ipsam solummodo dispositionem, quæ fit in loco statuti vel consuetudinis, rationi et juri consentaneum est, ut ea vim suam exerant etiam ad bona alibi sita: quoniam actuum solemnia ad eorum spectant jurisdictionem, in quorum territorio celebrantur; et alias contra rationem juris, testato decedere volenti, plura testamenta essent condenda, aut quod absurdum est, plurium locorum consuetudines in uno testamento exquirere oporteret, actumque unum atque individuum, qualis est testamenti, secundum diversa loca adjudicari. Ubi contraria scite expedit, et prudenter temperat, novam quandam distinctionem Fachinei adde, quæ nos, lib. 2, Select. Quest. C. 19. Plane si lex expresse testatores sequi jubeat jus loci, in quo bona sita sunt, aliud dicendum est. Talis est constitutio principum Brabantiæ, emissa anno 1611, cujus meminerunt Burgundus, &c. Vinn. ad Inst. lib. 2, tit. 10, s 14, n. 5; 1 Boullenois, obs. 21, p 426, 427. Gaill is equally explicit. Alibi statutum est, ut testamentum coram notario et duobus testibus factum valeat. Quæsitum, utrum tale testamentum ubique vires habeat, etiam extra territorium statuentium, ubi forte major solennitas requiritur, vel jus civile observatur. Conclusum quod sic; quia ex communi doctor. opinione, statutum disponens citra solemnitates testamenti, extendit se etiam extra territorium, ita ut hæres succedere possit in omnibus bonis, ubicunque sitis, et in universum jus testatoris; quia quoad solennitates attenditur consuetudo loci, in quo actus celebratur. Gaill, Pract. Obs. lib. 2, Obs. 123. p. 548. See Peckius, de Testam. Conjug. c. 28. n. 9, p. 620, who holds a similar opinion. Foelix, Conflit des Lois, Revue Étrang. et Franç. tom. 7, 1840, s. 37, p 307–312; ante, s. 426–428.

prescribes that no person shall dispose, by deed or by will, of more than half, or a third, or a quarter of his immovable property; or that he shall dispose only of a life-estate in such property; such laws are of universal obligation, and no other or further alienation thereof can be made.[1] It follows that if the local law prohibits the alienation of certain kinds of immovable property, or takes from the owner the power of charging them with liens or with mortgages, that law will exclusively govern in every such case. D'Aguesseau fully assents to this doctrine, and says that no one can be ignorant that, when the question is what portion of immovable property may be devised, it is necessary invariably to follow the law of the place where the property is locally situate.[2] (a)

---

[1] 1 Boullenois, Prin. Gén. 30, p. 8; Id. obs. 16, p. 205; and 1 Froland, Mém. 156; Rodenburg, de Div. Stat. tit. 2, c. 2, s. 1; 2 Boullenois, Appx. p. 14; post, s. 479.

[2] D'Aguesseau, Œuvres, tom. 4, p. 637, 638, 4to ed. Mr. Burge on this subject says: ' In a former part of this work it has been seen that the power to alienate immovable property by contract was a quality impressed on the property; that the law from which it was derived or by which it was regulated was a real law; and that the existence of this power and the validity of its exercise must be decided by the law of the country in which that property was situated. "Rebus fertur lex, cum certam iisdem qualitatem imprimit, vel in alienando, v. g. ut ne bona avita possint alienari, vel in acquirendo, v. g. ut dominium rei immobilis venditæ non aliter acquiratur, nisi facta fuerit judicialis resignatio." The power of making the alienation by testament is no less qualitas rebus impressa, than that of making the alienation by contract. When therefore the question arises whether the immovable property may be disposed of by testament, recourse must be had to the lex loci rei sitæ. That law must also decide whether the full and unlimited power of disposition is enjoyed, or whether it is given under restriction. The validity of the testamentary disposition depends in the latter case on its conformity to that restriction, whether the restriction consists in limiting the extent or description of property over which the power of disposition may be exercised, or the persons in whose favor the disposition is made, or in requiring that the testator should have survived a certain number of days after the execution of the act by which the disposition was made. The total or partial defect of the will on the ground that it did not institute heirs, or that it omitted to name the heirs, the disherison of the heirs, the grounds on which the disherison may be justified, are essentially connected with the power of disposing of immovable property by testament, and are therefore dependent on the law of its situs. Many of the restrictions on the power of disposing by testament have been considered by jurists expressly with reference to the operation of the law by which they were created. Rodenburg states the rule, " Unde certissima usu ac observatione regula est, cum de rebus soli agitur, et diversa sunt diversarum possessionum loca et situs

---

(a) See Thurston v. Rosenfield, 42 Mo. 474.

446. *Illustrations.* — An illustration of the doctrine may be borrowed from the English jurisprudence, prohibiting alienations spectari, semper cujusque loci leges ac jura, ubi bona sita esse proponuntur, sic ut de talibus nulla cujusquam potestas sit, præter territorii leges." He illustrates it by referring to a statute which prohibits a disposition of allodial property by testament. He considers such a statute a real law, which renders inoperative any testamentary disposition of the property in whatever place the testament is made. Ferriere has stated this doctrine: "Si je lègue unhéritage propre situé en coutume, qui en défende la disposition, tel legs est nul, et ne peut être parfourni sur les biens situés en cette coutume, quoi qu'acquest, parce qu'à l'égard des choses, dont on peut disposer par dernière volonté, on considère la coutume où elles sont situez. Celui, qui a son domicile en cette coutume peut instituer sa femme dans les biens, qu'il a dans le pays de droit écrit, comme il a été jugé par arrêt du 14 aoust, 1754 rapporté par Mariou au de ses plaidoyers, ce qui doit être sans difficulté." A testament made in a foreign country, bequeathing heritable subjects situated in Scotland, is not sustained in that kingdom, though by the law of the country where the testament was made heritage might have been settled by testament, because by the law of Scotland no heritable subject can be disposed of in that form. On this principle a Scot's personal bond taken to heirs and assignees, but "secluding executors," cannot be bequeathed by a foreign testament. But in all questions touching heritable subjects situate abroad, the foreign testament will be given effect to according to the lex loci. Dumoulin lays down the same doctrine respecting the restriction on the testamentary power over biens propres. "Unde statutum loci inspicietur, sive persona sit subdita, sive non; item si dicat, hæredia proventa ab una linea, redeant ad hæredes etiam remotiores lineæ, vel hæredes lineæ succedant in hærediis ab illa linea proventis. Vel quod illi de linea non possunt testari de illis in totum, vel nisi ad certam partem. Hæc enim omnia et similia spectant ad caput statuti agentis in rem, et præcedentem conclusionem." Again, the statute which prohibits a disposition to particular persons, or (which involves the same consequence) requires the disposition to be made in favor of persons, and therefore excludes all others, is a real law. "Directe enim in rerum alienationem scripta hæc lex realis omnino dicenda est: nec enim statutum reale sit, an personale metiri oportet a ratione, quæ a conjugali forsan qualitate fuerit ducta, sed ab ipsa re, quæ in prohibitione statuti ceciderit." So also it has been held that the law which requires that the testator should have survived the execution of his testament will control the disposition of property situated in the country where that law prevails, although the testament is made, or the testator domiciled, in a place where no such law exists. If a testator whose domicil and real estate were both in Normandy, made a will in some other place, in which he had occasion to be present, but where the law did not require that the testator should survive forty days, it was held that the survivorship was essential to the validity of the testament, so far as it related to the real property in Normandy. If these questions arise on the power to dispose of movable property by testament, the law by which they are decided is that of the domicil; "pour les meubles, ils suivent la loi du domicile, et il ne sauroit jamais y avoir de choc entre différentes coutumes, en sorte qu'il est assez inutile, quant aux meubles, d'agiter si le statut, qui permet de tester, ou qui le défend, est personnel, ou s'il est réel." The rule is stated by Grotius, "Ubi de forma sive solemnitate testamenti agitur, respici locum conditi testamenti; ubi

and devises of real estate in mortmain, or for charitable purposes. If an American citizen owning lands in England, or a Scotchman owning lands in England, should alienate or devise such lands in violation of the mortmain acts, the instrument, whether inter vivos or testamentary, would be held void. And the same principle would apply to a trust created in personal property, to be invested in lands in England for the like purposes.[1]

447. *What are Immovables.* — Fourthly, in relation to the subject-matter, or what are to be deemed immovables. Here, as we have already seen, not only lands and houses, (*a*) but servitudes and easements, and other charges on lands, as mortgages and rents, (*b*) and trust estates, (*c*) are deemed to be, in the sense of law, immovables, and governed by the lex rei sitæ.[2] But in

---

de persona antestari possit, jus domicilii; ubi de rebus quæ testamento relinqui possunt, vel non, respici locum domicilii in mobilibus, in rebus soli situm loci." ' 4 Burge, Col. & For. Law, pt. 2, c. 5, p. 217–220.

[1] Attor-Gen. *v.* Mill, 3 Russ. 328; s. c. 2 Dow & Cl. 393.

[2] Ante, s. 382; Poth. Cout. d'Orléans, c. 1, s. 2. P. Voet puts on this point the very sensible distinction, that whether rents are to be deemed personal or real depends upon the question whether they are charged on real property or not. ' Vel enim talium redituum nomine sunt affecta immobilia, id est, super immobilibus sunt constituti, et immobilibus erunt adscribendi, adeoque statutum loci spectabitur; vel immobilia affecta non sunt illis reditibus, tumque mobilibus poterunt accenseri; atque adeo statutum loci personæ, cujus illi sunt reditus, inspici debebit.' P. Voet, de Stat. s. 9, c. 1, n. 13, p. 259, ed. 1715; Id. p. 313, ed. 1661. And he includes among immovables all movables which are intentionally annexed permanently to the freehold. ' Nisi tamen perpetui usus gratia ex destinatione patris-familias in uno loco manere debeant; quo casu immobilibus comparabuntur.' Id. n. 8, p. 255, ed. 1715; Id. p. 309, ed. 1661. Rodenburg, speaking on this point, says: De reditibus peculiaris esto consideratio. Et illi quidem, qui a re præstantur, vel cujus nomine constituta hypotheca est, collocantur a doctoribus in immobilium numero, ita tamen, si perpetui sunt, secus si temporales, qua distinctione et Burgundus utitur. Sed vix est ut non utrobique idem sit dicendum; cum enim ob id ipsum annumerentur immobilibus, quod rei immobili per hypothecæ constitutionem innitantur, ponendi aliquin, vel si perpetui sint, in mobilium classe; nec hypothecæ immutetur natura, temporis aliqua ad redimendum præstitutione, nihilque ad summam rei intersit, certum an incertum luitionis sit tempus, consequens est dicere constitutos ad tempus reditus, æque atque perpetuos, immobilium nomine venire, maxime cum per hypothecæ constitutionem, res ad summam debiti habeatur quasi alienata, quæ per solutionem redimitur. Rodenburg, de

---

(*a*) Leasehold or chattel interests in land are classed as immovables. Freke *v.* Carbery, L. R. 16 Eq. 461; In bonis Gentili, Ir. R. 9 Eq. 541. But see Despard *v.* Churchill, 53 N. Y. 192.

(*b*) See Chatfield *v.* Berchtoldt, 25 Law Times, N. S. 121.

(*c*) See Knox *v.* Jones, 47 N. Y. 389.

addition to these, which may be deemed universally to partake of the nature of immovables, or (as the common-law phrase is) to savor of the realty, all other things, though movable in their nature, which by the local law are deemed immovables, are in like manner governed by the local law. For every nation having authority to prescribe rules for the disposition and arrangement of all the property within its own territory, may impress upon it any character which it shall choose ; and no other nation can impugn or vary that character. So that the question, in all these cases, is not so much what are or ought to be deemed, ex sua natura, movables or not, as what are deemed so by the law of the place where they are situated. If they are there deemed part of the land, or annexed (as the common law would say) to the soil or freehold, they must be so treated in every place in which any controversy shall arise respecting their nature and character.[1] In other words, in order to ascertain what is immovable or real property, or not, we must resort to the lex loci rei sitæ.[2]

448. *Interests acquired by Operation of Law.* — Hitherto we have spoken of alienations and acquisitions made by the acts of the parties themselves. The question next arises, whether the same principles apply to estates and rights acquired by operation of law. It may be affirmed without hesitation that, independent of any contract express or implied,[3] no estate can be acquired by operation of law in any other manner, or to any other extent, or by any other means, than those prescribed by the lex rei sitæ. Thus no estate in dowry, or tenancy by the curtesy, or inheritable estate or interest in immovable property, can be acquired, except by such persons, and under such circumstances, as the local law prescribes. Thus if the law of a state where a man is domiciled at his death should confer a title of dower on his wife though she were an alien, that would not prevail in any other state where an alien is not dowable, and where the intestate owned real estate.

449. *Matrimonial Rights.* — Many questions upon this subject

Div. Stat. tit. 2, c. 2, s. 2; 2 Boullenois, Appx. p. 15. See also Burgundus, tract. 2, n. 29, 30, p. 77–79.

[1] See Ersk. Institutes, b. 3, tit. 9, s. 4; ante, s. 382.
[2] Chapman *v.* Robertson, 6 Paige (N. Y.) 630.
[3] See Livermore, Dissert. s. 88, 89, p. 72, 73.

have arisen in the course of the discussions upon the matrimonial rights conferred by the lex domicilii over immovable property situate in foreign countries. In the different Italian states, and formerly in some of the provinces of France which were governed by the Roman law, there existed various regulations with regard to dowry or dotal property (lucrum dotis). By the laws and customs of some places, the husband gained by survivorship the whole of the dotal effects ; by others a third, by others a fourth, and by others nothing.[1] One of the questions which has been most elaborately discussed among foreign jurists is, whether in such a case, the law of the matrimonial domicil ought to govern the rights of the parties, as to immovable property in foreign countries, as it does in the matrimonial domicil.[2] It seems agreed on all sides, that where there is in the country rei sitæ a prohibitory law against any such dotal rights, and against any contract to create them, the law of the matrimonial domicil cannot prevail, if a different rule exists there.[3] But the question has been made, whether in the absence of any such prohibitory law, or any express contract, the law of the matrimonial domicil ought not to prevail, so as to give the same dotal rights in every other place.[4]

450. *Foreign Jurists.* — Baldus held that, in such cases, the law or custom of the matrimonial domicil ought to govern, as to property everywhere. 'Consuetudines et statuta,' said he, 'vigentia in domicilio mariti, non curo, ubi res sint positæ, quæ in dotem datæ sunt.'[5] Dumoulin asserted the same doctrine, upon his favorite theory that in all cases the law of the matrimonial

[1] Livermore, Dissert. s. 86, p. 71; 1 Domat, b. 1, tit. 9, s. 1; Code Civil of France, art. 1540–1573; 2 Boullenois, 89, 90.

[2] 1 Boullenois, obs. 29, p. 732–818.

[3] Livermore, Dissert. s. 85–91, p. 71–75; 2 Boullenois, 89–92; ante, s. 176–180, 184, 188; P. Voet, de Stat. s. 4, c. 3, s. 9, p. 134, 135, ed. 1715; 1 Froland, Mém. 62–64.

[4] Even Paul Voet, who is a strong advocate for the realty of statutes, admits that cases of express contract may govern, as to property locally situate in a foreign country. 'Si statuto in uno territorio contractus accesserit, seu partium conventio, etiam si in rem sit conceptum, sese extendit ad bona extra jurisdictionem statuentium sita; non ut afficiat immediate ipsa bona, quam ipsam personam, quoad illa.' P. Voet, de Stat. s. 4, c. 2, s. 15, p. 127, ed. 1715.

[5] Livermore, Dissert. s. 87, p. 71, 72; 1 Froland, Mém. 62.

domicil constituted a tacit contract between the parties.[1] There
are many jurists who maintain the same opinion.[2]

451. *Same.* — Boullenois, as we have seen,[3] does not admit the
existence of any such tacit contracts as Dumoulin contends for;
but he deems all laws real which respect property, making however a distinction in cases of laws which respect the rights of
married persons in each other's property, which he treats as laws
respecting the state or condition of the person.[4] But he contends
that, even if there be such a tacit contract, it does not render
the laws of the place in regard to dowry personal; for if that
were so, he adds, then the dowry of persons contracting at Paris
would be the same in all other provinces in the realm as it is in
Paris, which no one has ever yet contended for.[5] Rodenburg seems
to hold that where there is no matrimonial contract to govern the
case, the law of the situs is to govern in respect to dowry, ap-
proving the doctrine of D'Argentré and Burgundus on this point.[6]
D'Argentré says: 'Cum cautum est virum, uxore præmortua,
dotem, dotisve partem lucrari; cujus loci statutum spectamus, viri,
an uxoris, quod olim fuit, an quod nunc est? Nos rerum lucran-
darum situm spectandum dicimus; et quid ea de re statuta singu-
laria permittant, quid abnuant respiciendum.'[7] Burgundus boldly
asserts the opinion that the law rei sitæ must govern in all such
cases as to immovable property.[8] 'Nam si dotalitium rei immobilis

[1] Livermore, Dissert. s. 87, p. 73, 74; 1 Froland, Mém. 61–63. Dumoulin,
in treating of the question, what law ought to prevail in fixing the rights of
the husband, in regard to the dotal effects of his wife, in case of a change of
domicil before the dissolution of the marriage, ultimately decides in favor
of the law of the matrimonial domicil. His language is: ' Hinc infertur ad
quæstionem quotidianam de contractu dotis et .matrimonii, qui censetur fieri,
non in loco, in quo contrahitur, sed in loco domicilii viri; et intelligitur, non
de domicilio originis, sed de domicilio habitationis ipsius viri, de quo nemo
dubitat, sed omnes consentiunt.' Molin. Oper. tom. 3, ed. 1681, Com. ad
Cod. lib. 1, tit. 1, l. 1, Conclus. de Statut. p. 555; 1 Froland, Mém. 61, 62;
ante, s. 147.

[2] Ante, s. 145–156.

[3] Ante, s. 155; 1 Boullenois, obs. 29, p. 737–741.

[4] Ante, s. 155; 1 Boullenois, obs. 5, p. 121; Id. obs. 29, p. 737, 738.

[5] 1 Boullenois, obs. 5, p. 121; 2 Boullenois, p. 88–92. See ante, s. 155.

[6] Rodenburg, de Divers. Statut. pt. 2, tit. 2, c. 4, s. 5; 2 Boullenois,
Appx. p. 67.

[7] D'Argent. ad Briton. Leg. des Donations, art. 218, gloss. 6, n. 46, tom.
1, p. 664; Livermore, Dissert. s. 92–99, p. 75–78.

[8] 1 Boullenois, obs. 5, p. 121.

in controversiam veniat, ea antiquitus obtinuerit sententia, ut ad locum situs respicere oporteat; quæ cum usque ad nostra tempora, apud omnes, qui moribus reguntur, inviolabilis duret, non est committendum, ut illam dubiam faciam defensionis solicitudine.'[1] Many jurists concur with them in opinion.[2]

452. *Community and Donations between Husband and Wife.* — Similar questions have arisen in relation to the rights of community and of mutual donations between husband and wife, whether they extended to immovable property situate elsewhere than in the matrimonial domicil or not; and the general result of the reasoning among foreign jurists turns very much upon the same considerations which have been mentioned in relation to dowry. But this subject has been already discussed in another place, and it need not be here again examined.[3]

453. Similar questions have also arisen in considering the effect of mutual donations by married couples, when they are admitted by the law of the matrimonial domicil, but are unknown to, or prohibited by, the law of the place rei sitæ.[4] But they proceed upon the same general principles.[5] Cochin says that it is not the law of the place where an act is done which determines its effect. If, says he, property is situate in a place whose laws prohibit donations inter vivos, or reduce them to a particular portion, no one supposes the donation to be less a nullity, or less

[1] Burgundus, tract. 2, n. 10, p. 63, 64; Livermore, Dissert. s. 104-114, p. 80-87.

[2] Ante, s. 142, 148, 152, 153, 167, 168; 1 Froland, Mém. 66, 67, 156; Id. 316-323, 328, 341; 2 Froland, Mém. 816. Froland expresses himself in the following terms: ' La première (règle), que le statut réel ne sort point de son territoire. Et de là vient que dans le cas où il s'agit de successions, de la manière de les partager, de la quotité des biens dont il peut disposer entre vifs ou par testament, d'aliénation d'immeubles, de douaire de femme ou d'enfans, de légitime, retrait lignager, féodal ou conventionnel, de droit de puissance paternelle, de droit de viduité, et autres choses semblables, il faut s'attacher aux coutumes des lieux où les fonds sont situez.' 1 Froland, Mém. 156; Id. 49, 60-81.

[3] See ante, s. 143-158, s. 160-170, 174-177; 1 Froland, Mém. 66-69; Id. 177, pt. 2, c. 1, per tot.; Cochin, Œuvres, tom. 5, p. 80, 4to ed.; Merlin, Répertoire, Testament, s. 1, n. 5, art. 1, p. 309, 310. We have already seen Boullenois's view of this subject, ante, s. 155. See also ante, s. 451.

[4] Ante, s. 143-159.

[5] Livermore, Dissert. s. 181, 182, p. 114, 115; 1 Voet, ad Pand. lib. 1, tit. 4, n. 8, p. 89; 2 Froland, Mém. c. 18, p. 840, &c., c. 19, p. 904; Rodenburg, de Div. Stat. tit. 2, c. 5; 2 Boullenois, Appx. p. 33, 34; 1 Boullenois, 660, 661, 663; Id. obs. 29, p. 767; 2 Boullenois, obs. 44, p. 430-432; ante, s. 143-159.

subject to a reduction, because the act is done in a place where no such prohibition exists.[1]

454. *Rule of the Common Law.* — The doctrine of the common law seems uniformly to be, that in all cases of this sort, touching rights in immovable property, the law of the place rei sitæ is to govern.[2] Hence, if persons who are married in Louisiana, where the law of community exists, own immovable property in Massachusetts, where such community is unknown; upon the death of the husband, the wife would take her dower only in the immovable property of her husband, and the husband, upon the death of the wife, would take as tenant by the curtesy only, in the immovable property of his wife.

455. Another class of cases illustrating this subject may be derived from the known rights of fathers over the property of their children, according to the provisions of the Roman law, and the customary law of countries deriving their jurisprudence from the Roman law.[3] By the ancient Roman law all the sons were in subjection to the authority of the father until they were emancipated by the father, or by some other mode known to that law. During such subjection they were incapable of acquiring any property for themselves by succession, or donation, or purchase, or otherwise; and whatever they thus acquired belonged of right to their father, saving only what was called the son's peculium, which consisted of property acquired by his service in the army, or by his skill at the bar, or in the exercise of some public employment.[4] This sort of property was therefore known by the name of peculium castrense when it was acquired in war, and of peculium quasi castrense when it was acquired in any other manner.[5] In the time of Justinian the law was altered, and the father was no longer entitled to the property acquired by his unemancipated son; but he was entitled to the usufruct or profits thereof during his life. The rule, thus modified, has found its way, sometimes with and sometimes without modifications, into

[1] Cochin, Œuvres, tom. 5, p. 797, 4to ed.

[2] Ante, s. 157–159, 174–179, 186, 187.   [3] Ante, s. 139.

[4] 1 Domat, Civ. Law, Prelim. b. 2, tit. 2, s. 2, p. 24, note; Id. b. 2, tit. 2, s. 2, p. 667–670, n. 1, 2, 3; Bouhier, Cout. de Bourg. c. 16, s. 8–12, p. 295; 1 Brown, Civ. Law, p. 122, 123; 2 Froland, Mém. 806–813; 2 Henrys, Œuvres, par Bretonnier, lib. 4, quest. 127, p. 772, &c., 717; Merlin, Répert. Puissance Paternelle, s. 7, p. 142.

[5] 1 Domat, b. 2, s. 2, p. 668.

the jurisprudence of many provinces and states of continental Europe.[1]

456. *Paternal Power.* — Under this aspect of the law with regard to the paternal difficulty, the question has often been discussed among foreign jurists, whether the laws respecting the paternal power are personal or real ; or, in other words, whether the rights of the father, allowed and secured by the law of the place of his domicil, extend to the immovable property of his sons, situate in other countries whose jurisprudence confers no such paternal rights.[2]

457. *Foreign Jurists.* — Bretonnier holds the doctrine that all laws respecting the paternal power are personal, and consequently have effect upon all real property of the children, wherever it is situate, and especially as to the profits and usufruct of it; because the latter partake of the nature of movables. After stating the question whether fathers domiciled in a country using the Roman law (dans le pays de droit écrit), whose sons have real property in another country having a different customary law, are entitled to the profits of the latter, that is to say, whether the paternal power extends everywhere, he proceeds to say : ' Cette question ne me semble pas susceptible d'une grande difficulté; parceque la puissance paternelle est un droit personnel, et par conséquence il ne peut être borné par aucun territoire ; car c'est une maxime certaine même dans les pays de coutume, que les statuts personnels sont universels, et produisent leur effet partout. D'ailleurs, les fruits sont des choses mobiliaires. Or, constat inter omnes, que les meubles suivent les personnes, et se réglent suivant la coutume du domicile.' [3]

458. Hertius seems to hold a like doctrine as to the personality of such laws, and puts a question, whether a daughter, who is emancipated by marriage, may afterwards make a testament of property situate elsewhere ; and whether the father would have a right to the usufruct of her property, situate in a place where she would be deemed unemancipated. He answers : ' Quæstio

---

[1] 1 Domat, b. 2, s. 2, p. 668; Civil Code of France, art. 384–387; 1 Froland, Mém. 69; 2 Froland. Mém. c. 17, p. 789; Bouhier, Cout. de Bourg. c. 16, p. 294.

[2] 2 Froland, Mém. 808, 813–829.

[3] Henrys, Œuvres, par Bretonnier, tom. 2, p. 720. See 2 Boullenois, obs. 82, p. 46, 47.

hæc duplex est; verum ex eodem principio decidenda. Jus nempe datum est personæ, quod etiam per consequentiam in bona alterius civitatis, licet immobilia operatur.'[1] Yet Hertius, in another place, holds that an unemancipated son (filius-familias), who by the law of his domicil may make a testament, cannot make a testament of property situate in a foreign country. 'Nam statutum est in rem conceptum, et conditio filii-familiæ non est in dispositione.[2] Hinc juxta regulam Puduensis filius-familias de bonis alibi sitis testari non poterit.'[3] The ground of this opinion probably is, that the general incapacity is admitted to exist by the law of the domicil, and the special exception is local and real.[4] In this opinion Hertius admits that he differs from Huberus, whom he asserts to hold the opinion that, if a Batavian who is an unemancipated son, but has authority to make a testament in Holland, makes a testament in Holland of immovable property situate in Friesland, that testament will be valid in Friesland, although in Friesland the son, however rich and of whatever age, cannot make any testament of his property.[5]·

459. Bouhier maintains, with earnestness and ability, that the paternal power is altogether personal, and that it extends to the immovable property of the unemancipated child, situate in a foreign country where the like law as to the paternal authority does not exist.[6] And he is supported by the opinion of Le Brun, D'Argentré, and others.[7]

460. On the other hand, Froland maintains that the paternal power in regard to the immovable property of a child is purely real. 'Ce statut est constamment réel; il ne s'étend point sur les biens situez dans une coutume, qui n'a pas disposition pareille.'[8] Boullenois, while he admits that the laws which give

---

[1] 1 Hertii Opera, de Collis. Leg. s. 4, n. 17, p. 130, ed. 1737; Id. p. 185, ed. 1716.

[2] 1 Hertii Opera, de Collis. Leg. s. 4, n. 22, p. 133, ed. 1737; Id. p. 188, ed. 1716.

[3] Ibid.

[4] Merlin, Répert. Testament, s. 1, n. 5, art. 1, p. 310.

[5] Hertii Opera, de Collis. Leg. s. 4, n. 22, p. 133, ed. 1737; Id. p. 188, ed. 1716.

[6] Bouhier, Cout. de Bourg. c. 24, s. 37–87, p. 468–475.

[7] Bouhier, Cout. de. Bourg. c. 24, s. 41, p. 468; Le Brun, de la Communauté, lib. 1, c. 5; n. 8; D'Argent. de Briton. Leg. des Donations, art. 218, gloss. 6, n. 7, tom. 1, p. 648.

[8] 1 Froland, Mém. 69; Id. 39, 60, 156; 2 Froland, Mém. c. 17, p. 789–819.

the paternal power are personal so far as they respect the state or condition of the parties, contends, at the same time, that, so far as those laws give rights over immovable property, they are real, and are to be governed by the law of the place where the property is situate.[1] And he proceeds to vindicate his opinion in a most elaborate manner.[2]

461. D'Aguesseau says: 'That which characterizes a real statute, and distinguishes it essentially from a personal statute, is not that it relates to certain personal qualities, or to certain personal circumstances, or to certain personal events; otherwise we should be compelled to say that all laws which concern the paternal power, the right of guardianship, the right of widowhood (le droit de viduité), and the prohibition of donations between married persons, are all personal laws. And accordingly it is beyond doubt that in our jurisprudence all these laws are real, which are to be governed, not according to the law of the domicil, but according to that of the place where the property is situate.'[3]

462. Merlin has examined the same subject in a formal discussion; and he endeavors to hold a middle course between the opinions of Bouhier and Boullenois, agreeing with the latter that the usufruct arising under the paternal power is a real right, and governed by the lex rei sitæ, and at the same time holding with Bouhier that the father cannot possess the right unless, by the law of the place of his domicil, the paternal power is recognized. He then lays down three principles, which he supposes will remove all the difficulties upon this thorny subject. (1.) The law which subjects the son to the power of his father has no need of the aid (ministère) of man for its execution; and it is therefore personal from the very nature of its object. (2.) The law which declares an unemancipated son (un fils de famille) incapable of alienating his immovable property without the authority of his father is personal, although its object is real; because it determines the state of the person in regard to what he can and cannot do. (3.) The law which gives to a father the usufruct of the property of his son ought to be real; because its object is real, and it makes no regulation concerning the capacity or inca-

---

[1] 1 Boullenois, obs. 4, p. 68; 2 Boullenois, obs. 32, p. 30–33; Id. p. 39–47; Boullenois, Quest. Mixtes, quest. 20, p. 406.

[2] Ibid.   [3] D'Aguesseau, Œuvres, tom. 4, p. 660, 4to ed.

pacity of the unemancipated son to do anything.[1] In another
place he holds that a law which prohibits an unemancipated son

[1] Merlin, Répert. Puissance Paternelle, s. 7, p. 142, 144, ed. 1827. The
reasoning of Merlin on this subject is marked with uncommon clearness and
force of statement; and I have therefore thought that an extract from it might
not be unacceptable to the reader. ' Or, que trouvons nous dans la puissance
paternelle? Trois choses. Premièrement, elle détermine l'état des enfans; et
à cet égard, elle forme un statut personnel, qui suit les enfans partout. Ainsi,
une mère, domiciliée en Hainaut, conserve sous sa puissance les enfans qu'elle
a eu dans cette province, lors même que le hasard ou certaines circonstances
les ont fait passer dans une autre coutume, qui n'accorde pas les mêmes droits
aux femmes qu'aux hommes sur la personne de leurs enfans. En second lieu,
la puissance paternelle imprime dans les enfans, qui y sont assujetis, une incapacité de faire certains actes: comme cette incapacité est la suite de leur état,
elle les suit également partout et influe sur tous leurs biens, quelle qu'en soit la
situation. Ainsi, un fils de famille, né dans une coutume où il ne peut pas contracter sans l'autorité de son père, ne peut vendre de lui-même les biens qu'il
possède dans une autre coutume qui n'admet pas la puissance paternelle; et
reciproquement un fils de famille domicilié dans une coutume qui n'admet pas
la puissance paternelle, peut, sans l'autorisation de son père, aliéner les biens
qu'il possède dans les pays de droit écrit. Par la même raison, un fils né à
Senlis, où la coutume proscrit formellement toute puissance paternelle, quoique
nourri et entretenu par son père, peut acquérir pour lui-même en Hainaut et dans
les pays de droit écrit. Et réciproquement, un fils de famille né en Hainaut,
ou dans un pays de droit écrit, ne peut s'approprier les biens qu'il acquiert
dans la coutume de Senlis, lorsque ses acquisitions ne réunissent pas toutes les
circonstances requises pour qu'elles tombent dans le pécule castrense, et quasi-
castrense, ou adventice. Troisièmement, la puissance paternelle donne au
père dans les pays de droit écrit et dans quelques coutumes, la jouissance des
biens de ses enfans. Cette jouissance est, à la vérité, un accessoire de la puissance paternelle; mais elle ne forme dans les enfans ni capacité ni incapacité:
le statut, qui la défère, n'a pas besoin, pour son exécution, du ministère de
l'homme; il agit seul; l'homme n'a rien à faire. On ne peut donc pas appliquer ici les raisons, qui ont déterminé l'espèce de concordat tacite, dont nous
avons parlé. Quel inconvénience y a-t-il à restreindre cette jouissance au territoire des lois ou coutumes, qui l'accordent? Quoi! parcequ'un père jouira des
biens, que ses enfans ont dans une province, et qu'il ne jouira pas de ceux qu'ils
ont dans une autre, l'ordre public serait troublé, le commerce serait dérangé.
Non. Il n'y a pas en cela plus de trouble ni plus de confusion, qu'à succéder à
un défunt dans une coutume, et de ne pas lui succéder dans une autre. Il est
donc constant que le système du président Bouhier ne peut pas se soutenir, et que
le statut, qui donne à un père l'usufruit des biens des enfans, qu'il a sous sa puissance, n'est pas personnel. Mais est-il purement réel, comme le prétend Boullenois, ou bien est-il personnel réel, c'est-à-dire, faut-il, pour qu'il produise son effet,
que le père soit domicilié dans une coutume, qui admet la puissance paternelle?
C'est la difficulté, qui nous reste à résoudre. Le principal peut subsister sans
les accessoires: mais les accessoires ne peuvent jamais subsister sans le principal. Ce principe est aussi clair, qu'indubitable, et il nous conduit droit à
la décision de notre question. Ainsi, la puissance paternelle peut avoir lieu
sans l'usufruit dont nous parlons ici. La coutume de Douai nous en fournit

to make a testament is personal; but he at the same time asserts that this will not prevent him from making a testament of movable property in other countries where it is permitted; because this case is a mere exception from his general incapacity, and also falls within the rule that, in a conflict of real and personal laws, the latter must yield.[1]

463. *Rule of the Common Law.* — Without going further into an examination of the opinions of foreign jurists upon this subject, it is sufficiently obvious what difficulties they are compelled to encounter at almost every step, in order to carry into effect their favorite system of the division of laws into real and personal. The common law has avoided all these difficulties by a simple and uniform test. It declares that the law of the situs shall exclusively govern in regard to all rights, interests, and titles, in and to immovable property. Of course it cuts down all attempts to introduce all foreign laws, whether they respect persons or things, or give or withhold the capacity to acquire or to dispose of immovable property.[2]

463 *a.* This subject of the nature and extent of the paternal power and rights came recently under consideration in England, in a case somewhat complicated in its circumstances, and touching personal estate only. It may be briefly stated as follows. A marriage took place in Holland between the parties. At the time of the marriage, a marriage contract was there executed in the Dutch form, making certain provisions, and, among other things, provision for the distribution of the wife's property in the

---

un exemple, puisqu'elle admet l'une, chap. 7, art. 2, et qu'elle exclut l'autre par son silence, comme l'a décidé le parlement de Flandre par un arrêt du 27 Janvier 1739, rendu au rapport de M. de Casteele de la Briarde, en faveur du Marquis de Sin, contre les Sieurs et Demoiselles d'Aoust. Mais l'usufruit ne peut avoir lieu sans la puissance paternelle, dont il n'est l'accessoire. Un père ne peut donc en jouir, s'il n'a ses enfans sous sa puissance, et par conséquence s'il n'est domicilié dans une coutume, qui admet la puissance paternelle. Un père, qui émanciperait son fils au moment même de sa naissance, n'aurait certainement aucun droit à l'usufruit des biens, que cet enfant acquerrait ensuite, soit dans la coutume du domicile qu'il avait alors, soit dans tout autre province. Or, ce que ce père est supposé faire, la loi le fait elle-même dans les coutumes qui n'admettent pas la puissance paternelle; elle émancipe cet enfant dès qu'il voit le jour, et conséquement elle soustrait les biens, qu'il aura dans la suite, à l'usufruit que son père en aurait eu sans cette émancipation.' Merlin, Répert. Puissance Paternelle, s. 7, p. 145, 146, ed. 1827.

[1] Merlin, Répert. Testament, s. 1, n. 5, art. 1, p. 310.

[2] See Brodie *v.* Barry, 2 V. & B. 127.

event of her husband surviving her. They afterwards removed to and became domiciled in England, and had children born there. The wife died; and by her death the children became entitled, under a compromise in Holland, to one fourth of certain property of the wife in the public funds. By the French Code, which is the law of Holland also, when children are under the age of eighteen years, their surviving parent has the enjoyment of their property until they attain that age; and the father insisted that as the children were under that age, and the marriage contract and compromise under which they took one fourth were both made in Holland, the children must take it subject to his paternal rights by the law of Holland. The vice-chancellor held that the father was not so entitled. On that occasion the learned judge said: ' By the Code Napoléon, which is the law of Holland as well as of France, when children are under the age of eighteen, their surviving parent has the enjoyment of their property until they attain that age. But that is nothing more than a mere local right, given to the surviving parent by the law of a particular country, so long as the children remain subject to that law; and as soon as the children are in a country where that law is not in force, their rights must be determined by the law of the country where they happen to be. These children were never subject to the law of Holland; they were both born in this country, and have resided here ever since. The consequence is, that this judicial decree has adjudged certain property to belong to two British-born subjects domiciled in this country; and so long as they are domiciled in this country, their personal property must be administered according to the law of this country. The claim of their father does not arise by virtue of the contract, but solely by the local law of the country where he was residing at the time of his marriage; and therefore this property must be considered just as if it had been an English legacy given to the children; and all that the father is entitled to is the usual reference to the master, to inquire what allowance ought to be made to him for the past and future maintenance of his children.'[1]

[1] Gambier v. Gambier, 7 Sim. 263, 270.

CHAPTER XI.

WILLS AND TESTAMENTS.

464. *Preliminary Remarks.* — Having taken these general views of the operation of foreign law in regard to movable property and immovable property, and ascertained that the general principle, at least in the common law, adopted in relation to the former is, that it is governed by the law of the domicil of the owner, and in relation to the latter, that it is governed by the law of the place where it is locally situate ; we now come to make a more immediate application of these principles to two·of the most important classes of cases arising, constantly and uniformly, in all civilized human societies. One is the right of a person, by an act or instrument, to dispose of his property after his death ; the other is the right of succession to the same property, in case no such post-mortuary disposition is made of it by the owner. The former involves the right to make last wills and testaments ; and the latter the title of descent and the distribution of property ab intestato. We shall accordingly in this and the succeeding chapter exclusively discuss the subject of foreign law in relation to testaments, and to successions and distributions of movable and immovable property.

465. *Testaments of Movables.* — And first in relation to testaments of movable property.[1] So far as respects the capacity or incapacity of a testator to make a will of personal or movable property, we have already had occasion to consider the subject in another place. The result of that examination was, that the law of the actual domicil of the party, at the time of the making of his will or testament, was to govern as to that capacity or incapacity.[2] (a) We may therefore proceed to the consideration of

[1] See 4 Burge, Col. & For. Law, pt. 2, c. 12, p. 579–581; post, s. 466, 467.
[2] Ante, s. 52–62, 64–78, 101–106, 368, 430–484. See also 2 Boullenois, Appx. p. 38; 4 Burge, Col. & For. Law, pt. 2, c. 12, p. 577–579.

(a) See Lawrence v. Kitteridge, 21 Conn. 582.

41

the forms and solemnities by which wills of personal estates are to be governed. And here it may be stated now to be a well settled principle in the English law, that a will of personal or movable property, regularly made according to the forms and solemnities required by the law of the testator's domicil, is sufficient to pass his personal or movable property in every other country in which it is situated. But this doctrine, although now very firmly established, was for a great length of time much agitated and discussed in Westminster Hall.[1] On one occasion, Lord Loughborough laid down the doctrine that, with respect to the disposition of movable property, and with respect to the transmission of it, either by succession or by the act of the party, it follows the law of the person.[2] The owner in any country may dispose of his personal property. On another occasion Lord Thurlow asserted the same doctrine as to succession to personal property, and by implication as to wills.[3] Lord Ellenborough put it as clear in his day. He observed : ' It is every day's experience to recognize the law of foreign countries as binding on personal property; as in the sale of ships condemned as prize by the sentences of foreign courts, the succession to personal property by will or intestacy of the subjects of foreign countries.'[4] But antecedently to this period many learned doubts and discussions had existed on the subject.[5] In the Duchess of Kingston's Case, a will of personal property executed in France, but not in conformity to the laws of that country, was admitted to probate in the ecclesiastical courts of England in 1791, it being duly executed according to the English forms, although she was domiciled in France at the time of making the will, and also at the time of her death.[6]

[1] See Brodie v. Barry, 2 V. & B. 127, 131; Bempde v. Johnstone, 3 Ves. 198, 200; Price v. Dewhurst, 8 Sim. 279, 299, 300; Moore v. Budd, 4 Hagg. Ecc. 346, 352; Robertson on Successions, p. 99, 191, 214, 215, 285, 290, 297; The Case of the Goods of Marshall Bennett, before Sir H. Jenner Fust, July, 1840, London Monthly Law Magazine, Sept. 1840, p. 264.

[2] Sill v. Worswick, 1 H. Bl. 690. See also Ommaney v. Bingham, cited 5 Ves. 757; 3 Hagg. Ecc. 414, note; Stanley v. Bernes, 8 Hagg. Ecc. 373; Hogg v. Lashley, 3 Hagg. Ecc. 415, note.

[3] Bruce v. Bruce, 2 B. & P. 229, note.

[4] Potter v. Brown, 5 East, 130; Ferraris v. Hertford, 3 Curteis, 468, 7 Jur. 262.

[5] See Bempde v. Johnstone, 3 Ves. 198, 200; Somerville v. Somerville, 5 Ves. 750; Balfour v. Scott, 6 Bro. P. C. 550, Tomlin's ed.; 2 Add. Ecc. 15, note.

[6] See Curling v. Thornton, 2 Add. Ecc. 21. See 4 Burge, Col. & For. Law, pt. 2, c. 12, p. 588–590.

466. *Sir John Nicholl's Opinion.* — Even at so late a period as 1823, Sir John Nicholl doubted whether a will of personal property, made abroad by an English subject domiciled abroad, ought to be held valid, unless it was executed in conformity to the forms prescribed by the English law. The ground of his doubt was, whether an English subject was entitled to throw off his country (exuere patriam) so far as to select a foreign domicil in complete derogation of his native domicil, and thus to render his property in England distributable by succession or testament according to the foreign law. He took a distinction between testacy and intestacy (assuming, for the sake of argument, that in the latter case the foreign law might prevail), thinking that cases of testacy might be governed by very different considerations from those of intestacy. Even if a will, executed according to the law of the place of the testator's domicil, would in such a case be valid, he contended that it by no means followed universally, and upon principle, that a will, to be valid, must strictly conform to that law which would have regulated the succession to the testator's property if he had died intestate. And therefore he held that a will of personal property, made by a British subject in France, according to the forms of the English law, was good as to such property situate in England. He admitted that, as to British subjects domiciled in any part of the United Kingdom, the law of their domicil must govern in regard to successions and wills ; and so the like law must govern in regard to successions and wills of foreigners resident abroad. The restriction which he sought to establish was, that a British subject could not, by a foreign domicil, defeat the operation of the law of his own country as to personal property situate in the latter.[1]

467. *Reversal of his Decision.* — To this opinion the same learned judge firmly adhered in a still later case. But upon an appeal, the decision was overturned by the High Court of Delegates, and the doctrine fully established, that the law of the actual foreign domicil of a British subject is exclusively to govern in relation to his testament of personal property, as it would in the case of a mere foreigner.[2] (a) This case is the stronger, be-

[1] Curling v. Thornton, 2 Add. Ecc. 6, 10–25; 8 Sim. 310, 311.
[2] Stanley v. Bernes, 3 Hagg. Ecc. 373–465; Moore v. Darell, 4 Hagg. Ecc.

(a) See Bremer v. Freeman, 10 Moore, P. C. 358.

cause it was the case of a will and several codicils made according to the law of Portugal, and also of several codicils made not according to the law of Portugal, where the testator was domiciled. The will and codicils executed according to the Portuguese law were held valid; the others were held invalid. And this doctrine necessarily goes to the extent of establishing, not only whether there be an instrument called a will, but whether it constitutes a will in the sense of the lex loci. The doctrine also applies, whether the personal property be locally situate in the domicil of the testator or in a foreign country.[1]

468. *The Rule in America.* — The same doctrine is now as firmly established in America. The earliest case in which it was directly in judgment was argued in the Supreme Court of Pennsylvania in 1808;[2] and this case may be truly said to have led the way to the positive adjudication of this important and difficult doctrine. There a foreign testator domiciled abroad had made a will of his personal estate, invalid according to the law of his domicil, but valid according to the law of Pennsylvania; and the question was, whether it was competent and valid to pass personal property situate in Pennsylvania. The court decided that it was not, and asserted the general doctrine, that a will of personal estate must, in order to pass the property, be executed according to the law of the place of the testator's domicil at the time of his death. If void by that law, it is a nullity everywhere, although it is executed with the formalities required by the law of the place where the personal property is locally situate. The court asserted that in this respect there was no difference between cases of succession by testament, and by intestacy.[3] The same doctrine has been since repeatedly recognized by other American courts, and may now be deemed as of universal authority here.[4] (a)

346, 352; Price *v.* Dewhurst, 4 My. & Cr. 76, 80, 82; Ferraris *v.* Hertford, 7 Jur. 262; 3 Curteis, 468.

[1] Ibid.; Ferraris *v.* Hertford, 7 Jur. 262; 3 Curteis, 468.

[2] Desesbats *v.* Berquier, 1 Binn. (Pa.) 336.

[3] Ibid.; Moore *v.* Budd, 4 Hagg. Ecc. 346, 352; Grattan *v.* Appleton, 3 Story, 755.

[4] See Holmes *v.* Remsen, 4 Johns. Ch. (N. Y.) 460, 469; Harvey *v.* Richards, 1 Mason, 381, and cases cited, p. 408, note; Dixon *v.* Ramsay, 3 Cranch, 319; De Sobry *v.* De Laistre, 2 Harr. & J. (Md.) 193, 224; Armstrong *v.* Lear, 12 Wheat. 169; Harrison *v.* Nixon, 9 Pet. 483, 504, 505.

(a) See Rue High, App. 2 Doug. 226; Irwin's Appeal, 33 Conn. 128. In (Mich.) 522; Norris *v.* Harris, 15 Cal. re Lewis, 32 La. An. 385; Succession

469. *Scotch Law.* — In Scotland the doctrine was formerly involved in many doubts. By the law of Scotland, illegitimate persons are not deemed capable of making a will; and hence a will of movables in Scotland, made by such a person domiciled in England, was formerly held in Scotland to be invalid.[1] In like manner a nuncupative will, being in Scotland invalid, was formerly held invalid to pass movables in Scotland, although the will was made in England (where such a will is valid) by a person domiciled there.[2] But the general doctrine is now the same in Scotland as in England. The law of the domicil universally prevails as to successions and wills of movables in other countries.[3]

470. *Foreign Jurists.* — Foreign jurists are generally agreed as to the doctrine in regard to movables, upon the ground, maintained by all of them, that mobilia sequuntur personam.[4] John Voet lays down the rule in the following terms: ' In successionibus, testandi facultate, contractibus, aliisque, mobilia, ubicunque sita, regi debere domicilii jure, non vero legibus loci illius, in quo naturaliter sunt constituta. '[5] He adds: ' Ibique DD. (Doctores) mobilium tamen ratione in dispositionibus testamentariis, dum quæritur, an illæ in universum permittendæ sint, nec ne,

---

[1] Ersk. Inst. b. 3, tit. 2, s. 41, p. 515; 3 Kames, Eq. b. 3, c. 8, s. 3.

[2] 2 Kames, Eq. b. 3, c. 8, s. 3, p. 345.

[3] See Bempde v. Johnstone, 3 Ves. 198, 201; Somerville v. Somerville, 5 Ves. 757; Brodie v. Barry, 2 V. & B. 127, 131, and the cases cited ante, s. 495; Ersk. Inst. b. 3, tit. 2, s. 40, 41; 2 Kames, Eq. c. 8, s. 6.

[4] See 1 Boullenois, obs. 28, p. 696–721; Cochin, Œuvres, tom. 5, p. 85, 4to ed.; ante, s. 362, 362 a, 399; 4 Burge, Col. & For. Law, pt. 2, c. 12, p. 579, 580; Foelix, Conflit des Lois, Revue Étrang. et Franç. tom. 7, 1840, s. 40–50, p. 346–360; post, s. 481.

[5] J. Voet, ad Pand. 1, 4, ps. 2, s. 11, p. 44.

---

of Elliot, 27 La. An. 42; Holman v. Hopkins, 27 Tex. 88; In re Blithman, L. R. 2 Eq. 23; In re Hellmann's Will, Id. 363; Richards v. Miller, 62 Ill. 417; Townes v. Durbin, 3 Met. (Ky.) 352; Jones v. Gerock, 6 Jones, Eq. (N. C.) 190; Fellows v. Miner, 119 Mass. 541; Fay v. Haven, 3 Met. (Mass.) 109; Phelps v. Pond, 23 N. Y. 69; Bascom v. Albertson, 34 N. Y. 584; Chamberlain v. Chamberlain, 43 N. Y. 424. That domicil, not residence, is the test, see Caulfield v. Sullivan, 85 N. Y. 153; Manuel v. Manuel, 13 Ohio St. 458; Morris v. Morris, 27 Miss. 847; Sturdivant v. Neill, Id. 157; Wallace v. Wallace, 2 Green, Ch. 616. But where the law of the forum actually prohibits the particular kind of disposition in question made in the country of the domicil, the former law will prevail. Harper v. Stanbrough, 2 La. An. 377; Harper v. Lee, Id. 382.

uti et ab intestato successionibus, donationibus inter conjuges vetitis permissisve, et aliis similibus, de juris rigore communi quasi gentium omnium consensu laxatum est; sic ut ex comitate profecta regula praxi universali invaluerit, mobilia in dubio regi lege loci, in quo eorum dominus domicilium fovet, ubicunque illa vere exstiterint.'[1]

471. *Vattel.* — Vattel has spoken in terms admitting of more question as to the extent of their meaning. After observing that a foreigner in a foreign country has by natural right the liberty of making a will, he remarks : ' As to the forms or solemnities appointed to settle the validity of a will, it appears that the testator ought to observe those which are established in the country where he makes it, unless it be otherwise ordained by the laws of the State of which he is a member, in which case he will be obliged to observe the forms which they prescribe, if he would validly dispose of the property which he possesses in his own country. The foreign testator cannot dispose of his property, movable or immovable, which he possesses in his own country, otherwise than in a manner conformable to the laws of that country. But as to movable property, specie, and other effects, which he possesses elsewhere, which he has with him, or which follow his person, we ought to distinguish between the local laws, whose effect cannot extend beyond the territory, and those laws which peculiarly affect the character of citizens. The foreigner remaining a citizen of his own country is still bound by those last-mentioned laws wherever he happens to be, and is obliged to conform to them in the disposal of his personal property, and all his movables whatsoever. The laws of this kind, made in the country where he resides at the time, but of which he is not a citizen, are not obligatory with respect to him. Thus a man who makes his will and dies in a foreign country cannot deprive his widow of the part of his movable effects assigned to that widow by the laws of his own country. A Genevan, obliged by the laws of his country to

[1] J. Voet, ad Pand, 1, 4, ps. 2, s. 12, p. 45. See also J. Voet, ad Pand. 28, 1, n. 13, 15, 44; 4 Burge, Col. & For. Law, pt. 2, c. 12, p. 579, 580, 590; P. Voet, de Statut. s. 9, c. 1, n. 8, p. 255, ed. 1715; Id. p. 309, ed. 1661; Burgundus, tract. 1, n. 36; Id. tract. 6, n. 1–3; Foelix, Conflit des Lois, Revue Étrang. et Franç. tom. 7, 1840, s. 24–27, p. 204–216; Id. s. 32, 33, p. 221–227; ante, s. 381, note, s. 444 *a*; 4 Burge, Col. & For. Law, pt. 2, c. 5, p. 217, 218; Id. c. 12, p. 576–580; post, s. 479; Sand. Decis. Frisic. lib. 4, tit. 1, defin. 14, p. 142, 143.

leave a portion of his personal property to his brothers or cousins, if they are his next heirs, cannot deprive them of it by making his will in a foreign country while he continues a citizen of Geneva. But a foreigner, dying at Geneva, is not obliged in this respect to conform to the laws of the republic. The case is quite otherwise in respect to local laws. They regulate what may be done in the territory, and do not extend beyond it. The testator is no longer subject to them when he is out of the territory, and they do not affect that part of his property which is also out of it. The foreigner is obliged to observe those laws in the country where he makes his will, with respect to the goods he possesses there.' [1]

472. Vattel is in this passage principally considering the effect of the law of a foreign country upon a foreigner who is resident there. And there can be no doubt that every country may by its laws prescribe whatever rules it may please as to the disposition of the movable property of its citizens, either inter vivos, or testamentary. But it is equally clear that such rules are of no obligation as to movable property in any other country, and can be in force there only by the comity of nations. So that a will of such movable property, made in a foreign country where the testator is domiciled, and according to its laws, will be held valid, whatever may be the validity of such a will in the country to which he owes his allegiance by birth. (a) But the discussion in which we are engaged does not respect the effect of any local prohibitory laws over movable property within the particular territory, but the general principles which regulate the disposition of it when no such prohibitory laws exist. And here, by the general consent of foreign jurists, the law of the domicil of the testator governs as to transfers inter vivos and testamentary.[2]

[1] Vattel, b. 2, c. 8, s. 111. See post, s. 479.

[2] See ante, s. 465; Hertii Opera, de Collis. Leg. s. 4, n. 6, p. 112, ed. 1737; Id. p. 174, ed. 1710; Pothier, Cout. d'Orléans, c. 1, s. 2, n. 24. J. Voet, ad Pand. 2, 88, 17, s. 34; ante, s. 470. Very difficult questions however may still arise as to what is to be deemed the real domicil of a party who is a native of one country and who has yet been long resident in another. The quo animo with which such residence has been originally taken, or subsequently upheld, often becomes a very important element in the decision. See ante, s. 44, 49; Atty.-Gen. v. Dunn, 6 M. & W. 511; De Bonneval v. De Bonneval, 1 Curteis Ecc. 856; post, s. 481, note; Munro v. Munro, 7 Cl. & F. 842; 1 Rob. 493.

(a) See Mahorner v. Hooe, 9 Smedes & M. 247.

473. *Effect of Change of Domicil.* — But it may be asked, What will be the effect of a change of domicil after a will or testament is made of personal or movable property, if it is valid by the law of the place where the party was domiciled when it was made, and not valid by the law of his domicil at the time of his death? The terms in which the general rule is laid down would seem sufficiently to establish the principle that in such a case the will or testament is void; for it is the law of his actual domicil at the time of his death, and not the law of his domicil at the time of making his will or testament of personal property, which is to govern.[1](a) This doctrine is very fully recognized and laid down by John Voet. 'Tamen, si quis habitans in loco in quo minor annorum numerus in testatore requiritur, veluti in Hollandia, ibidem anno decimo quinto testamentum fecerit, deinde vero domicilium alio transtulerit, ubi necdum per ætatem testari licet, veluti Ultrajectum, ubi plena pubertas in masculo testatore exigitur, testamentum ejus quantum ad mobilia per talem migrationem irritum efficitur. Idemque eveniet, si Hollandus uxorem hæredem instituerit (quod ibi licitum), deinde vero ad aliam migret regionem, ibique domicilium figat, ubi gratificatio inter conjuges ne supremo quidem elogio permissa est; nam et hoc in casu mobilium intuitu in irritum deducitur voluntas ejus; cum mobilia in successione testata vel intestata regantur ex lege domicilii defuncti, adeoque res devenerit in hisce ad eum casum, a quo propter qualitatem testatoris, vel honorati, initium habere nequit. Neque enim sufficit in honorato, quod tempore facti testamenti capax sit, sed et tempore mortis testatoris eum capacem esse, necesse est.'[2] Again he adds: 'Quod si is, cujus testamentum migratione ex Hollandia ad regionem Ultrajectinam irritum factum fuerat, ibidem ætatem expleverit in testatore requisitam, de novo quidem repetere solenniter potest priorem voluntatem, atque ita de novo testari; sed si id non fecerit, testamentum, antea anno ætatis decimo quinto in Hollandia conditum, ipso jure

---

[1] See Desesbats *v.* Berquier, 1 Binn. (Penn.) 336; Potinger *v.* Wightman, 3 Meriv. 68; Henry on Foreign Law, Appx. p. 196; 2 Boullenois, c. 1, p. 2, &c.; Id. p. 7, 54, 57; ante, s. 55–74; 4 Burge, Col. & For. Law, pt. 2, c. 12, p. 580, 581.

[2] J. Voet, ad Pand. 28, 3, 2, s. 12, p. 292.

(a) See Moultrie *v.* Hunt, 23 N. Y. 394; Dupuy *v.* Wurtz, 53 N. Y. 556; Irwin's Appeal, 33 Conn. 128.

quantum ad mobilia vel immobilia Ultrajectina nequaquam convalescit; non magis, quam jure civili aut prætorio testamentum ab impubere conditum, si is pubes factus in fata concedat.'[1] If however he should afterwards return and resume his domicil, where his first will or testament was made, its original validity will revive also. ' Diversum esset, si testator talis iterum postea mutata mente in Hollandia rerum ac fortunarum suarum sedem reponat; tunc enim voluntas illa, quæ migratione in irritum deducta fuerat, quasi recuperata pristina ad testandum habilitate redintegratur ex æquitate; eo modo, quo sustinetur jure prætorio testamentum, a patrefamilias conditum, quod per arrogationem irritum factum fuerat, si is iterum postea sui juris factus in eadem perstiterit voluntate.'[2] (a)

473 a. *Power of Appointment.* — Another question may arise under this head. Suppose a power of appointment to be given to a party enabling him to dispose by will of personal estate situate in one country, and he has his domicil in another country, and he executes the power and complies with all the requisites of the power, making a will according to the law of the country where the power was created, and the personal estate is situated; but the will is not made according to the requisites prescribed by the law of the place of his domicil; the question would then arise, whether the power of appointment was well executed, and

---

[1] J. Voet, ad Pand. 28, 3, 2, s. 13, p. 293.

[2] J. Voet, ad Pand. 28, 3, 2, s. 13, p. 293; 4 Burge, Col. & For. Law, pt. 2, c. 12, p. 580, 591; Robinson on Succession, p. 95.

(a) The principle laid down in this section, viz., that a change of domicil after a will is made may revoke a prior will if the same be invalid according to the law of the new domicil, was modified in England by St. 24 & 25 Vict. c. 114, s. 3, — commonly called Lord Kingsdown's act, — which enacts that ' no will shall be held to be revoked, or to have become invalid, nor shall the construction thereof be altered by reason of any subsequent change of domicil of the person making the same.' Accordingly it was held in a recent case under that act, that when a man whose domicil was in Scotland made a will and afterwards married in Scotland, but subsequently moved to England and there acquired a new domicil and died there, his will was good in England, and was not revoked by his subsequent marriage in Scotland; though Sir J. P. Wilde observed that, ' but for Lord Kingsdown's act, the will would without doubt be invalid;' and he added that if the deceased, instead of marrying in Scotland, married in England after obtaining an English domicil, a question of some nicety would have arisen whether the act applied. Goods of Reid, L. R. 1 P. & D. 74.

the will entitled to probate as a will in the country where the personal property is situate. It has been held that it is.[1] (a)

[1] Tatnall v. Hankey, 2 Moore, P. C. 342.

(a) *Intention to appoint.* — The question whether a will is intended as an execution of a power of appointment may depend upon whether the will is interpreted according to the law of one place or that of another. By the statute law of England (1 Vict. c. 26, s. 27) a general devise or bequest without any reference to the power is construed to include property which the testator has power to appoint as he may think proper. In Massachusetts the same rule has been in part adopted by judicial decision. In Pennsylvania and Maryland, an intention to exercise the power is not inferred unless the will contains a reference to the power, or expressly disposes of the property subject to it, or would be inoperative except as an execution of the power. In Bingham's Appeal, 64 Pa. St. 345, a testator domiciled in England made a general devise and bequest of all his property; he had power under the will of his father, who was domiciled in Pennsylvania, to appoint by will, as he should think proper, a fund of personal estate which had been bequeathed by his father to trustees. The Pennsylvania court, applying its own rules of construction, held that the will showed no intention to execute the power, and therefore did not operate as an execution of it. In Sewall v. Wilmer, 132 Mass. 131, a married woman domiciled in Maryland likewise made a general devise and bequest of all her property; she had by the will of her father, who was domiciled in Massachusetts, a general power to appoint by deed or will certain real estate in Massachusetts which he had devised to trustees. A majority of the Massachusetts court, also applying its own rules of construction, held that an intention to execute the power was to be inferred, and that

the real estate passed by the will. In both of these cases the testators had other property upon which their wills operated.

The Pennsylvania court in Bingham's Appeal (supra) says with regard to the effect of the English statute, 'It is doubtless in the power of the parliament to say that a bequest of a testator's own estate shall be deemed to extend to the estate of another over which the testator has a power, unless he expresses the contrary intention. But this effect is produced by operation of law, not by the words of the will. It is manifest that no possible judicial interpretation of the words *my personal estate* can make them mean the estate of another. It is simply a legal effect or operation of law by statutory construction which can do so.' The English statute referred to provides that a general devise or bequest of the real or personal estate of the testator 'shall be construed to include' any real or personal estate respectively which he may have power to appoint as he may think proper. It seems clear that since that statute the words *my personal estate* in an English will do include in their meaning the property of another which the testator has a general power to appoint by will. The statute gives the words, when used in wills executed after it took effect, a meaning which they did not have before. It is obvious that it is not impossible for the words to have in some places a different meaning from that which they have in Pennsylvania. In Chandler v. Pocock, 15 Ch. D. p. 498, Jessel, M. R., speaking of this provision of the statute, said, 'Consequently, a bequest of " my personal estate " is, in my opinion, not only a bequest of the actual personal estate of the

474. *Wills of Immovables.* — We next pass to the consideration of wills made of immovable property.[1] And here the doctrine

[1] See 4 Burge, Col. & For. Law, pt. 2, c. 12, p. 586, 596; Foelix, Conflit des Lois, Revue Étrang. et Franç. tom. 7, 1840; s. 40–51, p. 346–360.

testator, but also a bequest of all the personal estate over which at the time of his death he shall have a general power of appointment by will. Accordingly such bequest should be read as if it included these words, " I appoint all the personal estate over which I shall have at my decease a general power of appointment by will." ' The testator in Bingham's Appeal therefore clearly expressed in the language of the country to which he belonged by domicil an intention to dispose of all the personal estate which he had a general power to appoint by will.

But except upon the question of the possibilities of judicial interpretation, the courts of Pennsylvania and Massachusetts substantially agree in the grounds of their decisions in these two cases. Both seem to admit that, as to personal property at least, the interpretation of a will is governed by the law of the testator's domicil; but both say that the testator whose property was in question was the testator who gave the power of appointment, and not the one to whom the power was given, and therefore the will of the latter was to be interpreted by the law of the domicil of the former.

The rule that a will is to be interpreted according to the law of the testator's domicil, is not limited to dispositions of his personal estate, but seems to apply in all cases, except where it appears that he expressed his meaning with reference to the law of some other place. Trotter v. Trotter, 4 Bligh, N.S. 502; 3 Wils. & S. 407; Wallis v. Brightwell, 2 P.W. 88; Maxwell v. Maxwell, L. R. 4 H. L. 506; Caulfield v. Sullivan, 85 N. Y. 153; post, s. 479 a, 479 h, 479 m. For example, in cases where a will is inope-

rative as to real estate in a foreign country, and the question is whether the testator has expressed an intention to dispose of it which will put the heir to his election, the interpretation is governed, not by the law of the foreign country where the real estate is, but by the law of the testator's domicil. Trotter v. Trotter, 4 Bligh, N.S. 502; 3 Wils. & S. 407; Maxwell v. Maxwell, 2 D. M. & G. 705; Orrell v. Orrell, L. R. 6 Ch. 802. A disposition of property in the technical forms of a foreign law will in some cases show an intention that it is to be construed according to that law. Chamberlain v. Napier, 15 Ch. D. 614; Mitchell v. Davies, Scotch Ct. Sess. Cas. 4th series, vol. 3, p. 208. Perhaps a specific disposition of real estate in a foreign country separately from other property may be presumed to have been made with reference to the law of that country, and may therefore be interpreted according to that law. See Yates v. Thomson, 3 Cl. & F. at p. 588. But no such presumption can arise where a testator makes a general disposition of all his property or all his real estate. In such a case the question being simply one of the intention expressed in the will, and not of the validity of the disposition, it is evident that the words express the same intention as to all the property or real estate wherever it may be. They ought not therefore to be interpreted even in the case of real estate so as to have different meanings in the different countries where the lands may be. Crusoe v. Butler, 36 Miss. 150; Wilson v. Cox, 49 Miss. 538, 545; Studd v. Studd, Scotch Ct. Sess. Cas. 4th series, vol. 8, p. 249. This has sometimes been done, however, but, as it is submitted, by a mis-

is clearly established at the common law, that the law of the place where the property is locally situate is to govern as to the capacity or incapacity of the testator, to the extent of his power to dispose of the property, and the forms and solemnities to give the will or testament its due attestation and effect.[1] (a)

---

[1] Coppin v. Coppin, 2 P. Wms. 291, 293; Curtis v. Hutton, 14 Ves. 537, 541; Birtwhistle v. Vardill, 1 Fonbl. Eq. p. 444, 445, note; United States v. Crosby, 7 Cranch, 115; Holmes v. Remsen, 4 Johns. Ch. (N. Y.) 460; 20 Johns. (N.Y.) 229; McCormick v. Sullivant, 10 Wheat. 192, 202; Wills v. Cowper, 2 Hamm. (Ohio) 124; Henry on Foreign Law, p. 13, 15; ante, s. 428, 434; 4 Burge, Col. & For. Law, pt. 2, c. 12, p. 576–580; Id. pt. 2, c. 4, s. 5, p. 169, 170; Id. pt. 2, c. 5, p. 217. Mr. Burge, speaking on this point (p. 217, 218), says: 'The power of making the alienation by testament is no less qualitas rebus impressa, than that of making the alienation by contract. When therefore the

application of the rule that the *validity* and *forms* of transfers of real estate are governed by the lex situs. Applegate v. Smith, 31 Mo. 166; Jennings v. Jennings, 21 Ohio St. 56. When the question is whether a general gift shows an intention to dispose of property over which the testator has a power of appointment, and which is subject to the law of a foreign country, it cannot be said that the gift should be interpreted according to the foreign law because it takes effect under that law, for the object of the interpretation is to ascertain whether it takes effect or not. It cannot be said that it should be interpreted according to the law of any place where there may be property which the testator has power to dispose of, for then the same words would in Massachusetts show that he intended to exercise all his powers of appointment, and in Maryland would not show that he intended to exercise any. Resort must be had in such cases to the law of the place in the language of which the testator would probably have expressed his meaning. The authorities seem to establish that that law is the law of the country in which he was domiciled. It is submitted therefore, with deference, that in each of these two cases (Bingham's Appeal, 64 Pa. St. 345; Sewall v. Wilmer, 132

Mass. 131) the will should have been interpreted according to the law of the domicil of the testator who made the will in question, and not of the testator who made the will containing the power. If this had been done, the will in Bingham's Appeal would have disclosed an intention to dispose of all property which the testator had a general power to appoint by will, and would have been effectual as an execution of the power. No intention to execute any power of appointment would have been found in the will in Sewall v. Wilmer, and accordingly the will would have had no effect as an execution of the power.

(a) See Ross v. Ross, 129 Mass. 243; Knox v. Jones, 47 N. Y. 389; White v. Howard, 46 N. Y. 144; Monroe v. Douglass, 5 N. Y. 447; Applegate v. Smith, 31 Mo. 166; Jennings v. Jennings, 21 Ohio St. 56 (as to these two cases see the last note, supra); Irwin's Appeal, 33 Conn. 128; Key v. Harlan, 52 Ga. 476; Kingsbury v. Burnside, 58 Ill. 310; Lynch v. Miller, 54 Iowa, 516; In re Lewis, 32 La. An. 385; Succession of Elliot, 27 La. An. 42; Holman v. Hopkins, 27 Tex. 38; Coohran v. Martin, 47 Ala. 525; Apperson v. Bolton, 29 Ark. 418; Richards v. Miller, 62 Ill. 417; Jones v. Gerock, 6 Jones, Eq. 190.

475. *Doctrine of Foreign Jurists.* — The doctrine of foreign jurists does not, as we have seen, entirely accord with that of the

question arises, whether the immovable property may be disposed of by testament, recourse must be had to the lex loci rei sitæ. That law must also decide, whether the full and unlimited power of disposition is enjoyed, or whether it is given under restriction. The validity of the testamentary disposition depends in the latter case on its conformity to that restriction, whether the restriction consists in limiting the extent or description of property over which the power of disposition may be exercised, or the persons in whose favor the disposition is made, or in requiring that the testator should have survived a certain number of days after the execution of the act by which the disposition was made. The total or partial defect of the will on the ground that it did not institute heirs, or that it omitted to name the heirs, the disherison of the heirs, the grounds on which the disherison may be justified, are essentially connected with the power of disposing of immovable property by testament, and are therefore dependent on the law of its situs.' Again, Mr. Burge says: ' By the jurisprudence of England and the United States, a will devising lands in England or the states, if the solemnities prescribed by the statute of frauds have not been observed, would be ineffectual to pass those lands. This doctrine is fully warranted by the qualification which has been given by jurists to the rule, lex loci regit actum. The statute of frauds, as regards real property situated in England and in the states of America, " est lex, quæ expresse testatores jubet jus loci sequi, in quo bona sita sunt." It may be said that the jurisprudence which allows a testament executed according to the solemnities prescribed by the lex loci actus to affect real property situate in the country where that jurisprudence prevails, does not depart from the general principle that the lex loci rei sitæ must determine whether the instrument is sufficient to dispose of real property. The difference between that jurisprudence and the doctrine of England and the United States is, that the effect of the latter is to require a particular form for the execution, whether it be made in England or in any other country, that is, it makes no provision for a will made in a foreign country, but the terms of its enactment are so comprehensive as to include all wills, in whatever country they are made, if they affect real property in England. In the other systems of jurisprudence, it is a part of the lex loci rei sitæ that its immovable property should pass by a testament executed with certain formalities, if it be made in the country where the property is situated, but that if it be made in another country, it may be executed with other solemnities; that is, with the solemnities required by the law of that country. The jurists whose opinions have been cited in support of the rule, that the testament is valid if the testator has complied with the forms and solemnities prescribed by the law of the place in which it was made, apply it to a testament of movable, as well as immovable, property. The decisions of the courts of England on the validity of testaments of personal estate made abroad are few. The two most important are on the testaments of the Duchess of Kingston and of Bernes. The former was resident in Paris; she obtained letter-patent from the King of France, which gave her the same power of devising as she would have had in England. Although she died in France, she had not relinquished her English domicil. She made her testament in Paris. It was clearly nul under the Coutume. But she had observed the forms required by the statute of frauds, and the will was valid according to

common law but even among them there is great weight of authority in favor of the general principle.[1] We have already had occasion to consider the opinions of foreign jurists as to the capa-

the law of England. It was the opinion of M. Turgot, an advocate of France, and his opinion was confirmed by the Court of Probate, that the testament, although made in Paris, was valid. This opinion proceeds on a principle which is admitted by jurists, that although a will made with the solemnities of the lex loci actus may be valid, yet if it were made with the solemnities of the locus rei sitæ in respect of immovables, and the locus domicilii in respect of movable property, it would also be valid. In Bernes's will it appeared that although an Irishman by birth, he had acquired a domicil in Madeira. He made a will and several codicils in that island, some of which were not executed with the solemnities required by the law of Portugal, but with those formalities which would satisfy the law of England. The decision given by Sir John Nicholl, that the latter codicils were valid, and that it was competent to have executed them in the manner which would be consonant to the law of England, was reversed by the delegates, and they were deemed invalid. Bernes in this case, had no longer a domicil in Ireland. His domicil was in Portugal. It was necessary to establish that fact to distinguish the case from that of the Duchess of Kingston. If he had still retained his domicil in Ireland, the codicils would, upon the principles referred to, and which will be presently more fully stated, have been valid. In neither of these cases did the question arise on a testament made with the solemnities required by the lex loci actus, although deficient in those required by the law of the domicil. In another case the testator was an Englishman by birth, and although he had been for many years residing in France, it did not appear that he had abandoned his English domicil. He came to England, and during his residence there made his will, which was a valid testamentary disposition in respect of forms and solemnities according to the law of England. It was contended that it ought not to be admitted to probate, because it was not made in the manner required by the law of France. Here the court adopted the lex loci actus, but, from the report of the case, the learned judge dwells so much on circumstances founded on the testator's domicil of origin, that it would be perhaps not correct to describe the decision as warranting the conclusion that if the testator had not been an Englishman, his will made in England would have been valid. In Nasmyth's Case, the testator was domiciled in Scotland, and his will was made and found there. He died in England in transitu. The Court of Probate in England held itself bound to defer to the law of Scotland. In giving effect to a testament made with the solemnities prescribed by the lex loci actus, jurists do not deny it to a testament made according to the forms required by the lex loci rei sitæ, if it be immovable, or the lex loci domicilii, if it be personal property, which is the subject of the disposition: " Proinde, si quis eo, quod ad testandum expeditius sua causa comparatum est, noluerit uti, quod ei forte promptius sit componere suprema ad loci leges, cui bona subjaceant, quo minus testamentum ejus valiturum sit, non video." Paul Voet and John Voet adopt this opinion.' 4 Burge, Col. & For. Law, pt. 2, c. 12, p. 586–590; Robertson on Succession, p. 95. See also Harrison v. Nixon, 9 Pet. 505; post, s. 479 g.

[1] See ante, s. 52–62, 430–435.

city and incapacity of the testator to make a testament of immovable property, whether it is to be governed by the law of his domicil, or by the law rei sitæ.[1] We have also had occasion to consider their opinions as to the law which ought to govern in respect to the forms and solemnities of testaments of immovable property, whether it is the law rei sitæ, or that of the domicil of the testator, or that of the place where the will was made.[2] Putting out of view these questions as to the forms and solemnities of acts, and the capacity and incapacity of the testator (upon which we have sufficiently commented), there seems to be a general coincidence of opinion among foreign jurists that the lex rei sitæ must in other respects govern as to wills and testaments of immovable property. Thus, John Voet says: ' Bona defuncti immobilia, et quæ juris interpretatione pro talibus habentur, deferri secundum leges loci, in quo sita sunt.'[3] Dumoulin's opinion is to the same effect. His language is: ' Aut statutum agit in rem, et quacunque verborum formula utatur, semper inspicitur locus, ubi res sita est.' And again : ' Quoties ergo statutum principaliter agit in personam et in ejus consequentiam, agit in res immobiles, non extenditur ad res sitas in locis, ubi jus commune vel statutum loci diversum est.'[4] Hertius is even more direct. ' Si lex directo rei imponitur, ea locum habet, ubicunque etiam locorum et a quocunque actus celebretur.'[5] He adds in another place : ' Rebus fertur lex, cum certam iisdem qualitatem imprimit, vel in alienando, v. g. ut ne bona avita possint alienari, vel in acquirendo, e. g. ut dominium rei immobilis venditæ non aliter acquiritur, nisi facta fuerit judicialis resignatio.'[6] D'Aguesseau deems it a mere waste of time to do more than to state the general rule.[7] Paul Voet has stated the doctrine in an expressive

[1] Ibid.

. [2] See ante, s. 363–373, 435–446; 1 Burge, Col. & For. Law, pt. 1, c. 1, p. 21–23; 4 Id. pt. 2, c. 12, p. 576–586; Id. c. 5, p. 217–221. See also Foelix, Conflit des Lois, Revue Étrang. et Franç. tom. 7, 1840, s. 40–50, p. 346–360; Sand. Decis. Frisic. lib. 4, tit. 1, defin. 14, p. 142, 143.

[3] J. Voet, ad Pand. 38, 17, s. 34, p. 596; ante, s. 424.

[4] Molin. Oper. Com. ad Cod. 1, 1, 1, de Conclus. Statut. tom. 3, p. 556, ed. 1681; ante, s. 443; 1 Froland. Mém. 65; Id. vol. 2, p. 779.

[5] 1 Hertii Opera, de Collis. Leg. s. 4, n. 9, p. 125, ed. 1737; Id. p. 177, ed. 1716.

[6] 1 Hertii Opera, de Collis. Leg. s. 4, n. 6, p. 122, ed. 1737; Id. p. 174, ed. 1716; 2 Burge, Col. & For. Law, p. 843; 4 Id. p. 217.

[7] D'Aguesseau, Œuvres, tom. 4, p. 636, 637. See Cochin, Œuvres, tom. 4, p. 555, 4to ed.

manner: 'Non tamen statutum personale sese regulariter extendit ad bona immobilia alibi sita.'[1] In another place he says: 'Immobilia statutis loci, ubi sita, mobilia loci statutis, ubi testator habuit domicilium.'[2] In another place he says : 'Quid, si itaque contentio de aliquo jure in re, seu ex ipsa re descendente; vel ex contractu, vel actione personali, sed ad rem scripta; an spectabitur loci statutum ubi dominus habet domicilium, an statutum rei sitæ? Respondeo; statutum rei sitæ.'[3] Boullenois cites another jurist as holding similar language: 'Sive in rem, sive in personam, loquatur statutum, ad bona extra territorium non extenditur. Consideratur namque bonorum dominus, ut duplex homo; quoad bona nempe sita in uno territorio est unus homo ; et quoad alterius territorii bona est alius homo.'[4] Again: 'Idem quod inferendum, quoad successionem testamentariam; finge enim testamentum hic fieri permissum esse, in Geldria non ita? Hinc si quispiam hic fecerit testamentum, non capiet vires, ratione bonorum, in Geldria jacentium. Tale quippe statutum spectat ipsa bona, adeoque erit reale, non exserens vires ultra statuentis territorium.'[5] Again he adds : 'Quid, si testamento bona immobilia relicta, diversis subjacent statutis? Idem dicendum; nihil enim interest, testatus quis, an intestatus decedat, ut locus sit regulæ. Extra territorium jus dicenti impune non paretur.'[6] This is certainly the doctrine of the common law ; for a man may have the capacity to take real estate in one country, when he is totally disabled to take it in another. Boullenois (as we have seen) lays it down among his general principles, that, when the personal laws of the domicil are in conflict with the real laws of the same country, or of a foreign country, the personal laws

[1] P. Voet, de Stat. s. 4, c. 2, n. 6, p. 123, ed. 1715; Id. p. 138, ed. 1661.
[2] Id. c. 3, n. 10, p. 135, ed. 1715; Id. p. 153, ed. 1661; ante, s. 442.
[3] Id. s. 9, c. 1, n. 2, p. 252, ed. 1715; Id. p. 305, ed. 1661. We are not to confound the opinion of Paul Voet, as here expressed, with what he has said in another place (ante, s. 442) that testaments are to be executed according to the forms and solemnities of the place where they are made, and not by those of the situs of the immovable property. He takes a distinction between the forms and solemnities of testaments and their operation on this point. Whether there be any solid foundation for such a distinction it is for the learned reader to decide. Ante, s. 442.
[4] Ibid.; 1 Boullenois, obs. 10, p. 154.
[5] P. Voet, de Stat. s. 4, c. 3, n. 11, p. 135, ed. 1715; Id. p. 153, ed. 1661.
[6] P. Voet, de Stat. s. 6, c. 1, n. 4, p. 253, ed. 1715; Id. p. 306, 307, ed. 1661.

are to yield; and that, when the real laws of the domicil are in conflict with the real laws of another country, both have effect within their own respective territories, according to the laws thereof.[1]

475 a. Rodenburg admits that, where the law rei sitæ prohibits married persons to devise their immovable estate by will or testament to each other, or where the law rei sitæ prohibits certain kinds of immovable property from being devised by will or testament, in such cases the law rei sitæ is to govern, notwithstanding the parties are domiciled, or make their will or testament in a place where no such prohibition prevails; because these are real laws.[2] 'Unde certissima usu ac observatione regula est, cum de rebus soli agitur, et diversa sunt diversarum possessionum loca et situs, spectari semper cujusque loci leges ac jura, ubi bona sita esse præponuntur, sic ut de talibus nulla cujusquam potestas præter territorii leges.'[3]

476. Huberus has expounded the subject at large. We have already had occasion to cite his remarks on the subject, so far as respects the forms and solemnities of testaments, which he insists are valid if made according to the forms and solemnities of the place where the testament is made, although not made according to the forms and solemnities required by the law of the situs of the property.[4] But he takes a distinction between the forms and solemnities of testaments, and the right to dispose of immovable property by testament. 'The foundation,' says he, 'of the whole of this doctrine which we have been speaking of, and hold, is the subjection of all persons to the laws of any territory as long as they act there, which settles it, that an act valid or invalid from the beginning will be accordingly valid or invalid everywhere else. But this reasoning does not apply to immovable property, when this is considered, not as depending upon the free disposition of the head of the family (paterfamilias), but as having certain marks impressed upon it by the laws of every commonwealth in which it is situate, which marks remain indelible therein,

1 1 Boullenois, Pr. Gén. 30, 31, p. 8.

[1] 1 Boullenois, Pr. Gén. 30, 31, p. 8.

[2] Rodenburg, de Div. Stat. tit. 2, c. 5, s. 1–5; 2 Boullenois, Appx. p. 35–38.

[3] Rodenburg, de Div. Stat. tit. 2, c. 5, s. 1; 2 Boullenois, Appx. p. 35; 4 Burge, Col. & For. Law, pt. 2, c. 5, p. 218; Id. c. 12, p. 582, 583. See also Burgundus, tract. 1, n. 40, 41, p. 41, 42.

[4] Ante, s. 443, 443 a.

whatever the laws of other governments, or whatever the dispositions of private persons, may establish to the contrary. For it would cause great confusion and prejudice to the commonwealth where immovable property is situate, that the laws promulgated concerning it should be changed by any other acts. Hence, a Frisian, having lands and houses in the province of Gröningen, cannot make a will thereof, because the laws there prohibit any will to be made of such real estate ; and the Frisian laws cannot affect real estate which constitutes an integral part of a foreign territory.'[1] 'Fundamentum universæ hujus doctrinæ diximus esse, et tenemus, subjectionem hominum infra leges cujusque territorii, quamdiu illic agunt, quæ facit, ut actus ab initio validus aut nullus, alibi quoque valere aut non valere non nequeat. Sed hæc ratio non convenit rebus immobilibus, quando illæ spectantur, non ut dependentes a libera dispositione cujusque patrisfamilias, verum quatenus certæ notæ lege cujusque reip. ubi sitæ sunt, illis impressæ reperiuntur ; hæ notæ manent indelebiles in ista republ., quicquid aliarum civitatum leges aut privatorum dispositiones secus aut contra statuant ; nec enim sine magna confusione præjudicioque reip. ubi sitæ sunt res soli, leges de illis latæ, dispositionibus istis mutari possent. Hinc Frisius habens agros et domos in provincia Groningensi, non potest de illis testari, quia lege prohibitum est ibi de bonis immobilibus testari, non valente jure Frisico adficere bona, quæ partes alieni territorii integrantes constituunt.' And yet, with this clear principle in view, he proceeds to declare that this does not contradict the rule which he had already laid down, that, if a will is valid by the law of the place where it is made, it ought to have effect even in regard to real property situate in foreign countries, by whose laws such property may be passed by a will ; because, says he, the diversity of laws in that respect does not affect the soil, neither speaks of it, but simply directs the manner of making the will, which being rightly done, the law of the commonwealth does not prohibit the instrument to have validity in regard to immovables, inasmuch as no characteristic or incident, impressed by the laws of the country, is injured or diminished.[2]

477. Burgundus lays down the doctrine in general terms, that, in everything which regards land and other real inheritances, it is

---

[1] Huberus, lib. 1, tit. 3, s. 15.
[2] Huberus, lib. 1, tit. 3, s. 15. The original is cited ante, s. 443 a.

the law of the situation which is to decide.[1] He takes the distinction between movable and immovable property, and between real and personal statutes. ' Proinde, in quantum (statutum) est reale, et immobilia dirigit, finis territorii non egreditur.'[2] And, again : ' Quando hoc unum generaliter obtineat ut in immobilibus situs semper spectandus veniat ; in mobilibus autem locus domicilii.'[3] And, as we have seen, he applies the rule specially to wills. 'Si quidem solemnitates testamenti ad jura personalia non pertinent ; quia sunt quædam qualitas bonis ipsis impressa, ad quam tenetur respicere, quisquis in bonis aliquid alterat.[4] Quare etiam mihi videtur consequens, juris civilis rationem exigere in testamentis exarandis adhibitionem solemnitatis, quam præscripserit consuetudo cujusque possessionis. Nam si ex solemni testamento nascitur jus in ipsa re, quomodo id potest præstare alterius regionis consuetudo, quæ alienis fundis alterationis necessitatem imponere non potest ? Hoc enim esset jus dicere extra territorium cui impune non paretur.'[5] There is a great deal of solid sense in these remarks ; and they form a satisfactory answer to the distinction propounded by Huberus.[6]

478. *Scotch Law.* — The Scottish law is in perfect coincidence with the common law on this subject. Erskine, in the passage already cited, has stated that in the conveyance of an immovable subject, or of any right affecting heritage, the owner must follow the solemnities established by the law, not of the country where he signs the instrument, but of the state in which the heritage lies.[7] And even if all due solemnities are observed, still no estate will pass, unless in conformity with the local law. Hence, he adds, a foreign testament bequeathing heritable subjects situate in Scotland is not sustained in Scotland, although by the law of the country where the testament was made a heritage might have been actually settled ; because by the Scottish law no heritable subject can be disposed of in that form.[8]

[1] Ante, s. 433. [2] Burgundus, tract. 1, n. 26, p. 38, 89.
[3] Burgundus, tract. 1, n. 41, p. 43.
[4] Burgundus, tract. 6, n. 3, p. 128 ; ante, s. 372, 438.
[5] Burgundus, tract. 6, n. 1–3, p. 129 ; Id. tract. 1, n. 36, p. 38, 89 ; ante, s. 372, 433, 438 ; 1 Boullenois, obs. 9, p. 151. See also Henry on Foreign Law, p. 97, 98.
[6] Ante, s. 476. See also 4 Burge, Col. & For. Law, pt. 2, c. 12, p. 582–586.
[7] Ante, s. 436.
[8] Ersk. Inst. b. 3, tit. 2, s. 41, p. 515, 516 ; 2 Kames, Eq. b. 3, c. 8, s. 3.

479. *Vattel.* — *Grotius.* — Vattel, as we have seen, adopts the same rule, as a general one of the jus gentium.[1] As to bequests, he asserts in the most positive terms that, when they respect immovables, they must be conformable to the law of the country where they are situated.[2] He adds : In the same manner the validity of a testament, as to its form, can only be decided by the judge of the domicil, whose sentence, delivered in form, ought to be everywhere acknowledged. But without affecting the validity of the testament itself, the bequest contained in it may be disputed before the judge of the place where the effects are situated; because those effects can only be disposed of conformably to the laws of the country.[3] Grotius makes a distinction between the personal capacity of making wills and testaments and the forms and solemnities thereof, and the right and power to dispose of property, whether movable or immovable, holding that the forms and solemnities are governed by the law of the place where the will or testament is made; (a) the capacity of the person is governed by the law of his domicil; and the right to dispose of property is governed in the case of movables by the law of the domicil, and in the case of immovables by the law of the situs rei. ' Ubi de forma sive solemnitate testamenti agitur, respici locum conditi testamenti ; ubi de persona antestari jus domicilii ; ubi de rebus, quæ testamento relinqui possunt, vel non, respici locum domicilii, in mobilibus, in rebus soli situm loci.'[4] If it were necessary, the opinions of many other foreign jurists might be cited to the same effect; but it would incumber these pages to give them a more extended review.[5]

[1] Ante, s. 471, 472.

[2] Vattel, b. 2, c. 7, s. 85, c. 8, s. 103, 110, 111.

[3] Vattel, b. 2, c. 7, s. 85. So also Id. c. 8, s. 110, 111; ante, s. 471.

[4] Grotius, Epist. 467, cited 4 Burge, Col. & For. Law, pt. 2, c. 5, p. 220.

[5] See 4 Burge, Col. & For. Law, pt. 2, c. 5, p. 217, 218; Id. c. 12, p. 576–585. Mr. Burge (vol. 4, p. 218–220, 581–585) states the opinions of many foreign jurists; and among others he says (p. 218–220): ' Ferricre has stated this doctrine: " Si je lègue un héritage propre situé en coutume qui en défende la disposition, tel legs est nul, et ne peut être parfourni sur les biens situez en cette coutume, quoi qu'acquest, parce qu'à l'égard des choses dont on peut disposer par dernière volonté, on considère la coutume où elles sont situées. Celui qui a son domicile en cette coutume peut instituer sa femme dans les biens qu'il a dans le pays de droit écrit, comme il a été jugé par arrêt du 14 aoust, 1751, rapporté par Marion au de ses plaidoyez ce qui doit être sans difficulté." A

(a) See Dannelli *v.* Dannelli, 4 Bush, (Ky.) 51.

479 *a. Interpretation.* — Passing from these considerations as to the law by which the forms and solemnities of wills and testa-

testament made in a foreign country, bequeathing heritable subjects, situated in Scotland, is not sustained in that kingdom, though by the law of the country where the testament was made, heritage might have been settled by testament; because by the law of Scotland no heritable subject can be disposed of in that form. On this principle a Scot's personal bond taken to heirs and assignees, but "secluding executors," cannot be bequeathed by a foreign testament. But in all questions touching heritable subjects situate abroad, the foreign testament will be given effect to according to the lex loci. Dumoulin lays down the same doctrine respecting the restriction on the testamentary power over biens propres. "Unde statutum loci inspicietur, sive persona sit subdita, sive non; item si dicat, hæredia proventa ab una linea, redeant ad hæredes etiam remotiores lineæ, vel hæredes lineæ succedant in hærediis ab illa linea proventis. Vel quod illi de linea non possunt testari de illis in totum, vel nisi ad certam partem. Hæc enim omnia et similia spectant ad caput statuti, agentis in rem, et præcedentem conclusionem." Again : the statute which prohibits a disposition to particular persons, or (which involves the same consequence) requires the disposition to be made in favor of certain persons, and therefore excludes all others, is a real law. "Directe enim in rerum alienationem scripta hæc lex realis omnino dicenda est: nec enim statutum reale sit, an personale metiri oportet a ratione quæ a conjugali forsan qualitate fuerit ducta, sed ab ipsa re, quæ in prohibitione statuti ceciderit." So also it has been held that the law which requires that the testator should have survived the execution of his testament will control the disposition of property situated in the country where that law prevails, although the testament is made, or the testator domiciled, in a place where no such law exists. If a testator whose domicil and real estate were both in Normandy made a will in some other place, in which he had occasion to be present, but where the law did not require that the testator should survive forty days, it was held that the survivorship was essential to the validity of the testament, so far as it related to the real property in Normandy. If these questions arise on the power to dispose of movable property by testament, the law by which they are decided is that of the domicil: "Pour les meubles, ils suivent la loi du domicile, et il ne sauroit jamais y avoir de choc entre différentes coutumes, en sorte qu'il est assez inutile quant aux meubles, d'agiter si le statut, qui permet de tester, ou qui le défend, est personnel, ou, s'il est réel." See also Foelix, Conflit des Lois, Revue Étrang. et Franç. tom. 7, 1840, s. 37, p. 307–312. The latter author says in this place: "Le second cas, où le statut personnel semble devoir prédominer sur le statut réel, est celui de la succession à toute la fortune d'un individu, soit ab intestat, soit par testament. Voici les arguments invoqués par les auteurs qui, dans ces deux hypothèses, prétendent faire régir la succession par la loi personnelle du défunt. Lorsque, par la mort d'un individu, il s'agit de succéder à tous ses droits actifs et passifs, à toute sa fortune (universum patrimonium), on regarde en droit cette fortune comme un ensemble (universitas juris), sans égard aux objets particuliers qui la composent; et cette universalité représente de droit le défunt, même avant l'appréhension faite par l'héritier. L'héritier succède ensuite dans cette universalité, et c'est alors seulement qu'il représente la personne du défunt. L'universalité des biens du défunt forment ainsi la continuation de

ments of movable property and of immovable property are to be regulated, in order to give them validity, let us proceed in the next

la personne de ce dernier, on doit, pour tout ce qui concerne la succession à cette universalité, suivre la loi de son domicile, c'est-à-dire son statut personnel; tous les objets compris dans la succession sont soumis à ce statut personnel. Ainsi la succession d'un Français est régie par le code civil, même à l'égard des immeubles appartenant au défunt et situés en Autriche; et on ne suit pas l'ordre des successions établi par le code autrichien. Cette doctrine a été professée par un grand nombre d'auteurs distingués; elle l'a été d'abord par Cujas, relativement à la succession testamentaire; ensuite la même opinion a été adoptée, quant a la succession ab intestat, par Puffendorf, Bachov, J. H. Boehmer, G. L. Boehmer, Helfeld, Glück, Hamm, Meier, par MM. Mittermaier, Eichhorn, Mühlenbruch, et Gründler. Toutefois, quatre des auteurs cités, Puffendorff, Hert, Glück, et Hamm, n'admettent le principe qu'avec deux restrictions; il ne sera pas applicable lorsqu'il existe une loi prohibitive au lieu de la situation des immeubles, ou lorsqu'une qualité spéciale se trouve imprimée aux biens; par exemple, s'ils sont féodaux, stemmatiques ou frappés d'un fidéicommis. En faveur de cette opinion on invoque, outre le principe que la succession représente le défunt, plusieurs considérations accessoires. D'après l'opinion commune des auteurs, la succession ab intestat repose sur la volonté présumée du défunt; le défunt n'ayant connu, en règle générale, d'autre loi que celle du lieu de son domicile, on doit admettre qu'il a entendu faire passer ses immeubles aux parents appelés par cette loi : si telle n'avait pas été son intention, il en aurait disposé par testament. On fait remarquer que toutes les nations admettent chez elles l'exécution des testaments consentis par un étranger dans sa patrie et dans les formes qui y sont prescrites; ces testaments ne sont autre chose que l'expression formelle de la volonté du défunt, sanctionée par la loi civile de sa patrie: à plus forte raison devra-t-on accorder un effet semblable à cette loi civile lorsque, sans un acte du défunt, elle prononce seule. On cite encore les inconvénients résultant de la division des patrimoines en différentes successions particulières, au préjudice des héritiers et des créanciers; enfin on fait observer que la chose publique est sans intéret dans la question, parce que les prohibitions, les charges et impositions pesant sur l'immeuble peuvent néanmoins produire leur effet, et que, du reste, peu importe à l'état quelle est la personne qui hérite de tel immeuble. D'autres auteurs non moins respectables n'admettent l'application du statut personnel en matière de succession qu'en ce qui concerne les meubles, et ils la rejettent par rapport aux immeubles; ils appliquent à ceux-ci la loi de la situation, sans distinguer s'il s'agit de succéder à un immeuble particulier ou à l'universalité de la fortune d'un individu; ils admettent autant de successions particulières qu'il a de territoires où sont situés les immeubles provenant du défunt (Quot sunt bona diversis territoriis obnoxia, totidem patrimonia intelliguntur). Nous citerons Burgundus, Rodenburg, Paul Voet, Jean Voet, Abraham à Wesel, Christin, Sande, Gail, Carpzov, Wernher, Mevius, Struve, Leyser, Huber, Hommel, Berger, Lauterbach, Vattel, Tittmann, Danz, Hauss, MM. Thibaut, Story, et Burge. Aucune législation positive ne s'est expliquée sur la question de savoir si c'est la loi réelle ou la loi personnelle qui doit régir la succession ab intestat. Nous pensons qu'il faut appliquer le statut de la situation des immeubles.. Le premier principe, en matière de conflit des lois, c'est que les lois de chaque état régissent les

place to the consideration of the rules by which such wills and testaments are to be interpreted. And in the first place in regard to wills and testaments of personal property. In such cases where the will or testament is made in the place of the domicil of the testator, the general rule of the common law is, that it is to be construed according to the law of the place of his domicil, in which it is made.[1] (a) A will therefore, made of personal estate in England, is to be construed according to the meaning of the terms used by the law of England; and this rule equally applies, whether the judicial inquiry as to its meaning and interpretation arises in England, or in any other country.[2] Thus, for

biens situés dans le territoire (v. supra, n⁰ˢ 9 et 10); il n'est nullement établi qu'une convention tacite s'est formée entre les nations pour l'application de la loi personnelle au cas de succession dans l'universalité des meubles et immeubles d'un individu: témoin la divergence des sentiments des auteurs. Les arguments invoqués en faveur de cette application sont fondés en partie dans le droit civil, en partie dans l'avantage commun des nations; mais on ne voit pas que l'usage des nations ait consacré cette opinion." ' See also Foelix, id. s. 27, p. 216–218; ante, s. 429–444.

[1] Yates v. Thomson, 3 Cl. & F. 544, 570; Robertson on Successions, p. 99, 100, 191–197, 214, 255; post, s. 490, 491.

[2] Trotter v. Trotter, 4 Bligh, N.S. 502; 3 Wils. & Shaw, 407. In this case the testator, a Scotchman, domiciled in the dominions of England in India, made his will there, he being possessed of Scotch heritable bonds as well as of personal property there. The will was ineffectual to carry a Scotch heritage according to the law of Scotland; and the question arose whether his heir in Scotland, who claimed the heritable bonds as heir, was also entitled to share in the movables, as a legatee under the will, without bringing in the heritable bonds or being put to his election. It was held that the will as to its terms must be interpreted according to the law of England; and that by the law of England the terms used were not such as to import an intention to convey real estate by the testator; and therefore that the heir was entitled to the whole heritable bonds, and also to his share of the movable property under the will. On that occasion the lord chancellor (Lord Lyndhurst) said: ' It was stated at the bar, and I see by the papers it was also argued below, that in cases of this description it is not unreasonable that when any technical points arise in the construction of a will of this description, the Court of Sessions should resort to the opinion of lawyers of the country where the will or instrument was executed, but that this applies only to technical expressions; that where a will is expressed in ordinary language, the judges of the court of Scotland are as competent to put a proper construction upon it as judges or lawyers of the country where the will was executed. But the judges below were not of that opinion; and it is impossible, as it appears to me, that such an opinion can be

(a) See Laneuville v. Anderson, 2 Sw. & Tr. 26; Dannelli v. Dannelli, 4 Bush (Ky.) 51; Enohin v. Wylie, 10 H. L. C. 1; Boyes v. Bedale, 1 Hem. & M. 803.

example, if the question should arise, whether the terms of a will include a bequest of real estate, or show on the part of the testa-

reasonably entertained. A will must be interpreted according to the law of the country where it is made, and where the party making the will has his domicil. There are certain rules of construction adopted in the courts, and the expressions which are made use of in a will, and the language of a will, have frequently reference to those rules of construction; and it would be productive therefore of the most mischievous consequences, and in many instances defeat the intention of the testator, if those rules were to be altogether disregarded, and the judges of a foreign court (which it may be considered in relation to the will) without reference to that knowledge which it is desirable to obtain of the law of the country in which the will was made, were to interpret the will according to their own rules of construction. That would also be productive of another inconvenience; namely, that the will might have a construction put upon it in the English courts different from that which might be put upon it in the foreign country. It appears to me that there is no solid ground for the objection; but that where a will is executed in a foreign country by a person having his domicil in that country, with respect to that person's property, the will must be interpreted according to the law of the country where it is made. It must, if it comes into question in any proceeding, have the same interpretation put upon it as would be put upon it in any tribunal of the country where it was made. It appears to me therefore that the judges were perfectly right in directing the opinion to be taken of English lawyers of eminence, with respect to the import and construction of this will according to the law of England. The main question that was ultimately put to the learned persons to whom I have referred is this: " Whether, on the supposition of the question having arisen for trial in England, the heir would have been put to his election if he had claimed money secured by heritable bond in Scotland, as well as his share of the personal estate under the will?" The answer is in these terms: " Considering heritable bonds in Scotland as real estates to which the heir at law is entitled, unless they are conveyed away with due solemnity by his ancestor, we think the heir at law would be entitled in this case to claim them without being put to his election, if the question had arisen in a court of justice in England." When that opinion was communicated to the court in Scotland, the court, immediately affirming that opinion, decided in favor of the heir at law. The heir at law was undoubtedly entitled to take the real estate, — that is, the heritable bond; and the sole question was, whether, when he came in to claim under the will his proportion of the personal estate, it was required by law that he should be put to his election, that is, whether he should take the one or the other; whether he should allow the real estate to be connected with the personal, so as to form one mass of the property, and the whole divided, or should take the real estate, and give up the personal estate? Whether he was obliged or not to do this, depended entirely on this consideration, whether upon the face of the will there was sufficient to manifest a clear intention that the testator designed by his will to dispose of his real estate; because if he intended to dispose of his real estate, although he had not carried that intention effectually into execution, the party taking under that will would not be entitled to have the benefit of the will, and at the same time to defeat the intention of the testator. The question was therefore simply a question of construction. Does it appear upon the face of the will that it was

tor an intention to bequeath real estate, as well as personal estate, the question must be decided according to the law of the place of his domicil and where the will was made; and the same interpretation must be put upon those terms in every other country, which would be put upon them by the law of that domicil.[1] (a) So what is to be deemed 'real estate' in the sense of a will, devising real estate to certain persons, must be decided by the law of the domicil of the testator. Thus, where a testator was domiciled in Jamaica, in which place he made his will, and the devise was in these words: 'I give, devise, and bequeath one moiety of the rents, issues, and profits of my estate named Islington and Cove's Penn, in the parish of St. Mary, to be divided equally amongst my grandchildren. The other moiety of the rents, issues, and profits of my said estate and Penn I give, devise, and bequeath to my son,' &c. According to the import of the words 'my estate,' as they are understood and used in Jamaica, not only the land, but the works, buildings, utensils, slaves, cattle, and stock on the plantation would be included. The court put this construction on the devise.[2]

479 b. In like manner, whether the words of a will give a legacy, or create a trust, in favor of a party, where the expressions used import a wish or desire, or other language of a similar sort

---

the intention of the testator to dispose of his real estate, that is, of those heritable bonds? Now the rule of law in England with respect to subjects of this kind is well ascertained and well defined, and it is this, — that you are not to proceed by probability or by conjecture, but that there must be a clear and manifest expression of the intention on the face of the will to include that property which is not properly devised, before the heir can be put to his election.' Ibid. See also Price v. Dewhurst, 8 Sim. 279, 299, 300; post, s. 489; Robertson on Successions, p. 189-197.

[1] Trotter v. Trotter, 4 Bligh, (N. S.) 502; 3 Wils. & Shaw, 407.

[2] Stewart v. Garnett, 3 Sim. 398; 4 Burge, Col. & For. Law, pt. 2, c. 12, p. 591.

(a) See Enohin v. Wylie, 10 H. L. C. 1; 1 Sw. & T. 118; 1 De G. F. & J. 410. In this case it appeared that a natural-born British subject died in Russia, leaving large real and personal estate there, and also a considerable sum in English funds, and made a will in the Russian language and form, disposing of 'all his movable and immovable property,' but without any other language excluding or including his English property. It was held that the executors appointed under the Russian law were entitled to probate of the will in England, and that the rule of construction adopted in Russia, as to the extent and meaning of the words 'all his movable and immovable property,' ought to govern.

is used, must be decided by the law of the place where the will is made, and the testator has his domicil.[1] So where a legacy is given in terms expressive of a currency in use in different countries, but of different values therein, the same rule will apply. Thus, for example, a will made in Ireland by a testator domiciled there, giving a legacy of £1,000, will be interpreted to be a legacy of £1,000, Irish currency, and payable accordingly, and not a £1,000 English sterling currency.[2] So legacies are deemed payable according to the law of the country, and in the currency of the country, where the will is made and the testator is domiciled.[3]

479 c. In like manner the question whether a legatee by the terms of a foreign will or testament takes an estate for life or in fee, is to be decided by the law of the place where the will is made and the testator is domiciled, and not by the law of the place where the controversy arises, or the testator was born.[4] So if the question arises whether it is competent to make a particular bequest of property, the validity of it must be decided by the law of the place where the will or testament is made and the testator is domiciled.[5] (a) So if a legacy is given by a will or testament to a party who dies in the lifetime of the testator, the question whether it is an ademption of the legacy, or whether the legacy goes to his personal representatives, is to be decided by the law where the will or testament is made, and he is domiciled.[6] (b)

479 d. *Validity of Devise to Charity.* — Another illustration may arise under a will which purports to direct the testator's real estate to be sold, and the proceeds to be applied to foreign

[1] Pierson v. Garnet, 2 Bro. C. C. 38; 2 Story Eq. Jur. s. 1068–1074.

[2] Id. p. 47.

[3] Ibid.; Saunders v. Drake, 2 Atk. 465; Pierson v. Garnet, 2 Bro. C. C. 39, 47; Malcolm v. Martin, 3 Bro. C. C. 50; Wallia v. Brightwell, 2 P. Wms. 88; Lansdowne v. Lansdowne, 2 Bligh, 60, 88, 89, 95; 4 Burge, Col. & For. Law, pt. 2, c. 12, p. 595, 596; ante, s. 259, 310–313.

[4] Brown v. Brown, 4 Wils. & Shaw, 28, 37; post, s. 490.

[5] Price v. Dewhurst, 8 Sim. 279, 299–301; 2 Boullenois, obs. 46, p. 505–508.

[6] Anstruther v. Chalmer, 2 Sim. 1; Thornton v. Curling, 8 Sim. 310; 2 Add. Ecc. 6, 10–25; post, s. 491.

(a) See Bible Society v. Pendleton, 7 W. Va. 79.

(b) See Boyes v. Bedale, 1 Hem. & M. 805.

charities, which devise is good by the law of the foreign country, but is prohibited by the law of the testator's domicil. In such a case the devise will be void, because it is against the law of his domicil. (a) This was held in a case where a testator in England by his will directed his real estate to be sold, and the produce to be laid out in lands or in the funds, for the maintenance of a charity in Scotland. On that occasion the Master of the Rolls (Sir William Grant) said: ' The statute (9 George II. c. 36) contains no express words prohibiting a bequest of money to be produced by the sale of land to charitable purposes ; but it is settled by construction that such a bequest is within the spirit and meaning of the law ; and it is clear that no charity in England, not within the exception of the statute, could have derived any benefit from the produce of the real estate. The question then is whether such produce may be given to what, in contemplation of the English law, is for a charitable purpose, when that purpose is to be carried into execution in another country. The validity of every disposition of real estate must depend upon the law of the country in which that estate is situated. The subject of this statute is real estate in England. The owners of such property are disabled from disposing of it to any charitable use, except by deed executed twelve months before the death of the owner, &c., to take effect from the execution. The words are perfectly general, " any charitable use whatsoever ; " and the object could not be to treat English charities less favorably than charities to take effect for the benefit of other countries. It would be somewhat incongruous to refuse to permit such a disposition for the most laudable and meritorious charitable institution in England; but if the party chose to carry his benevolent intention beyond England, to permit him to do so, to the effect of disinheriting his heir in his last moments. The disinheriting of the lawful heirs by languishing or dying persons, which is treated by the statute as a mischief, cannot be less so when the effect is to carry the property out of England. Therefore neither the words of this statute, nor the presumable intention, warrant me in declaring that it is to be confined to charitable purposes to be carried into execution in England. The statute not containing an exception in favor of the universities of Scotland, as it

(a) See Bible Society v. Pendleton, 7 W. Va. 79.

does with regard to the universities of England, I must consider this as a charitable disposition, by which nothing that is the produce of the testator's real estate can pass.' [1]

479 e. *Description of Persons intended to take.* — The same rule will apply to the ascertainment of the persons who are to take under a will or testament, when it is made by words designating a particular class or description of persons. Who are the proper persons entitled to take under the *designatio personarum* is a point to be ascertained by the law of the place where the will is made and the testator is domiciled. (a) Thus, for example, if a testator should bequeath his personal estate to his 'heir at law,' who is the person entitled to take under that description will depend upon the law of his domicil. If domiciled in England it will be the eldest son; if domiciled in most of the States of America, it will be all his children.[2] So if a person domiciled

[1] Curtis *v.* Hutton, 14 Ves. 537, 541. See also 3 Pet. Appx. p. 501-503.

[2] Harrison *v.* Nixon, 9 Pet. 483, 504. On this occasion the court said: ' No one can doubt, if a testator born and domiciled in England during his whole life should by his will give his personal estate to his heir at law, that the descriptio personæ would have reference to and be governed by the import of the terms in the sense of the laws of England. The import of them might be very different, if the testator were born and domiciled in France, in Louisiana, in Pennsylvania, or in Massachusetts. In short, a will of personalty speaks according to the laws of the testator's domicil, where there are no other circumstances to control their application; and to raise the question what the testator means, we must first ascertain what was his domicil, and whether he had reference to the laws of that place, or to the laws of any foreign country. Now the very gist of the present controversy turns upon the point, who were the person or persons intended to be designated by the testator, under the appellation of "heir at law." If at the time of making his will, and at his death, he was domiciled in England, and had a reference to its laws, the designation might indicate a very different person or persons from what might be the case (we do not say what is the case), if at the time of making his will, and of his death, he was domiciled in Pennsylvania. In order to raise the question of the true interpretation and designation, it seems to us indispensable that the country by whose laws his will is to be interpreted should be first ascertained; and then the inquiry is naturally presented, what the provisions of those laws are.' Mr. Burge has put a number of cases from the foreign law on the same subject. He says: ' The legal effect of the expression, "lawful heirs," will not be controlled by words which import an equality of distribution amongst the heirs; but those words will be understood as referring to the equality which is consistent with and recognized by that law which the testator is presumed to have invoked. The institution of heirs was thus expressed: " Fratrum et sororum filios ac nepotes hæredes legitimos ex æquis partibus." (Voet, lib. 28, tit. 5,

(a) See Dannelli *v.* Dannelli, 4 Bush (Ky.) 51.

in Holland should bequeath his property to the 'male children' of certain persons, and the question should arise, as well it might,

n. 17.) If the whole inheritance were to be divided amongst those heirs in equal parts, the qualification of legitimus hæres would be disregarded, because, according to the order of succession established by law, the grandsons of one brother succeeding with the sons of another do not take per capita, but per stirpes. The equality therefore to be observed in the distribution, and which must be presumed to have been that contemplated by the testator, is that which the law admits, namely, an equality between the stirpes, and not between the individuals. (Neostad, decis. 33.) A case arose, in the court at Brabant, of a father domiciled in Brabant, who had, in the institution of his son, desired him to allow that which he had left him to go to his lawful children. It was decided that the grandfather's estate would devolve on those children only who would take according to the law of Brabant in the case of intestacy, namely, the children of the first, to the exclusion of those of a second marriage. (Stockmans, Curiæ Brab. decis. 27.) Under an institution by the description of " brothers," brothers of the whole blood only will take, if according to the law in the place of the lex loci domicilii, the children of the father's or mother's side only are excluded from the succession. (Christin. ad Leg. Mech. tit. 16, art. 7, n. 5, 6; Voet, lib. 28, tit. 5, n. 18; Rodenb. de Jure, Quod Ori. de Stat. Divers. tit. 3, c. 2, n. 6, p. 135; Someren, de Repræs. c. 5, n. 4.) If a testator institute as his heirs those whom he calls proximi, without using any expression pointing to those who would by law succeed to him in case of intestacy, and he leaves no children, it is doubtful who are entitled to the succession; whether those who would take according to the law of the place of his domicil, or those who were really and naturally the nearest to the testator in blood, although according to that law they could not be his heirs. Thus if the testator were domiciled in a country where the relations of the deceased mother succeed in preference to the surviving father, the latter is the nearest in blood to the deceased, although he is not nearest in the order of succession. It seems that the term proximus would receive its natural signification, and consequently the father as the nearest in blood would succeed, and not the descendant in the maternal line. (Voet. lib. 28, tit. 5, n. 19, and lib. 36, tit. 1, n. 25; Someren, de Repræs. c. 6.) But it is said that this construction is made to depend on the degree in which the law of succession deviates from the natural sense of the word proximus. And where in cases of intestacy some of the nearest are admitted to the succession with some more remote in blood, the construction would be according to the legal sense. If therefore a testator, instituting his wife as his heir, should direct that the inheritance after his death should revert to the nearest, then according to the jus Scabinicum (Sen-Cons-Trebellianicum), the father would be entitled to one half, and all the brothers to the other half. (Ibid.; Sand. Decis. Fris. lib. 4, tit. 5, def. 6.) If the testator has called to the succession those who are nearest to him in case of intestacy, recourse must be had, not to the laws of the different countries in which his immovable property is situated, to decide who are the persons entitled to succeed, but to the lex loci domicilii. And then it may happen that those would succeed who will not be the nearest in blood. (Sand. Decis. Fris. lib. 4, tit. 5, def. 6, 8; Voet, lib. 36, tit. 1, n. 25, lib. 28, tit. 5, n. 20; Mantica, de Conj. ult. Volunt. lib. 8, tit. 14, n. 10; Van Leeuwen, Cens. For. pt. 1, lib. 3, c. 7, n. 19; Neostad, decis. 35; Jul. Clarus. s. Testam.

whether by 'male children' be meant male descendants, that is, descendants claiming through males only, the question would be decided by the interpretation put upon those words by the law of Holland.

479 f. *Will made at a Place other than that of Domicil.* — But the question may be asked in these and the like cases, what is to be the rule of construction if the will or testament is made by the party in the place of his domicil, but he is in fact a native of another country; or if the will or testament is made in a country of which the party is a native, and according to the forms of law in that country, and yet at the time his actual domicil is in another country, by whose laws the will or testament so made is equally good. The answer to both questions is the same. The law of the place of his actual domicil. Thus for example where a native of Scotland domiciled in England, having personal property only, executed during a visit to Scotland, and deposited a will there, prepared in the Scotch form, and died in England; it was held that the will was to be construed according to the English law.[1]

quæst. 76, n. 13; Someren, de Repræs. c. 5, n. 16; ante, vol. 2, p. 856.) In a bequest of a pecuniary legacy, where the will affords no direct evidence of the currency in which the testator intended it to be paid, his greater familiarity with the currency of the country in which he is domiciled, than with that of any other place, justifies the presumption that he has in view that currency, when he expresses no other currency in which his bequest is to be paid. The father of a family who was domiciled in a village in Peyrouse, in Italy, was on a visit to Ancona on business. He made his will in the latter place, and gave a legacy to one of his daughters of five hundred florins. Florins were of less value at Ancona than at Peyrouse, and the question raised was, whether the legacy should be paid according to the value of the florins at Ancona, or at Peyrouse; and it was determined it ought to be paid according to the value at Peyrouse, the place of the testator's domicil. Where a legacy consists of a certain number of modii of corn, Hertius says that the modii ought to be according to the measure of the place of the testator's domicil, and not according to that of the place where the testament was made. So if a testator, having lands in different places, devise a thousand acres without any other expression, such a devise must be understood according to the measurement prevailing in the place of his domicil.' 4 Burge, Col. & For. Law, pt. 2, c. 12, p. 591–594. See also 2 Id. pt. 2, c. 9, p. 855–860; ante, s. 271, 271 a, note; post, s. 484; Sand. Decis. Frisic. lib. 4, tit. 8, def. 7, p. 194.

[1] Anstruther *v.* Chalmer, 2 Sim. 1; Harrison *v.* Nixon, 9 Pet. 483, 504, 505, note. Mr. Burge on this subject says: 'The law of the place of domicil in many cases affords the rule of construction, when the testator has used expressions which are either ambiguous or of different significations in different countries. Thus if a testator does not institute his heirs by name, but by the

479 *g. Change of Domicil.* — Another question may also be propounded. Suppose, at the time of the making of a will or testament, the testator is domiciled in the place where it is made, and he afterwards removes to another place, where he is domiciled at his death ; does such removal change the rule of construction, so that if there is a difference between the law of the original domicil and that of the new domicil, as to the interpretation of the terms, the law of the new domicil is to prevail? or, does the interpretation remain as it was by the law of the original domicil? This question does not seem to have undergone any absolute and positive decision in the courts acting under the common law.[1] *(a)*

479 *h. Wills of Immovables.* — The same rules of construction will generally apply to wills and testaments of immovable pro-

description of those who would succeed to his estate in case he had died intestate, and the rules of succession where his real or immovable property is situated are different from those which prevail in the place of his domicil, or in that in which he made his will, or in that where the judicial tribunal is, which adjudicates on the will, the laws of succession which prevail in the place of his domicil are those which would be adopted. And the more general opinion is that, even with respect to the succession to real or immovable property, the laws of succession in the place of domicil, and not those in loco rei sitæ, prevail. The ground on which this rule rests is that, as it becomes necessary to ascertain the sense in which the testator has used the expression, and what laws of succession he contemplated, it is presumed that they were those of the country in which he was domiciled, because it must be supposed he was familiar with those laws. There are grounds for presuming he was acquainted with them; but there exist no grounds for presuming him to be acquainted with any other laws of succession. In affixing the sense in which he has used certain words, terms, or phrases, he is presumed to have adopted that which prevailed in the place of his domicil. It has been sometimes said that they ought to be understood in the sense in which they are accustomed to be used in the place where the will or contract was made. But it would be impossible to consider this as a general rule; for the residence of the party in the place may have been for so short a time as to negative the presumption that he was even acquainted with that sense.' 4 Burge, Col. & For. Law, pt. 2, c. 12, p. 590, 591. See also 2 Id. pt. 2, c. 9, p. 855–857.

[1] It was alluded to, and reserved for consideration, in Harrison *v.* Nixon, 9 Pet. 483, 502. See ante, s. 473; 4 Burge, Col. & For. Law, pt. 2, c. 4, s. 5, p. 169; Yates *v.* Thomson, 3 Cl. & F. 544, 583–589.

(a) See Laneuville *v.* Anderson, 2 Sw. & T. 24; Boyes *v.* Bedale, 1 Hem. & M. 805. It has been held however in such case, that unless the will was executed according to the law of the person's last domicil, and the place of his death, it would not be valid, although made according to the laws of the testator's domicil at the time it was made. Nat *v.* Coons, 10 Mo. 543.

perty, unless indeed it can be clearly gathered from the terms used in the will, that the testator had in view the law of the place of the situs, or used other language, which necessarily referred to the usages and customs, or language appropriate only to that situs.[1] (a) 'Thus' (to borrow an illustration from Mr. Burge), 'in case the limitation of a deed or will were made in England in favor of the heir of A., a person who had no children, and the settler or testator has property in England, Jamaica, and British Guiana, if the construction of the term heir was to be in conformity with the law of England, the father of A. would take, if according to the law of Jamaica the elder brother, and if according to the law of British Guiana his father, brothers, and sisters, would take his immovable property. It is not to be presumed that he used the expression in three different senses, or that he adopted the legal import given to it by the law of the one place, rather than that given to it by the law of either of the other two places. But if his domicil were in England, there is the presumption that he was acquainted with the sense attached to it by the law of England, and that he used it in this sense.'[2] So if a testator should devise his real property to his next of kin, who would be entitled would depend upon the construction given to the words by the law of his domicil.[3] (b)

479 i. *Boullenois.* — Foreign jurists have discussed this subject on various occasions.[4] Boullenois says: 'When the question is respecting the interpretation of clauses expressed in a contract or a testament, it is ordinarily the circumstances of the case which are to decide it.' In effect we sometimes find clauses or dispositions in contracts or testaments, which, from not being sufficiently developed, leave some uncertainty of knowing whether they are to be understood according to the law of the place where the acts are executed, or according to the law of the place where the goods are situated, or according to the law of the domi-

---

[1] Trotter v. Trotter, 3 Wils. & Shaw, 407; 4 Bligh, 502, 505; 2 Burge, Col. & For. Law, pt. 2, c. 9, p. 857, 858.

[2] 2 Burge, Col. & For. Law, pt. 2, c. 9, p. 858.   [3] Ibid.

[4] See Sand. Decis. Frisic. lib. 4, tit. 8, defin. 7, p. 194.

(a) See Enohin v. Wylie, 10 H. L. Cas. 1; Chamberlin v. Napier, 15 Ch. D. 614; Bible Society v. Pendleton, 7 W. Va. 79.

(b) Enohin v. Wylie, 10 H. L. Cas. 1; Dannelli v. Dannelli, 4 Bush (Ky.) 51.

cil of one or other of the contracting parties, or finally according to some other law. After citing the opinions of other jurists, he declares his own opinion to be, that the law of the place where the act is executed does not always furnish the proper rule of interpretation in all cases;[1] but that the only rule which can be prescribed is that of determining according to the different circumstances belonging to each case. These circumstances will sometimes compel us to follow the law of the place of the contract or testament, sometimes that of the situs rei, sometimes that of the domicil of the party, and sometimes the place where the payment or performance is to be. He adds that he finds no doctrine more reasonable than that which Dumoulin has laid down upon this subject.[2]

[1] 2 Boullenois, obs. 46, p. 489, 490.

[2] 2 Boullenois, obs. 46, p. 494, 503-518; Id. p. 537, 538. Mr. Burge has cited from 2 Boullenois, obs. 46, p. 534 et seq., a passage illustrating Boullenois's opinion. 'The terms,' says Mr. Burge, 'in which the contract is expressed may receive a construction, according to the law or usage of the place where the contract is made, different from that which is given to them by the law of the situs. If, by adopting the one sense, the contract would be brought within the prohibition of the law of the situs, that construction ought to be rejected. But if this would not be the consequence, and the adoption of either meaning would not afford a ground to prevent the contract from being completed by the law of the situs, it has been a question whether the construction given by the law or usage of the situs, or that given by the law of the place where the contract was made, ought to prevail. Thus in some countries, the limitation by gift or devise to a person, and " si sine liberis discesserit " to another, operates as a substitution. The children, " positi in conditione," are also considered as " positi in dispositione," and are entitled to take. Such was the law of Toulouse. But under the coutume of Paris, the expression, " si sine liberis," imported only a condition, and consequently, if there were no failure of children, there was no substitution. The following case occurred, on which M. Boullenois gave his opinion: The Comte de R., domiciled in Languedoc, made a settlement on the marriage of his son, who had resided in Paris many years, and the lady with whom he married was a native of and domiciled in Paris. The comte executed a general power of attorney to the Bishop of —— to arrange the marriage settlement. By this settlement he gave to his son a moiety of all his estate, movable and immovable, then belonging to him, or which should belong to him on the day of his death. " Sous la condition que, si le futur époux décède sans enfans mâles, nés de ce mariage, la moitié des biens à lui présentement donnés, retournera à l'aîné de ses frères, ou à l'aîné des enfans mâles du dit ainé; après toutes fois que les conventions de la dite demoiselle future épouse auront été payées et acquittées, et que déduction aura été faite de la légitime des filles." There were issue of the marriage, a son and daughter. The real property was situated in Toulouse. The son claimed it, insisting that his father had created a substitution, and that he took as a substitute. The daughter contended that no substitution was created, that the

479 *k. Foreign Jurists.* — We have already had occasion, in part, to refer to the opinions of Dumoulin on this subject.[1] He reproves the doctrine, maintained by many jurists, that the law and custom of the place where a contract is made are to govern the contract in all cases. 'Et advertendum, quod doctores pessime intelligunt, L. si fundus de evicti; quia putant ruditer et indistincte, quod debeat ibi inspici locus et consuetudo, ubi fit contractus, et sic jus in loco contractus. Quod est falsum; quinimo jus est in tacita et verisimiliter mente contrahentium.' And he explains himself thus. 'Aut statu-

condition had failed, and that consequently, the father having died without making any disposition, she was entitled with her brother as one of the heirs ab intestato. The opinion given by M. Boullenois was, that the import of the expression, given by the law of Paris, where the contract was made, and where two of the parties to it were domiciled, and the donor was present by his attorney, must prevail. This opinion was confirmed by sentence des Requêtes du Palais of the 21st of August, 1734, in favor of the daughter. But this sentence was reversed on appeal, and the decision was given in favor of the son. There is great force in the arguments by which this learned jurist maintains his opinion. The principal ground on which the decision proceeded was, that the domicil of the father, the donor, was in Toulouse, and that it must be presumed he contemplated the law with which he was acquainted, rather than that of Paris, with which he might be unacquainted; and that in donations the intention of the donor is principally to be considered, since the part of the donee is confined to the acceptance of the donation. But in the present case this consideration loses much of the weight to which it might otherwise be entitled, because the donor had granted a general power of attorney to a person resident in Paris to arrange the settlement, and had not prescribed the terms or conditions it should contain. It was not in this case insisted, nor is it the doctrine of jurists, that the situs of the property requires the application of its law to determine the legal import of any expression in the contract. The text of the civil law is, that "In stipulationibus, et in cæteris contractibus, id sequimur, quod actum est; et si non pateat quod actum est, erit consequens, ut id sequamur, quod in regione in qua actum est, frequentatur." It has been justly considered that this rule is too general; for that, if it were universally followed, the intentions of the contracting parties must be frequently defeated. It has been seen, in the passage already cited, that it was condemned by Dumoulin. In his opinion, and he is followed by Boullenois, the interpretation of expressions in a contract must depend, not on the place where it is made, but on those other circumstances from which the will or intention of the parties may be inferred. Generally the interpretation which it would receive in the place of their domicil is that which it is most probable will be conformable to their intention.' 2 Burge, Col & For. Law, pt. 2, c. 9, p. 855–857; 2 Boullenois, obs. 46, p. 518–533; ante, s. 275. Boullenois gives other illustrations of his doctrine. 2 Boullenois, obs. 46, p. 495–518. Bouhier seems to hold a similar opinion. Bouhier, Cout. de Bourg. c. 21, n. 220–222.

[1] Ante, s. 274, 441.

tum loquitur de his, quæ concernunt nudam ordinationem vel solemnitatem actus, et semper inspicitur statutum vel consuetudo, ubi actus celebratur, sive in contractibus, sive in judiciis, sive in testamentis, sive in instrumentis, aut aliis conficiendis.[1] Aut statutum loquitur de his, quæ meritum scilicet causæ vel decisionem concernunt; et tunc aut in his, quæ pendent a voluntate partium, vel per eas immutari possunt, et tunc inspiciuntur, circumstantiæ voluntatis quarum, una est statutum loci, in quo contrahitur, et domicilii contrahentium antiqui vel recentis, et similes circumstantiæ.'[2]

479 *l.* Hertius lays down the rule that the words of a testator are to be especially interpreted according to the custom of the place where the testator had his origin or domicil. 'Hinc jurisconsulti verba testatoris præcipue interpretantur secundum loci consuetudinem, ubi testator originem vel domicilium habeat.'[3] And he illustrates it by the case of a bequest of so many measures of wheat, or so many acres of land, where the question arises as to the quantity of the measures or of the acres, whether to be understood according to the lex loci of the testament, or the lex domicilii of the testator.[4] The like doctrine is adopted by John Voet, by Stockmans, by Christinæus, by Rodenburg, and by Sandius.[5] Stockmans uses the following language: 'Non exigua vis est communis regula, quæ dictat, testatorem in dubio censeri dispositionem suam aptare jure illius loci, ubi agit et testamentum condit, et consuetudinem ac leges municipales loci tacite influere, ac temperare generales testantium locutiones et dispositiones.'[6] Paul Voet says: 'In specie autem consuetudo legis verba ambigua interpretatur: et si non appareat, quid actum sit inter contrahentes, ad eam, tanquam rerum ac verborum dominam, recurritur. Quam etiam in perscrutanda testatoris voluntate.'[7]

---

[1] Molin. Opera, tom. 3, Comm. in Cod. 1, 1, p. 554, ed. 1681; ante, s. 260, 274, 441; 2 Boullenois, obs. 46, p. 495.

[2] Ibid.

[3] Hertii Op. de Collis. Leg. s. 6, n. 3, p. 222, ed. 1716; Id. p. 158, ed. 1737; 2 Burge, Col. & For. Law, pt. 2, c. 9, p. 859, 860.

[4] Ibid.; Molin. Opera, tom. 1, de Fiefs, s. 33, n. 86, p. 410, ed. 1661.

[5] See ante, s. 479 *e*, note; 4 Burge, Col. & For. Law, pt. 2, c. 12, p. 591-594, where the opinions of these jurists are cited.

[6] Stockm. Decis. 27, n. 1, p. 27.

[7] P. Voet, de Statut. s. 3, c. 1, n, 2, p. 100, ed. 1715; Id. p. 111, ed. 1661.

479 *m. General Rule.* — Indeed it may be laid down as a general rule, that wherever words of an ambiguous signification or different significations in different countries are used in a will, they are to be interpreted in the sense in which they are used in the law of the testator's domicil, which he may be presumed either to be most familiar with or to have adopted. Sandius says: 'In ambigua hac testatoris voluntate spectandum esse consuetudinem regionis, in qua testator versatus est.'[1] The same rule has been recognized in England, or rather it has been generalized ; for it has in effect been held that, in the construction of ambiguous instruments or contracts, the place of executing them, the domicil of the parties, the place appointed for their execution, and other circumstances, are to be taken into consideration.[2]

479 *n. Necessity of Probate.* — In respect to another point, whether a court of equity can enforce a foreign will, of which there has been no probate obtained from our own courts, the principle seems clear that it cannot. A court of equity can know nothing of a will of personalty in England, unless it has first been adjudged a will in the proper probate or ecclesiastical court. A fortiori the rule must apply to a foreign will.

---

[1] Sand. Decis. Frisic. lib. 4, tit. 8, defin. 7, p. 195.
[2] Lansdowne *v.* Lansdowne, 2 Bligh, 60, 87; 4 Burge, Col. & For. Law, pt. 2, c. 12, p. 590, 591. See Bunbury *v.* Bunbury (before Lord Cottenham) 3 Jur. p. 644; 1 Beav. 318.

CHAPTER XII.

SUCCESSION AND DISTRIBUTION.

480. *Subject of the Chapter.* — Having considered the operation of foreign law in regard to testaments of movable property and of immovable property, we next proceed to the right of succession in cases of intestacy, or, as the phrase is, of succession ab intestato. And here, the preceding discussions have left little more to be done, than to state the general principles applicable to each species of property.

481. *Movables.* — First in relation to movable property. The universal doctrine, now recognized by the common law, although formerly much contested, is that the succession to personal property is governed exclusively by the law of the actual domicil of the intestate at the time of his death.[1] (a) It is of no conse-

---

[1] Many of the authorities to sustain this point have been already cited, ante, s. 380–385, 465–474. But some others may be here referred to. Pipon *v.* Pipon, Ambler, 25; Thorne *v.* Watkins, 2 Ves. 35; 1 Chitty on Com. & Manuf. 661; Sill *v.* Worswick, 1 H. Bl. 690, 691; Bruce *v.* Bruce, 2 B. & P. 229, note; Hunter *v.* Potts, 4 T. R. 182; Potter *v.* Brown, 5 East, 130; Birtwhistle *v.* Vardill, 5 B. & C. 438, 450–455; 9 Bligh, 32–38; 2 Cl. & F. 571; Yates *r.* Thomson, 3 Cl. & F. 554; Robertson on Succession, c. 6, p. 104–117; Id. c. 8, p. 118–201; Thornton *v.* Curling, 8 Sim. 310; Price *v.* Dewhurst, 8 Sim. 279, 299; Moore *v.* Budd, 4 Hagg. Ecc. 346, 352; 4 Burge, Col. & For. Law. pt. 2, c. 4, s. 5, p. 156–170; ante, s. 362, 367, 378. For a long time the law of Scotland was unsettled on this point; but it now coincides with that of England. Robertson on Succession, *ubi supra;* 4 Burge, *ubi supra;* Stairs, Instit. b. 3, tit. 8, s. 35; Ersk. Instit. b. 3, tit. 9, s. 4; Livermore, Dissert. 162, 163; Olivier *r.* Townes, 2 Mart. N.S. (La.) 99; Shultz *v.* Pulver, 3 Paige (N. Y.) 182; De Sobry *v.* De Laistre, 2 Harr. & J. (Md.) 193, 224, 228; Holmes *v.* Remsen, 4 Johns. Ch. (N. Y.) 460; 20 Johns. (N. Y.) 229; De Couche *v.* Savetier, 3 Johns. Ch. (N. Y.) 190; Erskine, Inst. b. 3, tit. 2, s. 40,

(a) See Suarez *v.* New York, 2 Sandf. Ch. (N. Y.) 173; Ennis *v.* Smith, 14 How. 400; Lawrence *v.* Kitteridge, 21 Conn. 577; Holcomb *v.* Phelps, 16 Conn. 127; Lynch *v.* Ellett, 9 Wall. 740. Paraguay, L. R. 2 P. & M. 268; Russell *v.* Madden, 95 Ill. 485; Noonan *v.* Kemp, 34 Md. 73; Slaughter *v.* Garland, 40 Miss. 172; Wilkins *v.*

quence what is the country of the birth of the intestate, or of his former domicil, or what is the actual situs of the personal property at the time of his death; it devolves upon those who are entitled to take it, as heirs or distributees, according to the law of his actual domicil at the time of his death.[1] Hence if a Frenchman dies intestate in America, all his personal property, whether it be in America or in France, is distributable according to the statute of distribution of the state where he then resided, notwithstanding it may differ essentially from the distribution prescribed by the law of France. (a)

481 a. *Persons entitled.* — So the like rule prevails in the ascertainment of the person who is entitled to take as heir or distributee. The law of the domicil therefore is to decide whether primogeniture gives a right of preference, or an exclusive right to the succession, and whether a person is legitimate or not to take the succession. So whether persons are to take per capita or per stirpes; and the nature and extent of the right of representation. Thus, for example, in England and in some of the American states there is no right of representation beyond that of brothers' and sisters' children, as to the right of distribution, in cases of intestacy, of movable property. If therefore a man should die, leaving a brother and sister and the grandchildren of a deceased brother, the latter would not take anything in virtue of a representation of the deceased brother.[2]

41; Id. b. 3, tit. 9, s. 4; 2 Kames, Eq. b. 3, c. 8, s. 3, 4, p. 333, 345; 1 Boullenois, obs. 20, p. 358; 2 Boullenois, 54, 57; Fergusson on Marr. & Div. 346, 361; Vattel, b. 2, s. 85, 103, 110, 111; 1 Hertii Opera, de Collis. Leg. s. 4, n. 26, p. 135, ed. 1737; Id. p. 192, ed. 1716; Huberus, de Confl. Leg. lib. 1, tit. 3, s. 15; Henry on Foreign Law, p. 13–15, 46, 196; J. Voet, ad Pand. 38, 17, s. 34, p. 596; Harvey v. Richards, 1 Mason, 418; 2 Froland, Mém. 1294; 2 Dwarris on Statut. 649; Price v. Dewhurst, 3 My. & Cr. 76, 82; Preston v. Melville, 8 Cl. & F. 1, 12.

[1] Ibid.

[2] Burge, Col. & For. Law, pt. 2, c. 4, s. 5, p. 156–160. As in cases of movable property, the law of the domicil is thus held to regulate the succession and distribution thereof, the question may often become important, what

(a) So if a person dies abroad in the country of his domicil, and by the law of that country his natural son is entitled to inherit his father's property as heir at law, and the courts of that country have adjudicated upon such right, an English court is bound by that decision, and is bound to admit such natural son to dispute a will offered in the English court, disposing of his personal property in England to other parties. Doglioni v. Crispin, Law Rep. 1 H. L. 301. See Goods of Weaver, 36 Law J. Prob. & Mat. 41.

481 *b.* *Foreign Jurists.*—This same doctrine is maintained with equal broadness by foreign jurists. It is founded in a great measure upon the doctrine that movables have no situs, and accompany the person of the owner; so that in fictione juris, they are always deemed to be in the place of his domicil. 'Mobilia sequuntur personam, et ejus ossibus adhærent.'[1] Thus Rodenburg, referring to the effect of a change of domicil on succession, takes the very distinction between movable property and immovable property, founded upon its nature and character. 'Jus rebus succedendi immobilibus, semper a loco rei sitæ metiendum, huc non pertinet; succedendi mobilibus pertinet; quod ea certo loco non circumscripta, comitentur personam a domicilio ejus accipientia leges.'[2] Boullenois fully concurs in this opinion.[3] Burgundus holds the some opinion.[4] Perhaps it might, with quite as much accuracy, be said that the doctrine is founded in a great public policy, observed, ex comitate, by all nations, from a sense of its general convenience and utility, and its tendency to avoid endless embarrassments and conflicts, where personal pro-

is the actual domicil. As to this see ante, s. 44–50. Upon this subject many difficult questions may arise. See for example De Bonneval *v.* De Bonneval, 1 Curteis, 856; Attorney-General *v.* Dunn, 6 M. & W. 511. But the rule itself may require some modification, where the law of the domicil of the intestate is intended to take away the rights of persons who might otherwise succeed to movable property in another country by a sort of hostile perversity. Thus it has been said that under the Berlin and Milan decrees passed by Napoleon, Englishmen were rendered incapable of succeeding to the personal estates of intestates dying in Italy. Such a law might require England to disallow the operation of the general rule as to personal property of the same intestate situate in England. See Koster *v.* Sapte, 1 Curteis, Ecc. 691; ante, s. 472, note. Suppose a person should die in transitu from his acquired domicil, the question might then arise, whether the law of his native domicil, or of his acquired domicil, or of his intended domicil, was to govern. It seems clear that a domicil, whether native or acquired, is not lost by a mere abandonment. It is not defeated animo merely, but animo et facto, and necessarily remains until a subsequent domicil is acquired, at least unless the party dies in transitu to his intended domicil. This last qualification of the doctrine, though stated by a learned judge, may be exactly the point of a doubt whether it varies the rule. Munroe *v.* Douglas, 5 Madd. 379. See also 2 Boullenois, Appx. p. 59, 60; Jennison *v.* Hapgood, 10 Pick. (Mass.) 77, 99.

[1] See ante, s. 362, 377, 378; 4 Burge, Col. & For. Law, pt. 2, c. 4, s. 5, p. 157; Foelix, Conflit des Lois, Revue Étrang. et Franç. tom. 7, 1840, s. 32, p. 221, 222.

[2] Rodenburg, de Div. Stat. tit. 2, pt. 2, c. 2, s. 1; 2 Boullenois, Appx. p. 59; 2 Boullenois, c. 2, p. 54.

[3] 2 Boullenois, obs. 38, p. 57, 63, 64.

[4] Burgundus, tract. 2, n. 20, 21; Id. tract. 1, n. 26.

perty has often changed places; which is the view entertained by John Voet.[1]

482. Paul Voet has put the principle in a compendious manner. 'Idem ne inferendum de statutis, quæ spectant successiones ab intestato? Respondeo, quod ita; rem enim afficiunt, non personam, ut legibus loci, ubi bona sita sunt, vel esse intelliguntur, regi debeant. Immobilia statutis loci, ubi sita; mobilia loci statutis, ubi testator habuit domicilium.'[2] And again: 'Verum an, quod de immobilibus dictum, idem de mobilibus statuendum erit? Respondeo, quod non. Quia illorum bonorum nomine nemo censetur semet loci legibus subjecisse. Ut quæ res certum locum non habent, quia facile de loco in locum transferuntur; adeoque secundum loci statuta regulantur, ubi domicilium habuit defunctus.'[3]

482 a. Sandius, in speaking of successions, takes the like distinction between movables and immovables. 'Aliud judicium est de mobilibus quæ ex conditione personarum legem accipiunt, nec loco continuere dicuntur, sed personam sequuntur, et ab ea dependent; et ideo omnia ubicunque mobilia legibus domicilii subjiciuntur.'[4] Strykius affirms the same doctrine; as do Gaill and Christinæus and John Voet.[5] The latter says: 'Cæterum occasione variantium in successionem intestatam statutorum, generaliter observandum est, bona defuncti immobilia, et quæ juris interpretatione pro talibus habentur, deferri secundum leges loci, in quo sita sunt; adeo, ut tot censeri debeant diversa patrimonia, ac tot hæreditates, quot locis, diverso jure utentibus, immobilia existunt. Mobilia vero ex lege domicilii ipsius defuncti, vel quia semper domino præsentia esse finguntur, aut (ut exposui) ex comitate, passim usu.'[6] Bynkershoek is equally positive. 'Omnino

---

[1] J. Voet, ad Pand. 38, 17, n. 34, tom. 2, p. 596; post, s. 482 a, note.

[2] P Voet, de Stat. s. 4, c. 8, n. 10, p. 135, ed 1716; Id. p. 153, ed. 1661; ante, s. 475.

[3] P. Voet, de Stat. s. 9, c. 1, n. 8, p. 255, ed. 1715; Id. p. 309, ed. 1661. See also to the same point, J. Voet, ad Pand. 1, 1, 4, pt. 2, n. 11, p. 44; ante, s. 362, n. 3.

[4] Sand. Decis. Frisic. lib. 4, tit. 8, defin. 7, p. 194.

[5] Strykius, de Success. Diss. 1, c. 4, n. 3; Gaill. Pract. Obs. lib. 2, obs. 124, n. 18, p. 552; Christin. Decis. Cur. Belg. vol. 2, decis. 3. n. 2, 3, p. 4; J. Voet, ad Pand. 38, 17, de Success. ab Intestato, n. 34, tom. 2, p. 596; Foelix, Conflit des Lois, Revue Étrang. et Franç. tom. 7, 1840, s. 37, p. 307–311; 4 Burge, Col. & For. Law, pt. 2, c. 4, s. 5, p. 156–158.

[6] J. Voet, Com. ad Pand. 38, 17, n. 34, tom. 2, p. 596.

igitur interest scire non tam ubi quis decessit, quam ubi decedens domicilium habuit ; nam si hoc sciamus, secundum leges domicilii hæreditas intestati defertur, sive major, sive minor decesserit quod ad mobilia nempe, et quæ pro mobilibus habentur.' [1]

483. *Immovables.* — Secondly, in relation to immovable property. And here a very different principle prevails at the common law. The descent and heirship of real estate are exclusively governed by the law of the country within which it is actually situate. No person can take, except those who are recognized as legitimate heirs by the laws of that country ; and they take in the proportions and the order which those laws prescribe. This is the indisputable doctrine of the common law.[2]

· 483 *a. Foreign Jurists.* — Foreign jurists are not indeed universally agreed even as to this point, although certainly they differ less than in most other cases. It may truly be said that the generality of them (having a great weight of authority) unequivocally admit that the descent and distribution of real estate are, and ought to be governed by the lex rei sitæ.[3] On this head it might seem almost sufficient to adopt the language of John Voet in his classification of real and personal statutes. He reduces to the class of real statutes whatever regards inheritances. ' Quo pertinet jura successionum ab intestato ; quonam

[1] Bynkers. Quest. Privat. Jur. lib. 1, c. 16, p. 179, 180.

[2] 4 Burge, Col. & For. Law, pt. 2, c. 4, s. 5, p. 151, 152; Birtwhistle v. Vardill, 5 B. & C. p. 451, 452; 6 Bligh, 479, note; 9 Bligh, 82–88; 1 Rob. App. 627; ante, s. 364–366, 426–429; post, s. 483 a, note; Bunbury v. Bunbury, 3 Jur. 644; 1 Beav. 318.

[3] The authorities to this point also have been already cited, ante, s. 424–448. See Birtwhistle v. Vardill, 5 B. & C. 438; United States v. Crosby, 7 Cranch, 115; Kerr v. Moon, 9 Wheat. 556, 570; McCormick v. Sullivant, 10 Wheat. 192; Darby v. Mayer, 10 Wheat. 469; Hosford v. Nichols, 1 Paige (N. Y.) 220; Cutter v. Davenport, 1 Pick. (Mass.) 81; Wills v. Cowper, 2 Hamm. 124; 1 Hertii Opera, de Collis. Leg. s. 4, n. 26, p. 135; 1 Boullenois, 25, 223, &c. 1 Froland, Mém. 60, 61, 65; P. Voet, de Stat. s. 4, c. 2, n. 6, p. 123; J. Voet. ad Pand. 1. 4, pt. 2, s. 3, p. 39; Ersk. Inst. b. 3, tit. 2, s. 40, 41, p. 515; D'Aguesseau, Œuvres, tom. 4, p. 637; Huberus, lib. 1, tit. 3, s. 15; 2 Dwarris on Statut. p. 649; Rodenburg, pt. 2, tit. 2, c. 2; 2 Boullenois, Appx. p. 59, 63; 2 Boullenois, 54, 57, 383; 2 Froland, Mém. c. 7, p. 1288; Foelix. Conflit des Lois, Revue Étrang. et Franç. tom. 7, 1840, s. 37, p. 307-312; 4 Burge, Col. & For. Law, pt. 2, c. 4, s. 5, p. 151-156. Since the preceding sheets were worked off I have ascertained that the case of Birtwhistle v. Vardill, above cited, has been affirmed in the House of Lords. 1 Rob. App. 627. The ground was that by the law of England no person could inherit lands as heir who was not born after the marriage of his parents.

ordine ad bona quæque ab intestato, quisque in capita, vel stirpes, vel lineas, vel jura primogenituræ admittendus sit; qua ratione legitimi aut illegitimi, agnati, cognati vocentur; quæque his sunt similia plura.'[1] Rodenburg is equally decisive. 'Jus rebus succedendi immobilibus semper a loco rei sitæ metiendum.'[2] Froland gives the rule in the most concise but energetic terms, attributing the language to Dumoulin: 'Mobilia sequuntur personam; immobilia situm.'[3] Dumoulin says: 'Aut statutum datur in rem; puta, bona decedentis veniant ad primogenitum; et tunc attenditur statutum loci, in quo sita sunt bona.'[4] Bynkershoek in his bold and uncompromising manner asserts that the rule is so well established that no one dares to open his mouth against it. 'Immobilia enim deferri ex jure, quod obtinet in loco rei sitæ, adeo recepta hodie sententia est, ut nemo ausit contra hiscere.'[5]

483 b. Paul Voet says: 'Quid si circa successionem ab intestato, statutorum sit difformitas? Spectabitur loci statutum, ubi immobilia sita, non ubi testator moritur.'[6] Rodenburg, speaking of laws which are purely real (quæ quidem jure precipui mere realia sunt), says: 'Cujusmodi appellamus ea, quæ de modo dividendarum ab intestato hæreditatum tractant, territorium non egredientia; conspirant enim eo vota fere omnium, bona ut dijudicentur sua lege loci, in quo sita sunt vel esse intelliguntur.'[7] Burgundus, after remarking that there is a diversity of opinion upon this subject among jurists, some holding that the law of the

[1] J. Voet, ad Pand. 1, 4, 2, s. 3, tom, 1, p. 39; Id. 38, 17, n. 34, tom. 2, p. 596.

[2] Rodenburg, de Div. Stat. pt. 2, tit. 2, c. 2, p. 59; 2 Boullenois, Appx. p. 54, 57. See also Henrys, Œuvres, tom. 2, lib. 4, c. 6, quest. 105, Obs. Bretonnier, p. 613, 614, ed. 1771.

[3] 2 Froland, Mém. 1289. I cannot find any such expressive language used by Dumoulin in the passage cited by Froland, and therefore conclude that it is his own concise statement of Dumoulin's opinion, in which he is certainly correct. The passages cited Molin. Opera, tom. 2, p. 701, ed. 1681, Coutumes de Senlis, art. 140, 747, Coutumes d'Auvergne, art. 4; Id. Consil. 53, p. 964; Id. tom. 3, p. 554, Conclus. de Statut.

[4] Molin. Oper. Com. in Cod. 1, 1, 1, Conclus. de Statut. p. 556, ed. 1681.

[5] Bynkers. Quest. Privat. Jur. lib. 1, c. 16, p. 180; ante, s. 381.

[6] P. Voet, de Statut. s. 9, c. 1, n. 3, 4, p. 252, 253, ed. 1715; Id. p. 305-307, ed. 1661; ante, s. 433, 475. Paul Voet gives a long list of authorities, supporting the doctrine ut immobilia statutis loci regantur, ubi sita. P. Voet, s. 9, c. 1, n. 4, *ubi supra*.

[7] 2 Rodenburg, de Divers. Statut. tit. 2, c. 2, s. 1, n. 1; 2 Boullenois, Appx. p. 14; Id. p. 74.

situs of the property is to govern, some that the law of the domicil of the intestate, and some few that the law of the place where the intestate happened to die, then asserts his own opinion. 'Bonorum duæ sunt species; alia enim mobilia sunt, alia immobilia; illa a persona, hæc a situ cujusque provinciæ legem accipiunt; videlicet, ut nulla habita ratione originis, aut mortis, aut domicilii, tam hæredum, quam ipsius defuncti, dividantur secundum consuetudines locorum, ubi bona vel sunt, vel sita esse intelliguntur.'[1]

483 c. Boullenois treats the subject as so entirely free from doubt as to require no comment or explanation.[2] D'Argentré, as we have seen, resolutely maintains the same opinion.[3] Sandius says: 'Contra tamen vulgo a doctoribus receptum est, statuta de bonis et successione intestati disponentia esse realia, nec egredi fines territorii. Atque ita fieri, ut secundum diversitatem statutorum diversimode succedatur, non aliter, quam si per fictionem unius hominis diversa sunt patrimonia. Et immobilia sunt sub jurisdictione loci in quo jacent. Statutum igitur Hollandiæ non extendit se ad res immobiles in Frisia sitas; sed istæ subjacent dispositione juris communis quod in Frisia obtinet.'[4]

483 d. And not to dwell upon a point which, although not without controversy among foreign jurists, is generally established, we may quote the opinion of Huberus. His language is: 'Non potest heic omitti quæstio frequens in foris hodiernis, a juris Romani tamen aliena terminis: Quia sæpe sit, ut diversum jus succedendi ab intestato in locis, ubi defunctus habuit domicilium, atque in iis locis, ubi bona sita sunt obtineat, dubitatur, secundum utrius loci leges successio regenda sit. Communis et recta sententia est, in rebus immobilibus servandum esse jus loci in quo bona sunt sita; quia cum partem ejusdem territorii faciant, diversæ jurisdictionis legibus adfici non possunt. Verum in mobilibus nihil esse causæ, cur aliud quam jus domicilii sequamur; quia res mobiles non habent affectionem versus territorium, sed ad personam patrisfamilias duntaxat; qui aliud quam, quod in loco domicilii obtinebat, voluisse videri non potest.'[5]

---

[1] Burgundus, tract. 1, n. 36, p. 38.

[2] 1 Boullenois, obs. 20, p. 358; 2 Boullenois, obs. 41, p. 383.

[3] Ante, s. 438.

[4] Sand. Decis. lib. 4, tit. 8, defin. 7, p. 194.

[5] Huberus, vol. 1. lib. 3, de Success. n. (s), p. 278. See also 4 Burge, Col. & For. Law, pt. 2, c. 4, s. 5, p. 150–152, 154, 155.

484. *Persons entitled.* — We have already had occasion to state that, in the interpretation of wills of immovable property and of movable property, if the description of persons who are to take be by some general designation, such as 'heirs,' or 'next of kin, 'issue,' or 'children,' the rule of the common law is that they are to be ascertained by the lex domicilii, both in regard to immovable property and to movable property, unless the context furnishes some clear guide for a different interpretation.[1] The same rule will apply in cases of the descent and distribution of movable property ab intestato, for the reason already suggested, that it is deemed by fiction of law to be in the place of his domicil, and therefore to be distributable according to the lex domicilii; and consequently, who are the 'issue,' or 'children,' or 'heirs,' or 'next of kin,' is a matter to be ascertained by that law.[2] But in regard to immovable property a different rule prevails, founded upon the actual situs; and as the succession is to be according to the lex loci situs, the persons who are to take by succession can be ascertained only by reference to the same law.[3]

484 *a. Foreign Jurists.* — Foreign jurists generally, although not universally, maintain the same doctrine, and accordingly hold that in cases of succession ab intestato we are to ascertain the persons who are to take the inheritance, by the lex loci rei sitæ, whether the question respects legitimacy, or primogeniture, or right of representation, or proximity of blood, or next of kin. (*a*) John Voet is very full and explicit on this subject. He says: 'Posita ergo varietate, si quæras, cujus loci leges in repræsentatione observandæ sint? respondendum videtur eodem modo, quo supra in principali quæstione de successione; puta, mobilium intuitu spectandas esse leges domicilii defuncti, immo-

---

[1] Ante, s. 479 *a*, 479 *m*, 479 *n*; 2 Burge, Col. & For. Law, pt. 2, c. 9, p. 855-858.

[2] See Thorne *v.* Watkins, 2 Ves. 35; Brown *v.* Brown, or Gordon *v.* Brown, 3 Hagg. Ecc. 455, note; 4 Wils. & Shaw, 28; P. Voet, de Statut. s. 3, c. 1, n. 2, p. 100, ed. 1715; Id. p. 111, ed. 1661; Elliott *v.* Minto, 6 Madd. 16; Winchelsea *v.* Garetty, 2 Keen, 293, 309, 310; ante, s. 479 *e*; post, s. 490, 529.

[3] Birtwhistle *v.* Vardill, 5 B. & C. 438; 9 Bligh, 32; ante, s. 364-366, 426-429, 483; 4 Burge, Col. & For. Law, c. 4. s. 5, p. 150-156; Id. c. 15, s. 4, p. 722-734; Elliott *v.* Minto, 6 Madd. 16; Winchelsea *v.* Garetty, 2 Keen, 293, 309, 310; post, s. 529.

(*a*) See also Abston *v.* Abston, 15 Louis. Ann. 138.

bilium respectu leges cujusque loci, in quo illa sita sunt : eo quod jus repræsentationis omnino ad jus successionis intestatæ pertinet, imo successorem facit eum tanquam ex fictione legis proximum, qui vere atque naturaliter defuncto proximus non est.' [1]

485. *Remarks of Sir W. Grant.* — But these general principles still leave behind them, even in the common law, some very embarrassing difficulties ; and in the complex systems of foreign law, the difficulties are greatly multiplied. Sir William Grant adverted to this subject in an important case, and said : ' Where land and personal property are situated in different countries, and governed by different laws, and a question arises upon the combined effect of those laws, it is often very difficult to determine what portion of each law is to enter into the decision of the question. It is not easy to say how much is to be considered as depending on the law of real property, which must be taken from the country where the land lies, and how much upon the law of personal property, which must be taken from the law of the domicil, and to blend both together so as to form a rule applicable to the mixed question which neither law separately furnishes sufficient materials to decide.' [2]

486. *Balfour* v. *Scott.* — Two cases of a curious nature were on the same occasion mentioned by Sir William Grant as illustrative of his remarks, which cannot be better stated than in his own language. ' I have argued (said he) in the House of Lords, cases in which difficulties of that kind occurred. Two of the most remarkable were those of Balfour *v.* Scott,[3] and Drummond *v.* Drummond.[4] In the former a person domiciled in England died intestate, leaving real estate in Scotland. The heir was one of the next of kin, and claimed a share of the personal estate. To this claim it was objected that by the law of Scotland, the heir cannot share in the personal property with the other next of kin,

---

[1] J. Voet, ad Pand. tom. 2, 38, 17, n. 35, p. 597. See Id. 38, 18, n. 84, p. 639, where he adds: Denique prætermittendum non est, in eo, an jus primogenituræ admittendum sit, necne; immobilium quidem intuitu spectandam esse legem loci, in quo sita sunt; mobilium vero respectu consuetudinem domicilii defuncti.

[2] Brodie *v.* Barry, 2 V. & B. 130, 131.

[3] See Robertson on Successions, p. 202-207; 4 Burge, Col. & For. Law, pt. 2, c. 15, s. 4, p. 731; 6 Bro. P. C. 601, by Tomlins.

[4] 6 Bro. P. C. (Tomlins's ed.) 601; 4 Burge, Col. & For. Law, pt. 2, c. 15, s. 4, p. 729.

except on condition of collating the real estate, that is, bringing it into a mass with the personal estate, to form one common subject of division. It was determined however that he was entitled to take his share without complying with that obligation. There the English law decided the question.' [1]

487. *Drummond* v. *Drummond.* — He then added : ' In Drummond v. Drummond, a person domiciled in England had real estate in Scotland, upon which he granted a heritable bond to secure a debt contracted in England. He died intestate; and the question was, by which of the estates this debt was to be borne. It was clear that by the English law the personal estate was the primary fund for the payment of debts. It was equally clear that by the law of Scotland the real estate was the primary fund for the payment of the heritable bond. Here was a direct conflictus legum. It was said for the heir that the personal estate must be distributed according to the law of England, and must bear all the burdens to which it is by that law subject. On the other hand it was said that the real estate must go according to the law of Scotland, and bear all the burdens to which it is by that law subject. It was determined that the law of Scotland should prevail ; and that the real estate must bear the burden.' [2]

488. In conclusion he said : ' In the first case, the disability of the heir did not follow him to England ; and the personal estate was distributed as if both the domicil and the real estate had been in England. In the second, the disability to claim exoneration out of the personalty did follow him into England ; and the personal estate was distributed as if both the domicil and the real estate had been in Scotland.' [3]

489. *Election.* — Another illustration is furnished by the very case then in judgment before Sir William Grant, which turned upon the question whether an heir at law of heritable property in Scotland, being a legatee of personal property which was in England, under a will of the testator, which intended to dispose of all his real property in England and Scotland, but which will,

---

[1] Brodie v. Barry, 2 V. & B. 130, 131.

[2] Brodie v. Barry, 2 V. & B. 130, 131. See also Drummond v. Drummond, 6 Bro. P. C. (Tomlins's ed.) p. 601 ; post, s. 529; Robertson on Successions, p. 209, 214; 4 Burge, Col. & For. Law, pt. 2, c. 15, s. 4, p. 722-734.

[3] Brodie v. Barry, 2 V. & B. p. 132; ante, s. 266; post, s. 529.

not being conformable to the law of Scotland, was not capable of passing real estate there, should be put to his election to take the legacy under the will, or to surrender to the purposes of the will the Scotch heritable property. Sir William Grant decided in the affirmative; and said : 'Now what law is to determine whether an instrument of any given nature or form is to be read against an heir at law for the purpose of putting him to an election by which the real estate may be affected? According to Lord Hardwicke and the judges who have followed him, that is a question belonging to the law of real property; for they have decided it by a statute which regulates devises of land. Upon that principle, if the domicil were in Scotland and the real estate in England, an English will imperfectly executed ought not to be read in Scotland for the purpose of putting the heir to an election; and upon the same principle, if by the law of Scotland no will could be read against the heir, it would follow that a will of land situated in Scotland ought not to be read in England to put the Scotch heir to an election. Doubting much the soundness of that principle, I am glad that the case of Cunningham *v.* Gayner[1] relieves me from the necessity of deciding the question; as, whichever law is applied to the decision of the present case, the result will be the same, &c. If the law of Scotland is resorted to, the case alluded to determines that the English will may be read against the Scotch heir for the purpose of putting him to an election.'[2]

489 *a. Liability for Debts.* — Other questions of a very difficult and embarrassing nature may arise, as to the nature and extent of the liability of the heirs to the payment of debts and other charges of the intestate, chargeable on his real estate, situate in different countries, where different rules prevail as to the nature and extent of the liability of the heirs in respect to such real estate, and the real estate descends to different persons and in a different manner in the respective countries. The question may respect the exclusive or primary applicability of one or more of the real estates to the discharge of such debts or other charges; or the liability of the heirs in solido, or pro portione hæreditaria; or the right of the heirs or devisees of the real estates in one

---

[1] 1 Bligh, 27, note; Robertson on Successions, p. 219, 220.
[2] Brodie *v.* Barry, 2 V. & B. 127, 133; ante, s. 479 *a*, note; Robertson on Successions, p. 217, 218.

country to contribution or indemnity from the heirs or devisees of the real estate in another country; or the right of the creditors to proceed against them all in solido, or pro portione hæreditaria.[1]

489 b. *Rights of Creditors.* — Many cases of this sort have been discussed by foreign jurists, and decided by foreign tribunals. Thus for example, where one part of the succession has been situate in a country by whose laws the creditors are permitted to proceed against each heir in solido, and another part in the country of the domicil of the intestate, by whose laws the creditors are entitled to proceed against each heir pro portione hæreditaria; there has been no small diversity of judgment as to the rule which ought to be applied in favor of the creditors; whether the rule of the law rei sitæ, or of the law of the domicil, as to the nature and extent of the liability of the heirs.[2] Perhaps in such a case the right of the creditors against the heirs respectively may most properly be deemed to be governed by the lex rei sitæ; and the mode of proceeding against them be regulated by the law of the place where he seeks his remedy. If he seeks to enforce his rights in the place of the domicil of the intestate, he must recover against each heir pro portione hæreditaria. If he seeks to enforce them in the other country, then the heirs are there liable to him in solido. But this opinion is far from having the assent of several distinguished jurists. They hold that the creditors are entitled to proceed against the heirs in either country, according to the law of the domicil of the intestate; because it is there that they suppose the heirs to have contracted the debt to the creditors. Of this opinion are Paul de Castro, Christinæus, and Bouhier, as well as the judges of several foreign tribunals.[3] On the other hand, other jurists hold that in each country respectively the heirs contract with the creditors according to the law of the place where the succession is devolved upon and is assumed by

[1] See 1 Boullenois, obs. 17, p. 277–288, where the subject is much discussed. Bouhier, Cout. de Bourg. c. 21, s. 213, 214, p. 416.

[2] 4 Burge, Col. & For. Law, pt. 2, c. 15, s. 4, p. 722–724, who cites several authorities upon the subject. Among them are Christin. tom. 1, Decis. 283, n. 15, 16: J. Voet, 29, 2, n. 31; Merlin, Répert. tit. Dette, s. 4; 1 Boullenois, obs. 17, p. 278; Bouhier, Cout. de Bourg. c. 21, n. 213.

[3] 1 Boullenois, obs. 17, p. 277, 278; Bouhier, Cout. de Bourg. c. 31, n. 213, p. 416; Christin. tom. 1, Decis. 283, n. 15, 16, p. 353. See also J. Voet, ad Pand. 29, n. 31, 32, tom. 2, p. 376; Merlin, Répert. Dette, s. 4.

the heir, that is, the lex rei sitæ. Of this latter opinion are many distinguished jurists.[1] Merlin inclines strongly to this latter opinion.[2] Boullenois leaves the question without any expression of his own views, saying that it is a point full of difficulty.[3]

489 c. *Contribution between Heirs and Devisees.* — A question of another sort may arise between the heirs or devisees of the deceased party, who as between themselves, in cases of successions or wills of immovable property in different countries, governed by different laws, is ultimately to bear the debts of creditors or other charges for which such property is liable, and which some of the heirs have been compelled to pay. In such cases the question must first arise, which fund is primarily liable for the payment or discharge thereof inter sese; for it should seem that, as between themselves, the fund primarily liable should ultimately be held chargeable therewith in exoneration of all the other funds. If there is no such priority of liability, but all the funds are equally liable pari passu, then it should seem reasonable that each fund, wherever it is actually situate, should contribute pro rata, according to its value in the hands of each heir respectively, to the discharge of the common burden. If part of the funds are exempted from contribution, they should still possess that privilege, and the residue contribute. It will however be found difficult to affirm that foreign jurists and tribunals have given any uniform support to these doctrines.[4]

---

[1] Bouhier, Cout. de Bourg. c. 21, n. 213, 214, p. 416.
[2] Merlin, Répert. Dette, s. 4.
[3] 1 Boullenois, obs. 17, p. 279.
[4] Pothier appears to hold this doctrine. Pothier, des Successions, c. 5, s. 1, p. 223, 4to ed. He there cites a case of which Mr. Burge has given the substance, as follows: ' An inhabitant of Blois, where the coutume burdened the heir to the movable estate with all the movable debts, left in his succession biens propres situated in Blois, and others situated in Orleans. The coutume of the latter place makes all the different heirs subject to all the debts. He left an heir to his movable estate, and another heir to his biens propres, situated in Orleans and Blois. In this case Pothier says that the heir to the biens propres must, conformably to the coutume of Orleans, where he had succeeded to that part of the succession, bear his part of all the debts of the succession, even those which are movable, regard being had to the value which the real estate at Orleans would bear to the whole succession. By this apportionment effect is given to the coutume of Orleans as well as to that of Blois, for the heir to the real estate contributes only to the debts in respect to that part of the estate which is situated in Orleans, and he does not contribute in respect of that part which is situated in Blois.' 4 Burge, Col. & For.

490. *Interpretation of Wills.* — Other illustrations of the difficulties attendant upon the administration of this branch of law are to be found in the application of local rules to the interpretation of wills, whether arising from the lex domicilii or the lex rei sitæ, as the case may regard movable property or immovable property. We have already had occasion to discuss this subject in another place.[1] But it may not be without use to state one or two cases a little more fully than has been already done. A question of this sort was recently discussed in the House of Lords upon a will made in Virginia, by which the testator bequeathed to his sister, Mary Brown, ' the remaining one fourth share of the balance of his estate, at her death to be equally divided among her children, if she should have any.' The question was, what estate Mary Brown took under the will, whether a life estate or an absolute property. And it appearing that the courts of Virginia had construed the bequest to give her an absolute estate, upon the footing of that decree, the House of Lords,

Law, pt. 2, c. 15, s. 4, p. 724, 725. The same subject is discussed at large in 2 Froland, Mém. des Statut. c. 92, p. 1547–1573, and he cites several adjudications, and among others one stated by Basnage, Coutume de Normand. tom. 2, art. 408, p. 141. See also 1 Boullenois, obs. 17, p. 281, who cites Mornac, Com. on Dig. 5, 1, 50, 1, de Judiciis. Mr. Burge has expressed his own opinion in the following words: ' It may perhaps be stated as the correct rule that where an obligation or an exemption is annexed to the personal estate, but no similar obligation or exemption is annexed to the real estate, the lex loci domicilii will prevail in whatever country the rights or liabilities of the heir become the subject of adjudication. But if similar obligations or exemptions are annexed to the personal and real estate by the respective laws to which the succession to these two species of property is subject, and the effect of adopting the one law rather than the other would be to throw on the one estate a burden, or confer on it an exemption not annexed to it by the law of the country which governed the succession to it, it would be the more just and correct rule to adopt the lex loci rei sitæ, rather than the lex loci domicilii. The case of Drummond and Drummond would seem to warrant the adoption of such a rule, nor is the decision in the Bishop of Metz's succession at variance with it. The lex domicilii had alone annexed to the personal estate an exclusive liability to pay the debts, and no such liability was annexed to the real estate by the lex loci rei sitæ. The only liability which was annexed to the real estate by that law was an obligation to contribute with the personal estate; but such a contribution could not take place, because the personal estate was subject to a law which made it exclusively applicable, and therefore the liability to contribute could only exist when the personal estate was subject to the same law as the real estate.' 4 Burge, Col. & For. Law, pt. 1, c. 15, p. 732, 733.

[1] Ante, s. 479 *a*–479 *n*.

deeming it a question of American law, established the same construction.[1]

491. In another case, the same principle was adopted; and the court laid down the rule that, in the construction of a will, the lex domicilii must govern, unless there is sufficient on its face to show a different intention in the testator. The facts were these. A lady, a native of Scotland, was domiciled in England. On a visit to Edinburgh, she made a will entirely in the Scotch form, and it was deposited with the writer at Edinburgh. She had personalty in England only, and died in England. Scotland, then, was the domicilium originis et forum contractus; but on the other hand England was the forum domicilii and the locus rei sitæ. The question was, whether by the legatee's death in the lifetime of the testatrix the legacy lapsed according to the law of England, or survived to the legatee's representatives according to the law of Scotland. The court decided that, being domiciled in England, it was to be presumed that she intended the law of England to be applied, and that there was not enough in the will to repel that presumption.[2] (a)

[1] Gordon v. Brown, or Brown v. Brown, 3 Hagg. Ecc. 455, note; 4 Wils. & Shaw, 28; ante, s. 479 c.

[2] Anstruther v. Chalmer, 2 Sim. 1; 3 Hagg. Ecc. 455; Yates v. Thomson, 3 Cl. & F. 544, 570; ante, s. 479c.

(a) It has lately been decided in the English Court of Probate and Matrimonial Causes (Crispin v. Doglioni, 9 Jur. N.S. 653), affirmed in the House of Lords (L. R. 1 H. L. 304; and see Partington v. Att'y-Gen., L. R. 4 H. L. 104, 107; Enohin v. Wylie, 10 H. L. C. 1) that the right of succession to personal estate, and who is the person entitled, must be determined by the law of the place of domicil of the intestate; and that the decisions of the courts of that place are decisive upon these questions. Thus where one domiciled through life in Portugal, who died without ever having been married, leaving one natural son, left personal estate in England, it was held that, this son having instituted a suit in Portugal and obtained a decree by the Supreme Court of Lisbon, by which he was declared entitled to the whole movable and immovable property of the deceased father, the English courts would regard that decision, being made upon full hearing of all the parties interested, as conclusive of the right of succession to such personal estate in England.

So where one deceased in Connecticut domiciled there, leaving a will duly executed according to the law of that state, where his principal property was, also left personal estate in New York, which rendered it necessary to take administration there; after the funds within the latter state had been collected, some of the legatees, who had come to reside in that state after the testator's death, claimed that such funds should be there distributed, there being a difference of opinion between the surrogate there and the courts in Connecticut as to the construction of the will, — it was held by the Court of Appeals in New York that the surrogate should have remitted the funds in that state to the courts of Connecticut for distribution. Parsons *v.* Lyman, 20 N. Y. 103.

And in another case in the same court (Moultrie *v.* Hunt, 23 N. Y. 394) it was held that whether a deceased person died intestate or not must be determined by the law of the place where he was domiciled at the time of his death. That is the law which prescribes the requisites to the valid execution of a will of personal estate. Accordingly, where a citizen of South Carolina executed his will in such a manner as to create a valid bequest of personal estate by the law of that state, but not according to the law of New York, into which state he subsequently removed and died, having his domicil in that state, it was held that he died intestate as to personal estate within that jurisdiction.

CHAPTER XIII.

FOREIGN GUARDIANSHIPS AND ADMINISTRATIONS.

492. *Subject of the Chapter.* — The order of our subject next leads us to the consideration of the operation of foreign laws in relation to persons acting in autre droit, such as guardians, tutors, and curators, inter vivos, and executors and administrators, post mortem.

493. *Guardians.* — And first in relation to guardians.[1] By the Roman law, guardianship was of two sorts (1) *Tutela,* (2) *Cura.* The first lasted in males until they arrived at fourteen years of age, and in females until they arrived at twelve years of age, which was called the age of puberty of the sexes respectively. From the time of puberty until they were twenty-five years of age, which was their full majority, they were deemed minors and subject to curatorship. During the first period of tutelage their guardian was called tutor, and they were called pupils; during the second period their guardian was called curator, and they were called minors.[2] In England the guardian performs the offices both of a tutor and a curator under the Roman law.[3] In France the tutorship lasts until the full age of majority.[4]

494. *Questions arising.* — In treating of guardianship, two questions naturally arise : (1) Whether the authority of a guardian over the person of his ward is local, and confined to the place of his domicil, or extends everywhere? (2) Whether the authority of the guardian over the property of his ward is local, or extends everywhere?

---

[1] See 3 Burge, Col. & For. Law, pt. 2, c. 23, s. 5, p. 1001–1014.

[2] 1 Domat, Civil Law, b. 2, tit. 1, p. 260; Halifax, Analysis of Civil Law, c. 9, p. 15, 17, 18; 1 Brown, Civil Law, b. 1, c. 5, p. 129, 130. See also Ersk. Inst. b. 1, tit. 6, s. 1, p. 128.

[3] Halifax, Analysis of Civil Law, c. 9, p. 15, 17, 18; 1 Brown, Civil Law, b. 1, c. 5, p. 129, 130.

[4] 1 Domat, Civil Law, b. 2, tit. 1, p. 261.

495. *Authority over the Person.* — *Boullenois.* — In regard to the first point (the authority of the guardian over the person of his ward), Boullenois mantains that the laws which regulate it are strictly personal; and therefore that the authority extends to the ward in foreign countries, as well as at home, and is of equal validity and right, according to the law of the domicil, in every other place. 'Je mets,' says he, 'au nombre des statuts personnels, ceux qui mettent les enfants sous la puissance de leur père, où de leur tuteur.'[1] From this it would seem to follow that the tutor is to be recognized as fully entitled to assert any claims over the movable property of his ward, and to sue for the debts due to his ward in foreign countries, without having any confirmation of the guardianship by the local authorities.[2]

496. *Other Jurists.* — Merlin expressly holds the same doctrine, asserting that the foreign guardian in such a case is competent to maintain any suit for the debts due to his ward in France and in the Netherlands, without any interposition of the local authorities to confirm the guardianship.[3] 'Il est,' says he, 'de principe, que les procurations revêtues de la forme requise par la loi du lieu où elles se passent, ont leur effet partout. Aussi ne s'est-on jamais avisé de prétendre que le tuteur nommé à un mineur, ou à un interdit, par le juge de son domicile, ne pût agir dans un pays étranger contre les débiteurs d'un ou de l'autre, qu'après avoir fait déclarer le jugement de sa nomination exécutoire dans ce pays.'[4]

497. Vattel lays down a similar doctrine in more comprehensive terms. 'It belongs,' says he, 'to the domestic judge to nominate tutors and guardians for minors and idiots. The law of nations, which has an eye to the common advantage and the good harmony of nations, requires therefore that such nomination of a tutor or guardian be valid and acknowledged in all countries where the pupil may have any concerns.'[5] This is also the opinion of Huberus, as we have already seen;[6] and it is stoutly maintained by Hertius. After having stated the rule,

---

[1] 1 Boullenois, obs. 4, p. 51; Id. p. 68; ante, s. 57; 2 Boullenois, obs. 39, p. 320, 330.

[2] 3 Burge, Col. & For. Law, pt. 2, c. 23, s. 5, p. 1002, 1003.

[3] Merlin, Répert. Absens, c. 3, art. 3, p. 37; Id. Faillité, s. 2, n. 2, art. 9, 10, s. 2, p. 412. See also Id. Autorisation Maritale, s. 10, art. 2; ante, s. 53, 54.

[4] Merlin, Répert. Faillité, s. 2, n. 2, art. 10, p. 414; ante, s. 53, 54.

[5] Vattel, b. 2, c. 9, s. 85.　　　　　　[6] Ante, s. 60.

he adds : ' Ratio hujus regulæ est evidens. Persona enim subditi qua talis nemini alii est subjecta, quam summo imperanti, cui se submisit. Unde fit, ut leges, quæ personæ qualitatem sive characterem impuniunt comitari personam soleant, ubicunque etiam locorum versetur, tametsi in aliam civitatem migraverit, veluti si quis, magis infamis, vel prodigus declaretur.[1] Hinc tutor,' says he, ' datus in loco domicilii, etiam bona alibi sita administrat.' He applies this rule however solely to personal rights and personal incapacities, rights of property and power over movables. For in respect to immovables, he adds this important qualification: ' Quoniam ipsi patemur, si externa civitas circa bona immobilia aliquid directe disposuit, eam legem servari oportere.'[2] Stockmans holds a broader opinion. ' Tutor etiam pupilli a prætore auctoritatem et administrationem suam extra territoriam prætoris, et in bona ubicunque locorum sita exercet.'[3] Indeed this same doctrine is commonly asserted by all those foreign jurists who give to personal laws an ubiquity of operation.[4]

498. On the other hand there are jurists who maintain a different opinion. Paul Voet denies that laws respecting either per-

[1] 1 Hertii Opera, de Collis. Leg. s. 4, n. 8, p. 123, 124, ed. 1737; Id. p. 175; ed. 1716; ante, s. 51.

[2] Ibid.

[3] Stockman. Decis. 125, n. 6, p. 262. Dumoulin is thought to hold the same opinion; but it may well be doubted if it admits of that interpretation. Post, s. 502 a; Molin. Opera, tom. 3, Com. ad Cod. 1, 1, 1, Conclus. de Stat. p. 556, ed. 1681. Matthæus, who has also been cited on the same side, certainly does not hold the opinion. His language is: Sed etsi silentio suo quodammodo approbare videatur curatorem a judice domicilii datum, vix tamen est, ut curator illa prædia alibi sita proscribere ac vendere possit, sine speciali permissu ejus judicis, in cujus territoria sita sunt. Sic enim et tutor hodie a judice domicilii datur; nec tamen universorum negotiorum et bonorum administrationem consequitur, nisi cesset judex ejus territorii, in quo prædia sita sunt. Matthæus, de Auctionibus, lib. 1, c. 7, n. 10, p. 39. See also 3 Burge, Col. & For. Law, pt. 2, c. 23, s. 5, p. 1002, 1003. He says: ' The appointment of tutor or guardian, committees or curators, so far as it confers the care and custody of the person of the minor or lunatic, could not consistently with the principles of international jurisprudence be made by any other judicial tribunal but that of the country to which the minor or lunatic was by his residence subject. According to the opinion of foreign jurists every judicial tribunal is bound to recognize this appointment. They consider that the law which places the minor or lunatic sub tutela or sub cura is a personal law, affecting the status of the person, and that the relation of tutor and ward which it has constituted continues to exist notwithstanding the persons may have resorted to any other country.'

[4] 3 Burge, Col. & For. Law, pt. 2, c. 23, s. 5, p. 1004, 1005.

sons or property have, in the sense of the civil jurisprudence, any extra-territorial authority, and lays down, among others, the following rules: (1) That a personal statute does not affect the person beyond the territory of his domicil, so that he is not to be reputed such without the territory as he was within; (2) That a personal statute accompanies the person everywhere, in regard to property within the territory of the government where the person has his domicil, and to which he is subjected.[1] He adds that he makes no distinction, in this respect, whether the statute be in rem or in personam; or whether it purports to extend to property situate in a foreign territory or not, directly or indirectly; for the same rule applies in each case. 'Quia nullum statutum, sive in rem, sive in personam, si de ratione juris civilis sermo instituatur sese extendit ultra statuentis territorium.'[2] He qualifies his doctrine however by admitting that movables are always deemed to be in the place of the domicil of the party, and are therefore governed by the laws thereof.[3] John Voet, as we have seen, maintains a similar opinion in the broadest and most unqualified terms.[4]

499. *English and American Opinions.* —It would seem from Morrison's Case[5] that the House of Lords deemed the authority of an English guardian sufficient to institute a suit for the personal property of his ward in Scotland, upon the ground that the administration of his personal estate, granted by the usual authority where he resided, must be taken to be everywhere of equal force with a voluntary assignment by himself. The courts of Scotland had unequivocally decided the other way. Whether this decision has since been acted upon in England does not distinctly appear.[6] It has certainly not received any sanction in America, in the states acting under the jurisprudence of the common law. The rights and powers of guardians are considered as strictly local, and not as entitling them to exercise any authority over the person or personal property of their wards in other states, upon the same general reasoning and

---

[1] P. Voet, de Stat. s. 4, c. 2, n. 6, p. 123, ed. 1716; Id. p. 137, ed. 1661.
[2] Id. n. 7, p. 124, ed. 1716; Id. p. 138, ed. 1661; ante, s. 51 b, 52.
[3] Ante, s. 52, 377.   [4] Ante, s. 54 a.
[5] Cited in 4 T. R. 140, and 1 H. Bl. 677, 682.
[6] See Beattie v. Johnstone, 1 Ph. 17; 10 Cl. & F. 42, where the point is ruled the other way.

policy which have circumscribed the rights and ithorities of executors and administrators.[1] (a)

500. *Authority over Property.* — In regard to the other point, whether guardians appointed in foreign countries have any authority over the property of their wards situate in other countries, foreign jurists are generally, although not universally, of opinion [2] in respect to movable property, that, since it is deemed to be in the domicil of the owner, the law of the domicil is to govern, and the rights and powers of the guardian, tutor, or curator over it ought to be admitted to prevail everywhere to the same extent as they are acknowledged by the law of the domicil.[3] But in respect to immovable property, foreign jurists as generally, although not universally, maintain the doctrine (whatever may be

[1] Morrell *v.* Dickey, 1 Johns. Ch. (N. Y.) 153; Kraft *v.* Wickey, 4 Gill & J. (Md.) 332.

[2] See Muhlenbruch, Doctr. Pand. lib. 1, pt. 1, s. 72, p. 167, 168.

[3] Ante, s. 495–498; 3 Burge, Col. & For. Law, pt. 2, c. 23, s. 5, p. 1010, 1611.

(a) See Hoyt *v.* Sprague, 103 U. S. 631; Woodworth *v.* Spring, 4 Allen (Mass.) 324. But though a foreign guardian has no absolute rights as such in a foreign jurisdiction, the fact that he is such is entitled to great weight in the courts of another state, when called upon to determine, in their discretion, to whose custody a minor child shall be committed; and if it appears for the best interests of the child that he should be under the care and custody of a guardian appointed in a foreign state, the court may so decree, even though another guardian has been appointed in the state where the minor subsequently is found. Woodworth *v.* Spring, 4 Allen (Mass.) 324. And see Johnstone *v.* Beattie, 10 Cl. & F. 42, 113, 145; Stuart *v.* Moore, 4 Law Times, N.S. 382; 9 H. L. C. 463; 4 Macqueen, 1. And the same principle was recently acted upon in England. Nugent *v.* Vetzera, L. R. 2 Eq. 704. Although in a prior case, where an infant was taken from America to England, where her property was situated, by a paternal aunt with whom she resided, both parents being dead, the Lord Chancellor refused to order her to be delivered to a maternal aunt, who had also been appointed her guardian in America: being of opinion that as the minor was also a British subject, though born in America, he had no authority to send her out of the realm. Dawson *v.* Jay, 3 D. M. & G. 764. See this case explained in Stuart *v.* Bute, 9 H. L. C. 440. Johnstone *v.* Beattie, 10 Cl. & F. 42, was much criticised in the important case of the Bute Guardianship. Stuart *v.* Moore, 4 Macqueen, 1. And it was there declared that all that it decided was, that the status of guardian not being a status recognized by the law of England, unless constituted in that country, it was not a matter of course to appoint a foreign guardian to be the English guardian, but only a matter to be taken into consideration in that country. Upon the jurisdiction to appoint a guardian see In re Hubbard, 82 N. Y. 90; Johnstone *v.* Beattie, 10 Cl. & F. 42.

the rule as to movable property), that the rights and authority of guardians are circumscribed by the laws of the territory of their appointment, and do not extend to other countries where the immovable property is situated. In other words, the laws rei sitæ are to govern; and a guardian in one country can claim nothing in another, except in the form and manner, and under the regulations, prescribed by the local law. Burgundus states the doctrine with great clearness. Speaking of the capacity and incapacity of minors, he says : ' Proinde confitendum est, si aliquid circa rem alterare minor velit, ut puta, alienandi vel hypothecandi facultatem exigere, ibi sane veniam impetrari debere, ubi bona sunt sita.[1] Nam et Constitutio Diocletiani in alienatione manifeste requirit decretum præsidis ejus provinciæ, in quo prædium minoris est situm.' He then adds: ' Nec immerito Felinus scripsit, si facienda est dispensatio respectu rei, non ejus episcopi esse erit, cui persona subjecta est, sed ad eum spectare cui res supponitur.' He says that a different reason is given by others. 'Cujus rei rationem alii tradunt quia per ejusmodi dispensationem alteratur, et reinstatur natura ipsius beneficia et non persona.'[2] He then states a qualification of the doctrine in cases where the venia ætatis is obtained, saying : ' Ergo, e contra, si venia ætatis in hoc duntaxat impetretur, ut actus personales minor celebrare et peragere possit, veluti bonorum suorum administrationem consequi, contractus et obligationes inire, sane hoc casu postulare debebit a judice domicilii, cui in personas plenum jus est attributum.'[3] But whether it exists or not is immaterial, as Burgundus in another passage speaks directly on the present point. ' Unde fere obtinuit, ut judex domicilii, ubi et mobilia, rationesque et instrumenta reperiuntur, tutelam solus deferat. Sed non aliter universorum bonorum administrationem consequitur, quam si supersedente judice situs, solus ille constituatur.'[4] This however is a qualification by no means generally conceded or admissible.

500 a. *Foreign Jurists.* — We have already seen that Hertius and Matthæus and Paul Voet and John Voet hold the opinion that the guardian has not, by virtue of his appointment in the place of the domicil of his ward, any rights or authorities over the immovable property of his ward in a foreign country.[5] Paul

---

[1] Burgundus, tract. 1, n. 12, p. 23,   [2] Ibid. n. 13.
[3] Ibid. n. 14, p. 24; 1 Boullenois, obs. 9, p. 150; Id. obs. 6, p. 129.
[4] Burgundus, tract. 2, n. 18, p. 69.   [5] Ante, s. 497, 498.

Voet in another place adds : ' Verum a contractibus proprie sic dictis, me conferam ad quasi contractus, et quidem tutelæ vel curatelæ. Ubi sequentia examinanda. Quid si pupillo dandus sit tutor, illene dabit, ubi pupillus domicilium habet, an ubi bona pupilli immobilia sita sunt ? Respondeo ; Quamvis regulariter ab illo magistratu detur tutor, ubi pupillus domicilium habet, ubi parentes habitarunt ; etiam qui dat tutorem, eum primario personæ, non rei dedisse, censeatur ; adeoque is, qui simpliciter datus est, ad res omnes etiam in diversis provinciis sitas, datus intelligatur ; Id quod plerumque jure Romano obtinebat, quo diversarum provinciarum magistratus, uni suberant imperatori. Ne tamen videatur judex domicilii quid extra territorium fecisse, non præjudicabit judici loci, ubi nonnulla pupillaria bona sita, quin et tutorem pupillo ratione illorum bonorum, scilicet immobilium, ibidem recte dederit. Unde etiam si de prædiis minorum alienandis contentio ; si quidem in alia sita sint Provincia, tutius egerit tutor, qui datus est in loco domicilii, si decretum ab utroque judice curet interponi, et domicilii, pupilli, et rei sitæ.'[1] Even those jurists who contend that permission ought to be given by the local judge to such a guardian to administer such foreign immovable property, at the same time concede that, without such permission, the guardian cannot exercise any rights or authorities over it.[2] John Voet says : ' Non autem in loco originis vel situs rerum pupillarium, sed tantum in loco domicilii pupillaris tutores a loci illius camera pupillari aut magistratu creari, moris est ; qui hoc ipso dati intelliguntur universo pupilli patrimonio, ubicunque existenti. Quod tamen ex comitate magis, quam juris rigore sustinetur ; cum in casu, quo pupillus immobilia habet sita in eo loco, qui non subest eidem magistratui supremo, cui pupillus subest ratione domicilii, magistratus loci, in quo sita immobilia, rebus in suo territorio existentibus peculiarem posset tutorem dare.'[3]

501. Boullenois, after stating that in France the principal object of guardianship is not so much the custody of the person, as

[1] P. Voet, de Statut. s. 9, c. 2, n. 17; Id. n. 19, p. 270, 271, ed. 1715; Id. p. 329–331, ed. 1661.

[2] 3 Burge, Col. & For. Law, pt. 2, c. 23, p. 1004–1007.

[3] J. Voet, ad Pand. 26, 5, s. 5, tom. 2, p. 188; Id. 1, 4, pt. 2, s. 3, 7, tom. 1, p. 89, 40. See also other foreign jurists cited, 3 Burge, Col. & For. Law, c. 23, p. 1005–1007.

of property, adds that it has in view the administration and direction of property (biens), and that the rights which it grants are all real rights. ' La garde consiste, ou en droits de propriété, ou en droits d'usufruit ; et il n'y a rien de plus réel, que ces sortes de droits. Par conséquent elle ne peut être régie, que par la loi de la situation. C'est cette loi, qui donne, ou ne donne pas; qui appelle certaines personnes, ou qui ne les appelle pas. De là il semble qu'il faudroit nécessairement en conclure que chaque coutume qui admet la garde, et où il y a des biens, a seule le droit de déférer la garde, à qui bon lui semble ; et qu'il n'y a que ceux, à qui elle la défère, qui puissent être gardiens, quelque domicile d'ailleurs, qu'aient ceux qui tombent en garde et ceux qui sont appelés à la garde.' [1] He admits that there are jurists who assert the contrary.[2]

502. Hertius, as we have seen, asserts the same doctrine as to immovable property.[3] Froland arrays himself on the side of those who assert the reality of the laws which respect guardianship, distinguishing however as to the quality of persons entitled, the right of possessing the property, and the formalities accompanying it.[4]

502 a. Dumoulin holds the opinion that the lex rei sitæ is to govern in all such cases, and explains himself with unusual fulness on the point. ' Aut statutum agit in personam, et tunc non includit exteros, sive habiliter, sive inhabiliter personam, unde si statuto hujus urbis cavetur, quod contractus facti per minorem 25 annis non valeant sine consensu suorum propinquorum, et authoritate judicis, non intelligitur, nisi de subditis suæ jurisdictioni per text. l. 1, in fin. ff. de curat. et tutor. dat ab his. ' Unde minor dicti loci non poterit etiam extra locum prædia, in eo territorio sita, locare sine dicta solemnitate : Sed bene extra locum prædia alibi sita. Quia in quantum agit in personam, restringitur ad suos subditos ; et in quantum agit in res, restringitur ad sitas intra suum territorium. Exterus autem minor annis poterit etiam de sitis intra locum dicti statuti etiam inter locum illum disponere:

[1] 2 Boullenois, obs. 29, p. 320–322, 339, 340; 3 Burge, Col. & For. Law, pt. 2, c. 23, p. 1001, 1002.
[2] Ibid.
[3] Ante, s. 497; 1 Hertii Opera, de Collis. Leg. 4, n. 8, p. 123, 124, ed. 1737; Id. p. 175, ed. 1716.
[4] 1 Froland, Mém. c. 16, p. 717, 749, 750, 752.

Quamvis is, qui datus est tutor vel curator a suo competenti judice, sit inhabilitatus propter tutelam, et curam ubique locorum pro bonis ubicumque sitis. Quia non est in vim statuti solius, sed in vim juris communis, et per passivam interpretationem legis, quæ locum habet ubique.'[1] Everhardus holds the same opinion. 'Ubi ratione diversarum jurisdictionum et territoriorum diversi judices dant tutores, et unus non intromittat se de territorio alterius; semper enim inspicienda est consuetudo loci, ubi res sunt sitæ, maxime quoad immobilia.'[2]

503. *Scotch Law.* — Lord Kames lays down the Scottish doctrine to be, that it is of no importance in what place curators of minors are chosen; and accordingly a choice made in England of curators, whether English or Scotch, will be held effectual in Scotland. He admits that the powers of a guardian of a lunatic in England are limited, extending only to his person, and not to his estate; or rather, that different guardians are, or may be, appointed by the Court of Chancery for each. But the authority of any guardian or curator, however appointed, in a foreign country, is not understood by him to extend to any real estate in Scotland.[3]

504. *Common Law.* — *Immovables.* — There is no question whatsoever, that according to the doctrine of common law, the rights of foreign guardians are not admitted over immovable property situate in other countries. Those rights are deemed to be strictly territorial, and are not recognized as having any influence upon such property in other countries, whose systems of jurisprudence embrace different regulations, and require different duties and arrangements.[4] No one has ever supposed that a guardian, appointed in any one state of this Union, had any right to receive the profits, or to assume the possession, of the real estate, of his ward in any other state, without having received a due appointment from the proper tribunals of the state where it is situate. The case falls within the well-known principle that rights to real property can

---

[1] Molin. Opera, tom. 3, ad Cod. 1, 1, 1, Conclus. de Statut. p. 556, ed. 1681; ante, s. 497, note. See also Rodenburg, de Divers. Statut. tit. 2, c. 5, n. 16; 2 Boullenois, Appx. p. 47–51.

[2] Everhard. Consil. 185, n. 3, p. 406.

[3] 2 Kames, Eq. b. 3, c. 8, s. 1, p. 325; Id. s. 4, p. 348.

[4] See 3 Burge, Col. & For. Law, pt. 2, c. 23, s. 5, p. 1009–1011.

be acquired, changed, and lost only according to the law rei sitæ.[1] (a)

504 a. *Movables.* — The same rule is applied by the common law to movable property, and has been fully recognized both in England and in America. No foreign guardian can virtute officii exercise any rights or powers or functions over the movable property of his ward which is situated in a different state or country from that in which he has obtained his letters of guardianship. (b) But he must obtain new letters of guardianship from the local tribunals, authorized to grant the same, before he can exercise any rights, powers, or functions over the same. Few decisions upon the point are to be found in the English or American authorities, probably because the principle has always been taken to be unquestionable, founded upon the close analogy of the case of foreign executors and administrators.[2] (c)

505. *Change of the Ward's Domicil.* — Whether a guardian has authority to change the domicil of his ward from one country to another, seeing that it may have a most important operation as to the succession to his movable property in case of his death, is a matter which has been much discussed. In favor of the affirmative there are some distinguished foreign jurists, among whom we may enumerate Bynkershoek, Bretonnier, Rodenburg, and John Voet. Bynkershoek says: 'Posse tutorem pupilli sui domicilium mutare, perinde ut potest parens superstes, nescio quisquam serio dubitaverit, si successionis legitimæ causa non versetur; nam si hæc versetur, multa disputatio est. Sed an hæc quoque valebunt, si superstes parens vel tutor domicilium

[1] Ante, s. 424; 3 Burge, Col. & For. Law, pt. 2, c. 23, s. 5, p. 1005, 1006, 1009, 1010.

[2] 3 Burge, Col. & For. Law, pt. 2, c. 23, s. 5, p. 1011; Id. p. 1010; ante, s. 499; Morrell v. Dickey, 1 Johns. Ch. (N. Y.) 153; Kraft v. Wickey, 4 Gill & J. (Md.) 332, 340, 341; 4 Cowen, 529, note; post, s. 512, 513. But Mr. Chancellor Walworth seems to have thought otherwise in McNamara v. Dwyer, 7 Paige (N. Y.) 239, 241.

(a) But see McClelland v. McClelland, 7 Baxter (Tenn.) 210; Hickman v. Dudley, 2 Lea (Tenn.) 375.

(b) But see Ross v. Southwestern R. Co., 53 Ga. 514.

(c) Under what circumstances a foreign guardian may be preferred over one of the forum, see the suggestion in In re Rice, 42 Mich. 528, where a habeas corpus was applied for by the foreign guardian and refused. See also Townsend v. Kendall, 4 Minn. 412; Douglas v. Caldwell, 6 Jones Eq. (N. C.) 20; Nugent v. Vetzera, L. R. 2 Eq. 704.

minoris transferat, ut ejus intestati mortui alia sit successio quam ante fuit?' He proceeds then to discuss the question, and comes to the conclusion that he may. 'Sic puto. Scio impuberem, vel minorem proprio marte non recte domicilium suum mutare; sed quid ni non posset, qui eum repræsentat, et quid ni non posset cum omni effectu, nisi qua lex sit, quæ impediat?'[1] Rodenburg says; ' Quæramus et illud quod frequentioris est incursionis; Hollandus major viginti, minor viginti quinque annis transfert domicilium Ultrajectum, ubi vigesimo anno tutela vel cura finitur. Quid dicemus preventurum illum suam in tutelam? Respondi ex facto consultus minori hodie constituendi domicilii, facultatem non esse, tutori esse; qui ut contrahere, ita et domicilium potest constituere, quod collocetur illud per contractum, de quo mox latius. Proinde in proposita mihi specie, cum mater, quæ tutrix esset, mutato a morte viri domicilio, Ultrajectum concessisset, ibique infans adolevisset: dixi ex Ultrajectinis legibus æstimandos perfectæ ætatis annos; dummodo fraus absit, aut præjudicium tertii, extra quod vix est ut non dixeris tutori, maxime matri locum ad habitandum, pupillumque educandum, elegendi jus esse, illudque ipsum dubii veriti Batavi jurisconsulti tutori agnato auctores fuerunt, ut stipularetur a matre illa, cum cogitaret ex Hollandia concedere Trajectum, ne ea res infantis adspectu ullo modo domicilii mutationem induceret; quamquam fateor, si quid hoc ad rem pertinet, posita hac sententia, in potestate tutoris fore, tutela semet ocius exuere, nisi tum potius super fraude quærendum foret.'[2] John Voet says: 'Plane, si etiamnum minorennis sit, patre vel matre vidua domicilium mutante, filium etiam videri mutasse, si et ipse translatus sit, nec ex prioris sed novi domicilii, a patre matreve recenter constituti, jure censeri in dubio debere, rationis est. Utut enim haud difficulter admittendum sit, minorennem non magis posse domicilium mutare, quam contrahendo se obligare: tamen quemadmodum contrahere auctore tutore permissum ei est, ita et domicilium cum patre matreve, tanquam tutelæ ejus aut saltem educationi præposita, tutoribus cæteris non contradicentibus, mutare nihil vetat: nisi ex circumstantiis manifestum esset, talem domicilii pupillaris translationem in fraudem proximo-

---

[1] Bynkers. Quest. Privat. Juris. lib. 1, c. 16, p. 174-186, ed. 1744.

[2] Rodenburg, de Div. Stat. tit. 2, c. 1, s. 6; 2 Boullenois, Appx. p. 57, 58.

rum, spem successionis ex prioris domicilii lege habentium, factam esse.'[1]

505 *a*. Bynkershoek thinks it impracticable to make any such exception of cases of fraud from the intrinsic difficulty of ascertaining what circumstances shall constitute evidence of a fraudulent change of domicil.[2] Burgundus seems to hold with Bartolus, that the domicil of the guardian is also the domicil of the minor. 'Pupilli ipsi sibi constituere domicilium non possunt. Bartolus autem ibi sensit habere domicilium, ubi cum tutoribus, sive aliter habitaverint. Quæ sententia ita demum mihi vera videtur, nisi in academiam studiorum causa, vel alio profecti, remanendi animo ibi non steterint. Qui veniam ætatis impetravit, et proprie negotiationi commodisque subservit, ipse sibi minor domicilium instruere potest. Uxor ibi censetur habere domicilium, ubi maritus habitat. Legitima tori separatione facta, ipsa sibi domicilium instruet.'[3]

505 *b*. Boullenois has spoken with so little clearness and precision on this subject, that it is not very easy to say, with entire exactness, what is his opinion. From the best examination which I have been able to make of his various discussions of this subject in his different works, he seems to have thought: (1) That the law of the actual domicil of the parents of a minor constituted the rule to regulate the succession to the minor, if he died during his minority, although it was not the domicil of his birth, but was acquired by his parents afterwards. (2) That the like rule did not apply to the case of a minor under tutelage; and that his guardian could not by a change of domicil change the succession to the property of the minor. (3) That hence if a minor, following the change of domicil of his parents, should die, his movable estate would be governed by the law of succession of the new domicil, if there was no fraud in the removal. (4) But that there was no reason why a minor might not be reputed domiciled in the domicil of his guardian, so far as the law of that domicil would confer on him particular faculties or privileges; and that therefore, if the law of the domicil of the guardian would give him the power of making a testament of his movables, he might make one conformable to that law; for it is but just that in such

[1] J. Voet, ad Pand. 5, 1, s. 100, tom. 1, p. 847.
[2] Bynkers. Quest. Jur. Priv. lib. 1, c. 16, p. 182, 188, ed. 1744.
[3] Burgundus, tract. 2, n. 34, p. 80, 81.

a case, a person domiciled there, even although a minor, should be held subject to the real laws, or laws in rem, of the place where he is domiciled without fraud.[1]

[1] Boullenois, Dissert. sur Quest. de la Contrar. des Lois, Quest. 2, p. 59-62; 2 Boullenois, obs. 32, p. 49–53. It may not be unacceptable to give some extracts from Boullenois in this place. He says in his Dissertations: En effet, il y a plusieurs raisons, pour lesquelles le dernier domicile du père doit régler, la succession mobiliaire du fils, lorsqu'il décède en minorité. La première est, que le fils mineur tombant sous la puissance d'autrui, on n'a pas voulu qu'il put dépendre d'un tuteur de changer l'ordre de succéder au mineur en lui faisant changer de domicile; en sorte qu'on n'a pas cru qu'un tuteur dut avoir la liberté de donner ou d'ôter aux héritiers présomptifs. La seconde est, qu'un mineur à raison de sa minorité est toujours présumé grevé et chargé de fidéi-commis envers les héritiers de celui de qui il a reçu les biens qui doivent composer sa succession, et un tuteur ne doit pas avoir le pouvoir de déroger à cette espèce de fidéi-commis. Again he says: Sur le changement de domicile d'un mineur en ce qui touche ses biens, il semble qu'il y auroit quelque considération à faire. Il paroitroit assez convenable que la succession d'un mineur au dessus de la pleine puberté fut réglée par le domicile de ses père et mère. Que dès qu'il est pourvu par mariage, il puisse se choisir tel domicile que bon lui semblera, et que sa succession mobiliaire soit régie par ce domicile. Que le fils mineur en suivant le domicile du père, ou de la mère survivante, sa succession mobiliaire soit pareillement assujettie aux loix de ce nouveau domicile, pourvu que d'ailleurs il n'y ait point de fraude: Que peut faire de mieux un mineur que de continuer de vivre sous l'éducation de celui de ses père et mère que Dieu lui a conservé, et dès qu'il y a prudence et justice dans cette conduite, ce nouveau domicile devient une demeure juste et légitime pour le mineur, dont la succession mobiliaire doit suivre le sort. Que le fils mineur qui fait trafic de marchandises et qui pour ce, s'est choisi un domicile soit pareillement en ce qui touche ses biens mobiliers, assujetti à la loi du lieu qui a été le centre de sa fortune, et cela paroit indispensable quand le bien du mineur est un bien d'industrie. Il n'y a pas d'inconvénient qu'un mineur soit réputé domicilié au domicile de son tuteur, quant aux facultez particulières que la loi de ce domicile peut lui donner; c'est pourquoi si par la loi du domicile de son tuteur il a faculté de tester de ses meubles il pourra tester conformément à cette loi. Il est juste dans ce cas qu'un domicilié, même mineur, subisse les loix pures réelles du lieu où il est domicilié sans fraude. Mais quant à son état de majeur, ou de mineur on ne sçauroit le faire dépendre que de la loi de son origine, par les raisons qui ont été cy-devant alléguées. Boullenois, Diss. de la Contrar. des Lois, quest. 2, p. 59, 61, 62. In his larger Treatise, he says: Au surplus, ce que nous disons ici pour le cas de la succession mobiliaire ab intestat, doit-il avoir lieu pour le cas d'un testament? S'il s'agissoit, par exemple, de savoir si le mineur incapable de tester par la loi de son domicile de droit, le pourroit en vertu de la loi de son domicile de fait. L'auteur des Observations sur Henrys, observe loco citato, que si des enfants mineurs sont mises sous la tutelle d'un Lyonnois, ils pourront faire un testament, lorsqu'ils seront parvenus à la puberté, parce que les mineurs suivent, à cet égard, le domicile de leur tuteur. Il dit qu'il l'a ainsi décidé en consultation avec M. Severt, pour le testament du Servieres, fait à l'âge de dix-huit ans. Son père s'étoit marié et établi à Paris: après son décès et celui de sa femme, ses enfants, qui étoient en bas âge, fu-

505 c. On the other hand, Mornac, Christinæus, Bouhier, and Pothier maintain the opinion, in unequivocal terms, that the domicil of a minor, so far as it regards his succession to his estate, cannot be changed by his guardian. Mornac says : ' Quæsitum est, mortuo impubere, de cujus bonis mobilibus agitur, quod spectari debeat illius domicilium, utrum patris et matris, an tutoris, apud quem defunctus est; atque id, quia locus domicilii parentum, et locus domicilii tutoris contrarias, quoad successiones mobilium, diversasque consuetudines ferant. Videbatur nonnullis constituendum domicilium in ædibus tutoris, ut qui patrem refer-

rent mis sous la tutelle, de Charles Groflier, leur oncle paternel ; domicilié en Lyonnois. Le sieur Servieres fils avant que de partir pour l'armée, ou il fut tué, fit son testament au profit d'une de ses sœurs: il fut contesté par une autre sœur, et la décision fut pour le testament. M. le P. Bouhier, c. 21, n. 4, n'adopte pas cette décision, et j'avoue qu'elle n'est pas sans difficulté. En effet, puisque la loi détermine le domicile du mineur, par le domicile du père, je parle, d'un mineur non établi, pourquoi lui donner deux domiciles, l'un pour régler sa succession mobiliaire, et l'autre pour régler sa capacité personnelle de tester? Il n'y a, comme nous venons de le dire, que le domicile de la personne qui puisse rendre capable celui qui est incapable ; et puisque le domicile du mineur est fixé au domicile du père, comment celui de fait, qu'il peut avoir partout ailleurs, peut-il affecter sa personne, préférablement à son domicile de droit qui est nécessairement, selon la loi, son vrai domicile ? D'ailleurs un testament apporte toujours un changement dans la succession légale du testateur, et la loi du domicile de droit qu'a le mineur, ne lui permet pas de disposer de ses biens, et de changer rien dans sa succession. Mais pour le soutien de la décision de MM. Severt et Bretonnier, deux savants consultants, ne peut-on pas répondre que le mineur est dans son devoir, quand il demeure avec son tuteur qui est chargé de son éducation, qu'il y demeure nécessairement et sans fraude ? A la bonne heure que le domicile de son père règle sa succession ab intestat; c'est l'intérêt des héritiers qui l'a voulu ainsi, et c'est pour cela qu'il retient le domicile de son père. Mais si le mariage, si l'émancipation permettent à un mineur de changer de domicile, comme en convient M. Bouhier lui-même, et que dans ce cas, le mineur puisse tester conformément à la loi du domicile qu'il s'est choisi, pourquoi ne veut-on pas pareille chose dans le cas où le mineur passe, par nécessité, et sans fraude, dans le domicile de son tuteur ? Il est vrai que dans le cas du mariage et de l'émancipation, la succession mobiliaire de ce mineur se réglera par la loi de son domicile de choix, et que je n'en dirai pas de même par rapport à un mineur qui n'est ni marié ni émancipé; mais ce que je ne dirai pas pour le cas de la succession ab intestat, parce qu'il y a une jurisprudence formée à cet égard, je puis le dire pour le cas du testament, parce que la loi n'a rien décidé là-dessus, et qu'il semble juste de laisser à un mineur, que la mort prévient, une capacité que lui donne la loi où il demeure, actuellement, sans fraude. Néanmoins le premier avis me paroit le meilleur; un mineur hors le domicile de son père, avec son tuteur, habite avec lui; mais il n'est pas proprement domicilié avec lui; il séjourne en attendant sa majorité; c'est un plaideur qui attend là que le temps lui fasse gagner son procès. 2 Boullenois, obs. 32, p. 51--53; ante, s. 44, note 2, p. 44.

ret. Prævaluit vero eorum sententia, qui domicilium minoris præsertim eo casu in loco originis, id est, in ædibus paternis ac maternis collocandum dicerent. Cum enim domicilium quatuor modis contrahi soleat, natura, ac origine, item voluntate, ac concilio, deinde conventioue, aut ex necessitate muneris. Solum ex his naturale domicilium minori superest, locus scilicet, in quo ipse creverit, parentesque defecerint ; absurdumque aliud fuerit affingere minori in cæteris, quod ipse per ætatem non habeat illigendi nempe domicilii consilium. Imo et præstaretur ansa interdum tutoribus fraudandi veros mobilium minoris intereuntis hæredes transferentibus scilicet domicilium in loca, quibus successura sibi viderent ex patriis moribus, intereunte valetudinario minore desideria.'[1] Christinæus adopts the very language of Mornac on this subject.[2] Bouhier is equally direct and positive ; holding that the minor retains the domicil of his parents, and that it cannot be changed by his guardian. He says that the inviolable rule of the law in Burgundy is, that the domicil of minors, in respect to the succession to their property, cannot be changed by their guardians during their minority ; and he reasons out the doctrine at large.[3] Pothier takes a distinction between the change of the domicil of a parent and the change of domicil of a guardian ; and holds that in the former case, if a change is made without fraud, the minor follows the domicil of his parents and of the survivor. But in the case of a guardian no such effect follows ; for the minor is no part of the family of the guardian, but is like a stranger there, and only for a time (ad tempus).[4]

[1] Mornacci, obs. ad Cod. lib. 3, tit. 20, tom. 3, p. 558, ed. 1721.
[2] Christin. Decis. 176, tom. 2, p. 204.
[3] Bouhier, Cout. de Bourg. c. 21, s. 3, p. 383; Id. c. 23, s. 160–167, p. 441, 452.
[4] Pothier, Coutume d'Orléans, Introd. n. 17. He uses there the following language: ' ll nous suffit de dire, que les mineurs ne composent pas la famille de leur tuteur, comme les enfans composent la famille de leur père: ils sont dans la maison de leur tuteur comme dans une maison étrangère; ils y sont ad tempus, pour le temps que doit durer la tutelle; par conséquent le domicile de leur tuteur n'est pas leur vrai domicile, et ils ne peuvent être cénsés en avoir d'autre que le domicile paternel, jusqu'à ce qu'ils soient devenus en âge de s'en établir un eux-mêmes par leur propre choix, et qu'ils l'aient effectivement établi. Il n'en est pas de même de la mère: la puissance paternélle étant, dans notre droit, différent en cela du droit romain, commune au père et à la mère, la mère, après la mort de son mari, succède aux droits et à la qualité de chef de la famille, qu'avoit son mari vis-à-vis de leurs enfans: son domicile, quelque part qu'elle juge de la transférer sans fraude, doit donc être celui de

506. *Change of Domicil of Minors.* — The same question has occurred in England; and it was on that occasion held that a guardian may change the domicil of his ward, so as to affect the right of succession, if it is done bona fide and without fraud.[1] (a) In that case the father, a native of England, died intestate, domiciled in Guernsey, leaving a widow, and infant children by her, and also by a former wife. The widow, after his death, was appointed guardian of her own children, and, in conjunction with the guardian of the children of the first marriage, sold their estate in Guernsey, and invested the amount in the English funds, and afterwards removed to England with the children. On the death of some of the children under age, the question arose, whether their shares were distributable by the law of England, or by that of Guernsey; and it was decided by the Master of the Rolls, Sir William Grant, that it was to be by the law of England. On that occasion the learned judge said: ' Here the question is, whether, after the death of the father, children remaining under the care of the mother follow the domicil which she may acquire, or retain that which their father had at his death, until they are capable of gaining one by acts of their own. The weight of authority is certainly in favor of the former proposition. It has the sanction both of Voet and Bynkershoek; the former however qualifying it by a condition that the domicil shall not have been changed for the fraudulent purpose of obtaining an advantage by altering the rule of succession. Pothier, whose au-

ses enfans, jusqu'à ce qu'ils aient pu s'en choisir un, qui leur soit propre. Il y auroit fraude, s'il ne paroissoit aucune raison de sa translation de domicile, que celle de se procurer des advantages dans les successions mobiliaires de ses enfans. Les enfans suivent le domicile que leur mère s'établit sans fraude, lorsque ce domicile lui est propre, et que, demeurant en viduité, elle conserve la qualité de chef de famille; mais lorsqu'elle se remarie, quoiqu'elle acquière le domicile de son second mari en la famille duquel elle passe, ce domicile de son second mari ne sera pas celui de ses enfans, qui ne passent pas comme elle en la famille de leur beau-père; C'est pourquoi ils sont censés continuer d'avoir leur domicile au lieu où l'avoit leur mère avant que de se remarier, comme ils séroient censés le conserver, si elle étoit morte.'

[1] Potinger *v.* Wightman, 3 Mer. 67; Robertson on Personal Succession, 197-202.

(a) It should be observed that in this case it was the *mother* that was held to have the power to change the domicil of her minor children after the father's death. 3 Mer. 67; Johnstone *v.* Beattie, 10 Cl. & F. 42, 138; ante, s. 46, note.

either case might be onerous, as well as profitable, the law allowed the heir, whether he were so by testament or by intestacy, to renounce the inheritance if he pleased ; or he might accept it with the benefit of an inventory, the effect of which was to exonerate the heir from any further liability than the amount of the assets or property inventoried.[1] These explanations are important in order fully to understand the reasonings of foreign jurists, and to apply them to the present subject ; for the civil-law distinctions everywhere pervade the jurisprudence of continental Europe.

508. *Heirs by the Roman Law.* — It will be at once seen that the executor under the common law in many respects corresponds with the testamentary heir of the civil law, and that the administrator in many respects corresponds with the heir by intestacy. The principal distinction between them which is here important to be considered is, that executors and administrators have no right except to the personal estate of the deceased ; whereas the Roman heir was entitled to administer both the real estate and personal estate ; and all the assets were treated as of the same nature, without any distinction of equitable assets or of legal assets.[2]

509. *Immovables.* — From what has already been said, the heir, whether testamentary or by intestacy, of immovable property, can take only according to the lex loci rei ; or, in other words, he is not admissible as heir, so as to administer the estate in any foreign country, unless he is duly qualified according to the principles, rules, and forms of the local law.[3] In this respect he does not differ, either in regard to rights or to responsibilities, from an heir or devisee chargeable at the common law or by statute with the bond debts of his ancestor or testator. It is for the same reason that a power to sell immovable property, given to an executor, cannot be executed, unless upon due probate of the will in the place where the property is situate, and showing that it may be

frequently get the name of executors, because it is their office to execute the last will of the deceased.' See id. b. 3, tit. 9, s. 1, 2, 26.

[1] 1 Domat, b. 1, tit. 1, s. 4, n. 3, 4, p. 593.
[2] 1 Brown, Civil & Adm. Law, s. 344, note.
[3] See 2 Kames, Eq. b. 3, c. 8, s. 3, p. 332; Vattel, b. 2, c. 8, s. 109–111; 1 Boullenois, obs. 17, p. 242; Id. Prin. Gén. 87, p. 9; Lewis *v.* McFarland, 9 Cranch, 151.

lawfully done by the lex loci rei sitæ.[1] And if the party claims, not under a power, but as a devisee, in trust to sell it for the payment of debts, it is also necessary to have a like probate of the will. But it is not necessary in the latter case to take out letters of administration, although the devise be in trust to the party by the description of executor; for in such case he takes as devisee and not as executor, and his title is under the will, and not under the letters testamentary.[2]

510. *Movables.* — But in regard to movable estate a like rule does not necessarily prevail in foreign countries governed by a jurisprudence which is drawn from or modelled upon the civil law; for movables being treated as having no situs, and to be governed by the law of the domicil of the testator or intestate, the title of the heir, taking its effect directly from that law, is, or at least may consistently be, held to carry the right to such property, wherever it may be locally situated in the same manner as the title would or might pass by an assignment by the owner by an act inter vivos.[3]

511. *Scotch Law.* — Lord Kames seems to take a distinction between the case of a testamentary heir and that of an heir by intestacy, asserting that the nomination of an executor (hæres de mobilibus, or hæres fiduciarius[4]) by the testator in his testament, as to his movables, is effectual all the world over, jure gentium, and will be sustained in Scotland; whereas letters of administration in a foreign country are strictly territorial, and when granted in a foreign country are not recognized in Scotland unless they are confirmed there by a proper judicial proceeding.[5] It may be so; but Erskine lays it down as clear law, that in Scotland neither executors nor administrators, foreign or domestic, are entitled to administer the estate of the deceased, until they have been duly confirmed by the competent judge.[6] What perhaps Lord Kames meant to say was, that the title of executor was a good title, jure gentium, and when it was established in the manner and by the process prescribed by the law of

---

[1] Wills *v.* Cowper, 2 Hamm. (Ohio) 124.
[2] Lewis *v.* McFarland, 9 Cranch, 151.
[3] 2 Kames, Eq. b. 3, c. 8, s. 4.
[4] Ersk. Inst. b. 3, tit. 9, s. 2, 26.
[5] 2 Kames, Eq. b. 3, c. 8, s. 3; Id. s. 4, p. 347, 348.
[6] Ersk. Inst. b. 1, tit. 9, s. 27, 29. See Robertson on Succession, p. 263-273.

the place where it was sought to be exercised, it ought to be held of universal obligation. And so it probably is in all civilized nations, except such (if any such there now are), as adopt the Droit d'aubaine, and confiscate the movable property of all foreigners dying, and leaving such property within their territories.

512. *Title of Executors and Administrators.* — In regard to the title of executors and administrators, derived from a grant of administration in the country of the domicil of the deceased, it is to be considered that that title cannot de jure extend, as a matter of right, beyond the territory of the government which grants it, and the movable property therein. (*a*) As to movable property situated in foreign countries, the title, if acknowledged at all, is acknowledged ex comitate ; and of course it is subject to be controlled or modified, as every nation may think proper, with reference to its own institutions, and its own policy, and the rights of its own subjects. (*b*) And here the rule to which reference has been so often made applies with great strength, that no nation is under any obligation to enforce foreign laws prejudicial to its own rights, or to those of its own subjects. Persons domiciled and dying in one country are often deeply indebted to foreign creditors living in other countries, where there are personal assets of the deceased. In such cases it would be a great hardship upon such creditors to allow the original executor or administrator to withdraw those funds from the foreign country without the payment of such debts, and thus to leave the creditors to seek their remedy in the domicil of the original executor or administrator, and perhaps there to meet with obstructions and inequalities in the enforcement of their own rights from the peculiarities of the local law.

513. *Suits by and against them.* — It has hence become a general doctrine of the common law, recognized both in England and America, that no suit can be brought or maintained by any

(*a*) See Moore *v*. Field, 42 Penn. St. 472; Dial *v*. Gary, 14 S. C. 573; Sheldon *v*. Rice, 30 Mich. 296; Cabanne *v*. Skinker, 56 Mo. 357; Apperson *v*. Bolton, 29 Ark. 418. So of foreign receivers. City Ins. Co. *v*. Commercial Bank, 68 Ill. 348; Rutherford *v*. Clark, 4 Bush (Ky.) 27; Succession of De Roffignac, 21 La. An. 364; McNamara *v*. McNamara, 62 Ga. 200.

(*b*) An executor, duly qualified in England, of the estate of one domiciled abroad, may sell leasehold property in England like an ordinary English executor, though he could not do so in the country of the executor. Hood *v*. Barrington, L. R. 6 Eq. 218.

executor or administrator, or against any executor or administrator, in his official capacity, in the courts of any other country except that from which he derives his authority to act in virtue of the probate and letters testamentary, or the letters of administration there granted to him.[1] (a) But if he desires to maintain any suit in any foreign country, he must obtain new letters of administration, and give new security according to the general rules of law prescribed in that country, before the suit is brought.[2] (b)

[1] Bond v. Graham, 1 Hare, 482.

[2] Preston v. Melville, 8 Cl. & F. 1, 12; Whyte v. Rose, 3 Q. B. 498, 507; Spratt v. Harris, 4 Hagg. Ecc. 405; Price v. Dewhurst, 4 My. & Cr. 76. The authorities to this point are now exceedingly numerous and entirely conclusive.

(a) See Silver v. Stein, 21 L. J. Ch. 312; 9 Eng. L. and Eq. 216; Vermilya v. Beatty, 6 Barb. 431; Smith v. Webb, 1 Barb. 231; Swearingen v. Morris, 14 Ohio St. 429; Bell v. Nichols, 38 Ala. 678; Gilman v. Gilman, 54 Me. 453; Beatty v. Mason, 30 Md. 409; Baldwin's Appeal, 81 Penn. St. 441; Sherman v. Page, 85 N. Y. 123; Freeman's Appeal, 68 Penn. St. 151; Magraw v. Irwin, 87 Penn. St. 139; Vickery v. Beir, 16 Mich. 50; In re Ames, 52 Mo. 290; Hedenberg v. Hedenberg, 46 Conn. 30 (explaining Marcy v. Marcy, 32 Conn. 308); Burbank v. Payne, 17 La. An. 15; Wright v. Gilbert, 51 Md. 146; Barton v. Higgins, 41 Md. 539; Fogle v. Schaeffer, 23 Minn. 304; Klein v. French, 57 Miss. 662; Jefferson v. Glover, 46 Miss. 510; Riley v. Moseley, 44 Miss. 37; Carr v. Lowe, 7 Heisk. 84; Simpson v. Foster, 46 Tex. 618; Davis v. Phillips, 32 Tex. 566; Clopton v. Booker, 27 Ark. 482; Hatchett v. Berney, 65 Ala. 39. But see Bell v. Nichols, 38 Ala. 678; Manly v. Turnipseed, 37 Ala. 522; Johnson v. Jackson, 56 Ga. 326.

An important principle laid down in Newton v. Bronson, 13 N. Y. 587, should however be noticed here. It was there declared that the authority of an executor was not conferred by the Probate Court, but by the will. He is donee of a power, and though he must qualify as executor, still, when he has performed that condition, he acts, in conveying property, as devisee of a power created by the testator; and hence he may, if the will authorize, convey lands in another state. See also Conklin v. Egerton, 21 Wend. 430, 436.

It should be noticed that the change of domicil of an administrator or executor to another state annuls his official authority within the state of his appointment. Whittaker v. Wright, 35 Ark. 511.

Of course the courts of one state cannot remove an executor or administrator of another. Tillman v. Walkup, 7 S. C. 60.

(b) See Gilman v. Gilman, 54 Me. 453; Beatty v. Mason, 30 Md. 409; Succession of Butler, 30 La. An. 887; Sloan v. Frothingham, 65 Ala. 593; Williams v. Jones, 14 Bush (Ky.) 418; Lawrence v. Lawrence, 3 Barb. Ch. 71; Noonan v. Bradley, 9 Wall. 394; Mackey v. Coxe, 18 How. 100; Parsons v. Lyman, 20 N. Y. 103; Newton v. Bronson, 13 N. Y. 587; Conner v. Paul, 12 Bush (Ky.) 144. But see Crawford v. Graves, 15 La. An. 243; Brownlee v. Lockwood, 20 N. J. Eq. 239; Bowman v. Carr, 5 Lea (Tenn.) 571.

So, on the other hand, if a creditor wishes a suit to be brought in any foreign country, in order to reach the effects of a deceased testator or intestate, situated therein, it will be necessary that letters of administration should be there taken out in due form according to the local law, before the suit can be maintained; for the executor or administrator appointed in another country is not suable there, and has no positive right to or authority over those assets, neither is he responsible therefor. The right of a foreign executor or administrator to take out such new administration is

See Lee v. Moore, Palmer, 163; Tourton v. Flower, 3 P. Wms. 369, 370; Thorne v. Watkins, 2 Ves. 35; Attorney-General v. Cockerell, 1 Price, 179; Burn v. Cole, Ambl. 416; Lowe v. Farlie, 2 Madd. 101; 1 Hagg. Ecc. 93, 239; Mitford's Eq. Pl. 177 (4th ed.); Fenwick v. Sears, 1 Cranch, 259; Dixon v. Ramsay, 3 Cranch, 319, 323; Kerr v. Moon, 9 Wheat. 565; Armstrong v. Lear, 12 Wheat. 169; Thompson v. Wilson, 2 N. H. 291; Dickinson v. Mc-Craw, 4 Rand. (Va.) 158; Glenn v. Smith, 2 Gill & J. (Md.) 493; Stearns v. Burnham, 5 Greenl. (Me.) 261; Goodwin v. Jones, 3 Mass. 514; Borden v. Borden, 5 Mass. 67; Gaylord v. Stevens, 11 Mass. 256; Langdon v. Potter, 11 Mass. 313; Dangerfield v. Thruston, 8 Mart. N.S. (La.) 232; Riley v. Riley, 3 Day (Conn.) 74; Champlin v. Tilley, id. 303; Trecothick v. Austin, 4 Mason, 16, 32; Ex parte Picquet, 5 Pick. (Mass.) 65; Holmes v. Remsen, 20 Johns. (N. Y.) 229, 265; Smith v. Union Bank, 5 Pet. 518; Campbell v. Tousey, 7 Cowen (N. Y.) 64; Logan v. Fairlie, 2 Sim. & Stu. 285; Atty v. Bouwens, 4 M. & W. 171, 192, 193; Tyler v. Bell, 1 Keen, 826, 829; 2 My. & Cr. 89, 109. On this occasion Lord Cottenham said: ' That an estate cannot be administered in the absence of a personal representative, and that such personal representative must obtain his right to represent the estate from the ecclesiastical court in this country, has, I believe, never before been doubted. The cases of Tourton v. Flower, 3 P. Wms. 369; Atkins v. Smith, 2 Atk. 63; Swift v. Swift, 1 Ball & B. 326; Attorney-General v. Cockerell, 1 Price, 165; Lowe v. Farlie, 2 Madd. 101; Logan v. Fairlie, 2 Sim. & Stu. 284, all proceed upon this, that the courts in this country, for the security of property, will not administer the property of a person deceased in the absence of a person authorized to represent the estate; and that they look only to the judgment of the ecclesiastical courts in this country, in granting probate or letters of administration, to ascertain who are so authorized; and it is immaterial what ecclesiastical court in this country has granted probate or letters of administration, provided the state of the property was such as to give it jurisdiction.' But see Anderson v. Caunter, 2 My. & K. 763, which seems not a sound authority. Lord Cottenham. in Tyler v. Bell, 2 My. & Cr. 110, manifestly disapproved of it. 3 Burge, Col. & For. Law, pt. 2, c. 23, s. 5, p. 1010–1012. Mr. Chancellor Walworth, in McNamara v. Dwyer, 7 Paige (N. Y.) 239, 241, held that, although a foreign administrator could not sue, he might be sued in another state for an account of the assets received under the foreign administration. Can such a distinction be maintained? The Supreme Court of the United States, in Vaughan v. Northup, 15 Pet. 1, decided against it. S. P. Bond v. Graham, 1 Hare, 482; Price v. Dewhurst, 4 My. & Cr. 76, 80. See Preston v. Melville, 8 Cl. & F. 12, 14.

usually admitted as a matter of course, unless some special reason intervene to vary or control it (*a*) and the new administration is treated as merely ancillary or auxiliary to the original foreign administration, so far as regards the collection of the effects and the proper distribution of them.[1] (*b*)   Still however the new administration is made subservient to the rights of creditors, legatees, and distributees, who are resident within the country where it is granted, (*c*) and the residuum is transmissible to the foreign country only when a final account has been settled in the proper tribunal where the new administration is granted, upon the equitable principles adopted by its own law in the application and distribution of the assets found there.[2] (*d*)

---

[1] Harvey *v.* Richards, 1 Mason, 381; Stevens *v.* Gaylord, 11 Mass. 256; Case of Miller's Estate, 3 Rawle (Penn.) 312.

[2] Preston *v.* Melville, 8 Cl. & F. 12, 14.   See Harvey *v.* Richards, 1 Mason, 381; Dawes *v.* Boylston, 9 Mass. 337; Boston *v.* Boylston, 2 Mass. 384; Richards *v.* Dutch, 8 Mass. 506; Dawes *v.* Head, 3 Pick. (Mass.) 128; Hooker *v.* Olmstead, 6 Pick. (Mass.) 481; Davis *v.* Estey, 8 Pick. (Mass.) 475; Jennison *v.* Hapgood, 10 Pick. (Mass.) 77; Stevens *v.* Gaylord, 11 Mass. 256; Case of Miller's Estate, 3 Rawle (Pa.) 312; Gravillon *v.* Richards, 13 La. 293. Many complicated questions may grow out of original and ancillary administrations, some of which have been stated in the cases of Harvey *v.* Richards, 1 Mason, 381, and Dawes *v.* Head, 3 Pick. (Mass.) 128.   The following extract from the opinion of Mr. Chief Justice Parker in the latter case deserves an attentive perusal.   The question there arose, how assets under an ancillary administra-

(*a*) See Williams *v.* Jones, 14 Bush (Ky.)418; Woodruff *v* Schultz, 49 Iowa, 430; Goodman *v.* Winter, 64 Ala. 410.

(*b*) But see Carr *v.* Lowe, 7 Heisk. (Tenn.) 84; Carroll *v.* McPike, 53 Miss. 569.

(*c*) 'If a citizen of another country dies indebted to citizens of this country, and owns personal property here, we appropriate it to the payment of creditors in the order prescribed by our law, and not that of the domicil.' Carson *v.* Oates, 64 N. C. 115; Moye *v.* May, 8 Ired. (N. C.) Eq. 131. See also Fellows *v.* Lewis, 65 Ala. 343.

(*d*) See Succession of Cordeviolle, 24 La. An. 319; Barry's Appeal, 88 Penn. St. 131; Fretwell *v.* McLemore, 52 Ala. 124; Moses *v.* Hart, 25 Gratt. (Va.) 795; Wright *v.* Phillips, 56 Ala. 69; Miner *v.* Austin, 45 Iowa, 221; Findley *v.* Gidney, 75 N. C. 395; Par-

ker's Appeal, 61 Penn. St. 478. Though the same person conducts both the principal and the ancillary administration, he will not be liable on his ancillary administration bond for proceeds of land sold in the foreign state, though the money is brought into the state of the forum. State *v.* Osborn, 71 Mo. 86. The court of the State of ancillary administration may in its own discretion make distribution to those who, by the law of the decedent's domicil, are entitled. Partee *v.* Kortrecht, 54 Miss. 66.

A note given to a man to secure a debt in the state of his domicil belongs on his death to his representative there, and not to another representative of the estate in a foreign jurisdiction where the decedent may have happened to die. McIlvoy *v.* Alsop, 45 Miss. 365.

513 a. *English Administration.* — In England ' it is well established that, in the case of a British subject dying intestate in

tion were to be disposed of in cases of insolvency, and of debts due to creditors belonging to the same country as the deceased debtor. The Chief Justice, after disposing of these particulars, said: ' Thus this action is determined without touching the questions upon which it was supposed it would turn, which are of a novel and delicate nature, and, though often glanced at, do not appear to have been decided, either in this or any other state of the Union. We wish to avoid anything which may be construed into a conclusive adjudication, and yet are of opinion that it will be useful to throw out for consideration the results of our reasonings upon this subject. If the technical difficulties upon which this cause has been decided had not occurred, but the estate had been rendered insolvent here, and a decree of distribution for a proportion had been issued, or if the debt of Lenox and Sheafe had been ascertained by a·judgment, and the pleadings to a suit on the bond had been the same in that case as now, the question would be, whether the funds collected here by an ancillary administration should be appropriated to the payment of such debts as might be regularly proved here, notwithstanding it was made to appear that the whole estate was insufficient to pay all the debts, and that the effects here were wanted by the executor abroad to enable him duly to administer the estate. It has been contended that this should be done, because the administrator has given bond here in the same manner as if this were the original administration, and because the statute which authorizes this administration requires that the judge of probate shall settle the estate in the same way and manner as he would if the original will had been proved here. With respect to the bond, it will be saved by a faithful administration of the estate according to law; and with respect to the settlement by the judge of probate, this must be understood to authorize him to require the administrator to account, and that the due course of proceedings in the probate office shall be observed. It certainly cannot be construed to mean that in all cases a final settlement of the estate shall take place here; if it did, then if there were no debts here, and none to claim as legatees or next of kin, it would be necessary for all such to prove their right and receive their distributive shares here, notwithstanding the settlement must in such case be made according to the laws of the country where the deceased had his domicil. But we think in such case it would be very clear that the assets collected here should be remitted to the foreign executor or administrator; for it seems to be a well-settled principle that the distribution is to be made according to the laws of the country where the deceased was domiciled; and if any part is to be retained for distribution here, it will be only by virtue of some exception to this general rule, or because the parties interested seek their remedy here; in which case it might be within the legal discretion of the court here to cause distribution, or to remit, according to the circumstances and condition of the estate. An exception to the general rule grows out of the duty of every government and its courts to protect its own citizens in the enjoyment of their property and the recovery of their debts, so far as this may be done without violating the equal rights of creditors living in a foreign country. In relation to the effects found within our jurisdiction and collected by the aid of our laws, a regard to the rights and interests of our citizens requires that those effects should be made answerable for debts due

the colonies or in foreign countries, a prerogative administration
extends to all the personal property of the intestate, wherever

to them, in a just proportion to the whole estate of the deceased, and all the
claims upon it, whatever they may be. In the several cases which have come
before this court, where the legal character and effects of an ancillary administration have been considered, the intimations have been strong that the administrator here shall be held to pay the debts due to our citizens. The cases,
Richards v. Dutch, Dawes v. Boylston, Selectmen of Boston v. Boylston, and
Stevens v. Gaylord, are of this character. In all these cases however we must
suppose the court had reference to a solvent estate, and in such case there seems
to be no question of the correctness of the principle; for it would be but an idle
show of courtesy to order the proceeds of an estate to be sent to a foreign country, the province of Bengal for instance, and oblige our citizens to go or send
there for their debts, when no possible prejudice could arise to the estate or those
interested in it, by causing them to be paid here ; and possibly the same remark
may be applicable to legacies payable to legatees living here, unless the circumstances of the estate should require the funds to be sent abroad. Whether citizens of other states, claiming payment of their debts of the administrator here,
are to be put upon the same footing with citizens of Massachusetts, by virtue of
the privileges and immunities secured to them by the constitution of the United
States, is a point which we do not now decide. But without doubt the courts
of the United States, having full equity powers, would enforce payment upon
the principles above stated, where there is no suggestion of insolvency of the
estate. There would be no doubt, we think, that payment of debts by the
administrator here, after sufficient proof that they were due, and an allowance
of his account therefor by the Probate Court with proper notice, would be
faithful administration according to the condition of his bond, and would be a
proper way of accounting to the principal administrator abroad. In regard to
effects thus collected within our jurisdiction, belonging to an insolvent estate
of a deceased person having his domicil abroad, the question may be more
difficult. We cannot think however that in any civilized country advantage
ought to be taken of the accidental circumstance of property being found within
its territory, which may be reduced to possession by the aid of its courts and
laws, to sequester the whole for the use of its own subjects or citizens, where it
shall be known that all the estate and effects of the deceased are insufficient to
pay his just debts. Such a doctrine would be derogatory to the character of
any government. Under the English bankrupt system, foreigners as well as
subjects may prove their debts, and share in the distribution. Without doubt,
in other foreign countries, where there is a cessio bonorum, or other process
relating to bankrupt estates, the same just principle is adopted. It was so
under our bankrupt law, while that was in force, and no reason can be suggested why so honest and just a principle should not be applied in the case of
insolvent estates of deceased persons. It is always practised upon in regard to
persons dying within our jurisdiction, having had their domicil here; that is,
creditors of all countries have the same rights as our own citizens to file their
claims and share in the distribution. There cannot be then a right in any
one or more of our citizens, who may happen to be creditors, to seize the whole
of the effects which may be found here, or claim an appropriation of them to
the payment of their debts, in exclusion of foreign creditors. It is said this
is no more than what may be done by virtue of our attachment law, in regard

situate at the time of his death, whether in Great Britain, or in the colonies, or in any country abroad ; and, indeed, from the late case

to the property of a living debtor who is insolvent. But the justness of that law is very questionable, and its application ought not to be extended to cases, by analogy, which do not come within its express provisions. What then is to be done with the effects collected here belonging to an insolvent estate in a foreign country ? Shall they be sent home in order to be appropriated according to the laws of that country ? This would often work great injustice, and always great inconvenience, to our own citizens, whose debts might not be large enough to bear the expense of proving and collecting them abroad; and in countries where there is no provision for an equal distribution, the pursuit of them might be wholly fruitless; as in Great Britain, our citizens, whose debts would generally be upon simple contract, such as bills of exchange, promissory notes, accounts, &c., would be postponed to creditors by judgment, bond, &c., and even to other debts upon simple contract which might be preferred by the executor or administrator. It would seem too great a stretch of courtesy to require the effects to be sent home, and our citizens to pursue them under such disadvantages. What then shall be done to avoid, on the one hand, the injustice of taking the whole funds for the use of our citizens to the prejudice of foreigners, when the estate is insolvent, and, on the other, the equal injustice and greater inconvenience of compelling our own citizens to seek satisfaction of their debts in distant countries ? The proper course would undoubtedly be to retain the funds here for a pro rata distribution, according to the laws of our state, among the citizens thereof, having regard to all the assets, either in the hands of the principal administrator, or of the administrator here, and having regard also to the whole of the debts which by the laws of either country are payable out of those assets, disregarding any fanciful preference which may be given to one species of debt over another, considering the funds here as applicable to the payment of the just proportion due to our own citizens; and if there be any residue, it should be remitted to the principal administrator, to be dealt with according to the laws of his own country, the subjects of that country, if there be any injustice or inequality in the payment or distribution, being bound to submit to its laws. The only objection which can be made to this mode of adjusting an ancillary administration upon an insolvent estate is the difficulty and delay of executing it. The difficulty would not be greater than in settling many other complicated affairs, where many persons have interests of different kinds in the same funds. The powers of a court of chancery are competent to embrace and settle all cases of that nature, even if the powers of the Court of Probate are not sufficiently extensive; which however is not certain. The administrator here should be held to show the condition of the estate abroad, the amount of property subject to debts, and the amount of debts, and a distribution could be made upon perfectly fair and equitable principles. The delay would undoubtedly be considerable, but this would not be so great an evil as either sending our citizens abroad upon a forlorn hope to seek for the fragments of an insolvent estate, or paying the whole of their debts out of the property without regard to the claims of foreign creditors. And if the Probate Court has not sufficient power to make such an equitable adjustment, a bill in equity, in which the administrator here should be the principal respondent, would probably produce the desired result, and then time and opportunity could be given to make known the whole condition

of Scarth *v.* Bishop of London, it appears that, where the intestate dies abroad, not having goods in divers dioceses in England, but

of the estate, and all persons interested might be heard before any final decree; in the mean time the administrator could be restrained from remitting the funds until such decree should be passed.' Dawes *v.* Head, 3 Pick. (Mass.) 143–148.

The following extracts are made from the opinion of the court in Harvey *v.* Richards: 'One objection urged against the exercise of the authority of the court is, that, as national comity requires the distribution of the property according to the law of the domicil, the same comity requires that the distribution should be made in the same place. This consequence, however, is not admitted; and it has no necessary connection with the preceding proposition. The rule that distribution shall be according to the law of the domicil of the deceased is not founded merely upon the notion that movables have no situs, and therefore follow the person of the proprietor, even interpreting that maxim in its true sense, that personal property is subject to that law which governs the person of the owner. Nor is it perhaps founded upon the presumed intention of the deceased that all his property should be distributed according to the law of the place of his domicil, with which he is supposed to be best acquainted and satisfied; for the rule will prevail even against the express intention of the deceased, unless the mode in which that intention is expressed would give it legal validity as a will. It seems indeed to have had its origin in a more enlarged policy, founded upon the general convenience and necessities of mankind; and in this view the maxim above stated flows from, rather than guides, the application of that policy. The only reason why any nation gives effect to foreign laws within its own territory is the endless embarrassment which would otherwise be introduced in its own intercourse with foreign nations. The rights of its own citizens would be materially impaired, and in many instances totally extinguished, by a refusal to recognize and sustain the doctrines of foreign law. The case now under consideration is an illustration of the perfect justice and wisdom of this general practice of nations. A person may have movable property and debts in various countries, each of which may have a different system of succession. If the law rei sitæ were generally to prevail, it would be utterly impossible for any such person to know in what manner his property would be distributed at his death, not only from the uncertainty of its situation from its own transitory nature, but from the impracticability of knowing with minute accuracy the law of succession of every country in which it might then happen to be. He would be under the same embarrassment if he attempted to dispose of his property by a testament; for he could never foresee where it would be at his death. Nay, more, it would be in the power of his debtor, by a mere change of his own domicil, to destroy the best digested will; and the accident of a moment might destroy all the anxious provisions of an excellent parent for his whole family. Nor is this all. The nation itself to which the deceased belonged might be seriously affected by the loss of his wealth from a momentary absence, although his true home was in the centre of its own territory. These are great and serious evils, pervading every class of the community, and equally affecting every civilized nation. But in a maritime nation, depending upon its commerce for its glory and its revenue, the mischief would be incalculable. The common and spontaneous consent of nations, therefore, established this rule from the noblest policy, the promotion

only in the diocese of London, administration granted to such
intestate by the Consistory Court of the Bishop of London will be

of general convenience and happiness, and the avoiding of distressing difficulties equally subversive of the public safety and private enterprise of all. It
flowed from the same spirit that dictated judicial obedience to the foreign commissions of the admiralty. Sub mutuæ vicissitudinis obtentu, damus peti-
musque vicissim, is the language of the civilized world on this subject. There
can be no pretence that the same general inconvenience or embarrassment
attends the distribution of foreign effects according to the foreign law by the
tribunals of the country where they are situate. Cases have been already stated
in which great inconvenience would attend the establishment of any rule excluding such distribution. It may be admitted also that there are cases in
which it would be highly convenient to decline the jurisdiction and remit the
parties to the forum domicilii. Where there are no creditors here, and no
heirs or legatees here, but all are resident abroad, there can be no doubt that a
court of equity would direct the remittance of the property upon the application of any competent party. The correct result of these considerations upon
principle would seem to be, that whether the court here ought to decree distribution or remit the property abroad is a matter not of jurisdiction, but of judicial discretion, depending upon the particular circumstances of each case; that
there ought to be no universal rule upon this subject; but that every nation is
bound to lend the aid of its own tribunals for the purpose of enforcing the
rights of all persons having a title to the fund, when such interference will not
be productive of injustice or inconvenience, or conflicting equities. It is further
objected that a rule which is to depend for its application upon the particular
circumstances of each case is too uncertain to be considered a safe guide for
general practice. But this objection affords no solid ground for declining the
jurisdiction, since there is an infinite variety of cases in which no general rule
has been or can be laid down, as to legal or equitable relief in the ordinary controversies before judicial tribunals. In many of these the difficulty is intrinsic
in the subject-matter; and where a general rule cannot easily be extracted,
each case must, and indeed ought, to rest on its own particular circumstances.
The uncertainty, therefore, is neither more nor less than belongs to many other
complicated transactions of human life, where the law administers relief ex
æquo et bono. Another objection, addressed more pointedly to a class of cases
like the present, is the difficulty of settling the accounts of the estate, ascertaining the assets, what debts are sperate, what desperate; and finally ascertaining what is the residue to be distributed, and who are the next of kin
entitled to share. And to add to our embarrassment, we are told that we cannot compel the foreign executor to render any accounts in our courts. I agree
at once that this cannot be done if he is not here; but I utterly deny that the
administrator here cannot be compelled to account to any competent court for
all the assets which he has received under the authority of our laws. And if
the foreign executor chooses to lie by, and refuses to render any account of the
foreign funds in his hands so far as to enable the court here to ascertain
whether the funds are wanted abroad for the payment of debts or legacies or
not, he has no right to complain if the court refuses to remit the assets, and
distributes them among those who may legally claim them. And as to settling
the estate, or ascertaining who are the distributees, there is no more difficulty
than often falls to our lot in many cases arising under the ordinary probate

46

equally effectual.'[1] How far this doctrine is intended to be carried is not perhaps very clearly defined; and certainly, if carried fully out, it may materially impair the general doctrine as to the necessity of local administrations, as well as trench upon the rights of foreign creditors and foreign governments. Is it meant to be said that, if personal property is in a foreign country at the death of the intestate, it may be removed from thence, and administered under a prerogative administration in England, or administered in England without such a removal, and in either case be obligatory upon the foreign government, and pass a perfect title to the property?

514. *Administrator collecting Assets abroad.* — But although an executor or administrator, appointed in one state, is not in virtue of such appointment entitled to sue, nor is he liable to be sued, in his

proceedings. All these objections are, in fact, reasons for declining to exercise the jurisdiction in particular cases, rather than reasons against the existence of the jurisdiction itself. It seems indeed admitted by the learned counsel for the defendant that, if there be no foreign administration, it would be the duty of the court to grant relief upon an administration taken here. Yet every objection already urged would apply with as much force in that as in the present case. The property would be to be distributed according to the foreign law of the deceased's domicil. The same difficulty would exist as to ascertaining the debts and legacies, and the assets and distributees entitled to share. But it is said, in the case now put, the administration here would be the principal administration, whereas in the case at bar it is only an auxiliary or ancillary administration. I have no objection to the use of the terms principal and auxiliary, as indicating a distinction in fact as to the objects of the different administrations; but we should guard ourselves against the conclusion that therefore there is a distinction in law as to the rights of parties. There is no magic in words. Each of these administrations may be properly considered as a principal one, with reference to the limits of its exclusive authority; and each might, under circumstances, justly be deemed an auxiliary administration. If the bulk of the property, and all the heirs and legatees and creditors, were here, and the foreign administration were only to recover a few inconsiderable claims, that would most correctly be denominated a mere auxiliary administration for the beneficial use of the parties here, although the domicil of the testator were abroad. The converse case would of course produce an opposite result. But I am yet to learn what possible difference it can make, in the rights of parties before the court, whether the administration be a principal or an auxiliary administration. They must stand upon the authority of the law to administer or deny relief, under all the circumstances of their case, and not upon a mere technical distinction of very recent origin.' Harvey *v.* Richards, 1 Mason, 381. See also Granvilon *v.* Richards, 13 La. 293. (a)

[1] Whyte *v.* Rose, 3 Q. B. 498, 507; Scarth *v.* Bishop of London, 1 Hagg. Ecc. 625.

(a) Banta *v.* Moore, 2 McCarter (N. J.) 101.

official capacity, in any other state or country; yet there are many other questions which may require consideration, and in which a conflict of laws may arise in different countries. In the first place let us suppose that an executor or administrator should go into a foreign country, and, without there taking out new letters of administration, should there collect property, effects, and debts of his testator or intestate, found or due there; the question might arise, whether he would not thereby, to the extent of his receipt and collection of such assets, be liable to be sued in the courts of that country by any creditor there. Upon general principles it would seem that he would so be liable; and, upon the principles of the common law, he would be liable as an executor de son tort, or person intermeddling with such assets without any rightful authority derived from the local authorities under a new grant of administration there. For it would not lie in his mouth to deny that he had rightfully received such assets; and he could not rightfully receive them except as executor.[1] (a) It would be quite a different question whether the payment of any such debts, or the delivery of any such property or effects to him by the debtors, or by other persons owing or possessing the same, would be a valid payment or discharge of such persons therefrom, or would confer any title to the same upon such executor or administrator, at least against any executor or administrator, subsequently appointed in such foreign state or country, and contesting the right or title.[2] Upon that question there is much room for discussion and doubt, notwithstanding what has been asserted in some of the tribunals acting under the common law.[3] (b) For it is exceedingly clear that the probate grant of letters testamentary or of letters of administration in one country give authority to collect the assets of the testator or intestate only in that country, and do not extend to the collection of assets in foreign countries;

[1] Campbell v. Tousey, 7 Cowen (N. Y.) 64.
[2] Preston v. Melville, 8 Cl. & F. 1, 12, 14.
[3] Doolittle v. Lewis, 7 Johns. Ch. (N. Y.) 45, 49; post, s. 515.

(a) See Hutchins v. State Bank, 12 Met. (Mass.) 421, 425; Mackey v. Coxe, 18 How. 100; Middlebrook v. Merchants' Bank, 3 Abb. App. Dec. (N. Y.) 295; Hedenberg v. Hedenberg. 46 Conn. 30.

(b) See, in support of the validity of such payment, Citizens' Bank v. Sharp, 53 Md. 521, referring to Wilkins v. Ellett, 9 Wall. 740; Williams v. Storrs, 6 Johns. Ch. 353; Rand v. Hubbard, 4 Met. (Mass.) 255: Hutchins v. State Bank, 12 Met. (Mass.) 421.

for that would be to assume an extra-territorial jurisdiction or authority, and to usurp the functions of the foreign local tribunals in those matters.[1] It is no answer to the objection, to say

[1] See Pond v. Makepeace, 2 Met. (Mass.) 114; Preston v. Melville, 8 Cl. & F. 1, 12, 14. See Attorney-General v. Bouwens, 4 M. & W. 171, 190-192. On this occasion Lord Abinger said: ' Whatever may have been the origin of the jurisdiction of the ordinary to grant probate, it is clear that it is a limited jurisdiction, and can be exercised in respect of those effects only which he would have had himself to administer in case of intestacy, and which must therefore have been so situated as that he could have disposed of them in pios usus. As to the locality of many descriptions of effects, household and movable goods, for instance, there never could be any dispute. But to prevent conflicting jurisdictions between different ordinaries, with respect to choses in action and titles to property, it was established as law that judgment debts were assets for the purposes of jurisdiction, where the judgment is recorded; leases, where the land lies; specialty debts, where the instrument happens to be; and simple-contract debts where the debtor resides at the time of the testator's death; and it was also decided that as bills of exchange and promissory notes do not alter the nature of the simple-contract debts, but are merely evidences of title, the debts due on these instruments were assets where the debtor lived, and not where the instrument was found. In truth, with respect to simple-contract debts, the only act of administration that could be performed by the ordinary would be to recover or to receive payment of the debt, and that would be done by him within whose jurisdiction the debtor happened to be. These distinctions being well established, it seems to follow that no ordinary in England could perform any act of administration within his diocese, with respect to debts due from persons resident abroad or with respect to shares or interest in foreign funds payable abroad, and incapable of being transferred here: and therefore no duty would be payable on the probate or letters of administration in respect of such effects. But on the other hand it is clear that the ordinary could administer all chattels within his jurisdiction; and if an instrument is created of a chattel nature, capable of being transferred by acts done here, and sold for money here, there is no reason why the ordinary or his appointee should not administer that species of property. Such an instrument is in effect a salable chattel, and follows the nature of other chattels as to the jurisdiction to grant probate. In this case, assuming that the foreign governments are liable to be sued by the legal holder, there is no conflict of authorities; for their governments are not locally within the jurisdiction, nor can be sued here; and no act of administration can be performed in this country, except in the diocese where the instruments are, which may be dealt with, and the money received by their sale in this country. Let us suppose the case of a person dying abroad, all whose property in England consists of foreign bills of exchange, payable to order, which bills of exchange are well known to be the subject of commerce, and to be usually sold on the Royal Exchange. The only act of administration which his administrator could perform here would be to sell the bills and apply the money to the payment of his debts. In order to make titles to the bills to the vendee, he must have letters of administration; in order to sue in trover for them, if they are improperly withheld from him, he must have letters of administration (for even if there were a foreign administration, it is an established rule that an

that the effects of the testator or intestate are assets wherever they are situated, whether at home or abroad; and that such effects as are in a foreign country at the time of the death of the testator or intestate, although they remain and are wholly administered there by the executor, are equally assets. Doubtless this is true; but the question is not whether they are assets or not, but who is clothed with authority to administer them; and this must be decided by the local jurisdiction where they are situated; for the original administration has no extra-territorial operation.[1] (a)

514 a. *Liability to account at Home.* — In the next place, let us suppose that an executor or administrator, appointed in the state where his testator or intestate died, should go into a foreign country, and should, without taking out new letters of administration, collect assets in such foreign country, and bring them home to the state from which he had received his original letters testamentary or letters of administration; the question might arise, whether, in such a case, he would be liable to account in the courts of the latter state for all the assets which he had so received in the foreign country, in the same way and under the like circumstances as he would be liable to account for them if he had received them in the home state. In other words, whether they would constitute a part of the home assets which he is bound to administer, and for which he is liable to account under the domestic administration according to the domestic laws. It has been said that

administration is necessary in the country where the suit is instituted); and that these letters of administration must be stamped with a duty according to the salable value of the bills; the case of Hunt v. Stevens is an express authority.' See also Doolittle v. Lewis, 7 Johns. Ch. (N. Y.) 45–47; Morrell v. Dickey, 1 Johns. Ch. (N. Y.) 153.

[1] Attorney-General v. Dimond, 1 Cr. & J. 356, 370; ante, s. 513.

(a) By the English law if a married woman becomes entitled to property from a deceased relative, which is situated in England, and she and her husband both die, without any step taken by him to reduce the property into possession during her lifetime, or taking out administration on her estate after her death, their child must take out two administrations, one on his father's and the other on his mother's estate, as being two distinct devolutions of property. And the same course must be pursued if the parents and child are all domiciled in America, although the property when once obtained is to be distributed in America, where the law might not require this double authority of administration. Partington v. Attorney-General, Law. Rep. 4 H. L. 100.

the assets, so received and collected are to be so administered and accounted for as home assets by such executor or administrator. And the doctrine laid down in an ancient case is relied on for this purpose; where it is asserted to have been held by the court that, 'if the executor have goods of the testator in any part of the world, they shall be charged in respect of them; for many merchants and other men who have stocks and goods to a great value beyond sea are indebted here in England; and God forbid that those goods should not be liable to their debts; for otherwise there would be a great defect in our law.'[1] Now this language in its broad import is certainly unmaintainable in our day; for it goes to the extent of making a domestic executor or administrator liable for all assets of the testator or intestate which are locally situate abroad; although, as we have seen, he has not in virtue of the domestic letters of administration any authority to collect them, or to compel payment or delivery thereof to himself.[2] But the circumstances of the case called for no such doctrine. The case was of a testator who died in Ireland, and the defendant, who was his executor, collected and administered in Ireland certain property of the deceased. Afterwards he came to England, and was sued there by a creditor as executor; and the question arose, whether he was liable to the creditor in such suit for the assets collected and received by him in Ireland under the administration there. With reference therefore to the actual facts of the case, the more general question did arise. But according to the doctrine maintained in England in modern times, he was not at all liable to be sued in England as executor, under letters testamentary taken out in Ireland; and a fortiori not for the assets received and administered in Ireland under that appointment.[3] The authority of the case may therefore well be doubted in both of its aspects.[4]

[1] Dowdale's Case, 6 Rep. 47, 48; Cro. Jac. 55; cited and approved also in Evans v. Tatem, 9 Serg. & R. (Penn.) 252, 259.

[2] Ante, s. 314.   [3] Ante, s. 314; post, s. 515.

[4] 'If after such administration shall have been completed, any surplus should remain, and it shall appear that there are trusts to be performed in Scotland, to which it was devoted by Sir Robert Preston, it will be for the Court of Chancery to consider whether such surplus ought or ought not to be paid to the pursuers, for the purpose of being applied in the performance of such trusts; and in considering that question every attention ought to be paid to the authority under which the pursuers have been appointed trustees, and the consent which led to such appointment. It is premature to decide that

514 b. *Liability of a Foreign Administrator.* — Some of the American courts have gone the length of recognizing, to its full extent, the doctrine asserted in this case ; and have held that a foreign executor or administrator coming here, having received assets in the foreign country is liable to be sued here, and to account for such assets, notwithstanding he has taken out no new letters of administration here, nor has the estate been positively settled in the foreign state.[1] (a)   The doctrine asserted in these courts is, that such a foreign executor or administrator is chargeable here, as executor, for all the assets which he still retains in his hands, or which he has expended or disposed of here, unless expended or disposed of here in the due course of administration, whether they were received here or in a foreign country, although he has not taken out any new letters of administration here.[2] There is very great difficulty in supporting these decisions to the extent of making the foreign executor or administrator liable here for assets received by him abroad in his representative character, and brought here by him.   If a foreign executor or administrator cannot sue in his representative character in another state for the assets of the deceased situate there, without new letters of administration, because he derives his authority solely from a foreign government, which has no authority to confer any right upon him, except to collect and receive the assets found within its own territorial jurisdiction, and to which therefore he is properly and directly responsible for the due administration of the assets actually collected and received in such foreign country

point, it being at present unascertained whether there will be any surplus of the personal estate in this country, or what will be the amount of it, and no declaration of right by the Court of Session would be binding upon the Court of Chancery, under whose jurisdiction the property in England is placed by the suits which have been instituted.'   Preston v. Melville, 8 Cl. & F. 14.

[1] Swearingen v. Pendleton, 4 Serg. & R. (Penn.) 389, 392; Evans v. Tatem. 9 Serg. & R. (Penn.) 252, 259; Bryan v. McGee, 2 Wash. C. C. 337; Campbell v. Tousey, 7 Cowen (N. Y.) 64.

[2] Ibid.

(a) See Baker v. Smith, 3 Met. (Ky.) 264; Johnson v. Jackson, 56 Ga. 326; s. c. 34 Ga. 511; Crawford v. Graves, 15 La. An. 243 (that a foreign administrator may sue in Louisiana for property wrongfully brought there); Dillard v. Harris, 2 Tenn. Ch. 196.   The text no longer states the rule in Pennsylvania.   See Magraw v. Irwin, 87 Penn. St. 139; Sayre v. Helme, 61 Penn. St. 299.   As to the cases of Campbell v. Tousey, 7 Cowen (N. Y.) 64, and Marcy v. Marcy, 32 Conn. 308, see Hedenberg v. Hedenberg, 46 Conn. 30, which follows the text.

under its exclusive appointment, it is not easy to perceive how he can be suable in such state for such assets in his hands, received abroad by him under the sanction of the foreign administration, and by the authority of the foreign government, to which he is thus accountable for all such assets. One of the learned courts however which decided the point seems to have taken it for granted that a foreign executor or administrator was of course suable here for all assets found in his hands. ' If a foreign executor,' said the court, ' is liable to be sued here, of which we apprehend there can be no question, he must, from the very nature of the case, prima facie, be responsible for the assets which are shown to have been in his possession within this state.' With great deference, that was the very point to be established by some just reasoning, founded upon the principles of international jurisprudence generally recognized by foreign jurists, or by the uniform established doctrine of the common law on this subject in modern times. It will be found exceedingly difficult to cite any modern authorities at the common law in support of such doctrine,[1] since no authority could be shown which supported it. On the other hand, there are other American authorities which indicate a very different doctrine.[2] The modern English authori-

---

[1] In the cases of Swearingen v. Pendleton, 4 Serg. & R. 389, 392, and Evans v. Tatem, 9 Serg. & R. 252, 259, the Supreme Court of Pennsylvania contented itself with merely affirming the doctrine in Dowdale's Case (6 Coke, 47), without any general reasoning on the subject.

[2] The very recent case of Fay v. Haven, 3 Met. (Mass.) 109, is directly in point. See Boston v. Boylston, 2 Mass. 384: Goodwin v. Jones, 3 Mass. 514; Davis v. Estey, 8 Pick. (Mass.) 475 ; Dawes v. Head, 3 Pick. (Mass.) 128; Doolittle v. Lewis, 7 Johns. Ch. (N. Y.) 45, 47; McRae v. McRae, 11 La. 571. In the case of Boston v. Boylston, 2 Mass. 384, 391, Mr. Justice Sedgwick, in delivering the opinion of the court after adverting to the fact that the testator died in England, and that administration was there granted of his estate to the defendant cum testamento annexo, and that the defendant took out ancillary letters of administration in Massachusetts, where the suit was brought, and in respect whereof he was called upon to account with the plaintiffs for the assets both in England and America, said: ' The judge of probate has, in this case, proceeded, and in all similar cases must proceed, according to the powers which are delegated to him by this statute. He can exercise no other powers. He has granted to the respondent administration on the estate of Thomas Boylston, lying in this government, with the will annexed. All the authority then given to the administrator is over the estate lying in this government. The judge is to settle the said estate. What estate? Clearly I think the estate lying in this government. And it will neither consist with the intention of the legislature nor the purposes of justice, because the administrator

ties are to the same effect. They fully establish the doctrine that, if a foreign executor or administrator brings or transmits property

with the will annexed is here, to proceed upon the fiction that, by his relation to the testator in the same capacity, in England, we ought to consider all the assets possessed by him there as the estate of the testator lying in this government; because the estate by the statute subjected to the control of the Court of Probate, and to be settled by it, was that which was lying here before granting the letters of administration. To that, and to that only, do the words, and as I think, the meaning of the legislature extend. The argument from the inconveniences of admitting the construction for which the counsel for the appellants have contended is strong and irresistible. It may reasonably be presumed that the largest part of the testator's estate lies in the country where the original administration is granted; and that there also is the greatest portion of claims upon it. For what purpose of utility is the property to be transported to a distant region, and those to whom it belongs compelled to follow it for the satisfaction of their demands? The expense and trouble of such a procedure, while wholly unnecessary, could not fail to be considerable. Suppose an English merchant of great property and extensive dealings to have been the testator; suppose this property to be principally in England, but portions of it to be left in several foreign countries, and that the administrator appointed there goes to collect it, and seeks the aid of the foreign governments for that purpose; and they, under pretence of giving this aid, claim an authority of drawing within their jurisdiction all the personal property of the testator, and all those who have demands upon it or are interested in it. All these governments are independent of each other; and what is to establish a right of precedence? The commencement of a prosecution? How is this to be known? How are the other authorities to be controlled? If this is to be the construction, who will become bound for the administrator? By what means can the liability of the administrator and his sureties be known? In terms they only guarantee the settlement of the estate lying within the commonwealth; but in effect, if this construction be admitted, estate lying in every part of the globe. It is, in our opinion, impossible that such could have been the intention of the legislature. There are innumerable other inconveniences which might be, but which it is unnecessary should be, pointed out.' In Goodwin v. Jones, 3 Mass. 514, 519, 520, Mr. Chief Justice Parsons, in delivering the opinion of the court, said: ' When any person, an inhabitant of another state, shall die intestate, but leaving real estate within this commonwealth, if administration should not be granted by some judge of probate of a county in which the estate lies, there would be no legal remedy for the creditors of the deceased to avail themselves of his real estate for the payment of the debts due them. Therefore, to prevent a failure of justice, administration in such case must be granted by some probate court here; and the administrator so appointed will, by virtue of his letters of administration and of the laws, also have the administration of all the goods, chattels, rights, and credits of the intestate, which were within the state. And if a foreign administrator of that intestate should also have the administration of his personal estate here, there would exist two administrators of the same goods of the same intestate, independent of each other, and deriving their authority from different states, a consequence which cannot be admitted. But the granting of administration here cannot divest the foreign administrator of

here, which he has received under the administration abroad, or if he is personally present he is not, either personally or in his representative capacity, liable to a suit here ; nor is such property liable here to creditors; but they must resort for satisfaction to the fo-

any rights already vested in him; and the necessary inference is, that whether administration be or be not granted in this state, an administrator appointed in another state cannot legally claim any interest in the goods of his intestate which are subject to an administration granted in this state. And it is no objection to this reasoning, that debts due to the intestate on simple contract are to be considered as goods situate where he dies. For if the position be admitted, contrary to the authority of Wentworth, in his Executor (page 46), where it is supposed that such debts are bona notabilia where the debtor lives; yet the administrator, if he recover judgment on such contract in this state, may satisfy it by an extent on lands, which certainly in their disposition are exclusively subject to the control of the laws of the commonwealth. We have no particular statute relating to foreign administrators; but the manner in which an executor of a will proved without the state may execute his trust within, is regulated by the statute of 1785, June 19, c. 12. The executor, or any person interested in any will proved without the state, may produce a copy of it, and of the probate under the seal of the foreign court which proved it, before the judge of probate of any county where the testator had real or personal estate whereon the will may operate, and request to have the same filed and recorded, which the judge, after notice and hearing all parties, may order to be done; and he may then take bonds of the executor, or may grant administration cum testamento annexo of the testator's estate lying in this government not administered, and may settle the estate, as in cases where the will has been proved before him. This statute needs no explanation. The executor of a will proved without the state cannot intermeddle with the effects of the testator in the state but with the assent of a judge of probate, to whom he must first give bond. Neither can an administrator with the will annexed intermeddle, unless he is appointed by some judge within the state who has authority to settle the whole estate within his jurisdiction. And it would be inconsistent with the manifest intent of the statute to allow an administrator of an intestate, not an inhabitant or resident within the state at his death, an authority derived from a foreign administration which he could not have under the foreign probate of a will of which he was the executor.' In Doolittle v. Lewis, 7 Johns. Ch. (N. Y.) 45, 47, Mr. Chancellor Kent said: 'It is well settled that a party cannot sue or defend in our courts, as executor or administrator, under the authority of a foreign court of probate. Our courts take no notice of a foreign administration; and before we can recognize the personal representative of the deceased in his representative character, he must be clothed with authority derived from our law. Administration only extends to the assets of the intestate within the state where it was granted; if it were otherwise, the assets might be drawn out of the state, to the great inconvenience of the domestic creditors, and be distributed, perhaps, on very different terms, according to the laws of another jurisdiction. The authorities on this subject were cited by me in the case of Morrell v. Dickey (1 Johns. Ch. (N. Y.) 154); and I presume there is no dispute about the general rule, and the only difficulty lies in the application of it to this particular case.'

rum of the original administration.[1] (*a*)   So where property is remitted by a foreign executor to this country to pay legacies, no suit can be maintained for it, if there is no specific appropriation of it, without an administration taken out here.[2] (*b*)

[1] Currie *v.* Bircham, 1 D. & R. 35; Davis *v.* Estey, 8 Pick. (Mass.) 475; Att.-Gen. *v.* Bouwens, 4 M. & W. 171, 191; Tyler *v.* Bell, 1 Keen, 826, 829; 2 My. & Cr. 89, 109, 110; Att.-Gen *v.* Dimond, 1 Cr. & J. 356, 371; Spratt *v.* Harris, 4 Hagg. Ecc. 408; Att.-Gen. *v.* Hope, 2 Cl. & F. 84, 90, 92; 8 Bligh, 44; 1 C. M. & R. 538.   But see Dowdale's Case, 6 Rep. 47, and Anderson *v.* Caunter, 2 My. & K. 763; Spratt *v.* Harris, 4 Hagg. Ecc. 405, 408; ante, s. 513, 514 *a.*   In Scrimshire *v.* Scrimshire (2 Hagg. Cons. 420), Sir Edward Simpson said: 'If an Englishman makes a will abroad, and makes a foreigner executor, and has no effects in England, and the executor proves the will lawfully abroad, that probate, or sentence of the proper court, establishing the will as to effects there of a man domiciled there, would be a bar to a discovery in chancery of effects abroad.'

[2] Logan *v.* Fairlie, 2 Sim. & Stu. 284.

(*a*) Campbell *v.* Sheldon, 13 Pick. (Mass.) 8; but see Hervey *v.* Fitzpatrick, Kay, 421; Orr Ewing *v.* Orr Ewing, 22 Ch. D. 456 (C. A.); McNamara *v.* Dwyer, 7 Paige (N. Y.) 239; Brown *v.* Knapp, 17 Hun (N. Y.) 160.

(*b*) *Trusts under Foreign Wills.* — A court of equity will enforce the trusts created by a foreign will, if the trustee is within the jurisdiction. Davis *v.* Morriss, 76 Va.   ; 14 Reporter, 286; Bright *v.* Bright, 3 Baxt. (Tenn.) 109, 112, 114. This is simply an application of the general principle, that equity, as it acts in personam, may enforce any equitable right where the person against whom relief is sought is within the jurisdiction. Penn *v.* Lord Baltimore, 1 Ves. 444; 2 Wh. & T. L. C. (5th ed.) 939, 955; Kildare *v.* Eustace, 1 Vern. 419; Massie *v.* Watts, 6 Cranch, 148. 159; Shattuck *v.* Cassidy, 3 Edw. Ch. (N. Y.) 152; Newton *v.* Bronson, 13 N. Y. 587; Vaughan *v.* Barclay, 6 Whart. (Pa.) 392. When a testator bequeaths a fund to a trustee in a foreign country for charitable purposes to be executed in that country, the court of the testator's domicil will direct the transfer of the fund to the trustee selected by the testator, and leave it to the foreign tribunals to enforce the execution of the trust.   Att.-Gen. *v.* Lepine, 2 Swans. 181; Emery *v.* Hill, 1 Russ. 112; Chamberlain *v.* Chamberlain, 43 N. Y. 424, 432; Burbank *v.* Whitney, 24 Pick. (Mass.) 146, 154; Fellows *v* Miner, 119 Mass. 541; Silcox *v.* Harper, 32 Ga. 639; Story, Eq. Jur. s. 1186. In In re Liddiard, 14 Ch. D. 310, where the trusts of an English will were for the benefit of persons resident in Australia, the court appointed as trustees two persons who resided in Australia, and who intended to sell the English investments and invest the money in Australia. See also Bright *v.* Bright, 3 Baxt. (Tenn.) 109. But in Massachusetts, in Campbell *v.* Wallace, 10 Gray, 162, which was followed in Jenkins *v.* Lester, 131 Mass. 355, it was held that the court had no jurisdiction to enforce a trust created by a foreign will which had not been proved in Massachusetts. In these cases the property constituting the trust fund was not in Massachusetts at the testator's decease, nor afterwards until it was received by the trustee; it therefore gave no jurisdiction to grant probate of the will in Massachusetts, and

515. *Voluntary Payment to a Foreign Administrator.*—But although an executor or administrator is not entitled to maintain

no probate granted there could affect that property. The decision in Campbell *v.* Wallace was placed simply upon the ground that the case was covered by the decision of the same court in Campbell *v.* Sheldon, 13 Pick. (Mass.) 8. That case however only decided that a suit could not be brought in Massachusetts against a foreign executor or administrator concerning the administration of the estate. In applying it to the facts of Campbell *v.* Wallace, the court seems to treat the execution of the trusts of the will as if it were a part of the administration of the testator's effects. But when a fund bequeathed to a trustee is received by him, the administration, so far as relates to that fund, is at an end, just as when any other legatee receives his legacy. The trustee takes it with the obligation of applying it according to the trust, and this obligation is one which the beneficiaries may enforce in a court of equity. It is difficult to see any reason why they may not enforce it in any country where the trustee may be, just as they may enforce other equitable rights. It is admitted that they can do so when the trust is created by deed. The title, rights, and obligations of the trustee and of the beneficiaries are precisely the same whether the trust is created by deed or will. In Jenkins *v.* Lester, 131 Mass. p. 357, it is said, as a reason why the trust should not be enforced against the trustee, that ' The trust on which the property is held by her having been created by judicial decree of a court of another state having jurisdiction of the matter, she is accountable in the courts of that state for the due execution of the trust.' The only decree mentioned in the case was the probate of the will. The reason therefore would not apply to a French or German will, for what is called pro-

bate by us is unknown on the continent of Europe, and wills take effect there without it. It seems also hardly correct to say that the trust was created by a judicial decree. The probate was only a decree declaring that the will had been duly proved, and, though the will would not be allowed to have effect without probate, it was the will that gave the property to the trustee and created the trust. Cf. 1 Wms. Ex. (8th ed.) 297; Crusoe *v.* Butler, 36 Miss. 150, 170. But if the trust was created by a judicial decree, that seems to be no reason why the trust should not be enforced by the courts of another state against a trustee within their jurisdiction who has received the trust-fund by virtue of the decree. It is not a recognized principle that courts will not enforce the judgments or decrees of foreign courts. It can make no difference that the trustee is also accountable to the courts of the state where the will was proved. He is not more accountable to those courts than he would be if the trust had been created in that state by deed, unless some special statute makes him so. Certainly it is no part of the jurisdiction of a court of probate to administer the trusts of a will, unless such jurisdiction is specially conferred by statute. The Massachusetts court recognizes that foreign tribunals will administer a charitable trust created by a Massachusetts will and to be executed in the foreign country (Burbank *v.* Whitney, 24 Pick. p. 154), and it would be inferred that the tribunals of Massachusetts would administer a charitable trust to be executed in that state, although it were contained in a foreign will which could not be proved in Massachusetts because there was no property there for it to operate upon. It follows that the same jurisdiction exists in respect of private

a suit in a foreign court, in virtue of his original letters of administration, yet it has been said that, if a debtor chooses voluntarily there to pay him a debt which he may lawfully receive under that administration, the debtor will be discharged. [1] (a) This proposition is, or at least may be, true to the extent in which it is thus guardedly laid down and limited. For if an administration should be taken out on a creditor's estate in the country where both the creditor and debtor resided at the time of his death, there, inasmuch as a debt is properly due in that country, and properly falls within that administration, it may be paid voluntarily by the debtor in another country, if he should afterwards change his domicil to that country, or if he should be found

[1] The proposition is thus guardedly laid down in Stevens v. Gaylord, 11 Mass. 256. But the question may also arise, whether the voluntary payment of a debt by a domestic debtor in a foreign country to a foreign administrator, when there is no domestic administrator appointed, will be a good discharge of the debtor. Debts are due not only in the domicil of the debtor, but in the domicil of the creditor; and indeed, unless a particular place of payment is appointed, they are due and may be demanded anywhere. If a debtor be found in the foreign country where the creditor died, and where an administrator is appointed, he would certainly be suable there, and could not protect himself by a plea that he was liable to pay only to the administrator appointed in the place of his (the debtor's) domicil. Lord Hardwicke, in Thorne v. Watkins (2 Ves. 35), said that all debts follow the person, not of the debtor in respect of the right or property, but of the creditor to whom due. In Doolittle v. Lewis, 7 Johns. Ch. (N. Y.) 49, Mr. Chancellor Kent held that a voluntary payment to a foreign executor or an administrator was a good discharge of the debt. See Shultz v. Pulver, 3 Paige (N. Y.) 182; Hooker v. Olmstead, 6 Pick. (Mass.) 481; Atkyns v. Smith, 2 Atk. 63; Trecothick v. Austin, 4 Mason, 16, 33.

trusts. The existence of such jurisdiction is recognized when the court allows the trust fund to be taken to a foreign country by a trustee residing in that country. A trustee of a will ought not to be able, any more than a trustee of a deed, to escape performance of the trust by leaving the country where it originated and taking the fund with him. It is no answer to say that security might have been required of him. Security can only be required under the provisions of local statutes, which exist in comparatively few places. And if security is taken, there is no principle of law by which the beneficiary must not follow the trust-fund or the trustee, but must look only to the security. A refusal by the foreign tribunals to enforce the trust under such circumstances would seem very like a denial of justice.

As to the appointment of new trustees, see Curtis v. Smith, 60 Barb. (N. Y.) 9; Curtis v. Smith, 6 Blatch. C.C. 537; Chase v. Chase, 2 Allen (Mass.) 101; Dorsey v. Thompson, 37 Md. 25.

(a) A foreign administrator can give a good discharge to a debtor of the decedent in the foreign state, if there are no creditors there or persons entitled as distributees, against an administrator in the foreign state. Wilkins v. Ellett, 9 Wall. 740.

there; and the discharge of the administrator will be held a good discharge everywhere else, although no new administration be taken out; because the right to receive it primarily attached where the original administration was granted. Thus, for example, if an intestate should die in Ireland, leaving a bond debt there due by a debtor, residing there at the time of his death, that bond debt would be bona notabilia there, and a payment afterwards by the debtor made in England to such administrator would or might be a good discharge, notwithstanding no administration was taken out in England.[1]

515 a. There is however (as has been already stated[2]) much reason to doubt whether the doctrine be maintainable to the extent which the proposition has been sometimes understood to justify; that is to say, so as to apply it to a debt due by a debtor, who at the death of the creditor is actually domiciled in and owes the debt in the foreign country, where no administration is taken out. Suppose an administration should afterwards be granted in a foreign country; would it be any bar to an action brought by the foreign administrator against the debtor for the same debt, that the debtor had already paid it to another administrator, who had no right to demand it in virtue of his original administration, and who therefore might properly be deemed a stranger to the debt? Suppose a contest to arise between the original administrator and the foreign administrator in relation to the administration of the debts, so received as assets of the deceased, could the original administrator retain it against the will of the foreign administrator; or thereby subject it to a different application in the course of administration and marshalling assets from that which would otherwise exist? It seems difficult to answer these questions in the affirmative, without shaking some of the best-established principles of international law on this subject.[3] (a)

---

[1] Huthwaite v. Phaire, 1 Man. & G. 159, and particularly what is said by Lord Chief Justice Tindal in page 162.

[2] Ante, s. 514. See Preston v. Melville, 8 Cl. & F. 1, 14.

[3] See Currie v. Bircham, 1 D. & R. 35; Tyler v. Bell, 1 Keen, 826; 2 My. & Cr. 89, 109, 110; Attorney-General v. Dimond, 1 Cr. & J. 356, 370; contra, Anderson v. Caunter, 2 My. & K. 763. But the latter case seems overruled. Ante, s. 513; post, s. 518-521, 525; Huthwaite v. Phaire, 1 Man. & G. 159, 164, 165.

(a) See McNamara v. McNamara, 62 Ga. 200.

516. *Title acquired by the Lex Situs.* — And here it may be necessary to attend to a distinction important in its nature and consequences. If a foreign administrator has, in virtue of his administration, reduced the personal property of the deceased, there situated, into his own possession, so that he has acquired the legal title thereto according to the laws of that country ; if that property should afterwards be found in another country, or be carried away and converted there against his will, he may maintain a suit for it there in his own name and right personally, without taking out new letters of administration; for he is, to all intents and purposes, the legal owner thereof, although he is so in the character of trustee for other persons. (*a*) In like manner, if a specific legacy of personal property is bequeathed in a foreign country, and the legatee has, under an administration there, been admitted to the full possession and ownership by the administrator, he may afterwards sue in his own name for any injury or conversion of such property in another country, where the property or wrong-doer may be found, without any probate of the will there.[1] (*b*) The plain reason in each of these cases is, that the executor and the legatee have, each in his own right, become full and perfect legal owners of the property by the local law ; and a title to personal property, duly acquired by the lex loci rei sitæ, will be deemed valid, and be respected as a lawful and perfect title in every other country. (*c*)

[1] See Commonwealth *v.* Griffith, 2 Pick. (Mass.) 11; Bollard *v.* Spencer, 7 T. R. 358; Shipman *v.* Thompson, Willes, 103 ; Slack *v.* Walcott, 3 Mason, 508, 513.

(*a*) Jefferson *v.* Glover, 46 Miss. 510. In similar cases receivers may sue in their individual capacity. Cagill *v.* Wooldridge, 8 Baxter (Tenn.) 580.

(*b*) See Brown *v.* Knapp, 79 N. Y. 136.

(*c*) For a similar reason it was recently held that where a widow by the law of France, where her husband was domiciled and died, became entitled to all the debts, claims, and causes of action, left by him, and to enforce them in her own name, she might do so in England without taking out administration there, the law of the parties' domicil attaching to them. Vanquelin *v.* Bouard, 15 C. B. N. S. 341. So a foreign administrator who has obtained judgment as such in the state of his appointment may sue upon the judgment in other states without new administration. Barton *v.* Higgins, 41 Md. 539; Cherry *v.* Speight, 28 Tex. 503; Rucks *v.* Taylor, 49 Miss. 552. So the sole devisee of an estate may after settlement thereof bring suit in another state (the testator owing no debts there) in his own name to recover a sum due the plaintiff individual under the will. Morton *v.* Hatch, 54 Mo. 408.

517. *Negotiable Securities.* — The like principle will apply where an executor or administrator, in virtue of an administration abroad, becomes there possessed of negotiable notes belonging to the deceased, which are payable to bearer; for then he becomes the legal owner and bearer by virtue of his administration, and may sue thereon in his own name; and he need not take out letters of administration in the state where the debtor resides, in order to maintain a suit against him.[1] (a) And for a like reason it would seem that negotiable paper of the deceased, payable to order, actually held and indorsed by a foreign executor or administrator in the foreign country, who is capable there of passing the legal title by such indorsement, would confer a complete legal title on the indorsee, so that he ought to be treated in every other country as the legal indorsee, and allowed to sue thereon accordingly, in the same manner that he would be if it were a transfer of any personal goods or merchandise of the deceased, situate in such foreign country.[2]

517 a. *Fund sent from Abroad for Distribution.* — And when an executor appointed abroad has remitted to another country (as, for example, to England) that fund, to be distributed between legatees there domiciled, the distribution may be made either voluntarily by the remittee, or enforced by a court of equity in such country, without any administration being taken there, or making the legal representative of the testator a party to the suit.[3]

518. *Principal and Ancillary Administration.* — Where there are different administrations granted in different countries, that is deemed the principal or primary administration which is granted in the country of the domicil of the deceased party; for the final distribution of his effects among his heirs or distributees is to be decided by the law of his domicil. Hence any other administration which is granted in any other country is treated as in its nature ancillary merely, and is, as we have seen, generally

---

[1] Robinson v. Crandall, 9 Wendell (N. Y.) 425. But see Stearns v. Burnham, 5 Greenl. (Me.) 261; Thompson v. Wilson, 2 N. H. 291; McNeilage s. Holloway, 1 B. & A. 218; ante, s. 354, 358, 359.

[2] Ib. and ante, s. 358, 359.

[3] Arthur v. Hughes, 4 Beav. 506.

(a) See Barrett v. Barrett, 8 Greenl. 187; Sanford v. McCreedy, 28 Wis. (Me.) 353; Purple v. Whithed, 49 Vt. 103; Rucks v. Taylor, 49 Miss. 552.

held subordinate to the original administration.[1] (a) But each administration is nevertheless deemed so far independent of the others, that property received under one cannot be sued for under another, although it may at the moment be locally situate within the jurisdiction of the latter. Thus if property is received by a foreign executor or administrator abroad, and it is afterwards remitted here, an executor or administrator appointed here could not assert a claim to it here, either against the person in whose hands it might happen to be, or against the foreign executor or administrator.[2] The only mode of reaching it, if necessary for the purposes of due administration in the foreign country, would be to require its transmission or distribution, after all the claims against the foreign administration had been duly ascertained and settled.[3] (b)

519. *Goods in Transitu.* — But suppose a case where the personal estate of the deceased has not, at the time of his decease, any positive locality in the place of his domicil or in any foreign territory, but it is strictly in transitu to a foreign country, and afterwards arrives in the country of its destination. It may be asked, in such case to whom would the administration of such property rightfully belong? Would it belong to the administrator in the place of the domicil of the deceased, or to the administrator appointed in the place where it had arrived? And if (as may well happen in case of a ship and cargo sent abroad) the property, or its proceeds, should afterwards return to the domicil of the original owner, would the administrator there appointed be entitled to take it, and bound to account for it in the due course of administration? Practically speaking, no doubt is entertained on this subject ; and the property, whenever it returns to the country of the domicil of the owner, whether by remittance or otherwise, is understood to be under the administration of the

---

[1] Ante, s. 514.

[2] Currie v. Bircham, 1 D. & R. 35. See Jauncy v. Sealey, 1 Vern. 397; ante, s. 513, 515, 515 a. See Huthwaite v. Phaire, 1 Man. & G. 159.

[3] See Dawes v. Head, 3 Pick. (Mass.) 128–148; Harvey v. Richards, 1 Mason, 381; ante, s. 513, and note, s. 514; Boston v. Boylston, 2 Mass. 384; Goodwin v. Jones, 3 Mass. 514; Dawes v. Boylston, 9 Mass. 337.

(a) Shegogg v. Perkins, 34 Ark. 117. But see Carroll v. McPike, 53 Miss. 569; Carr v. Lowe, 7 Heisk. (Tenn.) 84, under statutory law.

(b) See Lynes v. Coley, 1 Redf. (N. Y.) 407; Banta v. Moore, 2 McCarter (N. J.) 101.

administrator appointed there. Nor has there been a doubt hitherto judicially expressed, that property, so sent abroad and returned, might and should be so administered, and that all parties would be protected in their doings in regard to it.

520. *Ships and Cargoes. — Debts.* — Indeed according to the common course of commercial business, ships and cargoes, and the proceeds thereof, locally situate in a foreign country at the time of the death of the owner, always proceed on their voyages and return to the home port without any suspicion that all the parties concerned are not legally entitled so to act ; and they are taken possession of and administered by the administrator of the forum domicilii, with the constant persuasion that he may not only rightfully do so, but that he is bound to administer them as part of the funds appropriately in his hands. A different course of adjudication would be attended with almost inextricable difficulties, and would involve this extraordinary result, that all the personal property of the deceased must be deemed to have a fixed situs where it was at the moment of his death ; and, if removed from it, must be returned thither for the purpose of a due administration. Nay, debts due in a foreign country would be absolutely required to be retained there until a local administration was obtained, and could not without peril be voluntarily remitted to the creditor's domicil. And if the debtor should in the mean time remove to another country, it might become matter of extreme doubt whether a payment to a local administrator there would discharge him from the debt.[1] But it may perhaps, after all, be doubtful whether, with a strict regard to the principles of international law, the personal property of the deceased testator or intestate, whether it consisted of goods or of debts, situate at the time of his death in a foreign country, could be lawfully disposed of except under an administration granted in that country, although they had since been removed or transmitted to the domicil of the deceased, and had been received by his administrator appointed there.[2]

521. *Crowat v. Orms.* — A case illustrative of these remarks has recently occurred. The personal estate of an intestate consisted in a considerable degree of stage-coaches and stage-horses, belonging to a daily line, running from one state to another ; and letters

[1] See Stevens v. Gaylord, 11 Mass. 256; ante, s. 515, 515 a.
[2] See ante, s. 513–518; post, s. 525.

of administration were taken out by the same person in both states, one being that of the intestate's domicil. A question arose under which administration the property was to be accounted for, part of it being in one state and part in the other, and part in transitu from one to the other at the moment of the intestate's death. The learned Chancellor of New York said, that if administration had been granted to different individuals in the two states, the property must have been considered as belonging to that administrator who first reduced it to possession within the limits of his own state. But that in the case before him, as both administrations were granted to the same person, if an account of administration were to be taken, it would be necessary to settle that by ascertaining what had been inventoried and accounted for by him under the administration in the other state.[1]

522. *Relation between Different Administrations.* — Where administrations are granted to different persons in different states, they are so far deemed independent of each other that a judgment obtained against one will furnish no right of action against the other, to affect assets received by the latter in virtue of his own administration; for in contemplation of law there is no privity between him and the other administrator.[2] (a) It might be different if the same person were administrator in both states.[8] On the other hand, a judgment recovered by a foreign administrator against the debtor of his intestate will not form the foundation of an action against the debtor by an ancillary administrator appointed in another state.[4] But the foreign administrator himself might in such a case maintain a personal suit against the debtor in any other state; because the judgment would, as to him, merge

---

[1] Orcutt v. Orms, 3 Paige (N. Y.) 459.
[2] Lightfoot v. Bickley, 2 Rawle (Penn.) 431.
[8] Ibid.   [4] Talmage v. Chapel, 16 Mass. 71.

(a) This seems to be the settled law as to administrators (Low v. Bartlett, 8 Allen, 259; Ela v. Edwards, 13 Allen, 48; Merrill v. New England Mut. Life Ins. Co., 103 Mass. 245; McLean v. Meek, 18 How. 16; Pond v. Makepeace, 2 Met. (Mass.) 114. See Bigelow, Estoppel, 99, 100, 255, 256, 3d ed.), although it may not be as to *executors*. And if a testator by will appoints different executors in different states, there may be such a privity between them that a judgment against one in one state may be evidence, but not conclusive evidence, against another in a different state. Hill v. Tucker, 13 How. 458, distinguishing Aspden v. Nixon, 4 How. 467.

the original debt, and make it personally due to him in his own right, he being responsible therefor to the estate.[1] (a)

[1] Ibid. But see Smith v. Nicholls, 5 Bing. (N. C.) p. 208; post, s. 607.

(a) In Aspden v. Nixon, 4 How. 467, it was determined that a foreign administrator or executor, who was also the administrator or executor of the same estate in one of the American states, duly appointed, could not be held liable to account in the place of the principal foreign administration for any of the effects belonging to the estate which he had received under the American administration; and that consequently a decree of the court of chancery in England, where the principal administration was, exonerating such administrator or executor from all responsibility to account for any effects of the estate in his hands, was no bar to a similar proceeding in this country against the same person, claiming to charge him with effects of the estate received here, which were in his hands at the time of the adjudication in England. This decision proceeds upon the ground that a person who is administrator of the same estate in different states, and who has received assets under both administrations, cannot be compelled to account for any such effects except in the place where they were received.

The same doctrine has since been repeatedly reaffirmed by the same court. Thus it was afterwards held (Stacy v. Thrasher, 6 How. 44) that there was such a want of privity between different administrators in different states, that an action of debt would not lie in one state against an administrator on a judgment recovered against a different administrator of the same intestate appointed under the authority of another state. And the subject is further discussed very much at length by Mr. Justice Wayne, with similar conclusions, in a later case. Hill v. Tucker, 13 How. 458. It is also held by the same court that the record of a debt against an administrator in one state is not sufficient evidence of the debt against an administrator in another state. Hill v. Meek, 18 How. 16. So also must be regarded allowances by commissions of insolvency in the different states, if the decision last stated is to be followed; those allowances being merely for the purpose of reaching the estate within that particular jurisdiction.

The subject came again under consideration before the same court in Mackey v. Coxe, 18 How. 100, where it was decided that an administrator appointed in the Cherokee Territory might receive payment of a debt in the District of Columbia, and his discharge, or that of his authorized attorney, would be valid. But this is upon the ground that by the act of Congress he might sue in the courts of that district. He did however out of abundant caution take new letters of administration in that district. The true law in regard to ancillary administrations is here stated, that this being an ancillary administration, it depended upon the discretion of the orphans' court which granted it, whether the money remaining in the hands of the ancillary administrator, after the satisfaction of all claims in this jurisdiction, should be distributed here by the ancillary administrator, or remitted to the principal administrators for distribution, and until that direction shall be executed, and the ancillary administrator directed which course to pursue, he is in no default.

Concerning remedies in regard to the distribution of the estates of deceased persons in the national tribunals, where the parties in interest

523. *Real Securities.* — So strict is the principle that a foreign administrator cannot do any act as administrator in another state,

reside in different states, it is settled that a creditor cannot have an execution in a court of the United States, so as to levy upon the property of an estate reported as insolvent, which is in the course of settlement as such. Williams *v.* Benedict, 8 How. 107; Peale *v.* Phipps, 14 How. 368; Bank of Tennessee *v.* Horn, 17 How. 157. Whether it is competent for state authority to compel foreign creditors in all cases to seek their remedies in the state courts against the estates of decedents, to the exclusion of the jurisdiction of the United States courts, seems not to have been fully determined. Green *v.* Creighton, 23 How. 90, 107. But upon principle it would not seem competent for the several states to exclude the jurisdiction of the·national tribunals in matters of this kind, any more than in common-law actions. But the mode of enforcing remedies in the United States courts will undoubtedly be attended with some embarrassments. And where the state laws provide that suits pending at the decease of a debtor whose estate is represented insolvent shall be discontinued and brought before the commissioners of insolvency, this, it would seem, must extend to the national courts, the same as a statutory bar.

It would seem to be the established rule however in the national tribunals to allow a foreign creditor to pursue his claim to judgment there, without regard to state laws conferring exclusive jurisdiction in the settlement of estates upon particular state courts. But such judgments must be brought into the probate court before any distribution is there decreed, or else it would seem impracticable to entitle them to an equal share in the distribution, where the assets prove insufficient to pay all the creditors.

But in a case where all the creditors had been paid, and the administrators still held assets in their hands, the creditor, having recovered judgment in the courts of the United States, was held entitled to maintain a bill in equity in those courts to enforce the payment of his judgment before any distribution to the heirs, notwithstanding such judgment had not been presented before the commissioners of insolvency appointed to audit all claims against the estate, and the provision in the state statutes that all claims not presented to such commissioners should be forever barred after a certain time, which in this case had already expired. Union Bank *v.* Jolly, 18 How. 503; Green *v.* Creighton, 23 How. 90.

The question of the right of those claiming title through deceased parties to maintain an action in a foreign forum to enforce those rights, without having taken letters of administration there, in a recent case came before the court of common pleas; where it was held that the widow of a French subject, who became donee of the universality of the real and personal estates of the succession of her husband, and in whom, as such, all his rights by the law of France vested, and who was entitled to enforce the same in her own name, and who also became liable for all her husband's liabilities, and who was compelled to pay the amount of certain bills of exchange, of which her husband was drawer and the defendant acceptor, and who had recovered judgment thereon in France against the defendant,—was not bound to take out letters of administration in England in order ·to entitle her to maintain an action upon such judgment. Vanquelin *v.* Bouard, 10 Jur. N.S. 566; 15 C. B. N.S. 341.

The last case seems to proceed upon the ground that the plaintiff claimed

that where the local laws convert real securities in the hands of an administrator into personal assets, which he may sell or assign, he cannot dispose of such real securities until he has taken out letters of administration in the place rei sitæ.[1] Thus mortgages are declared by the laws of Massachusetts to be personal assets in the hands of administrators, and disposable by them accordingly. But the authority cannot be exercised by any except administrators who have been duly appointed within the state.[2] On the other hand, if an administrator sells real estate for the payment of debts, pursuant to the authority given him under the local laws rei sitæ, he is not responsible for the proceeds as assets in any other state; but they are to be disposed of and accounted for solely in the place and in the manner pointed out in the local laws.[3]

524. *Modes of Administering.* — In relation to the mode of administering assets by executors and administrators, there are in different countries very different regulations. The priority of debts, the order of payments, the marshalling of assets for this purpose, and, in cases of insolvency, the mode of proof, as well as the mode of distribution, differ in different countries.[4] In some countries all debts stand in an equal rank and order, and in cases of insolvency the creditors are to be paid pari passu. In others, there are certain classes of debts entitled to a priority of

[1] Goodwin v. Jones, 3 Mass. 514, 519. See Bissell v. Briggs, 9 Mass. 467, 468. But see Doolittle v. Lewis, 7 Johns. Ch. (N. Y.) 45, 47; Attorney-General v. Bouwens, 4 M. & W. 171, 191, 192.

[2] Cutter v. Davenport, 1 Pick. (Mass.) 81. But see Doolittle v. Lewis, 7 Johns. Ch. (N. Y.) 45, 47.

[3] Peck v. Mead, 2 Wendell (N. Y.) 471; Hooker v. Olmstead, 6 Pick. (Mass.) 481, 483; Goodwin v. Jones, 3 Mass. 514, 519, 520.

[4] Harvey v. Richards, 1 Mason, 421; ante, s. 323–328, 401–403.

in her own right, and not in the right of the deceased. This might have been placed upon the mere ground of judgment recovered in the name of the plaintiff. But the court put the case mainly upon the ground that the plaintiff by paying the debts of her husband had become the owner, in her own right, of all the effects belonging to his estate, and might enforce those rights in her own name. This may be true of personal estate in the hands of a foreign executor, which is afterwards converted in a foreign state (Bullock v. Rogers, 16 Vt. 294), but is more questionable in regard to choses in action, which can only be sued by some personal representative of the deceased appointed by the probate courts in the forum where the action is brought. Whyte v. Rose, 3 Q. B. 493.

payment; and they are therefore deemed privileged debts. Thus in England, bond debts and judgment debts possess this privilege; and the like law exists in some of the states of this Union.[1] Similar provisions may be found in the law of France in favor of particular classes of creditors.[2] On the other hand, in Massachusetts, and in many other states of the Union, all debts except those due to the government possess an equal rank, and are payable pari passu. Let us suppose then that a debtor dies domiciled in a country where such priority of right and privilege exists, and he has personal assets situate in a state where all debts stand in an equal rank, and administration is duly taken out in the place of his domicil, and also in the place of the situs of the assets. What rule is to govern in the marshalling of the assets, — the law of the domicil, or the law of the situs? The established rule now is that in regard to creditors the administration of assets of deceased persons is to be governed altogether by the law of the country where the executor or administrator acts, and from which he derives his authority to collect them, and not by that of the domicil of the deceased. The rule has been laid down with great clearness and force on many occasions.[3] (a)

525. *Ground of the Doctrine.* — The ground upon which this doctrine has been established seems entirely satisfactory. Every nation, having a right to dispose of all the property actually situated within it, has (as has often been said) a right to protect itself and its citizens against the inequalities of foreign laws which are injurious to their interests. The rule of a preference or of an

[1] Smith v. Union Bank, 5 Pet. 518.

[2] Merlin, Répertoire, Privilège; Civil Code of France, art. 2092-2106.

[3] See Harrison v. Sterry, 5 Cranch, 299; Milne v. Moreton, 6 Binn. (Penn.) 353, 361; Olivier v. Townes, 2 Mart. N.S. (La.) 93, 99; ante, s. 388; De Sobry v. De Laistre, 2 Harr. & J. (Md.) 193, 224; Smith v. Union Bank, 5 Pet. 518, 523; Dawes v. Head, 3 Pick. (Mass.) 128; Holmes v. Remsen, 20 Johns. (N. Y.) 265; Case of Miller's Estate, 3 Rawle (Penn.) 312; McElmoyle v. Cohen, 13 Pet. 312. Where there are administrations and assets in different states, and the estate is insolvent, the general principle adopted by the courts of Massachusetts is to place creditors there, as to the assets in the state, upon a footing of equality with other creditors in the state where the party had his domicil at his death. Davis v. Estey, 8 Pick. (Mass.) 475.

(a) See St. John v. Hodges, 9 Baxter (Tenn.) 334. But see Dial v. Gary, 14 S. C. 573.

equality in the payment of debts, whether the one or the other course is adopted, is purely local in its nature, and can have no just claim to be admitted by any other nation which, in its own domestic arrangement, pursues an opposite policy. And in a conflict between our own and foreign laws, the doctrine avowed by Huberus is highly reasonable, that we should prefer our own. ' In tali conflictu magis est, ut jus nostrum, quam jus alienum, servemus.' [1]

526. *Opinions of Foreign Jurists.* — It seems that many foreign jurists, but certainly not all,[2] maintain a different opinion, holding that in every case the privileges of debts, and the rank and order of payment thereof, are to be governed by the law of the domicil of the debtor at the time of his contract or of his death. They found themselves upon the general rule that the creditor must pursue his remedy in the domicil of the debtor, and that debts follow his person, and not that of the creditor.[3] This rule was acknowledged in matters of jurisdiction in the Roman law, in which it is said : ' Juris ordinem converti postulas, ut non actor rei forum, sed reus actoris sequatur. Nam, ubi domicilium reus habet,

---

[1] Huberus, de Confl. Leg. lib. 1, tit. 3, s. 11. See also Smith *v.* Union Bank, 5 Pet. 518; ante, s. 322–327.

[2] See ante, s. 325 *a*–325 *o*, and 1 Boullenois, p. 684–690; Rodenburg, Diversit. Statut. tit. 2, c. 5, 16; 2 Boullenois, Appx. p. 47–50.

[3] Livermore, Dissert. p. 164–171; ante, s. 323–328. See also s. 401–403. Mr. Livermore has, in his Dissertations (p. 164–171), controverted the correctness of the American doctrine; and he holds that the law of the debtor's domicil at the time when the debt was contracted furnishes the true rule. Mr. Henry lays down the rule that when the laws of the domicil of the creditor and debtor differ, as to classing debts and rights of action among personal or real property, the law of the domicil of the debtor must prevail in suits on them. Henry on Foreign Law, 34, 35. Mr. Dwarris states the same rule, and quotes the maxims: ' Actor sequitur forum rei,' and ' Debita sequuntur personam debitoris.' He admits indeed that debts and rights of action attend upon the person of the creditor, ' Inhærent ossibus creditoris; ' but, to recover them, one must follow the forum rei, and person of the debtor. If the question regard the distribution of the creditor's estate, the law of his domicil is to be observed. If the question is, in what degree or proportion the representatives of the debtor should be charged with payment from his effects, then it is of a passive nature, and the law of the domicil of the debtor should be followed. Dwarris on Statut. 650. It would be difficult to point out in the English law any authority in support of this doctrine. See also Dumoulin's and Casaregis's opinions cited in Livermore, Dissert. 162, 163; Molin, Opera, tom. 1. In Consuetud. Paris. de Fiefs. tit. 1, s. 1, gloss. 4, n. 9, p. 56, 57, ed. 1681; Casaregis in Rubr. Stat. Civ. Genuæ de Success. ab Intest. n. 64, tom. 4, p. 42, 43; ante, s. 322–328.

vel tempore contractus habuit, licet hoc postea transtulerit, ibi tantum eum conveniri oportet.'[1] But it by no means follows that because this was the rule in the municipal jurisprudence of Rome, therefore it ought to be adopted as a portion of modern international law. Nor does it necessarily follow, even if the rule were admitted to govern as to the forum where the suit should be brought against the debtor in his lifetime, that upon his death, in a conflict of the rights and privileges of creditors (concursus creditorum) of different countries, the municipal law of the country of the debtor should overrule the jurisprudence of the situs of the effects.[2]

527. This however seems to be the doctrine of Coquille, Mævius, Carpzovius, Burgundus, Rodenburg, Matthæus, and Gaill.[3] But it is manifest from the language used by them that it is a matter of no small difficulty ; and a diversity of laws and opinions may well be presumed to exist in regard to it. Boullenois holds the same doctrine.[4] Hertius seems in one passage to affirm it, saying : ' Si de re immobili agitur, spectandas esse leges situs rei indubium est, etiamsi privilegium in ea propter qualitatem personæ tribuatur. At in rebus mobilibus, si ex contractu vel quasi agatur, locus contractus inspiciendus esset. Enimvero, quia antelatio ex jure singulari vel privilegio competit, non debet in præjudicium illius civitatis, sub qua debitor degit, et res ejus mobiles contineri censeatur, extendi. Ad jura igitur domicilii debitoris, ubi fit concursus creditorum, et quo omnes cujuscunque generis lites adversus illum debitorem propter connexitatem causæ trahuntur, regulariter respiciendum erit.'[5] Yet he afterwards ad-

---

[1] Cod. 3, 13, 2.   [2] Ante, s. 332–337.

[3] Livermore, Dissert. s. 254–257, p. 166–171; Rodenburg, de Div. Stat. tit. 2, c. 5, s. 16; 2 Boullenois, Appx. p. 47; ante, s. 324–325 o ; 1 Boullenois, p. 686–687; I. obs. 30, p. 818–834; Bouhier, Cout. de Bourg. c. 21, s. 204, c. 22, s. 151; Mævius, Comm. in Jus. Lubesence, lib. 3, tit. 1, art. 11, n. 24–27, p. 39, 40; Id. art. 10, n. 51, p. 33; Matthæus, de Auction. lib. 1, c. 21, s. 35, n. 10, p. 294, 295; Gaill, obs. Pract. lib. 2, obs. 130, n. 12–14, p. 563; Burgundus, tract. 2, n. 21, p. 72, ed. 1621; ante, s. 324–327. Not having access to the works of Carpzovius and Coquille, I am obliged to rely on the citations which I find in Livermore's Dissertations of Coquille's opinion, and upon Rodenburg, Mævius (ubi supra), and Hertius for the citations from Carpzovius. The other authors I have examined, and the citations are correct. Ante, s. 324–327; post, s. 782.

[4] 1 Boullenois, p. 818; Id. obs. 30, p. 834.

[5] 1 Hertii Opera, de Collis. Leg. s. 4, n. 64, p. 150, ed. 1737; Id. p. 211, ed. 1716; ante, s. 325 b.

mits that cases may exist where undue preferences, given by the local laws of one state in favor of its own subjects, may be met with a just retaliation by others.[1] He cites a passage from Huberus,[2] which would seem to show that the latter was of a different opinion. A creditor (says Huberus) upon a bill of exchange, exercising his right in a reasonable time, has a preference in Holland over all other creditors upon the movable property of his debtor. He has property of the like kind in Friesland, where no such law exists. Will such a creditor be there preferred to other creditors? By no means; since those creditors, by the laws there received, have already acquired a right.' 'Creditor ex causa cambii, jus suum in tempore exercens, præfertur apud Batavos omnibus aliis debitoribus [creditoribus?] in bona mobilis debitoris. Hic habet ejusmodi res in Frisia, ubi hoc jus non obtinet. An ibi creditor etiam præferetur aliis creditoribus? Nullo modo; quoniam heic creditoribus, vi legum hic receptarum jus pridem quæsitum est.'[3] Upon this Hertius remarks: 'Nimirum recte disceret in sect. antec. non teneri potestates sequi jus alienum in fraudem sui juris, et civium suorum. Hinc in quibusdam Germaniæ regionibus cives et incolæ in concursu creditorum antehabentur exteris, et pro consuetudine, quæ Biberaci est, ut cives chirographiarii præferantur extraneis forensibus, anteriorem hypothecam habentibus, pronunciatum in camera imperiali.'[4] Now, this seems a virtual surrender of the main ground in all cases where there is a conflict of laws, as to the priorities and preferences of creditors, between the law of the domicil of the debtor, or of the contract, and that of the situs of the movables.

528. *Primary Fund for Payment of Debts.* — In the course of administration also in different countries, questions often arise as to particular debts, whether they are properly and ultimately payable out of the personal estate, or are chargeable upon the real estate of the deceased.(a) In all such cases the law of the

---

[1] Ibid.   [2] Huberus, J. P. Univers. c. 10, s. 44.

[3] I quote the passage as I find it in Hertius, not having access to the work of Huberus here referred to. Huberus, J. P. Univers. c. 10, s. 44; 1 Hertii Opera, de Collis. Leg. s. 4, n. 64, p. 150, ed. 1737; Id. p. 211, ed. 1716. See ante, s. 325 a. Should not *debitoribus* be *creditoribus?*

[4] 1 Hertii Opera, de Collis. Leg. s. 4, n. 64, p. 150, ed. 1737; Id. p. 211, 212, ed. 1716; ante, s. 325 b.

(a) See Rice *v.* Harbeson, 63 N. Y. 493.

domicil of the deceased will govern in cases of intestacy; and in cases of testacy the intention of the testator. A case illustrating this doctrine occurred in England many years ago. A testator who lived in Holland, and was seised of real estate there, and of considerable personal estate in England, devised all his real estate to one person, and all his personal estate to another, whom he made his executor. At the time of his death he owed some debts by specialty, and some by simple contract in Holland, and he had no assets there to satisfy those debts; but his real estate was by the laws of Holland made liable for the payment of simple-contract debts, as well as specialty debts, if there were not personal assets to answer the same. The creditors in Holland sued the devisee, and obtained a decree there for the sale of the lands devised for the payment of their debts. And then the devisee brought a suit in England against the executor (the legatee of the personalty) for reimbursement out of the personal estate. The court decided in his favor, upon the ground that in Holland, as in England, the personal estate was the primary fund for the payment of debts, and that it should come in aid of the real estate, and be in the first place charged.[1]

529. *Scotch Law.* — In the Scottish law the same doctrine is recognized; that is to say, that the fund which is primarily chargeable with the debt shall ultimately bear it in exoneration of all other funds. But in its application under the local law to particular cases, an opposite result may be produced from that in the case just mentioned; for the personal estate is in such cases exonerated, and the real estate made to bear the debt. Thus, for example, in Scotland heritable bonds are primarily payable out of the real estate; and, as we have seen, the personal estate of a person domiciled and dying in England is held exonerated from the charge of such a heritable bond, made by him upon real estate in Scotland to secure a debt contracted in England; and the Scottish estate is compellable to bear the burden.[2] On the other hand, by the law of Scotland, movable debts (in contradistinction to heritable bonds) are primarily and pro-

---

[1] Anonymous, 9 Mod. 66; Bowaman v. Reeve, Prec. Ch. 577.

[2] Ante, s. 486-488; Drummond v. Drummond, 6 Bro. P. C. 601 (Tomlins's ed.); cited 2 V. & B. 131; Winchelsea v. Garetty, 2 Keen, 293, 310; Robertson on Succession, 209, 214; 4 Burge, Col. & For. Law, pt. 2, ch. 15, s. 4, p. 722-734; ante, s. 266 a, 366, 486, 487.

perly chargeable upon the personal estate. The creditor may indeed enforce payment against the real estate in the hands of the heir; but if he does so, the heir is entitled to relief against the executor out of the personal estate. In other words, according to the law of Scotland, the real estate, though subject to the payment of movable debts, is only a subsidiary fund for the purpose of payment. Payment therefore by the heir does not extinguish the debt in his hands, but vests in him a right to recover the amount against the personal estate.[1] The question has arisen whether under such circumstances the heir is entitled to enforce a payment out of the personal estate of his ancestor, not only in Scotland, but in England (where he died domiciled), according to whose laws the personal estate is also the primary fund for the payment of debts; and it has been held that he is so entitled, upon the ground that, as between the heir and the persons entitled to the distribution of the personal estate, the primary fund must in all cases ultimately bear the burden.[2]

[1] Winchelsea v. Garetty, 2 Keen, 293, 308.
[2] Winchelsea v. Garetty, 2 Keen, 293, 310–312. See Lord Langdale's opinion cited at large, ante, s. 266 a.

CHAPTER XIV.

JURISDICTION AND REMEDIES.

530. *Classification.* — We are next led to the consideration of the subject of remedies, or the modes of redress for the violation of the rights of other persons by proceedings in courts of justice. And in the nature of things these may well be classed into three sorts: first, those remedies which purely regard property, movable and immovable; secondly, those which purely regard persons; and thirdly, those which regard both persons and property. The Roman jurisprudence took notice of this distinction, and accordingly divided all remedies, as to their subject, into three kinds: (1) Real actions, otherwise called *vindications*, which were those in which a man demanded something that was his own, and which were founded on dominion, or jus in re; (2) Personal actions, denominated also *condictions*, which were those in which a man demanded what was barely due to him, and which were founded on some obligation, or jus ad rem; (3) Mixed actions, which were those in which some specific thing was demanded, and where also some personal obligations were claimed to be performed.[1] The real actions of the Roman law were not, like the real actions of the common law, confined to real estate, but they included personal as well as real property. But the same distinction, as to classes of remedies and actions, equally pervades the common law as it does the civil law. Thus we have in the common law the distinct classes of real actions, personal actions, and mixed actions; the first embracing those which concern real estate, where the proceeding is purely in rem; (a) the next em-

---

[1] Halifax on the Roman Law, b. 3, c. 1, s. 4, 5, p. 25, 28; 1 Brown, Civil & Adm. Law, p. 439, 440. In Pothier's work on the Customs of Orléans, there will be found a correspondent division of actions into the same classes. Pothier, Coutumes d'Orléans, Introd. Gén. c. 4, art. 109–122.

(a) This use of the term "in rem," as will appear hereafter (post, s. 592 a, note a), though common to the older books of English law, — the result per-

bracing all suits in personam for contracts and torts; and the last embracing those mixed suits where the person is liable by reason of, and in connection with, property.[1]

531. *Questions of Jurisdiction.* — In considering the nature of actions, we are necessarily led to the consideration of the proper tribunal in which they should be brought; or, in other words, what tribunal is competent to entertain them in point of jurisdiction. And here the subject naturally divides itself into the consideration of matters of jurisdiction in regard to the administration of mere municipal and domestic justice; and matters of jurisdiction in regard to the administration of justice inter gentes, founded upon principles of public law.

532. *Roman Law.* — *Place of Jurisdiction.* — In the Roman jurisprudence, and among those nations which have derived their jurisprudence from the civil law, many embarrassing questions as to jurisdiction seem to have arisen.[2] The general rule of the Roman Code is, that the plaintiff must bring his suit or action in the place where the defendant has his domicil, or where he had it at the time of the contract. 'Juris ordinem,' said the Emperor Diocletian, 'converti postulas; ut non actor rei forum, sed reus actoris sequatur. Nam ubi domicilium reus habet, vel tempore contractus habuit, licet hoc postea tanstulerit, ibi tantum eum conveniri oportet.'[3] But it is not to be understood that this rule applied to all cases where the party defendant was found, without any regard to the situation of the thing sought, as if its object were to show more favor to the party defendant than to the plaintiff. Its sole object was that the adjudication might be made where it could be enforced. Thus we find the doctrine laid down in the Code, that although the general rule is

---

[1] 3 Black. Com. 294; Com. Dig. Action, N.

[2] See 1 J. Voet, ad Pand. 5, 1, 303; Id. 64, 66, 74, 91, 92; Huberus, lib. 5, tit. 1, de Foro Compet. tom. 2, s. 38–52, p. 722–730; Strykius, tom. 6, 11, p. 1, 8, tom. 7, 1, p. 5; 1 Boullenois, obs. 25, p. 601, 618, 619, 635.

[3] Cod. 3, 13, 2; ante, s. 526.

---

haps of a confusion between the real actions of the English law and the actions in rem of the Roman law, — is now becoming obsolete, except in a sense which permits its application to personalty as well as to realty. In the proper sense a proceeding in rem is one instituted without relation to individual rights, in perfect contrast to a proceeding in personam; and the most familiar example of a proceeding in rem in this sense is found in cases of personalty, as for example in the case of a ship libelled as prize of war.

that the plaintiff must bring his suit in the domicil of the defendant, yet this was dispensed with in certain suits in rem, which might be brought in the place rei sitæ. 'Actor rei forum, sive in rem, sive in personam sit actio, sequitur. Sed et in locis, in quibus res, propter quas contenditur, constitutæ sunt, jubemus in rem actionem adversus possidentem moveri.'[1]

533. *Huberus. — Forum Domicilii, Rei Sitæ, Rei Gestæ.* — Huberus thus explains the doctrine. 'Cujus ratio non tam est, quod reus sit actore favorabilior, etsi verissima; sed quod necessitatis vocandi et cogendi alium ad jus æquum, non nisi a superiore proficisci queat: superior autem cujusque non est alienus, sed proprius rector. Vocandi, inquam, et cogendi; quandoquidem sine coactione judicia forent elusoria; nec alibi forum lege stabilitur, quam ubi illa cogendi facultas adhiberi potest; non tamen, ut ubicunque illa valet, sit forum, sed ubi res et æquitas patitur. Vis illa compellandi partes ad æquum jus, imprimis est in loco domicilii, est etiam in loco rei sitæ, et rei gestæ, si reus illic haberi possit, alias secus. Hinc tria sunt loca fori in jure nostro, domicilii, rei sitæ, rei gestæ.'[2] And hence he thinks that the rule of the civil law rei sitæ applies not only to immovables, but to movables, although many jurists confine it to the former.[3] 'Sed heic aliam potius rationem sequimur; quod in foro stabiliendo maxime consideretur, an in promptu sit effectum dare citationi, in cogendis partibus ad obsequium jurisdictionis; quæ facultas æque locum habet in mobilibus, ubi detinentur, quam in immobilibus, ubi sitæ sunt.'[4]

534. But he admits that, as the forum domicilii was of universal operation, actions in rem might be brought in the forum domicilii, as well as in the forum rei sitæ. 'Videlicet, hoc semper tenendum, domicilii forum esse generale, quod in cunctis actionibus, adeoque etiam in actionibus in rem, obtinere, sciendum est, ut de dd. legibus constat.'[5] Again he says: 'Summa igitur hæc

[1] Cod. 3, 19, 3; 1 Boullenois, obs. 25, p. 618, 619; post, s. 551.

[2] Huberus, lib. 5, tit. 1; De Foro Compet. s. 38, tom. 2, p. 722. See also 1 Boullenois, obs. 25, p. 618, 619; post, s. 551.

[3] The subject is a good deal controverted among the civilians; but the present work does not require me to engage in the task of discussing the various opinions which are held by them. The learned reader will find many of them referred to in J. Voet, ad Pand. 1, 5, s. 77, &c., p. 337.

[4] Huberus, tom. 2, lib. 5, tit. 1, s. 48, p. 727.

[5] Id. s. 49, p. 728.

esto. Domicilium in omnibus rebus et actionibus præbet forum. Res sita præterea in actionibus in rem singularibus, non excluso domicilio.'[1] And he supposes the same rule to apply in modern times in the civil-law countries. 'Hæc ego de foro domicilii, reique sitæ alterne conjuncto, moribus hodiernis eodem modo putem obtinere, quemadmodum jure Cæsaris præscriptum est; ut maxime in rem agatur, ubi res sita est; possit tamen omnino etiam, ubi reus habitat.'[2]

535. *Mixed Actions.* — In regard to mixed actions, although there is no text of the Roman law directly in point, Huberus thinks that they may be brought either in the place of domicil of the defendant or of the rei sitæ. 'De mixtis actionibus, excepta hæreditatis petitione, quæ partim in rem, partim in personam, esse dicuntur, non sunt textus speciales, ubi sint instituendæ. Ideoque id ex earum proprietate colligunt interpretes, cum partim imitentur naturam personalium, partim in rem actiones, illas et apud domicilium et apud rem sitam esse movendas, etc. Proinde sic est statuendum. Posse quidem illas actiones utroque loco, domicilii, situsque, moveri; verum, si faciendæ sunt adjudicationes manuque divisio regenda sit, partes ad judicem loci remittendas esse, res ipsa loquitur.'[3]

536. *Forum Rei Gestæ.* — The civil law contemplated another place of jurisdiction; to wit, the place where a contract was made or was to be fulfilled, or where any other act was done, if the defendant or his property could be found there, although it was not the place of his domicil. 'Illud sciendum est, eum, qui ita fuit obligatus, ut in Italia solveret, si in provincia habuit domicilium, utrubique posse conveniri, et hic, et ibi.'[4] Huberus explains this thus : 'Sequitur causa fori tertia, quam rem gestam esse diximus, eamque vel ex contractu vel ex delicto admisso, etc. Sed contractus ita forum tribuit, si contrahens in eodem loco reperiatur; quod convenit, requisito communi inde ab initio collocato, nullam esse fori causam, nisi cum facultate cogendi conjunctam; qualis non est ex historia contractus, si vel reus ibi non inveniatur, vel bona duntaxat sita non habeat, in quæ missio fieri possit, quando reus se in loco contractus non sistit.'[5] These distinctions of the

[1] Huberus, tom. 2, lib. 5, tit. 1, s. 50, p. 728. [2] Id. s. 50.
[3] Id. s. 51, p. 729.
[4] Dig. 5, 1, 19, 4. See also, as to all these distinctions, Pothier, Pand. 5, 1, n. 29–44; Cod. 3, 18, 1.
[5] Huberus, tom. 2, lib. 5, tit. 1, s. 53, 54, p. 729, 730.

Roman law have found their way into the jurisprudence of most, if not all, of the continental nations of modern Europe.

537. *General Doctrine of Foreign Jurists.* — Accordingly we find it laid down by foreign jurists generally that there are, properly speaking, three places of jurisdiction: first, the place of domicil of the party defendant, commonly called the *forum domicilii ;* secondly, the place where the thing in controversy is situate, commonly called the *forum rei sitæ ;* and thirdly, the place where the contract is made or other acts done, commonly called *forum rei gestæ,* or *forum contractus.* 'Vis illa compellandi partes ad æquum jus,' says Huberus, 'imprimis est in loco domicilii; est etiam in loco rei sitæ; et rei gestæ, si reus illic haberi posse; alias secus.'[1] The same distinctions are fully laid down by John Voet and Boullenois, to whom we may generally refer for more copious information.[2] They are also recognized in the Scottish law.[3] They have been here brought into view because they constitute the basis of the reasoning of many of the foreign jurists in discussing the great doctrines respecting the competency of tribunals to hold jurisdiction of causes, and the proper operation of judgments and decrees rei judicatæ. They are also known as fundamental elements in the actual jurisprudence of many of the modern nations of continental Europe.[4]

538. *Common Law. — Local and Transitory Actions.* — In the

[1] Huberus, tom. 2, lib. 5, tit. 1, de Foro Compet. s. 38, p. 722.

[2] J. Voet, ad Pand. 5, 1, de Judiciis, p. 303, s. 64–149; 1 Boullenois, obs. 25, p. 601; Id. p. 618, 619; Id. p. 635; Henry on Foreign Law, c. 8, p. 54, c. 9, p. 63.

[3] Erskine, Inst. b. 1, tit. 2, s. 16–22, p. 29–39.

[4] See Code de Procédure Civile of France, b. 1, tit. 1, art. 1–4; Henry on Foreign Law, c. 8, p. 54, c. 9, p. 63, c. 10, p. 71; Pardessus, Droit Comm. tom. 5, art. 1353; 1 Boullenois, obs. 25, p. 601, 618, 619; Id. 635. In France, jurisdiction would seem generally to belong either to the place of domicil, or to the place rei sitæ. Jurisdiction in the place of the contract, or of the other act done, does not seem to have been recognized under the old jurisprudence, and it does not exist in the modern Code. Code de Procédure Civile, art. 1, 2. 'Le lieu,' says Boullenois, 'où se passent les actes, celui où les parties s'obligent de payer, et leur soumission, ne déterminent pas la justice où elles doivent plaider.' 1 Boullenois, obs. 30, p. 829–832; 2 Boullenois, p. 455–457. Dumoulin says: 'Cæterum ex eo solo, quod quis promisit solvere certo loco, licet ibi conveniri possit de jure, sicut si ibi contraxisset; tamen hoc non observatur in hoc regno; quia in hoc regno non sortitur quis forum ratione contractus, etiam vere et realiter facti in loco.' Molin. Opera, Comm. in Decii, tom. 3, p. 837, ed. 1681; 1 Boullenois, obs. 30, p. 829. See also Pothier, Traité de la Procédure Civile, c. 1.

corresponding distribution of actions by the common law into personal actions and real actions and mixed actions,[1] the two latter are, in point of jurisdiction, confined to the place rei sitæ; and the former are generally capable of being brought wherever the party can be found. Or, as the judicial phrase is, in the common law, real actions and mixed actions are *local*, and personal actions are *transitory*.[2]

539. *Foundation of Jurisdiction.* — Considered in an international point of view, jurisdiction, to be rightfully exercised, must be founded either upon the person being within the territory, or upon the thing being within the territory; for otherwise there can be no sovereignty exerted, upon the known maxim, 'Extra territorium jus dicenti impune non paretur.'[3] (*a*) Boullenois puts this rule among his general principles. The laws of a sovereign rightfully extend over persons who are domiciled within his territory, and over property which is there situate.[4] Vattel lays down the true doctrine in clear terms. ' The sovereignty,' says he, ' united to domain, establishes the jurisdiction of the nation in its territories, or the country which belongs to it. It is its province, or that of its sovereign, to exercise justice in all places under its jurisdiction, to take cognizance of the crimes committed, and the differences that arise in the country.'[5] On the other hand, no sovereignty can extend its process beyond its own territorial limits to subject either persons or property to its judicial decisions. Every exertion of authority of this sort beyond this limit is a mere nullity, and incapable of binding such persons or property in any other tribunals.[5] (*b*) This subject however deserves a more exact consideration.

540. *Jurisdiction as regards Persons.* — In the first place let us consider the subject of jurisdiction a little more particularly in regard to persons. These may be either citizens, native or natu-

[1] 3 Black. Com. 117, 118.
[2] 3 Black. Com. 294; Com. Dig. Action, N.; 1 Chitty, Com. & Manuf. p. 647–649.
[3] Dig. 2, 1, 20.   [4] 1 Boullenois, Pr. Gén. 1, 2, p. 2, 3.
[5] Vattel, b. 2, c. 8, s. 84.

(*a*) See Yelverton *v.* Yelverton, 1 Sw. & T. 586; Warrender *v.* Warrender, 9 Bligh, 144.
(*b*) Picquet *v.* Swan, 5 Mason, 35, 42. See Russel *v.* Smyth, 9 M. & W. 819; De Witt *v.* Burnett, 8 Barb. 96; Gilbreath *v.* Bunce, 65 Mo. 349.

ralized, or foreigners. In regard to the former, while within the territory of their birth or of their adopted allegiance, the jurisdiction of the sovereignty over them is complete and irresistible. It cannot be controlled; and it ought to be respected everywhere. But as to citizens of a country domiciled abroad, the extent of jurisdiction which may be lawfully exercised over them in personam is not so clear upon acknowledged principles. It is true that nations generally assert a claim to regulate the rights and duties and obligations and acts of their own citizens, wherever they may be domiciled. And so far as these rights, duties, obligations, and acts afterwards come under the cognizance of the tribunals of the sovereign power of their own country, either for enforcement or for protection or for remedy, there may be no just ground to exclude this claim. (a) But when such rights, duties, obligations, and acts come under the consideration of other countries, and especially of the foreign country where such citizens are domiciled, the duty of recognizing and enforcing such a claim of sovereignty is neither clear, nor generally admitted. The most that can be said is, that it may be admitted ex comitate gentium. But it may also be denied ex justitia gentium, whenever it is deemed injurious to the interests of such foreign nations, or subversive of their own policy or institutions. No one, for instance, would imagine that a judgment of the parent country, confiscating the property or extinguishing the personal rights or personal capacities of a native subject, on account of such a foreign residence, would be recognized in any other country. And it would be as little expected, as a matter of right, that any other country would enforce a judgment against such persons in the parent country, obtained in invitum, on account of a supposed contumacy in remaining abroad, to which suit he had never appeared, and of which he had received no notice, however the proceedings might be in conformity to the local laws. This is the just result deducible from the axioms of Huberus already quoted; and especially from the first and second of these axioms.[1] Whatever authority should be given to such judgments must be purely ex comitate, and not as matter of absolute or positive right on one side, and of duty on the other.

[1] Ante, s. 29.

(a) Deck v. Deck, 2 Sw. & Tr. 90; and see Bond v. Bond, id. 93.

541. *Foreigners.* — In regard to foreigners resident in a country, although some jurists deny the right of a nation generally to legislate over them, it would seem clear, upon general principles of international law, that such a right does exist; (a) and the extent to which it should be exercised is a matter purely of municipal arrangement and policy. Huberus lays down the doctrine in his second axiom. All persons who are found within the limits of a government, whether their residence is permanent or temporary, are to be deemed subjects thereof.[1] Boullenois says that the sovereign has a right to make laws to bind foreigners in relation to their property within his domains; in relation to contracts and acts done therein; and in relation to judicial proceedings, if they implead before his tribunals.[2] And further, that he may of strict right make laws for all foreigners who merely pass through his domains, although commonly this authority is exercised only as to matters of police.[3] Vattel asserts the same general doctrine, and says that foreigners are subject to the laws of a state while they reside in it.[4] And in relation to disputes which may arise between foreigners, or between a citizen and a foreigner, he holds that they are to be determined by the judge of the place, and according to the laws of the place of the defendant's domicil.[5]

542. *Policy of some Nations.* — There are nations indeed which wholly refuse to take cognizance of controversies between foreigners, and remit them for relief to their own domestic tribunals, or to that of the party defendant, and especially as to matters originating in foreign countries. Thus in France, with few exceptions, the tribunals do not entertain jurisdiction of controversies between foreigners respecting personal rights and interests.[6] (b) But this is a matter of mere municipal policy and

---

[1] Ante, s. 29; Huberus, tom. 2, lib. 1, tit. 3, s. 2, p. 538; ante, s. 29, note 3; Henry on Foreign Law, c. 8, p. 54, c. 9, p. 63, c. 10, p. 71.

[2] 1 Boullenois, Pr. Gén. 4, 5, p. 3. [3] Id. 5, p. 3.

[4] Vattel, b. 1, c. 19, s. 213; Id. b. 2, c. 8, s. 90, 101, 103. (See Caldwell *v.* Van Vlissengen, 16 Jur. 115; 9 Eng. Law & Eq. 51.)

[5] Id. b. 2, c. 8, s. 103.

[6] See Pardessus, Droit Comm. tom. 5, art. 1470–1478, p. 238; Henry on Foreign Law, Appendix, p. 214–216.

(a) Peabody *v.* Hamilton, 106 Mass. 217.   (b) See Lang *v.* Reid, 12 Moore, P. C. 86.

convenience, and does not result from any principles of international law. In England and America, on the other hand, suits are maintainable, and are constantly maintained, between foreigners, where either of them is within the territory of the state in which the suit is brought.

543. *Property in other Countries.* — But although every nation may thus rightfully exercise jurisdiction over all persons within its domains, yet we are to understand that, in regard thereto, the doctrine applies only to suits purely personal, or to suits connected with property within the same sovereignty. For although the person may be within the territorial jurisdiction, yet it is by no means true that, in virtue thereof, every sort of suit may there be maintainable against him. A suit cannot, for instance, be maintainable against him, so as absolutely to bind his property situate elsewhere ; and, a fortiori, not so as absolutely to bind his rights and titles to immovable property situate elsewhere. It is true that some nations do, in maintaining suits in personam, attempt, indirectly, by their judgments and decrees, to bind property situate in other countries ; but it is always with the reserve, that it binds the person only in their own courts in regard to such property. And certainly there can be no pretence that such judgments or decrees bind the property itself, or the rights over it which are established by the laws of the place where it is situate. If a Court of Chancery in England should compel a bankrupt, by its decree, to convey his personal and real estate, situate in foreign countries, to the assignees under the commission (as it was at one time thought they might do, although now the doctrine is repudiated[1]) ; yet such a decree would not operate to transfer the property, so as to affect the rights of creditors, or the regular operation of the laws of the state rei sitæ. So a foreign court cannot, by its judgment or decree, pass the title to land situate in another country ; neither can it bind such land by a judgment or decree that, in default of the defendants in the suit conveying, it shall be conveyed by the deed of its own officers to the plaintiffs. Such a conveyance made by its officers would be treated in the country where the land is situate as a mere nullity.[2]

---

[1] *Ex parte* Blakes, 1 Cox, 898; Selkrig *v.* Davies, 2 Rose, 79, 291; 2 Dow, 281.

[2] Watts *v.* Waddle, 6 Pet. 389, 400.

544. *Chancery Jurisdiction.* — The doctrine of the English Courts of Chancery on this head of jurisdiction seems carried to an extent which may perhaps in some cases not find a perfect warrant in the general principles of international public law; and therefore it must have a very uncertain basis, as to its recognition in foreign countries, so far as it may be supposed to be founded in the comity of nations. (*a*) That doctrine is, that the Court of Chancery, having authority to act upon the person (agere in personam) may indirectly act upon real estate situate in a foreign country, through the instrumentality of this authority over the person; and that it may compel him to give effect to its decree respecting such property, whether it goes to the entire disposition of it, or only to affect it with liens or burdens.[1] (*b*) Lord Hardwicke asserted the jurisdiction in several cases.[2] At a more recent period the Court of Chancery asserted the jurisdiction over a British creditor who had fraudulently obtained a judgment in the British West Indies against his debtor, and had on an execution sold his debtor's real estate there, and become the purchaser thereof; and the court set aside the purchase for the fraud.[3] It is observable that in this last case all the parties were British subjects, and the original judgment was in a British island. The Master of the Rolls, Sir R. P. Arden, on that occasion said: 'Upon the whole, it comes to this, that, by a proceeding in the island, an absentee's estate might be brought to sale, and for whatever interest he has, without any particular upon which they are to bid; the question is, whether any court will permit the transaction to prevail to that extent. It is said this court has no jurisdiction, because it is a proceeding in the West Indies. It has been argued very sensibly that it is strange for this court to say it is void by the laws of the island for want of notice. I admit I am bound to say that according to those laws a creditor may do this. To that law he has had

[1] See 1 Eq. Abr. 133; Arglasse *v.* Muschamp, 1 Vern. 75, 135; Kildare *v.* Eustace, 1 Vern. 419.

[2] See Foster *v.* Vassall, 3 Atk. 589; Penn *v.* Lord Baltimore, 1 Ves. 444.

[3] Cranstown *v.* Johnston, 3 Ves. 170; 5 Ves. 277.

(*a*) See Norris *v.* Chambers, 29 Beav. 253.

(*b*) See Loney *v.* Penniman, 43 Md. 131; Keyser *v.* Rice, 47 Md. 203; Western Union Tel. Co. *v.* Pacific Tel. Co. 49 Ill. 90 (injunction refused); Snook *v.* Snetzer, 25 Ohio St. 516; Muller *v.* Dows, 94 U. S. 444.

recourse and wishes to avail himself of it; the question is, whether an English court will permit such an use to be made of the law of that island or any other country. It is sold, not to satisfy the debt, but in order to get the estate, which the law of that country never could intend, for a price much inadequate to the real value; and to pay himself more than the debt for which the suit was commenced, and for which only the sale could be holden. It was not much litigated that the courts of equity here have an equal right to interfere with regard to judgments or mortgages upon the lands in a foreign country, as upon lands here. Bills are often filed upon mortgages in the West Indies. The only distinction is, that this court cannot act upon the land directly, but acts upon the conscience of the person living here. Archer v. Preston, Lord Arglasse v. Muschamp, Lord Kildare v. Eustace (1 Eq. Abr. 133; 1 Vern. 75, 135, 419). Those cases clearly show that with regard to any contract made, or equity between persons in this country, respecting lands in a foreign country, particularly in the British dominions, this court will hold the same jurisdiction as if they were situated in England. Lord Hardwicke lays down the same doctrine (3 Atk. 589). Therefore without affecting the jurisdiction of the courts there, or questioning the regularity of the proceedings, as in a court of law, or saying that this sale would have been set aside either in law or equity there, I have no difficulty in saying, which is all I have to say, that this creditor has availed himself of the advantage he got by the nature of those laws, to proceed behind the back of the debtor upon a constructive notice, which could not operate to the only point to which a constructive notice ought, that there might be actual notice without wilful default; that he has gained an advantage which neither the law of this nor of any other country would permit. I will lay down the rule as broad as this: this court will not permit him to avail himself of the law of any other country to do what would be gross injustice.'[1]

545. *Its Limits.* — To the extent of this decision perhaps there may not be any well-founded objection;[2] and the same doctrine has been repeatedly acted upon by the equity courts of

[1] Cranstown v. Johnston, 3 Ves. 170; 5 Ves. 277.
[2] Jackson v. Petrie, 10 Ves. 164.

America.[1] (a) But even in England the Court of Chancery will not act directly upon lands in the plantations, so as to affect the title, or the possession, or the rents and profits thereof.[2] Nor will it entertain jurisdiction over contracts with regard to lands in foreign colonies, so as to touch the title there, or to prevent a sale thereof by an injunction;[3] although it has been repeatedly held, in very general terms, that there is no doubt of the jurisdiction of the Court of Chancery, as to land in the West Indies, or in other foreign places, if the persons are in England.[4]

546. *Actions against Non-Residents.* — But it is not an uncommon course for a nation by its own municipal code to provide for the institution of actions against non-resident citizens, and against non-resident foreigners, by a citation viis et modis, as it called, or by an attachment of their property, nominal or real, within the limits of its own territorial sovereignty; and to proceed to judgment against the party defendant, whether he has any actual notice of the suit or not, or whether he ever appears to the suit or not. In respect to such suits, in personam, by a mere personal citation, viis et modis, such as by posting up such a citation on the Royal Exchange in London, as is done in the Admiralty in England, or by an edictal citation, as it is called, posted up at the quay in Leith, at the market-cross of Edinburgh, and the pier and shore of Leith, according to the practice of Scotland,[5] there is no pretence to say that such modes of proceeding can confer any legitimate jurisdiction over foreigners who are non-residents, and

---

[1] See Massie v. Watts, 6 Cranch, 148, 158; Ward v. Arredondo, Hopkins, 213; Mead v. Merritt, 2 Paige (N. Y.) 402; Mitchell v. Bunch, 2 Paige (N. Y.) 606.

[2] Roberdeau v. Rous, 1 Atk. 543. See 1 Vern. 75, 135, 419; post, s. 551.

[3] White v. Hall, 12 Ves. 321. See Massie v. Watts, 6 Cranch, 148, 156.

[4] Jackson v. Petrie, 10 Ves. 165.

[5] Ersk. Inst. b. 1, tit. 2, s. 17, 18; Id. b. 4, tit. 1, s. 8. After a decree is obtained in personam in Scotland, it seems that letters of horning, as they are called, issue, requiring the defendant to comply with the decree, which may be served by personal service, or, if the party cannot be found, by application at his place of domicil or dwelling-house, and if he is out of the kingdom, then he is charged by a copy put up at the market-cross in Edinburgh, and at the pier and shore of Leith. Ersk. Inst. b. 2, tit. 5, s. 55; Id. b. 4, tit. 3, s. 9. See Douglas v. Forrest, 4 Bing. 686, 690.

(a) See Olney v. Eaton, 66 Mo. 563. So one may be enjoined from suing in another state for debt in a proper case. Snook v. Snetzer, 25 Ohio St. 516.

do not appear to answer the suit, whether they have notice of the suit or not. The effects of all such proceedings are purely local; and elsewhere they will be held to be mere nullities. (a)

547. *Buchanan* v. *Rucker.* — Lord Ellenborough put this doctrine with great clearness and force, in a case before the court where a judgment was obtained, in the island of Tobago, against a party stated in the proceedings to be ' formerly of the city of Dunkirk, and now of the city of London, merchant,' and who was cited to appear at the ensuing court to answer the plaintiff's action by a summons, which was returned served ' by nailing up a copy of the declaration at the court-house door,' and on which service judgment was afterwards given by default of the defendant to appear and defend it. It was attempted to maintain the judgment as authorized by the local law, in cases of persons absent from the island. Lord Ellenborough, in delivering the judgment of the court, said : ' By persons absent from the island must necessarily be understood persons who have been present and within the jurisdiction, so as to have been subject to the process of the court; but it can never be applied to a person who, for aught appears, never was present within or subject to the jurisdiction. Supposing however that the act had said in terms that, though a person sued in the island had never been present within the jurisdiction, yet that it should bind him, upon proof of nailing up the summons at the court door; how could that be obligatory upon the subjects of other countries? Can the Island of Tobago pass a law to bind the rights of the whole world? Would the world submit to such an assumed jurisdiction? The law itself however, fairly construed, does not warrant such an inference; for " absent from the island " must be taken only to apply to persons who had been present there, and were subject to the jurisdiction of the court out of which the process issued; and as nothing of that sort was in proof here to show that the defendant was subject to the jurisdiction at the time of commencing the suit, there is no foundation for raising an assumpsit in law upon the judgment so obtained.'[1]

[1] Buchanan *v.* Rucker, 9 East, 192, 194. See Cranstown *v.* Johnston, 3 Ves. 170; 5 Ves. 277; Cavan *v.* Stewart, 1 Stark. 525; Becquet *v.* McCarthy, 2 B. & Ad. 951; Ferguson *v.* Mahon, 11 A. & E. 179, 182. In Smith *v.* Nicolls,

(a) See Schibsby *v.* Westenholz, L. R. 6 Q. B. 153; Bischoff *v.* Wethered, 9 Wall. 812.

Douglas v. *Forrest.* — In a recent case the validity of a
rendered in a foreign country in a suit against persons
non-residents, and had no actual notice of the suit, and
appear and answer the same, came before the Court of
Pleas in England, upon a Scottish judgment rendered
a Scottish absentee, upon a due attachment of his herita-
in Scotland, and due proclamation, by what is tech-
called ' horning ' in Scotland, which judgment was rendered
the defendant by default for his non-appearance to answer
The question was, whether the judgment so rendered
void or not. It was held that the judgment was valid.
This decision was founded partly upon the construction of the
articles of union between Scotland and England, and partly upon
the recognition of such a practice as valid by a British act of parliament, and partly upon the fact that the judgment was against
a Scottish subject.[1] On that occasion Lord Chief Justice Best, in
delivering the opinion of the court, said ; ' A natural-born subject
of any country, quitting that country, but leaving property under
the protection of its laws, even during his absence owes obedience
to those laws, particularly when those laws enforce a moral obligation. The deceased, before he left his native country, acknowledged, under his hand, that he owed the debts ; he was under a
moral obligation to discharge those debts as soon as he could.' [2]
And after adverting to the case of Buchanan *v.* Rucker, and some
others, he added : ' To be sure, if attachments, issued against any
persons who were never within the jurisdiction of the court issuing them, would be supported and confirmed in the country in
which the person attached resided, the legislature of any country

case, which was an action in an English court on a Scotch judgment of horning against a Scotchman born, the court guards itself against a general inference from the decision. The Chief Justice, in delivering the judgment of
the court, says (4 Bing. 703): " We confine our judgment to a case where the
party owed allegiance to the country in which the judgment was so given
against him, and by the laws of which country his property was, at the time
those judgments were given, protected." Beckett *v.* McCarthy (2 B. & Ad.
951) has been supposed to go to the verge of the law; but the defendant in that
case held a public office in the very colony in which he was originally sued.'
In the still more recent case of Ferguson *v.* Mahon, 11 A. & E. 179 ; 3 P. & D.
143, the Court of King's Bench in England held, in an action on an Irish
judgment, that it was a good plea in bar that the defendant was never served
with, nor had notice of, any process in the action.

[1] Douglas *v.* Forrest, 4 Bing. 686, 702, 703.

might authorize their courts to decide on the rights of parties who owed no allegiance to the government of such country, and were under no obligation to attend its courts or obey its laws. We confine our judgment to a case where the party owed allegiance to the country in which the judgment was so given against him, from being born in it, and by the laws of which country his property was, at the time those judgments were given, protected. The debts were contracted in the country in which the judgments were given, whilst the debtor resided in it.[1]

548 a. *Becquet* v. *McCarthy.* — Another case also occurred at a later period which presented a similar question. An action was brought and a judgment recovered in the island of Mauritius against a party who had been a former resident in the island, but who was absent from the island during the whole course of the proceedings. By a law of the colony it was provided that if a suit was instituted against an absent party, process should be served upon the king's procurator-general in the colony; but it was not expressly provided that the procurator-general should communicate with the absent party. It appeared that the process was served on the procurator-general, but it did not appear that the absent party had any notice thereof. The court held that the judgment was valid. Lord Tenterden, on that occasion, in delivering the opinion of the court, said: ' Another objection, and not an unimportant one, was, that the testator, when the proceedings were instituted against him, was absent from the island; and it was urged that it was contrary to the principles of natural justice that any one should be condemned unheard and in his absence. Proof however was given that by the law of the colony, in the case of a person formerly resident in the island absenting himself, and not leaving any attorney upon whom process in a suit might be served, the procurator-general or his deputy was bound to take care of the interest of such absent party. It was said that the law of the island did not provide any means whereby the procurator-general or his deputy might be required to hold communication with, or receive directions from, an absent person. There may perhaps be some deficiency in the law in that respect; but as the law of the island is that the process shall

[1] Douglas *v.* Forrest, 4 Bing. 686, 702, 703. See also Becquet *v.* McCarthy, 2 B. & Ad. 951; Don *v.* Lippmann, 5 Cl. & F. 1, 21; Plummer *v.* Woodburne, 4 B. & C. 625.

be served upon the public officer, it must be presumed that he would do whatever was necessary in the discharge of that public duty; and we cannot take upon ourselves to say that the law is so contrary to natural justice as to render the judgment void in a case where the process was so served."[1]

549. *Proceedings by Attachment of Property.* — A still more common course in many states and nations is to proceed against non-residents, whether they are citizens or whether they are foreigners, by a seizure or attachment of their property situate or found within the territory. Sometimes the seizure or attachment is purely nominal, as, for example, of a chip, or a cane, or a hat. In other cases the seizure or attachment is bona fide of real property or personal property within the territory, or of debts due to the non-resident persons in the hands of their debtors who live within the country.[2] In such cases, for all the purposes of the suit, the existence of the property so seized or attached within the territory constitutes a just ground of proceeding to enforce the rights of the plaintiff to the extent of subjecting such property to execution upon the decree or judgment. But if the defendant has never appeared and contested the suit, it is to be treated to all intents and purposes as a mere proceeding in rem, and not as personally binding on the party as a decree of judgment in personam; or, in other words, it only binds the property seized or attached in the suit, to the extent thereof, and is in no just sense a decree or judgment binding upon him beyond that property. In other countries it is uniformly so treated, and is justly considered as having no extra-territorial force or obligation.[3] (a)

---

[1] Becquet v. McCarthy, 2 B. & Ad. 951, 958, 959. It has been justly remarked by Lord Brougham in Don v. Lippmann, 5 Cl. & F. 21, that that case 'has been supposed to go to the verge of the law; but the defendant in that case held a public office in the very colony in which he was originally sued.' Perhaps a stronger doubt of its correctness might upon principles of public justice have been pronounced. Boullenois manifestly deems an exercise of jurisdiction against an absent foreigner to be unfounded in point of authority. 1 Boullenois, obs. 25, p. 610.

[2] See Henry on Foreign Law, c. 8–10, p. 54, 63, 71; Douglas v. Forrest, 4 Bing. 686, 700, 701.

[3] See Phelps r. Holker, 1 Dall. 261; Kilburn v. Woodworth, 5 Johns. (N. Y.) 37; Pawling v. Bird, 13 Johns. (N. Y.) 192; Bissell v. Briggs, 9 Mass. 462; Robinson v. Ward, 8 Johns. (N. Y.) 86; post, s. 592. But see Douglas v.

(a) See Galpin v. Page, 18 Wall. 174; Cooper v. Reynolds, 10 Wall. 350; D'Arcy v. Ketchum, 11 How. 308.

550. *Jurisdiction as regards Property.* — In the next place let us consider the subject of jurisdiction in regard to property. It

Forrest, 4 Bing. 686, 702, 703; Shumway *v.* Stillman, 6 Wend. (N. Y.) 447; 1 Boullenois, obs. 25, p. 609, 610, 619, 620, 622, 623, 624, 628; 6 Harr. & J. (Md) 191; Taylor *v.* Phelps, 1 Harr. & G. (Md.) 492. Mr. Chief Justice Parsons, in his very able opinion in Bissell *v.* Briggs, 9 Mass. 468, has made some pointed remarks on this subject, from which the following extract is made: ' To illustrate this position, it may be remarked that a debtor, living in Massachusetts, may have goods, effects, or credits in New Hampshire, where the creditor lives. The creditor there may lawfully attach these, pursuant to the laws of that state, in the hands of the bailiff, factor, trustee, or garnishee of his debtor, and on recovering judgment, those goods, effects, and credits may lawfully be applied to satisfy the judgment; and the bailiff, factor, trustee, or garnishee, if sued in this state for those goods, effects, or credits, shall, in our courts, be protected by that judgment, the court in New Hampshire having jurisdiction of the cause for the purpose of rendering that judgment, and the bailiff, factor, trustee, or garnishee producing it, not to obtain execution of it here, but for his own justification. If however those goods, effects, and credits are insufficient to satisfy the judgment, and the creditor should sue an action on that judgment in this state to obtain satisfaction, he must fail; because the defendant was not personally amenable to the jurisdiction of the court rendering the judgment. And if the defendant, after the service of the process of foreign attachment, should either in person have gone into the state of New Hampshire, or constituted an attorney to defend the suit, so as to protect his goods, effects, or credits from the effect of the attachment, he would not thereby have given the court jurisdiction of his person; since this jurisdiction must result from the service of the foreign attachment. It would be unreasonable to oblige any man living in one state, and having effects in another state, to make himself amenable to the courts of the last state, that he might defend his property there attached.' See post, s. 584, 592, 598–618. Mr. Burge has made the following remarks on the same subject: 'In order that it may produce the effect of res judicata in the country in which it is pronounced, and a fortiori in a foreign country, the sentence must be given by a competent tribunal. It must put a final termination to the matter in litigation, and it must be certain. The want of either of these requisites is such a defect as to render the sentence null and void, and this defect is called a nullity. The judicial tribunal must be competent to entertain jurisdiction of the subject-matter of the suit. If, according to the constitution of the tribunal, the subject-matter of the sentence was excluded from its cognizance, the sentence pronounced by the individuals composing it would possess the weight which belonged to an arbitrament made by those to whom the litigating parties had submitted their differences, but it would not possess the authority of res judicata. Where a limited tribunal takes upon itself to exercise a jurisdiction which does not belong to it, its decision amounts to nothing, and does not create any necessity for an appeal. Such a defect in the sentence cannot be cured by the appearance of the party. Another nullity in the sentence is a decision given upon that which was not demanded or not contested, or when more has been adjudged than was demanded, for in either case the judge has exceeded his jurisdiction: " Ultra id, quod in judicium deductum est, potestas judicis nequaquam potest excedere.'' The party against whom the sentence has been obtained must be subject to the jurisdic-

will be unnecessary to discuss the matter at large, as to personal property, since the general doctrine is not controverted that,

tion of that tribunal. Such a jurisdiction is founded either in respect of the defender's domicil in the territory of the tribunal, ratione domicilii, or in respect of his being possessed of some estate or subject within it, ratione rei sitæ, or on the arrestment made by the decree of the court of the party's movable effects, arrestum causa fundandæ jurisdictionis. A jurisdiction acquired by the arrest of the defender's property was not known to the civil law, but it was admitted in the jurisprudence of Holland, Spain, France, and Scotland, in all personal actions in which the defender is bound, "ad dandum, faciendum, et præstandum." It is not allowed in order to compel the defender to appear before any other judicial tribunal than that of the place in which the immovable property, the subject of the suit, is situated. By the law of Scotland the jurisdiction is founded not only on the defendant's domicil, but on his personal residence in a place for forty days. It admits jurisdiction ratione rei sitæ, unless it has for its object a question merely personal, as of status. Where a foreigner not otherwise subject to the jurisdiction of the courts of Scotland is possessed of movable property there, the jurisdiction is acquired by arresting his goods, and so fixing them within the judge's territory, or by their being already a subject of competition in a court of that kingdom. By the civil law the jurisdiction was acquired in respect of the place in which the contract was entered into, or in which it was to be performed; but the codes founded on the civil law do not admit a jurisdiction in either of these cases unless the defendant is found in that place. The citation of the defender, the vocatio in jus, juris experiendi causa vocatio, is essential to the validity of the sentence, because otherwise he has not had the opportunity of defending himself against the claim of his adversary. That citation need not have been served on him personally; it is sufficient if it be left at his house. When the tribunal acquires jurisdiction either ratione rei sitæ, or by arrestment in consequence of the defender having no domicil in loco fori, this citation is necessarily a merely formal act. By the Code Civil, the public minister is specially charged with the duty of watching over the interest of those who are presumed to be absent, and he is to be heard upon all demands which concern them. The Code de Procédure makes provision for delivering to certain public officers copies of the process, which may be issued against foreigners. The jurisdiction exercised by the courts of England is in general founded on the personal service of the process on the defendant. Indeed, according to the ancient law, the plaintiff could not proceed in an action before the defendant had actually appeared in court to answer him; and even if he pertinaciously neglected or refused to appear, the only course was to issue continued process, or to distrain upon his goods, in order thereby, as it was expected, to induce him to appear, or to outlaw him, by which process he incurred a qualified forfeiture of his land and goods, and all his civil rights as a subject were suspended. But in certain cases, after actual personal service, the plaintiff was, by the aid of certain statutes, permitted to enter an appearance for the defendant. But if the defendant were abroad, or avoided the service of process, and had no goods (the distraining of which was considered nearly equivalent to actual service, because it was supposed the defendant would hear of that proceeding), then the only course was, and still is, to proceed to outlawry, which however does not enable the plaintiff to proceed in his action, or to obtain judgment therein,

although movables are for many purposes to be deemed to have no situs, except that of the domicil of the owner, yet this being but a legal fiction, it yields whenever it is necessary for the purpose of justice that the actual situs of the thing should be examined. (a)   A nation within whose territory any personal property is actually situate has as entire dominion over it while therein, in point of sovereignty and jurisdiction, as it has over immovable property situate there.   It may regulate its transfer, and subject it to process and execution, and provide for and control the uses and disposition of it, to the same extent that it may exert its authority over immovable property.[1]   One of the grounds upon which, as we have seen, jurisdiction is assumed over non-residents, is through the instrumentality of their personal property, as well as of their real property, within the local sovereignty.[2]   Hence it is that, whenever personal property is taken by arrest, attachment, or execution within a state, the title so acquired under the laws of the state is held valid in every other state;[3] and the same rule is applied to debts due to non-residents, which are subjected to the like process under the local laws of a state.[4] (b)

551. *Immovables.* — In respect to immovable property every attempt of any foreign tribunal to found a jurisdiction over it must, from the very nature of the case, be utterly nugatory, and its decree must be forever incapable of execution in rem.   We

but only causes a seizure of the lands, goods, and property of the defendant, as forfeited to the king for the defendant's contumacy and disrespect of his process.   But the plaintiff may thereupon, by application to the Court of Exchequer or by petition, when his claim exceeds fifty pounds, obtain satisfaction of his debt by sale of the defendant's property seized under his outlawry, unless previously the defendant appears to the action, and enables the plaintiff to try the merits.' 3 Burge, Col. & For. Law, pt. 2, c. 24, p. 1016, 1019.

[1] See ante, s. 423 a.   [2] Ante, s. 549.

[3] Lord Kenyon expressed his opinion to the following effect in Ogden v. Folliott, 3 T. R. 733: 'I have always understood it to be clear,' said he, 'that all judicial acts done in one country over the property of the subjects within their jurisdiction are conclusive on the property of those parties in any other country.'

[4] See Bissell v. Briggs, 9 Mass. 462, 468, 469.   But see Folliott v. Ogden, 1 H. Bl. 124, 135; 3 T. R. 726, 733.   See Don v. Lippmann, 5 Cl. & F. 1, 19.

(a) Graham v. First National Bank, 84 N. Y. 393; Green v. Van Buskirk, 5 Wall. 307; 7 Wall. 139; note to s. 383, ante.

(b) See Denny v. Faulkner, 22 Kans. 89.

have seen indeed that by the Roman law a suit might in many cases be brought, either where the property was situate or where the party had his domicil.[1] This might well be done within any of the vast domains over which the Roman empire extended; for the judgments of its tribunals would be everywhere respected and obeyed. But among the independent nations of modern times there would be insuperable difficulties in such a course. And hence, even in countries acknowledging the Roman law, it has become a very general principle that suits in rem should be brought where the property is situate; and this principle is applied with almost universal approbation in regard to immovable property.[2] The same rule is applied to mixed actions, and to all suits which touch the realty.[3]

552. *Boullenois.* — Boullenois has treated this whole subject with becoming fulness and accuracy. He has divided actions into those which are purely personal, those which are purely real, and those which are mixed and partake of the character of both, following in these respects, as he avows, the division of Burgundus.[4] The first (personal actions), respect the quality, state, or condition of persons, and pronounce against them judgments purely personal, ad dandum, vel faciendum, aut non faciendum. The next (real actions), respect things, either the proprietary right or ownership, or the right of possession, or the right or title of a creditor, or some other right or title. The last (mixed actions), respect both persons and things, either in adjudging the property to one, or pronouncing against him a personal judgment for the profit of the other, or adjudging the property to one, and adjudging the other to make restitution of the profits to him; so that it is the title of the action which char-

---

[1] Ante, s. 582, 545; post, s. 586, 591.

[2] The jurisdiction as to the rights of real property is local, the subject being fixed and immovable. Lord Chief Justice de Grey in Rafael v. Ferelst, 2 W. Bl. 1058.

[3] Henry on Foreign Law, c. 8, s. 3, p. 59, c. 9, s. 1, p. 63; 1 Boullenois, obs. 25, p. 601, &c.; Id. p. 618, 619; Id. p. 635, &c.

[4] The language of Burgundus is: Omnium condemnationum summa divisio, pariter in tria genera deducitur. Aut enim in rem, aut in personam, aut in utramque concipiuntur. In rem, quoties alicui res asseritur, hoc est ejus esse dicitur, vel jure creditoris, aut alio modo possidenda datur. In personam, si condemnetur ad aliquid dandum aut patiendum, faciendum aut non faciendum, vel, si personæ statum afficiat. In utramque si et res, et personæ simul in condemnationem veniant. Burgundus, tract. 3, n. 1, 2, p. 84, 85.

49

acterizes the action.[1] Personal actions may rightfully be brought between natives in any competent tribunal of the realm; and between foreigners also, who have submitted to the jurisdiction, wherever the laws allow its exercise; and between natives and foreigners in like manner.[2] But in all these cases the domicil of the party defendant is commonly supposed to be within the jurisdiction.[3] Real actions ought to be brought in the place rei sitæ; and this is the rule, not only when the property in controversy is situate in the same kingdom, but also when the parties, being domiciled in one country, engage in a litigation as to property locally situate in another country.[4] If therefore a judgment should be rendered in one country respecting property in another, it will be of no force in the latter. It is true that property within a country does not make the owner generally a subject of the sovereign where it is locally situate; but it subjects him to his jurisdiction 'secundum quid, et aliquo modo.'[5] Mixed actions, so far as they regard the realty, are to be brought in the place rei sitæ; but if the personal damages or claims be separable in their nature and character, they may be sued for as personal actions.[6] There are many other jurists who adopt the like distinctions.[7]

553. *Vattel.* — Vattel explicitly avows the same doctrine. 'The defendant's judge' (that is, the competent judge), says he, 'is the judge of the place where the defendant has his settled abode, or the judge of the place where the defendant is when any sudden difficulty arises, provided it does not relate to an estate in

[1] 1 Boullenois, obs. 25, p. 601, 602.

[2] Boullenois makes a distinction in suits between natives and foreigners to this effect. If a foreigner sues a native, then the jurisdiction is well founded against the latter in the place of his domicil, and the foreigner is bound by the judgment. If the foreigner is defendant and has submitted to the jurisdiction, then the same result follows. If he has not submitted or has not appeared to the suit, then the judgment is not obligatory. 1 Boullenois, obs. 25, p. 609, 610. He founds himself in this opinion upon the general rule, Actor sequitur forum rei; and he quotes with approbation the remark of J. Gaill: Quis manens extra regnum non tenetur in parlamento respondere super actione personali. Id. p. 612.

[3] 1 Boullenois, obs. 25, p. 601–603, 606, 609, 610. See also Id. Prin. Gén. 34, p. 8, 9.

[4] Id. obs. 25, p. 618–620, 622, 623; Id. Prin. Gén. 35, 37, p. 9.

[5] Id. obs. 25, p. 623–625.   [6] Id. obs. 25, p. 635, 636.

[7] Id. obs. 25, p. 601–651; 1 Hertii Opera, de Collis. Leg. s. 70, p. 132, ed. 1737; Id. p. 215, ed. 1716; J. Voet, ad Pand. 1, 4, 1, s. 28, p. 241.

land, or to a right annexed to such an estate. In such a case as property of this kind is to be held according to the laws of the country where it is situated, and as the right of granting it is vested in the ruler of the country, controversies relating to such [real] property can only be decided in the state in which it depends.'[1]

554. *Injuries to Immovables.* — It will be perceived that, in many respects, the doctrine here laid down coincides with that of the common law. It has been already stated that, by the common law, personal actions, being transitory, may be brought in any place where the party defendant can be found;[2](a) that real actions must be brought in the forum rei sitæ; and that mixed actions are properly referable to the same jurisdiction.[3] Among the latter are actions for trespasses and injuries to real property which are deemed local; so that they will not lie elsewhere than in the place rei sitæ. This distinction was recognized as long ago as 1665, in a case[4] where the twelve judges certified, that for torts to the person and the personal property done abroad, a remedy lay in a suit in personam in England; but that

[1] Vattel, b. 2, c. 8, s. 103.

[2] Personal injuries are of a transitory nature, et sequunter forum rei. Lord Chief Justice de Grey in Rafael v. Ferelst, 2 W. Bl. 1058. See Mostyn v. Fabrigas, Cowp. 161, 176, 177; Robinson v. Bland, 2 Burr. 1077; 1 W. Bl. 259; ante, s. 364.

[3] Ante, s. 364; 4 Cowen, 527, note. Lord Mansfield in Mostyn v. Fabrigas, Cowp. 161, 176, said: 'There is a formal and a substantial distinction as to the locality of trials. I state them as different things. The substantial distinction is, where the proceeding is in rem; and where the effect of judgment cannot be had, if it is laid in a wrong place. That is the case of all ejectments, &c. With regard to matters that arise out of the realm there is a substantial distinction of locality too; for there are some cases that arise out of the realm which ought not to be tried anywhere but in the country where they arise. As if two persons fight in France, and both happening casually to be here, one should bring an action of assault against the other, it might be a doubt whether such an action could be maintained here; because though it is not a criminal prosecution, it must be laid to be against the peace of the king; but the breach of the peace is merely local, though the trespass against the person is transitory.' His lordship here doubtless alluded to a case of a personal trespass between foreigners; for in a subsequent part of the same opinion he expressly held that, as between subjects, not only upon contracts, but for personal torts, an action might be maintained in England; and indeed that was the very point decided in the case then in judgment.

[4] Skinner v. East India Company, cited in Cowp. 167, 168.

(a) Peabody v. Hamilton, 106 Mass. 217.

for torts to real property or to fixtures abroad no suit lay. Lord Mansfield and Lord Chief Justice Eyre held at one time a different doctrine, and allowed suits to be maintained in England for injuries done by pulling down houses in foreign unsettled regions, viz., in the desert coasts of Nova Scotia and Labrador.[1] But this doctrine has been since overruled as untenable according to the actual jurisprudence of England,[2] (a) however maintainable it might be upon general principles of international law, if the suit were for personal damages only.[3] (b)

555. *Grounds of Exclusive Jurisdiction.* — The grounds upon which the exclusive jurisdiction is maintained over immovable property are the same upon which the sole right to establish, regulate, and control the transfer, descent, and testamentary disposition of it has been admitted by all nations. The inconveniences of an opposite course would be innumerable, and would subject immovable property to the most distressing conflicts arising from opposing titles, and compel every nation to administer almost all other laws except its own, in the ordinary administration of justice.[4]

556. *Procedure.* — Having stated these general principles in relation to jurisdiction (the result of which is, that no nation can rightfully claim to exercise it, except as to persons and property

[1] Cited by Lord Mansfield in Mostyn v. Fabrigas, Cowp. 180, 181.

[2] Doulson v. Matthews, 4 T. R. 503.

[3] The doctrine of this last case was very fully examined and affirmed by Mr. Chief Justice Marshall in the case of Livingston v. Jefferson, before the Circuit Court of Virginia, in 1811, 4 Hall's Am. Law Journal, 78; 1 Brock. 203. It was an action quare clausum fregit, brought against Mr. Jefferson on account of an alleged trespass to lands (the Batture) in New Orleans, by his order, while he was President of the United States. The suit was dismissed for want of jurisdiction.

[4] Ante, s. 364, 365.

(a) See Watts v. Kinney, 6 Hill (N. Y.) 82; 23 Wend. (N. Y.) 484.

(b) It has been determined however in a late case in America, that a person residing in Pennsylvania, and owning real estate situated there, might maintain an action in the Circuit Court of the United States, in the state of New Jersey, against a canal corporation chartered by the latter state, for consequential injuries done to such real estate by the defendant's canal, situated also in New Jersey. Rundle v. Delaware Canal, 1 Wall. jun. 275. See also Holmes v. Barclay, 4 Louis. Ann. 63. So it has been determined in Ohio, that an action on the case for diverting water from the plaintiff's mill, situated in Ohio, might be sustained in the courts of that state, although the act of diversion took place in another state. Thayer v. Brooks, 17 Ohio, 489.

within its own domains), we are next led to the consideration of the question, in what manner suits arising from foreign causes are to be instituted, and proceedings to be had until the final judgment. Are they to be according to the law of the place where the parties, or either of them, live? Or are they to be according to the modes of proceeding and forms of suit prescribed by the laws of the place where the suits are brought? Fortunately here there is scarcely any ground left open for controversy, either at the common law or in the opinions of foreign jurists, or in the actual practice of nations. It is universally admitted and established that the forms of remedies and the modes of proceeding and the execution of judgments are to be regulated solely and exclusively by the laws of the place where the action is instituted; or, as the civilians uniformly express it, according to the lex fori.[1] (a)

557. *Reasons for the Doctrine.* — The reasons for this doctrine are so obvious that they scarcely require any illustration. The business of the administration of justice by any nation is, in a peculiar and emphatic sense, a part of its public right and duty. Each nation is at liberty to adopt such forms, and such a course of proceeding, as best comport with its convenience and interests, and the interests of its own subjects, for whom its laws are particularly designed. The different kinds of remedies, and the modes of proceeding best adapted to enforce rights and guard against wrongs in any nation, must materially depend upon the structure of its own jurisprudence. What would be well adapted to the jurisprudence, either customary or positive, of one nation, for rights which it recognized, or for duties which it enforced, or for wrongs which it redressed, might be wholly unfit for that of another nation, either as having gross defects or steering wide of the appropriate remedial justice. A nation acknowledging the

[1] See, on this point, 1 Burge, Col. & For. Law, pt. 1, c. 1, p. 24; Fergusson *v.* Fyffe, 8 Cl. & F. 121; General Steam Navigation Co. *v.* Guillou, 11 M. & W. 877.

(a) See Freeman's Bank *v.* Ruckman, 16 Gratt. (Va.) 126; Collins Iron Co. *v.* Burkam, 10 Mich. 283; Laird *v.* Hodges, 26 Ark. 356; Scudder *v.* Union Bank, 91 U. S. 406; Rice *v.* Harbeson, 63 N. Y. 493; Adams *v.* Wait, 42 Vt. 16; Peters *v.* Stewart, 45 Conn. 103; Burchard *v.* Dunbar, 82 Ill. 450; Mineral Point R. Co. *v.* Barron, 83 Ill. 365; Halley *v.* Ball, 66 Ill. 250; Denny *v.* Faulkner, 22 Kans. 89; Lindsay *v.* Hill, 66 Me. 212. And see especially Rice *v.* Merrimack Hosiery Co., 56 N. H. 114.

existence of peculiar rights and privileges, either personal or real, such as seigniorial rights, or trusts in the realty, would naturally introduce correspondent remedies. While other nations, in which such rights and privileges and trusts did not exist, might well dispense with the formalities which they might require. The jurisprudence of one nation may be very refined and artificial, with a multitude of intricate and perplexed proceedings; that of another may be rude, uninformed, and harsh, consisting of an undigested mass of usages. It would be absolutely impracticable to apply the process and modes of proceeding of the one nation to the other. Besides there would be an utter confusion in all judicial proceedings by attempting to engraft upon the remedies of one country those of all other countries whose subjects should be parties or be interested therein. No tribunal on earth, however learned, could hope, by any degree of diligence, to master the laws and processes and remedies of all other nations, and the qualifications and limitations properly belonging thereto. A whole life might be passed in obtaining little more than a few unconnected elements; and litigation would thus become immeasurably complicated, if not absolutely interminable. All that any nation can therefore be justly required to do, is to open its own tribunals to foreigners, in the same manner and to the same extent as they are open to its own subjects, and to give them the same redress, as to rights and wrongs, which it deems fit to acknowledge in its own municipal code for natives and residents.[1]

[1] Lord Brougham, in delivering his judgment in Don v. Lippmann, 5 Cl. & F. 1, 13, 14, made some striking remarks on this subject. ' The law on this point is well settled in this country, where this distinction is properly taken, that whatever relates to the remedy to be enforced, must be determined by the lex fori, the law of the country to the tribunals of which the appeal is made. This rule is clearly laid down in the British Linen Co. v. Drummond, 10 B. & C. 903; De la Vega v. Vianna, 1 B. & Ad. 284; and in Huber v. Steiner, 2 Scott, 304; 1 Hodges, 206; 2 Bing. N. C. 202; 2 Dowl. Pr. 781; 4 M. & Scott. 328, though the reverse had previously been recognized in Williams v. Jones, 13 East, 439. Then, assuming that to be the settled rule, the only question in this case would be, whether the law now to be enforced is the law which relates to the contract itself, or to the remedy. When both the parties reside in the country where the act is done, they look of course to the law of the country in which they reside. The contract being silent as to the law by which it is to be governed, nothing is more likely than that the lex loci contractus should be considered at the time the rule; for the parties would not suppose that the contract might afterwards come before the tribunals of a foreign country. But it is otherwise when the remedy actually comes to be enforced. The parties do

558. *Rule of the Common Law.* — The doctrine of the common law is so fully established on this point, that it would be useless to do more than to state the universal principle which it has promulgated; that is to say, that, in regard to the merits and rights involved in actions, the law of the place where they originated is to govern : ‘ In iis, quæ spectant decisoria causæ, et litis decisionem, inspiciuntur statuta loci, ubi contractus fuit celebratus.’ [1] But the form of remedies and the order of judicial proceedings are to be according to the law of the place where the action is instituted, without any regard to the domicil of the parties, the origin of the right, or the country of the act.[2]

not necessarily look to the remedy when they make the contract. They bind themselves to do what the law they live under requires; but as they bind themselves generally, it may be taken as if they had contemplated the possibility of enforcing it in another country. That is the lowest ground on which to place the case. The inconvenience of pursuing a different course is manifest. Not only the principles of the law, but the known course of the courts, renders it necessary that the rules of precedent should be adopted, and that the parties should take the law as they find it, when they come to enforce their contract. It is true that there may be no difficulty in knowing the law of the place of the contract, while there may be a great difficulty in knowing that of the place of the remedy. But that is no answer to the rule. The distinction which exists as to the principle of applying the remedy exists with even greater force as to the practice of the courts where the remedy is to be enforced. No one can say that, because the contract has been made abroad, the form of action known in the foreign court must be pursued in the courts where the contract is to be enforced, or the other preliminary proceedings of those courts must be adopted, or that the rules of pleading, or the curial practice of the foreign country, must necessarily be followed. No one will assert that, before the jury court in Scotland, the English creditor of a domiciled Scotchman would have the right to call for a trial of the case by a jury; or, take the converse, that a Scotchman might refuse the intervention of a jury here, and insist on having the case tried as in Scotland, by the judge only. No one will contend in terms that the foreign rules of evidence should guide us in such cases; and yet it is not so easy to avoid that principle in practice, if you once admit that, though the remedy is to be enforced in one country, it is to be enforced according to the laws which govern another country.’

[1] 2 Boullenois, obs. 46, p. 462; ante, s. 260; Bank of the United States *r.* Donnally, 8 Pet. 361, 372; Andrews *v.* Pond, 13 Pet. 65; Wilcox *v.* Hunt, 13 Pet. 378. See also Bouhier, Coutume de Bourg. c. 18, n. 10; ante, s. 242, 260–273.

[2] The authorities are exceedingly numerous. Among them we may cite the following: Andrews *v.* Herriot, 4 Cow. (N. Y.) 508; and see id. 528, n. (10), and authorities there cited; 2 Kent, Comm. 118, &c.; Robinson *v.* Bland, 2 Burr. 1084; De la Vega *v.* Vianna, 1 B. & Ad. 284; Trimbey *v.* Vignier, 1 Bing. N. C. 159–161; Don *v.* Lippmann, 5 Cl. & F. 1, 13, 19, 20; ante, s. 557, note; Fenwick *v.* Sears, 1 Cranch, 259; Nash *v.* Tupper, 1 Caines (N. Y.)

559. *Foreign Jurists.* — Nor are the foreign jurists less pointed in their recognition of it. Thus Bartolus, in speaking upon con-

402; Pearsall v. Dwight, 2 Mass. 84; Smith v. Spinolla, 2 Johns. (N. Y.) 198; Van Reimsdyk v. Kane, 1 Gallis. 371; Lodge v. Phelps, 1 Johns. Cas. (N. Y.) 139; Trasher v. Everhart, 3 Gill & J. (Md.) 234; Hyde v. Goodnow, 3 Comstock (N. Y.) 270; Wood v. Watkinson, 17 Conn. 510; Peck v. Hozier, 14 Johns. (N. Y.) 346; Ohio Ins. Co. v. Edmondson, 5 La. 295–300; Warren v. Lynch, 5 Johns. (N. Y.) 239; Jones v. Hook, 2 Rand. (Va.) 303; Wilcox v. Hunt, 13 Pet. 378, 379; French v. Hall, 9 N. H. 137; Bank of the United States v. Donnally, 8 Pet. 361, 370–373. This last case was an action brought in Virginia on a promissory note made in Kentucky, not under seal, but which by the law of Kentucky was deemed a specialty. The statute of limitations of Virginia was pleaded in bar; and one question was, whether it was a good bar or not. On that occasion the court said: ‘ The other point, growing out of the statute of limitations, pleaded to the fourth and fifth counts (for as to the three first counts it is conceded to be a good bar), involves questions of a very different character as to the operation and effect of a conflict of laws in cases governed by the lex loci. The statute of limitations of Virginia provides that “all actions of debt, grounded upon any lending or contract without specialty,” shall be commenced and sued within five years next after the cause of such action or suit, and not after. This being the language of the act, and confessedly governing the remedy in the courts of Virginia, the bar of five years must apply to all the cases of contract which are without specialty, or in other words are not founded on some instrument acknowledged as a specialty by the law of that state. The common law being adopted in Virginia, and the word “ specialty ” being a term of art of that law, we are led to the consideration whether the present note is deemed in the common law to be a specialty. And certainly it is not so deemed. It is not a sealed contract, nor does it fall under any other description of instruments or contracts or acts known in the common law as specialties. The argument does not deny this conclusion; but it endeavors to escape from its force, by affirming that the note is a specialty according to the laws of Kentucky; and if so, that this constitutes a part of its nature and obligation; and it ought everywhere else, upon principles of international jurisprudence, to be deemed of the like validity and effect. The act of Kentucky of the 4th of February, 1812, provides “ that all writings hereafter executed without a seal or seals, stipulating for the payment of money or property, or for the performance of any act, duty, or duties, shall be placed upon the same footing with sealed writings, containing the like stipulations, receiving the same consideration in all courts of justice, and to all intents and purposes having the same force and effect, and upon which the same species of action may be founded, as if sealed.” Now it is observable that this statute does not in terms declare that such writings shall be deemed specialties; nor does it say that they shall be deemed sealed instruments. All that it affirms is, that they shall be put upon the same footing as sealed instruments, and have the same consideration, force, effect, and remedy, as sealed instruments. So that it is perfectly consistent with the whole scope and object of the act, to give them the same dignity and obligation as specialties, without intending to make them such. A state legislature may certainly provide that the same remedy shall be had in a promissory note as on a bond or sealed instrument; but it will not thereby make the note a bond or sealed

tracts, says : ' Quæro, quid de contractibus ? Pone contractum celebratum per aliquem forensem in hac civitate ; litigium ortum est, et agitatur lis in loco originis contrahentis. Cujus loci statuta debent servari vel spectari ? Distingue ; Aut loquimur de statuto, aut de consuetudine, quæ respiciunt ipsius contractus solennitatem, aut litis ordinationem, aut de his, quæ pertinent ad jurisdictionem ex ipso contractu evenientis executionis. Primo casu, inspicitur locus contractus. Secundo casu, aut quæris de his, quæ pertinent ad litis ordinationem, et inspicitur locus judicii ; aut de his quæ pertinent ad ipsius litis decisionem, et tunc, aut de his, quæ oriuntur secundum ipsius contractus naturam tempore contractûs, aut de his, quæ oriuntur ex post facto, propter negligentiam vel moram ; primo casu inspicitur locus contractus,' &c.[1]

---

instrument. It may declare that its obligation and force shall be the same as if it were sealed; but that will still leave it an unsealed contract. But whatever may be the legislation of a state as to the obligation or remedy on contract, its acts can have no binding authority beyond its own territorial jurisdiction. Whatever authority they have in other states depends upon principles of international comity and a sense of justice. The general principle adopted by civilized nations is, that the nature, validity, and interpretation of contracts are to be governed by the law of the country where the contracts are made or are to be performed. But the remedies are to be governed by the laws of the country where the suit is brought; or, as it is compendiously expressed, by the lex fori. No one will pretend that, because an action of covenant will lie in Kentucky on an unsealed contract made in that state, therefore a like action will lie in another state, where covenant can be brought only on a contract under seal. It is an appropriate part of the remedy, which every state prescribes to its own tribunals, in the same manner in which it prescribes the times within which all suits must be brought. The nature, validity, and interpretation of the contract may be admitted to be the same in both states; but the mode by which the remedy is to be pursued, and the time within which it is to be brought, may essentially differ. The remedy, in Virginia, must be sought within the time, and in the mode, and according to the descriptive characters of the instrument known to the laws of Virginia, and not by the description and characters of it prescribed in another state. An instrument may be negotiable in one state which yet may be incapable of negotiability by the laws of another state; and the remedy must be in the courts of the latter on such instrument, according to its own laws. If, then, it were admitted that the promissory note now in controversy were a specialty by the laws of Kentucky, still it would not help the case, unless it were also a specialty and recognized as such by the laws of Virginia; for the laws of the latter must govern as to the limitation of suits in its own courts, and as to the interpretation of the meaning of the words used in its own statutes.' Post, s. 567.

[1] Bartolus, Comm. ad Cod. 1, 1, 1; Bart. Oper. tom. 7, p. 4, ed. 1602; 2 Boullenois, obs. 46, p. 455, 456; ante, s. 301.

560. Rodenburg asserts the same distinction. 'Primum utamur vulgata doctorum distinctione, qua separantur ea, quæ litis formam concernunt ac ordinationem, ab iis, quæ decisionem aut materiam. Lis ordinanda secundum morem loci in quo ventilatur.'[1] Boullenois affirms the same doctrine. 'A l'égard,' says he, 'du principe de décision, quantum ad litis decisoria, il se tire, ou de la loi du contrat, ou de la loi de la situation, ou de la volonté présumée des parties, lorsqu'elles ont contracté ensemble ; en un mot la loi seule de la jurisdiction n'y influe point comme telle. Diversitas fori non debet meritum causæ variare. A l'égard des formalités judiciaires, quantum ad litis ordinationem, la règle est de suivre la procédure et les usages observés dans le lieu où l'on plaide.'[2] Hertius states the same point in his compendious way. 'Expedita est doctorum responsio, jura judicii tantum in illis observanda esse, quæ ad ordinem processus judicialis pertinent, etsi lis sit de bonis immobilibus, in alio territorio sitis.'[3]

561. Strykius states it in the following language: 'Quotiescunque circa judicii ordinationem controvertitur, statuta loci judicii, omnibus cæteris posthabitis, introspiciantur. In modo procedendi consuetudo judicii attendenda, ubi lis agitatur. In modo vero decidendi, seu in ipsa causæ decisione, consuetudo litigantium, seu ubi actus est gestus, attendendus.'[4] Huberus says : 'Adeoque receptum est optima ratione, ut in ordinandis judiciis loci consuetudo, ubi agitur, etsi de negotio alibi celebrato, spectetur.'[5] Dumoulin says : 'Unde an instrumentum habeat executionem, et quo modo debeat exequi, attenditur locus ubi agitur, vel fit executio. Ratio, quia fides instrumenti concernit meritum, sed virtus executoria et modus exequendi concernit processum.'[6] Again he adds : 'Quod in his, quæ pertinent ad processum judicii, vel executionem faciendam, vel ad ordinationem judicii, semper sit observanda consuetudo loci in quo judicium

---

[1] Rodenburg, de Div. Stat. tit. 2, p. 5, n. 16; 2 Boullenois, Appx. p. 47; 1 Boullenois, 660, 685, 818; ante, s. 325 c, 325 d, 325 h, note 2.

[2] 1 Boullenois, obs. 33, p. 535–546; Id. Prin. Gén. 49, p. 11.

[3] 1 Hertii Opera, de Collis. Leg. s. 4, n. 70, p. 152, 153, ed. 1737; Id. p. 215, ed. 1716.

[4] Strykii Tract. et Disp. tom. 2, p. 27; De Jure Princ. ext. Territ. c. 3, n. 34; ante, s. 205.

[5] Huberus, tom. 2, lib. 1, tit. 3, de Confl. Leg. s. 7.

[6] 1 Boullenois, obs. 23, p. 523, 524; Molin. Oper. Comm. ad Cod. 1, 1, tom. 3, p. 554, ed. 1681.

agitatur.'[1] Emerigon says : 'Pour tout ce qui concerne l'ordre judiciaire, on doit suivre l'usage du lieu où l'on plaide. Pour ce qui est de la décision du fond, on doit suivre, en règle générale, les lois du lieu où le contrat a été passé. Cette distinction est consignée dans tous nos livres.'[2]

562. We may conclude this reference to the opinions of foreign jurists by a citation from John Voet, who states at once the rule and the reason of it. 'Quia vero regionum, civitatum, vicorum varia, imo contraria sæpe jura sunt, observandum est, quantum quidem ad ordinem judicii formamque attinet, judicem nullius alterius sed sui tantum fori leges sequi. Sed in litis ipsius definitione, si de solennibus contractus, testamenti, vel negotii alterius quæstio sit, validum pronunciare debet ac solenne negotium, quoties adhibita invenit solennia loci, in quo illud gestum est, licet aliæ, aut majores, in loco judicii ad talem actum solennitates requisitæ essent.'[3]

563. There are many questions however which may arise as to what are, and what are not, matters properly belonging to the remedy (ad litis ordinationem), and what are, and what are not, matters properly belonging to the merits (ad litis decisionem). Many cases of this sort may be found collected and discussed by foreign jurists upon the peculiarities of their own jurisprudence. But they could not be made intelligible to a lawyer under the common law, without occupying a space in explanations wholly disproportionate to their importance in a treatise like the present.[4]

564. *Cases arising under the Common Law.* — It may be of more utility to introduce a few illustrations of the doctrine arising peculiarly under the common-law modes of proceeding, first, in regard to persons who may sue ; secondly, in regard to process and proceedings ; and thirdly, in regard to certain defences against actions arising from matters ex post facto, and founded on local law or customary practice.

565. *Persons who may sue.* — *Transfer of Claim.* — In the first

[1] 1 Boullenois, obs. 23, p. 523, 524; Molin. Oper. Comm. Cod. 6, 32, tom. 3, p. 735, ed. 1681.

[2] 1 Emerigon, Traité des Assur. c. 4, s. 8, n. 2, p. 122; Le Roy v. Crowninshield, 2 Mason, 163. See also to the same effect, P. Voet, de Stat. s. 10, c. 1, n. 1, 6, p. 281, 285, 286, ed. 1715; Id. p. 839–341, ed. 1661.

[3] J. Voet, ad Pand. 1, 5, 1, s. 51, p. 328.

[4] See 1 Boullenois, obs. 23, p. 535–569.

place, in regard to persons who may sue. It may be laid down as a general rule that all foreigners, sui juris, and not otherwise specially disabled by the law of the place where the suit is brought, may there maintain suits to vindicate their rights and redress their wrongs. The same doctrine applies to foreign sovereigns (a) and to foreign corporations.[1] (b) But questions may arise where the party suing is not the original party to the debt or claim, but he

[1] Foreign corporations may also be sued in all cases where they have property within the jurisdiction. Libbey v. Hodgson, 9 N. H. 394; but quære of some of the doctrines in the case. (c) Story, Eq. Pl. s. 55; Hullett v. King of Spain, 2 Bligh, N.S. 51; 1 Dow & Cl. 169; 1 Cl. & F. 333; Colombian Government v. Rothschild, 1 Sim. 94; South Carolina Bank v. Case, 8 B. & C. 427; Berne v. Bank of England, 9 Ves. 347; Silver Lake Bank v. North, 4 Johns. Ch. (N. Y.) 370; Bank of Augusta v. Earle, 13 Pet. 519, 588, 589. (d)

(a) See The Sapphire, 11 Wall. 164; Hullett v. King of Spain, 1 Dow & Cl. 169. It was recently decided in England, after much discussion, that the United States of America might maintain a suit in England in its own name, and not merely in the name of the President. United States v. Wagner, Law Rep. 2 Ch. 582, overruling the decision of Wood, V.C., in Law Rep. 8 Eq. 724.

As to suits against foreign sovereigns, see Duke of Brunswick v. King of Hanover, 2 H. L. C. 1; De Haber v. Queen of Portugal, 17 Q. B. 171.

(b) Railroad Co. v. Harris, 12 Wall. 65. Such corporations may sue in contract, or in trover, or in real actions. British America Land Co. v. Ames, 6 Met. (Mass.) 391; Society for Propagating Gospel v. Wheeler, 2 Gall. 105; Runyan v. Coster, 14 Pet. 122; American Ins. Co. v. Owen, 15 Gray (Mass.) 493. And they may levy upon the judgment like natural persons. See Bard v. Poole, 2 Kern. 495; New York Dry Docks v. Hicks, 5 McLean, 111; Lathrop v. Commercial Bank, 8 Dana, 114; Lumbard v. Aldrich, 8 N. H. 31; Merrick v. Van Santvoord, 34 N. Y. 208. For, as we have elsewhere seen, whatever may be said concerning corporations created by a

foreign power, their existence will be recognized and respected if not inconsistent with domestic law. Ante, s. 106, note; Merrick v. Van Santvoord, supra; Christian Union v. Yount, 101 U. S. 352; Cowell v. Springs Co., 100 U. S. 55; Williams v. Creswell, 51 Miss. 817.

The rights of foreign receivers will also be recognized when not in conflict with the claims of domestic attaching creditors, in case perhaps there is no intervention by creditors of the party represented by the receiver. Hurd v. Elizabeth, 41 N. J. 1; Cooke v. Orange, 48 Conn. 401; Pond v. Cooke, 45 Conn. 126; Blake Crusher Co. v. New Haven, 46 Conn. 473. Bagby v. Railroad Co. 86 Penn. St. 291, where a foreign creditor's claim was rejected in favor of the foreign receiver, on grounds of res judicata.

(c) See Danforth v. Penny, 3 Met. (Mass.) 564; Peckham v. North Parish in Haverhill, 16 Pick. (Mass.) 274; McQueen v. Middletown Manuf. Co. 16 Johns. (N. Y.) 5.

(d) But if the foreign corporation has no place of business in the state, and is not doing business there, it cannot be sued there upon a foreign contract. Camden Mill Co. v. Swede Iron Co., 32 N. J. 15.

takes a derivative title only from the original party, as where he is an assignee or grantee or donee of the debt or other claim. We have already had occasion to take notice of a peculiarity of the common law, that debts and choses in action are not, with the exception of negotiable promissory notes and bills of exchange, assignable.[1] Hence if any other debt or chose in action, such as a bond, or a covenant, or other contract, is assigned, no action can be maintained thereon in a common-law court by the assignee in his own name.[2] The same rule has been applied to assignments of debts or choses in action, made in foreign countries, although the assignee might be entitled to found an action thereon in such foreign country in his own name, in virtue of such assignment.[3] For (it has been said) the inquiry in whose name the suit is to be brought, belongs not so much to the right and merit of the claim, as to the form of the remedy. No distinction seems to have been made in England as to the right to sue, between the case of an assignee by the private voluntary act of the assignor, and an assignee by operation of law by an assignment in invitum under the bankrupt laws. Thus it has been held that a Scotch assignee of a bankrupt could not maintain a suit in his own name in England for a chose in action of the bankrupt, which was admitted to pass under the assignment.[4] In America contradictory

---

[1] Ante, s. 354, 355, 395–400.

[2] 3 Burge, Col. & For. Law, pt. 2, c. 20, p. 777, 778; Wolff v. Oxholme, 6 M. & S. 99; ante, s. 354, 355.

[3] Wolff v. Oxholme, 6 M. & S. 99; Folliott v. Ogden, 1 H. Bl. 131; Innes v. Dunlop, 8 T. R. 595; Jeffrey v. McTaggart, 6 M. & S. 126.

[4] Jeffery v. McTaggart, 6 M. & S. 126, and Wolff v. Oxholme, 6 M. & S. 99. But see, in Smith v. Buchanan, 1 East, 11, the dictum of Lord Kenyon to the contrary. In Alivon v. Furnival, 1 C. M. & R. 277, two out of three syndics of a French bankrupt sued a debtor of the bankrupt in their own names in England; and the objection was taken that they had no title to sue. The court overruled the objection. Mr. Baron Parke, in delivering the judgment of the court, said: 'Lastly, it is said that, though two may act and bring an action, yet they must sue in the name of all. Now the effect of the testimony of Colin is that two may sue in France without a third, and the witness for the defendant does not prove the contrary, and there seems no reason why it should not be so. The property in the effects of the bankrupt does not appear to be absolutely transferred to these syndics in the way that those of a bankrupt are in this country; but it should seem that the syndics act as mandatories or agents for the creditors, the whole three, or any two or one of them, having the power to sue for and recover the debts in their own names. This is a peculiar right of action, created by the law of that country; and we think it may by the comity of nations be enforced in this, as

decisions have been made upon the same point, some courts affirming, and others denying, the right of the assignee to sue in his own name, although the weight of authority must now be admitted to be against the right.[1]

566. The reasoning of these decisions seems equally to apply to the case of a foreign assignee by the voluntary act of the party, even where he could sue in his own name in the country in which the assignment was made, although certainly there is room for a distinction in such a case, and it has sometimes been recognized. Thus in a case where the assignee of an Irish judgment brought a suit in his own name in England, such a judgment being assignable in Ireland, so as to vest a title at law in the assignee, the Court of Common Pleas held that he was entitled to recover; because (as it should seem) a legal title by the lex loci vested in him, and the case was not to be governed by the law of England, as the assignment was in Ireland.[2] The distinction, although nice, is at the same time clear; for the remedy is sought upon a legal right, vested ex directo by the local law in the assignee against the judgment debtor. There does not seem therefore any solid ground upon principle why a right confessedly legal in the country where it originated, and passing a direct and positive fixed title in the assignee, should not have the same remedy in every other country which legal fixed titles in the party are there entitled to. It is assuming the very ground in controversy to assert that it is a mere equitable

much as the right of foreign assignees or curators, or foreign corporations appointed or created in a different way from that which the law of this country requires. Dutch West India Company v. Moses, 1 Str. 612; National Bank v. De Bernales, 1 Ry. & M. 190; Solomous v. Ross, 1 H. Bl. 131, n. We do not pronounce an opinion, whether this objection is available on the plea of nil debet, or ought to have been pleaded in abatement (though we were much struck with the argument of the learned counsel for the plaintiff), as we think it is not available at all upon the evidence in this case.' See also ante, s. 419, 420.

[1] See ante, s. 358, 359, 419, 420; Milne v. Moreton, 6 Binn. (Pa.) 374; Goodwin v. Jones, 3 Mass. 514, 519; Dawes v. Boylston, 9 Mass. 357; Orr v. Amory, 11 Mass. 25; Ingraham v. Geyer, 13 Mass. 146, 147; Byrne v. Walker, 7 Serg. & R. (Pa.) 483; Bird v. Caritat, 2 Johns. (N. Y.) 342; Bird v. Pierpont, 1 Johns. (N. Y.) 118; Murray v. Murray, 5 Johns. Ch. (N. Y.) 60; Brush v. Curtis, 4 Conn. 312; Raymond v. Johnson, 11 Johns. (N. Y.) 488; Holmes v. Remsen, 4 Johns. Ch. (N. Y.) 460, 485.

[2] O'Callaghan v. Thomond, 3 Taunt. 82, 84; ante, s. 855; 3 Burge, Col. & For. Law, pt. 2, c. 20, p. 777, 778.

title; for the local law has adjudged it otherwise, and vested the original title ex directo in the assignee. In the common case where an executor or administrator indorses negotiable paper in the country from which he derives his administrative authority, no one will doubt that the legal title passes to the indorsee, and that he may sue thereon in any other country in his own name; and yet such an indorsement in another country by the executor or administrator would not be admitted to have any such validity or effect.[1] However, the doctrine of this case has been much doubted; and therefore it can scarcely be thought to be unexceptionable in point of authority. There are certainly dicta and decisions which are pointedly the other way, and in which it is said that the suit must be brought in the name of the assignor, if the lex fori requires it.[2] (a)

[1] Ante, s. 353 a, 354, 358, 359; Trimbey v. Vignier, 1 Bing. N. C. 151, 159, 160.

[2] The dictum of Lord Loughborough in Folliott v. Ogden, 1 H. Bl. 135, and that of Lord Ellenborough in Wolff v. Oxholme, 6 M. & S. 92, 99, are to this effect. But the recent case of Alivon v. Furnival, 1 C. M. & R. 277, 296, certainly as far as it goes upholds it. Ante, s. 565, note. See also Robinson v. Campbell, 3 Wheat. 212. The case of Wolff v. Oxholme, 6 M. & S. 92, 99, may perhaps be distinguishable in its circumstances, as well as in the reasoning of the court. Lord Ellenborough's language in the last case was as follows: 'One of the points insisted upon in the argument for the defendant was that this assignment and the suit instituted upon it were a bar to the plaintiff's demand; but we think that they cannot have that effect. The assignee could not sue in the courts of this country in his own name; the action must have been brought here in the names of the original creditors, even if they had assigned the debt for a valuable consideration; and although the assignment gave the assignee a right to sue in his own name in Denmark, yet the defendant does not appear to have been prejudiced by that measure even there, nor has any material consequence resulted therefrom. And we consider the case to stand now just as it would have done if no assignment had been made, and if the suit in Denmark had been brought by the plaintiffs themselves, instead of being instituted by their trustees.' See ante, s. 358, 359, 399, note. See Trasher v. Everhart, 3 Gill & J. (Md.) 234; McRae v. Mattoon, 10 Pick. (Mass.) 52; Pearsall v. Dwight, 2 Mass. 84; 3 Burge, Col. & For. Law, pt. 2, c. 20, p. 777, 778. This subject is ably discussed on different sides in two articles in the American Jurist, viz.: in the number for January, 1833 (vol. 9, p. 42), and in the number for January, 1834 (vol. 11, p. 101), to which I gladly refer as giving a more satisfactory view of this subject than, with reference to the plan of the present work, I have been able to give. It may be thought that the case of foreign executors and administrators, as assignees by operation of law of the deceased's estate, stands upon a similar ground. But it appears

(a) See Foss v. Nutting, 14 Gray, 484; Richardson v. New York Cent. R. Co., 98 Mass. 85, 92.

567. *Instruments under Seal.* — Another illustration may be taken from the forms of action upon instruments under seal. Thus in Virginia a contract to pay money, with a scrawl instead of a seal, is treated as a sealed instrument, so that debt lies upon it in that state. But in New York, where such a scrawl is not treated as a seal, the remedy must be as upon an unsealed simple contract.[1] (*a*) The same doctrine has been maintained in England upon an instrument executed in Jamaica, where there was no seal, but a mark or scrawl in the place where the seal is usually affixed.[2] On the other hand, a single bill is deemed in Virginia not to be a specialty ; in Maryland it is otherwise. A remedy brought in Maryland upon such a single bill, executed in Virginia, cannot be by an action of assumpsit, as upon a simple contract, but must be by action of debt, as upon a specialty.[3]

568. *Process.* — *Melan v. Fitz James.* — In the next place as to process and proceedings. There is no controversy that in a general sense the mode of process constitutes a part of the remedy. But the question has arisen whether, upon contracts made in a foreign country, and which by the laws of that country are precluded from being enforced by a personal arrest or imprisonment, the like exemption applies in suits to enforce them in another country where such process constitutes a part of the remedial justice. Such a contract existed, or was supposed to exist, in a case where a bond given in France, and sued in England, was understood to bind the property and not the person of the party in France.[4] On that occasion Lord Chief Justice Eyre said: ' If it appears that this contract creates no personal obligation, and that it could not be sued as such by the laws of France, on the principle of preventing arrests so vexatious as to be an abuse of the process of the court, there seems

to me to proceed on principles materially different, applicable to rights, and not merely to remedies. Ante, s. 399, note, s. 420, 512, 513.

[1] Warren *v.* Lynch, 5 Johns. (N. Y.) 239. See also Andrews *v.* Herriot, 4 Cow. (N. Y.) 508. But see Meredith *v* Hinsdale, 2 Caines (N. Y.) 362.

[2] Adam *v.* Kerr, 1 B. & P. 360. See also Bank of the United States *v.* Donnally, 8 Pet. 361; ante, s. 558, note.

[3] Trasher *v.* Everhart, 3 Gill & J. (Md.) 234; Bank of the United States *v.* Donnally, 8 Pet. 361; ante, s. 558, note.

[4] Melan *v.* Fitz James, 1 B. & P. 138; 3 Burge, Col. & For. Law, pt. 2, c. 20, p. 766–768.

(*a*) See Le Roy *v.* Beard, 8 How. 464.

to be a fair ground on which the court may interpose to prevent a proceeding so oppressive as a personal arrest in a foreign country, at the commencement of a suit, in a case which, as far as one can judge at present, authorizes no proceeding against the person in the country in which the transaction passed. If there could be none in France, in my opinion there can be none here. I cannot conceive that what is no personal obligation in the country in which it arises, can ever be raised into a personal obligation by the laws of another. If it be a personal obligation there, it must be enforced here in the mode pointed out by the law of this country. But what the nature of the obligation is, must be determined by the law of the country where it was entered into; and then this country will apply its own law to enforce it.'[1] And accordingly the court discharged the party from the arrest.

569. *The Principle.* — There does not seem the least reason to doubt the entire correctness of the doctrine thus laid down. If the contract creates no personal obligation, but an obligation in rem only, it cannot be that its nature can be changed, or its obligation varied, by a mere change of domicil. That would be to contradict all the principles maintained in all the authorities, that the validity, nature, obligation, and interpretation of a contract are to be decided by the lex loci contractus.[2] A suit in personam in England could not be maintained except upon some contract which bound the person. If it bound the property only, the proceeding should be in rem; and if in express terms the party bound his property only, and exempted himself from a personal liability, no one would doubt that a suit in personam would not be maintainable. The same principle would apply, if the laws of a country should declare that certain classes of contracts should not bind the person at all, but only property, or a particular species of property. Such laws do probably exist in some countries. But it does not follow, because a personal remedy is not given by the laws of a country, that therefore there is no personal obligation in a contract.[3] (a)

[1] Ibid. See also Ohio Ins. Co. v. Edmondson, 5 La. 295, 300.
[2] Ante, s. 263–273; 3 Burge, Col. & For. Law, pt. 2, c. 20, p. 765, 766, 776.
[3] Talleyrand v. Boulanger, 3 Ves. 447; Flack v. Holm, 1 Jac. & W. 405.

(a) See Liverpool Credit Co. v. Hunter, L. R. 3 Ch. App. 479, commenting on Talleyrand v. Boulanger, supra.

570. *Its Application.* — The real difficulty lies not in the principle itself, but in its application. There is a great distinction between a contract which ex directo excludes personal liability, and a contract made in a country which binds the party personally, but where the laws do not enforce the contract in personam, but only in rem. In the latter case the remedy constitutes no part of the contract. The liability is general, so far as the acts of the parties go, and the mode of enforcing is a mere matter of municipal regulation. It is strictly a part of the lex fori, and may be changed from time to time, as the legislature may choose.[1] This was the view of the matter taken by Mr. Justice Heath in the case alluded to ; for he, in dissenting from the opinion of the court, did not deny the principles of the decision, but held that the contract was personal. ' We all agree,' said he, ' that in construing contracts we must be governed by the laws of the country in which they are made, for all contracts have reference to such laws. But when we come to remedies, it is another thing. They must be pursued by the means which the law points out where the party resides. The laws of the country where the contract was made can only have reference to the nature of the contract, not to the mode of enforcing it. Whoever comes voluntarily into a country subjects himself to all the laws of that country, and therein to all the remedies directed by those laws on his particular engagements.'[2]

571. *The Better Opinion.* — The doctrine of this case has been sometimes followed in America.[3] But the better opinion now established both in England and America is, that it is of no consequence whether the contract authorizes an arrest or imprisonment of the party in the country where it was made, if there is no exemption of the party from personal liability on the contract. He is still liable to arrest or imprisonment in a suit upon it in a foreign country, whose laws authorize such a mode of proceeding as a part of the local remedy.[4] In a recent case in England, where

[1] See Ogden v. Saunders, 12 Wheat. 213.

[2] Melan v. Fitz James, 1 B. & P. 142; Hinkley v. Marean, 3 Mason, 88; Titus v. Hobart, 5 Mason, 378.

[3] Symonds v. Union Ins. Co., 4 Dall. (Penn.) 417.

[4] See Imlay v. Ellefsen, 2 East, 453; Peck v. Hozier, 14 Johns. (N. Y.) 346; Robinson v. Bland, 2 Burr. 1089; Hinkley v. Marean, 3 Mason, 88; Titus v. Hobart, 5 Mason, 378; Smith v. Spinolla, 2 Johns. (N. Y.) 198, 200; De la Vega v. Vianna, 1 B. & Ad. 284; 3 Burge, Col. & For. Law, pt. 2, c. 20, p. 766—

the plaintiff and defendant were both foreigners, and the debt was contracted in a country by whose laws the defendant would not have been liable to arrest, an application was made to discharge the defendant from arrest on that account; but the court refused the application. Lord Tenterden on that occasion, in delivering the opinion of the court, said: ' A person suing in this country must take the law as he finds it. He cannot by virtue of any regulation in his own country enjoy greater advantages than other suitors here. And he ought not therefore to be deprived of any superior advantage which the law of this country may confer. He is to have the same rights which all the subjects of this kingdom are entitled to.' [1] (a) The same doctrine has been solemnly promulgated by the House of Lords on a still more recent occasion.[2]

572. *Judgments and Executions.* — The like principles apply to the form of judgments to be rendered, and of executions to be granted in suits. They must conform to the lex fori, although the party defendant may, in his domestic forùm, have been entitled to a judgment exempting his person from imprisonment, in virtue of a discharge under an insolvent law existing there, and of which he had there judicially obtained the benefit.[3] And it will make no difference in such case whether the contract sued on was made in a state granting such discharge or not, or whether the parties were citizens of that state or not. The effect of such a discharge is purely local. It is addressed solely to the courts of the state under whose authority the exemption is allowed. But it has nothing to do with the process, proceedings, or judgments of the courts of other states, which are to be governed altogether by their own municipal jurisprudence. Wherever a remedy is sought, it is to be administered according to the

---

769; Atwater v. Townsend, 4 Conn. 47; Woodbridge v. Wright, 3 Conn. 523, 526 ; Smith v. Healy, 4 Conn. 49.

[1] De la Vega v. Vianna, 1 B. & Ad. 284. See also Whittemore v. Adams, 2 Cowen (N. Y.) 626; Willings v. Consequa, 1 Pet. C. C. 317; Courtois r. Carpentier, 1 Wash. C. C. 376; Bird v. Caritat, 2 Johns. (N. Y.) 345; Wayman v. Southward, 10 Wheat. 1. See Henry on Foreign Law, p. 81–86.

[2] Don v. Lippmann, 5 Cl. & F. 1, 13–15; ante, s. 557, note.

[3] Hinkley v. Marean, 3 Mason, 88; Titus v. Hobart, 5 Mason, 378; Atwater v. Townsend, 4 Conn. 47; Woodbridge v. Wright, 3 Conn. 523, 526; Smith v. Healey, 4 Conn. 49; 3 Burge, Col. & For. Law, pt. 2, c. 21, s. 7, p. 878, 879.

(a) See Noonan v. Kemp, 34 Md. 73.

lex fori, and such a judgment is to be given as the laws of the state where the suit is brought, authorize and allow, and not such a judgment as the laws of other states authorize or require.[1] (a)

573. *Foreign Jurists.* — The general doctrine is stated in ample terms by Paul Voet. 'Quid, si actiones sint intentandæ, et quidem personales, an sequemur statutum domicilii debitoris, an statutum loci ubi exigi vel intentari poterunt? Respondeo, etsi bene multi velint tales actiones certo loco non circumscribi, inspecta tantum illa corporali circumscriptione, ut tamen eas velint censeri de loco ubi agi et exigi possunt.'[2] Again he adds : 'Sed revertar, unde fueram digressus, ad concursum statutorum variantium circa judicia. Ubi occurrunt nonnulla circa solemnia in judiciis servanda, circa tempora, cautiones, probationes, causarum decisiones, executiones, et appellationes. Finge, enim, alia servari solemnia, in loco domicilii litigatoris, alia in loco contractus, alia in loco rei sitæ, alia in judicii loco. Quænam spectanda solemnia? Respondeo ; Spectanda sunt solemnia, id est, stylus judicis fori illius, ubi litigatur. Idque in genere verum est, sive loquamur de civibus, sive forensibus ; statuta quippe circa solemnia meo sensu mixti erant generis ; adeoque vires exserunt tam intraquam extra territorium, tam in ordine ad incolas, quam ad exteros.'[3]

574. The same doctrine is fully confirmed by John Voet, as a received doctrine of foreign law. 'Multis præterea in locis id obtinet, ne duo ejusdem provinciæ seu territorii incolæ se invicem,

[1] Hinkley *v.* Marean, 3 Mason, 88; Titus *v.* Hobart, 5 Mason, 378; Atwater *v.* Townsend, 4 Conn. 47; Smith *v.* Healey, 4 Conn. 49; Woodbridge *v.* Wright, 3 Conn. 523. See also Suydam *v.* Broadnax, 14 Pet. 67.

[2] P. Voet, ad Stat. s. 10, c. 1, n. 2, p. 281, ed. 1715; Id. p. 340, ed. 1661.

[3] Id. n. 6, p. 285, ed. 1715; Id. p. 345, 346, ed. 1661.

(a) See Toomer *v.* Dickerson, 37 Ga. 440. And it often happens that, by reason of the form of a judgment rendered in a foreign jurisdiction, no adequate remedy can be found out of the particular place where rendered. Thus in regard to bonds with penalty for the performance of successive or continuing obligations or duties: where upon default the obligee has brought suit and obtained judgment for the penalty, with an assessment of damages for past breaches, the judgment for the penalty remaining as a pledge for future performance, upon which, by the local law, the obligee is entitled to bring scire facias, from time to time, as successive breaches occur, and obtain a reassessment of damages and another execution for each; no recovery upon the judgment for the penalty can be had, the adjudication in that form not importing an absolute debt. Dimick *v.* Brooks, 21 Vt. 569; Battey *v.* Holbrook, 11 Gray, 212; post, s. 609.

aut bona, sistant in alio territorio. Sic duo Brabantini se invicem non extra Brabantiam ; duo Hollandi non extra Hollandum, etc. Quod si quis, neglecta statuti dispositione, concivem aut bona ejus alibi stiterit, litis movendæ gratia, non peccabunt quidem istius loci judices, si arrestum confirment ; cum non ligentur alieni territorii legibus talem arrestationem concivium vetantibus. Sed, qui ita detentus litigare coactus est, recte petet a suo judice, condemnari concivem, ut arresti vinculum, contra statuti domicilii prohibitionem alibi impositum, remittat, litique alibi cœptæ cum impensis renunciet, ac solvat mulctam statuto dictatam.'[1] And he proceeds to add that in some places the practice is in suits between two foreigners belonging to one and the same country, to remit the parties to their domestic forum ; which however is done, not as a matter of right or duty, but of comity, or from policy, to prevent injurious delays to the suits of their own citizens. ' Quod tamen vel ex comitate magis, quam necessitate fit, vel magis ad declinandam nimiam litium frequentiam judicibus molestam, civibus inde suaram litium protelationem patientibus damnosam.'[2]

574 a. Dumoulin also affirms a similar doctrine in the passages already cited. ' Unde, an instrumentum habeat executionem, et quomodo debeat exequi, attenditur locus, ubi agitur, vel fit executio. Ratio, quia fides instrumenti concernet meritum ; sed virtus executoria et modus exequendi concernit processum.[3] Quod in his, quæ pertinent ad processum judicii, vel executionem faciendam, vel ad ordinationem judicii, semper sit observanda consuetudo loci, in quo judicium agitatur.'[4] Burgundus is equally expressive. ' Eodem modo dicemus, in contexanda actione, fori consuetudines observandas esse, ubi contenditur, quia et in judiciis quasi contrahitur. Idem in arrestis seu manuum injectionibus tenendum est, ut scilicet consuetudinem loci spectemus, ubi facta est manus injectio : quia arrestatio apud nos ingressus est judicii, et duntaxat litis pendentiam, non executionem generet.'[5]

---

[1] J. Voet, ad Pand. 2, 4, s. 45, p. 129 ; cited also 1 B. & Ad. 288, note ; ante, s. 562.

[2] Ibid.

[3] Molin. Opera, tom. 3, Com. ad Cod. 1, 1, 1, p. 559, ed. 1681 ; ante, s. 561.

[4] Id. 6, 32, p. 735 [741], ed. 1681 ; 1 Boullenois, obs. 23, p. 523, 524 ; ante, s. 561.

[5] Burgundus, tract. 5, n. 1, p. 118, 119 ; 1 Boullenois, obs. 23, p. 524, 526 ; 2 Boullenois, obs. 46, p. 488. But see Burgundus, tract. 4, n. 27, p. 116, cited post, s. 574 c, note.

This indeed seems, with few exceptions, to be the general doctrine maintained by foreign jurists; and Boullenois has collected their opinions at large.[1] He treats the question of imprisonment as purely one modus exequendi; and he applies the same principle to mesne process and to process of execution.[2] He accordingly puts the case where a Frenchman contracts a common debt in a country by whose laws such a debt imparts a right to arrest the body, and says that this right is a mere mode of enforcing the contract, modus exequendi, and consequently it depends upon the law of the place where the execution of it is sought; so that if it is sought in a place where no such arrest of the body is allowable, the creditor has no right to claim any restraint by such a rigorous course.[3]

574 b. But a distinction is taken by some foreign jurists between a contract made in a country between a stranger and a citizen thereof, or between two citizens, and a contract made in the same country between two foreigners belonging to another country, when the law of the place where the contract is made allows an arrest of the person, and the law of the place where the suit is brought or to which the two foreigners belong, disallows such an arrest. Thus in Brabant there is a law of Charles the Fourth which prohibits any Brabanter from arresting another Brabanter in a foreign jurisdiction; and Peckius puts the question, whether in a case of this sort any Brabanter may arrest another Brabanter in Spain, Italy, England, France, or other foreign country. And he holds that he may not: first, because the prohibitory law is absolute, and comprehends subjects even in a foreign territory; secondly, because the power of establishing a law between subjects is not limited to the territory of the sovereign; thirdly, because if the sovereign may bind his subjects everywhere, this privilege equally binds them everywhere, as a part of the law; fourthly, because a sentence of excommunication would bind the subjects in a foreign territory; and a fortiori, then, this privilege does bind them; and fifthly, because the incapacity of the prodigal binds him in a foreign territory, and this case of privilege is as strong or stronger. Hence he concludes that

---

[1] 1 Boullenois, obs. 23, p. 523–525, 528, 529; Id. p. 535–543, 544–569. See Henry on Foreign Law, p. 81–85.
[2] Id.; Henry on Foreign Law, p. 55, 56, 81–85.
[3] 1 Boullenois, obs. 23, p. 525, 528, 529; Id. obs. 25, p. 601, &c.

not only the person, but the movables of the Brabanter (which follow his person) also, would be free from arrest. 'Unde sicut persona arrestari non potest, ita nec bona mobilia ejusdem.'[1]

574 c. There is great reason to doubt both the premises and the conclusions of Peckius in asserting this distinction; and certainly it now has no admitted recognition in the common law.[2] Peckius asserts another distinction, in which he has apparently the support of Christinæus and Everhardus, and some other jurists, that where the law of the place of contract allows an arrest, but the law of the place of payment does not (and so e contra in the converse case), the law of the latter is to prevail: He quotes the language of Everhardus on the same point with approbation: 'Quod si in loco celebrati contractus sit statutum, quod debitor possit capi et incarcerari, vel quod instrumenta notariorum habeant executionem paratam; in loco vero destinatæ solutionis, non sit simile statutum, sed servetur jus commune, attendatur, quoad hoc, mos, observantia, statutum, aut lex, destinatæ solutionis. Quippe, quod in his, quæ concernunt judicariam executionem, inspicitur locus destinatæ solutionis.'[3] He then adds in the converse case: 'Quod et in arrestatione, si similis casus occurrat, locus destinatæ solutionis et judicii spectari debeat.'[4] Christinæus uses similar language.[5] The common law of England and America however does not recognize any such distinction.[6]

[1] Peck. de Jure Sist. c. 8, n. 1–6; Peckii Opera, p. 753, ed. 1666.

[2] Ante, s. 568–571. Mr. Henry however thinks the distinction sound, and deems it supported by the case of Melan v. Fitz James, 1 B. & P. 138; ante, s. 568–572. Burgundus says: Affinia solutioni sunt, præscriptio, oblatio rei debitæ, consignatio, novatio, delegatio, et ejus modi. Burgundus, tract. 4, n. 28, p. 116.

[3] Everhard. Consil. 78, n. 22, p. 208; Peck. de Jure Sist. c. 11, p. 758, ed. Peck. Oper. 1666.

[4] Peck. Oper. de Jur. Sist. c. 11, n. 1, p. 758, 759, ed. 1666.

[5] Christin. tom. 1, decis. 283, n. 12, p. 355; 1 Boullenois, obs. 28, p. 525; 2 Boullenois, obs. 46, p. 488.

[6] Post, s. 581; Campbell v. Stein, 6 Dow, 116; Don v. Lippmann, 5 Cl. & F. 1, 19, 20. In this latter case, Lord Brougham said, speaking on this point: 'All the authorities, Huber (De Confl. Leg. in Div. Imp.), Voet (Dig. 24, 3, 12), and Lord Kames (Kames's Principles of Equity, 3, 8, 6, 1, 5, 3), are cited in that case. Campbell v. Stein, 6 Dow, 116, was an action for a bill of costs for business done in this House. The court below there allowed the rule of Scotch prescription. That judgment was affirmed by Lord Eldon, who however said that he moved it with regret. He said that it had been ruled that the debtor being in Scotland, and the creditor in England, the debtor

574 *d.* Peckius then puts another case, where the contract of indebtment is made in a country where an arrest is not allowed, and the debtor has not promised to pay in another country where an arrest is allowed, but he is found there; whether in such a case he may nevertheless be arrested there, the debt being then due. He thinks he may; because to this extent it may be truly said that the law and usage of the place of the judgment ought in this matter to be observed; and that in those things which concern the proceedings in suits, foreigners are bound by the laws of the place where they are liable to be sued. 'Sed quid, si quis contraxit in loco, in quo illius loci homines non utuntur arresto, neque promisit solvere in patria arresti, sed tamen illice reperitur; utrum nihilominus arrestari possit? Existimo, quod sic, si vel tempus solutionis elapsum vel in mora periculum sit; quia adhuc verum est dicere, quod statutum et consuetudo loci judicii servari debet in isto modo; et in his, quæ ad ordinationem judiciorum pertinent, forenses ligantur statutis loci, ubi conveniuntur.'[1]

575. *Defences ex post Facto.* — In the next place as to defences arising from matters ex post facto. These may be of the nature of counter-claims or set-offs to actions, analogous to compensation in the Roman and foreign law;[2] or they may be matters of discharge, such as discharges under insolvent laws, arising at a

---

might plead the Scotch rule of prescription; that that was against some of the old authorities, but was in accordance with those of later date. That case cannot be reconciled with the principle that the locus solutionis is to prescribe the law. It has nothing to do with the case. Why is it then that the law of the domicil of the debtor was there allowed to prevent the plaintiff from recovering? It was because the creditor must follow the debtor, and must sue him where he resides; and by the necessity of that case was obliged to sue him in Scotland. In that respect therefore there was in that case no difference between the lex loci solutionis and the lex fori; and it must be admitted that in such case the rules of evidence, and, if so, the rules of practice, may be varied, as they are applied in one court or the other. But governing all these cases is the principle that the law of the country where the contract is to be enforced must prevail in enforcing such contract, though it is conceded that the lex loci contractus may be referred to, for the purpose of expounding it. If therefore the contract is made in one country, to be performed in a second, and is enforced in a third, the law of the last alone, and not of the other two, will govern the case.'

[1] Peckii Opera, de Jure Sist. c. 11, p. 758, 759, ed. 1666. The same point was held in Don *v.* Lippmann, 5 Cl. & F. 1, 20; ante, s. 574 *c*, note.

[2] Pothier, Oblig. n. 587, 588.

subsequent period; or they may be laws regulating the time of instituting suits, called in the foreign law *statutes of prescription*, and in the common law *statutes of limitation*. The latter defence will deserve a very exact consideration. The former may be disposed of in a few words. The subject of discharges from the contract, either by the act of the parties or by operation of law, has been already sufficiently considered.[1] As to set-off or compensation, it is held in the courts of common law that a set-off to any action, allowed by the local law, is to be treated as a part of the remedy; and that therefore it is admissible in claims between persons belonging to different states or countries, although it may not be admissible by the law of the country where the debt which is sued was contracted.[2] (a) The liens, and implied hypothecations, and priorities of satisfaction, given to creditors by the law of particular countries, and the order of payment of their debts, are, as we have already seen,[3] generally treated as belonging to the proceedings in suits (ad litis ordinationem), and not to the merits of the claim.[4]

576. *Statutes of Limitation.* — In regard to statutes of limitation or prescription of suits, and lapse of time, there is no doubt that they are strictly questions affecting the remedy, and not questions upon the merits. They go ad litis ordinationem, and not ad litis decisionem, in a just juridical sense.[5] The object of them is to fix certain periods within which all suits shall be

---

[1] Ante, s. 330–352. See also 3 Burge, Col. & For. Law, pt. 2, c. 21, s. 7, p. 874–886.

[2] Gibbs v. Howard, 2 N. H. 296; Ruggles v. Keeler, 3 Johns. (N. Y.) 263. See Pothier on Oblig. n. 641, 642.

[3] Ante, s. 322 b–328, 423 a.

[4] Rodenburg, de Div. Stat. tit. 2, c. 5, n. 15, 16; 2 Boullenois, Appx. p. 47, 49; 1 Boullenois, obs. 25, p. 634, 635, 639; Id. p. 685, 818. See also P. Voet, de Stat. s. 10, c. 1, n. 2–6, p. 282–289, ed. 1715; Id. p. 340–346, ed. 1661.

[5] 1 Boullenois, obs. 23, p. 530; Fergusson v. Fyffe, 8 Cl. & F. 121, 140.

(a) See Mineral Point R. Co. v. Barron, 83 Ill. 365; Second National Bank v. Hemingray, 31 Ohio St. 168; Davis v. Morton, 5 Bush (Ky.) 160; Carver v. Adams, 38 Vt. 500; Bank of Gallipolis v. Trimble, 6 B. Mon. (Ky.) 601. But see Bliss v. Houghton, 13 N. H. 126; Harrison v. Edwards, 12 Vt. 648. Exemption laws also relate to the remedy. Mineral Point R. Co. v. Barron, supra; Leiber v. Union Pacific R. Co. 49 Iowa, 688. So of Statutory law abolishing the distinction between sealed and simple contracts. Williams v. Haines, 27 Iowa, 251. So of mere registration laws. Ex parte Melbourn, L. R. 6, Ch. 64. But comp. dictum in Hicks v. Powell, L. R. 4 Ch. 741. So of forfeiture laws. Lindsay v. Hill, 66 Me. 212.

brought in the courts of a state, whether they are brought by or against subjects, or by or against foreigners. And there can be no just reason, and no sound policy, in allowing higher or more extensive privileges to foreigners than are allowed to subjects. Laws thus limiting suits are founded in the noblest policy. They are statutes of repose to quiet titles, to suppress frauds, and to supply the deficiency of proofs arising from the ambiguity and obscurity, or the antiquity of transactions. They proceed upon the presumption that claims are extinguished, or ought to be held extinguished, whenever they are not litigated in the proper forum within the prescribed period. They take away all solid grounds of complaint, because they rest on the negligence or laches of the party himself. They quicken diligence, by making it in some measure equivalent to right. They discourage litigation, by burying in one common receptacle all the accumulations of past times which are unexplained, and have now from lapse of time become inexplicable. It has been said by John Voet, with singular felicity, that controversies are limited to a fixed period of time, lest they should be immortal while men are mortal: 'Ne autem lites immortales essent, dum litigantes mortales sunt.' [1] (a)

577. *Foreign Jurists.* — It has accordingly become a formulary in international jurisprudence, that all suits must be brought within the period prescribed by the local law of the country where the suit is brought (lex fori), otherwise the suits will be barred ; and this rule is as fully recognized in foreign jurisprudence as it is in the common law.[2] (b)   Not indeed that there

---

[1] J. Voet, ad Pand. 5, 1, 53, p. 328.

[2] The authorities in the common law are very numerous. A considerable number of them are cited in 4 Cowen (N. Y.) 528, note 10; Id. 530; Van Reimsdyk *v.* Kane, 1 Gallis. 371; Le Roy *v.* Crowninshield, 2 Mason, 151, British Linen Co. *v.* Drummond, 10 B. & C. 903; De la Vega *v.* Vianna, 1 B. & Ad. 284; Huber *v.* Steiner, 2 Bing. N. C. 202, 209–212; Don *v.* Lippmann, 5 Cl. & F. 1, 13–17; Medbury *v.* Hopkins, 3 Conn. 472; Woodbridge *c.* Wright, 3 Conn. 523; Bank of the United States *v.* Donnally, 8 Pet. 361; Bulger *v.* Roche, 11 Pick. (Mass.) 36; De Couche *v.* Savetier, 3 Johns. Ch. (N. Y.) 190; Lincoln *v.* Battelle, 6 Wend. (N. Y.) 475.

(a) And the statute of frauds is, like the statute of limitations, a matter affecting the remedy merely; and if by the law of the forum no action can be maintained on a particular oral contract if made in that country, the like rule will obtain as to a contract made abroad, although it was valid by the law of the place where made. Leroux *v.* Brown, 12 C. B. 801; 14 Eng. L. and Eq. 257.

(b) See Brown *v.* Stone, 4 La. An-

are no diversities of opinion upon this subject; but the doctrine is established by a decisive current of well-considered authorities.[1] Thus Huberus lays down the doctrine in clear terms, applying it to the very case of a prescription; and he assigns the reason : ' Ratio hæc est, quod prescriptio et executio non pertinent ad valorem contractus, sed ad tempus et modum actionis instituendæ, quæ per se, quasi contractum, separatum negotium constituit. Adeoque receptum est optima ratione, ut ordinandis judiciis, loci consuetudo, ubi agitur, etsi de negotio alibi celebrato, spectatur, ut docet Sandius, ubi tradit, etiam in executione sententiæ alibi latæ, servari jus loci, in quo fit executio, non ubi res judicata est.' [2] Paul Voet says: ' Ubi quoad actionis intentationem, occurrit illa difficultas, an si diversa sint statuta circa actionis finitionem seu terminum, spectandus sit terminus statuti debitoris, an creditoris? Respondeo; quia actor sequitur forum rei, ideo extraneus petens a reo, quod sibi debetur, sequetur terminum statuti præscriptum actioni in foro rei. Et quia hoc statutum non exserit vires extra territorium statuentis, ideo, etiam reo alibi convento, tale statutum objicere non poterit.' [3] Boulle-

---

[1] See Ersk. Inst. b. 3, tit. 7, n. 49, p. 633, 634.

[2] Huberus, tom. 2, lib. 1, tit. 3, de Conflict. Leg. s. 7; 1 Hertii Opera, de Collis. s. 4, n. 65, p. 150, 151, ed. 1787; Id. p. 312, ed. 1716. Hertius seems of a different opinion; saying that if the prescription only of the place where the suit is brought could prevail, the times of prescription would be very uncertain; for a man might frequently be sued in different places. 1 Hertii Opera, de Collis. Leg. s. 4, n. 65, p. 150, ed. 1737; Id. p. 212, ed. 1716. See also the opinions of other jurists to the same point in 1 Boullenois, obs. 23, p. 528–530; 2 Boullenois, obs. 46, p. 487, 488; Ersk. Inst. b. 3, tit. 7, s. 48, p. 633, 634; J. Voet, ad Pand. 2, 44, 3, s. 10, 12; 3 Burge, Col. & For. Law, pt. 2, c. 21, s. 7, p. 878, 879.

[3] P. Voet, de Stat. s. 10, c. 1, n. 1, p. 281, ed. 1715; Id. p. 340, ed. 1661.

235; Young v. Crossgrove, ib. 233; Miller v. Brenham, 68 N. Y. 83; Scudder v. Union Bank, 91 U. S. 406; Paine v. Drew, 44 N. H. 306; Ruckmaboye v. Mottichund, 8 Moore, P. C. 36; Pinney v. Cummings, 26 Ohio St. 46; McMerty v. Morrison, 62 Mo. 140; Carson v. Hunter, 46 Mo. 467; Langston v. Aderhold, 60 Ga. 376; Mineral Point R. Co. v. Barron, 83 Ill. 365; Hoggett v. Emerson, 8 Kans. 262; Swickard v. Bailey, 3 Kans. 507; O'Bannon v. O'Bannon, 13 Bush (Ky.) 583; McDonald v. Underhill, 10 Bush (Ky.) 584; Bigelow v. Ames, 18 Minn. 527; Fletcher v. Spaulding, 9 Minn. 64; Perkins v. Guy, 55 Miss. 153; Hubbard v. Epps, 9 Baxter (Tenn.) 231. But see Wilson v. Demers, 12 L. Can. Jur. 222. The rule in regard to actions barred in the foreign state has been changed by statute in many states. Van Dorn v. Bodley, 38 Ind. 402 (see Harris v. Harris, ib. 423); Webster v. Rees, 23 Iowa, 269; Sloan v. Waugh, 18 Iowa, 224; Mass. Pub. Stat. c. 197, s. 11.

nois holds a similar doctrine, asserting that the bar of prescription is a part of the modus procedendi.[1] It is in vain, he adds, to assert that the bar of prescription is a peremptory exception (exceptio peremptoria), and that, according to Baldus, 'exceptio peremptoria pertinent ad decisionem causæ;' that remark properly applies to a peremptory exception which falls upon the contract, and not to one which falls only upon the action or proceedings in a suit.[2] Many other jurists might be cited in support of this doctrine, if it were necessary to go at large into the subject.[3] The doctrine of the Scottish courts is in precise conformity to that of the common law.[4]

578. *Necessity of the Rule.* — But if the question were entirely new, it would be difficult upon principles of international justice or policy to establish a different rule. Every nation must have a right to settle for itself the times and modes and circumstances within and under which suits shall be litigated in its own courts. There can be no pretence to say that foreigners are entitled to crowd the tribunals of any nation with suits of their own which are stale and antiquated, to the exclusion of the common administration of justice between its own subjects. As little right can foreigners have to insist that the times and modes of proceeding in suits provided by the laws of their own country shall supersede those of the nation in which they have chosen to litigate their controversies, or in whose tribunals they are properly parties to any suit.

579. *Objections of Foreign Jurists.* — The reasoning sometimes insisted upon by foreign jurists, in opposition to this plain and intelligible doctrine, is, in the first place, that the statute of limitations or prescription really operates as a peremptory bar, and therefore does not in fact touch the mode of proceeding, but the merits of the case; 'non tangit modum simplicem procedendi,

---

[1] 1 Boullenois, obs. 23, p. 530; post, s. 579.
[2] Ibid.
[3] See 1 Boullenois, obs. 23, p. 530, 550; 2 Boullenois, obs. 46, p. 455, 456; Casaregis, Disc. 179, s. 59, 60; P. Voet, de Stat. s. 10, c. 1, s. 1, p. 281, ed. 1715; Id. p. 339, 340, ed. 1661. See 3 Burge, Col. & For. Law, pt. 2, c. 10, s. 5, p. 122–124; Id. c. 21, s. 7, p. 878–880; Ersk. Inst. b. 3, tit. 7, s. 48, p. 633, 634.
[4] Ersk. Inst. b. 3, tit. 7, s. 48, p. 633; Le Roy v. Crowninshield, 2 Mason, 174; Kames on Equity, b. 3, c. 8, s. 4, 6; P. Voet, de Stat. s. 10, c. 1, n. 1, p. 280, 281, ed. 1715; Id. p. 339, 340, ed. 1661.

sed tangit meritum causæ;'[1] and, in the next place, that it subjects the party to different prescriptions in different places, and therefore leaves his rights in uncertainty.[2] The latter objection may be answered by the obvious consideration, that if the party chooses to reside within any particular territory, he thereby subjects himself to the laws of that territory, as to all suits brought by or against him. It may be added that, as the law of prescription of a particular country, even in case of a contract made in such country, forms no part of the contract itself, but merely acts upon it ex post facto in case of a suit, it cannot properly be deemed a right stipulated for, or included in the contract. Even these foreign jurists do not pretend that the prescription of a country where a contract is made constitutes a part of the contract. What they contend for amounts at most only to this, that the prescription of the lex loci contractus acts upon, and appertains to, the decision of the cause. 'Hoc pertinet ad decisionem causæ,' says Baldus. 'Prescriptio utique ad contractum et meritum causæ pertinet, non ad processum,' says Gerhard Titius.[3] This objection indeed is fully and satisfactorily answered by Boullenois in the passage above cited.[4]

580. The other objection is well founded in its form, but it

---

[1] 1 Boullenois, obs. 23, p. 529, 530; ante, s. 577.

[2] 1 Hertii Opera, de Collis. Leg. s. 4, n. 65, p. 150, 151, ed. 1737; Id. p. 212, ed. 1716.

[3] 1 Boullenois, obs. 23, p. 529, 530; Ersk. Inst. b. 3, tit. 7, s. 48, p. 633, 634.

[4] Ante, s. 577. Lord Brougham also in delivering his judgment in Don v. Lippmann, 5 Cl. & F. p. 1, 15, 16, met the very objection. His language on that occasion was (it being the case of a bill of exchange accepted and payable in France, and sued afterwards in Scotland, and the Scottish prescription set up as a bar): 'It is said that the limitation is of the very nature of the contract. First, it is said that the party is bound for a given time, and for a given time only. That is a strained construction of the obligation. The party does not bind himself for a particular period at all, but merely to do something on a certain day, or on one or other of certain days. In the case at the bar, the obligation is to pay a sum certain at a certain day; but the law does not suppose that he is, at the moment of making the contract, contemplating the period at which he may be freed by lapse of time from performing it. The argument that the limitation is of the nature of the contract supposes that the parties look only to the breach of the agreement. Nothing is more contrary to good faith than such a supposition, that the contracting parties look only to the period at which the statute of limitations will begin to run. It will sanction a wrong course of conduct, and will turn a protection against laches into a premium for evasiveness.'

does not shake the ground of the general doctrine. It is true, as Baldus contends, that the statute of limitations or prescription does go to the decision of the cause: ' Exceptio peremptoria pertinet ad decisionem causæ.' But that is not the question. The question is, whether it is a matter of the original merits, as for example a question of the original validity, or interpretation, or discharge of a contract, or whether it is a matter touching the time and mode of remedial justice, which is provided by law to redress grievances, or to prevent wrongs, or to suppress vexatious litigation. Suppose a nation were to declare (as France has done in regard to foreigners in some cases) that no suits should be maintained in its own courts between foreigners.[1] This would be a peremptory exception. But could it be denied that France had a right so to regulate the jurisdiction of its own tribunals? or that it was an enactment touching remedies? Considered in their true light, statutes of limitation or prescription are ordinarily simple regulations of suits, and not of rights. They regulate the times in which rights may be asserted in courts of justice, and do not purport to act upon those rights. Boullenois has truly said : ' L'exception ne tombe, que sur l'action et la procédure intentée.'[2] Pothier very properly treats prescription (fin de non recevoir), not so much as an extinguishment of the debtor claim, as an extinguishment of the right of action thereon.[3] And this is precisely the manner in which the subject is contemplated at the common law as well as by many foreign jurists.[4] (a)

581. *Another Doctrine of Foreign Jurists.* — And here again upon the same mistaken foundation already discussed, some foreign jurists (as we have seen[5]) maintain the doctrine in rela-

[1] Ante, s. 542.

[2] 1 Boullenois, obs. 23, p. 530; ante, s. 577; Ersk. Inst. b. 3, tit. 7, s. 48, p. 633, 634.

[3] Pothier on Oblig. n. 640–642.

[4] Sturges v. Crowninshield, 4 Wheat. 122, 200, 207; J. Voet, ad Pand. 44, 3, 10; D'Aguesseau, Œuvres, tom. 5, p. 374, 4to ed.; Le Roy v. Crowninshield, 2 Mason, 170, 171; Merlin, Répert. tit. Prescription, sect. I. s. 3, n. 7. Corporations are deemed to be domiciled in the country from which they derive their act or charter of incorporation; and therefore the same rule applies to them as applies to private persons in cases of prescription. 3 Burge, Col. & For. Law, pt. 2, c. 21, s. 7, p. 881, 882. (b)

[5] Ante, s. 574 c.

(a) See Ruckmaboye v. Mottichund, 8 Moore, P. C. 36.

(b) See Louisville R. Co. v. Letson, 2 How. 497.

tion to contracts (a doctrine repudiated by the common law[1]), that if they are made in one place, and to be performed or paid in another place, the law of prescription of the latter place is to govern. Such is the opinion of Everhardus. 'Aut quærimus,' says he, 'quis locus inspiciatur, quoad extinctionem actionis propter præscriptionem statutoriam, vigentem in uno loco, et non in alio, ubi statuta locorum sunt diversa. Et certum est, quod inspicitur locus destinatæ solutionis.'[2] Bartolus, Burgundus, and Christinæus hold the same opinion.[3] Of course, the doctrine of these authors must be understood to be limited to prescription in personal actions; for as to prescription in cases of immovable property, it is beyond reasonable doubt that it is and ought to be governed purely by the lex loci rei sitæ.[4] Dumoulin has laid down the distinction in broad but exact terms. 'Aut statutum disponit de præscriptione, vel usucapione rerum corporalium, sive mobilium, sive immobilium, et tunc indistincte inspicitur locus, ubi res est. Idem in rebus sive juribus incorporalibus limitatis ad res corporales, sive quatenus ad illas res limitantur; secus si de juribus, vel actionibus personalibus, sive momentaneis, sive annuis personæ adhærentibus, id est non limitatis ad certas res, etiamsi illis actionibus adhæreat hypo-

---

[1] Ibid.   [2] Everhard. Consil. 78, p. 208; 2 Boullenois, obs. 46, p. 488.

[3] 2 Boullenois, obs. 46, p. 488. It is surprising that Mr. Henry should have cited this doctrine of foreign authors as sound law (apparently copying it from Boullenois) without considering that the whole course of English opinions on this subject disclaimed it. Henry on Foreign Law, c. 8, s. 1, 2, p. 54, 55. Pardessus says that, when a debtor pleads a statute of prescription, the right to use this plea, and the time within which it should be pleaded, will be regulated by the law of the place where he has promised to pay; or if this place has not been determined, then at the domicil of the debtor, at the time when he contracted the obligation; because prescription being a plea given to the debtor against the demand of his creditor, it is naturally in the domicil of the debtor or of his government that he should find this protection. Pardessus, tom. 5, pt. 6, tit. 9, c. 2, s. 2, art. 1445, p. 275; Henry on Foreign Law, Appendix, p. 237. Pardessus goes on to state that these rules apply to the case where several sureties for the same debt reside in jurisdictions where the laws respecting prescriptions are different. Each in becoming a surety must be supposed to have intended to enjoy all the real pleas or exceptions existing in favor of the principal debtor, without renouncing the particular prescription in his own favor, to extinguish his obligation as surety, which is regulated by the law of his domicil at the moment when he signed the contract. Pardessus, id. art. 1495, p. 275, 276; Henry on Foreign Law, 238. This is certainly pressing the doctrine to a very great extent.

[4] 1 Boullenois, obs. 20, p. 350; J. Voet, ad Pand. 44, 3, 12.

certainly been thought that, in such a case, the title of the possessor cannot be impugned.[1] If it cannot, the next inquiry is, whether the bar of a statute extinguishment of a debt, lege loci, ought not equally to be held a peremptory exception in every other country? This subject may be deemed by some persons still open for future discussion. It has however the direct authority of the Supreme Court of the United States in its favor;[2] and its correctness has been recently recognized by the Court of Common Pleas in England.[3] In the American courts other than the Supreme Court, it does not seem hitherto to have obtained any direct approval or recognition. But in all the cases in which the question might have been incidentally discussed in these courts, the statutes under consideration did not purport to extinguish the right, but merely the remedy.[4]

582 a. *Limitation of Actions upon Judgments.* — A question of a kindred character has been discussed of late years both in England and America; and that is, whether the statute of limitations or prescription of the country where a suit is brought is a good defence and bar to a suit brought there to enforce a foreign judgment. In both countries it has been held that it is a good defence and bar.[5] In America the case was stronger than it was as presented in England, for it was a judgment rendered in one of the United States which was sought to be enforced in another state of the Union, and therefore fell within the clause of the constitution which declares that full faith and credit and effect shall be given in each state to the judicial proceedings of every other. It was thought that this clause did not

---

[1] See Beckford v. Wade, 17 Ves. 88; Newby v. Blakey, 3 Hen. & Mun. 57; Brent v. Chapman, 5 Cranch, 358; Shelby v. Guy, 11 Wheat. 361, 371, 372. But see Dudley v. Warde, Amb. 113.

[2] Shelby v. Guy, 11 Wheat. 361, 371, 372.

[3] Huber v. Steiner, 2 Bing. N. C. 202, 211. See also Don v. Lippmann, 5 Cl. & F. 1, 16, 17; 3 Burge, Col. & For. Law, pt. 2, c. 10, s. 5, p. 123. 124.

[4] On this subject see De Couche v. Savetier, 3 Johns. Ch. (N. Y.) 190, 218, 219; Van Reimsdyk v. Kane, 1 Gallis. 371; Le Roy v. Crowninshield, 2 Mason, 151, and the cases there cited; Lincoln v. Battelle, 6 Wend. (N. Y.) 475; 1 Domat, b. 3, s. 4, art. 1, p. 464; Id. art. 10, p. 466. John Voet says in one place: 'Si præscriptioni implendæ alia prefinita sint tempora in loco domicilii actoris, alia in loco, ubi reus domicilium fovet, spectandum videtur tempus, quod obtinet ex statuto loci, in quo reus commoratur.' J. Voet, ad Pand. 44, 3, 12, p. 877.

[5] Don v. Lippmann, 5 Cl. & F. 1, 19–21; McElmoyle v. Cohen, 13 Pet. 312.

in the slightest degree vary the application of the general principle, that in all matters of proceedings in courts the lex loci was to govern.[1] (a)

[1] McElmoyle v. Cohen, 13 Pet. 312, 327, 328. Mr. Justice Wayne, in delivering the opinion of the court, after adverting to the clause of the constitution of the United States, and the interpretation thereof, said: 'Such being the faith, credit, and effect to be given to a judgment of one state in another by the constitution and the act of congress, the point under consideration will be determined by settling what is the nature of a plea of the statute of limitations. Is it a plea that settles the right of a party on a contract or judgment, or one that bars the remedy? Whatever diversity of opinion there may be among jurists upon this point, we think it well settled to be a plea to the remedy; and consequently that the lex fori must prevail. Higgins v. Scott, 2 B. & Ad. 413; 4 Cowen (N. Y.) 528, note 10; Id. 530; Van Reimsdyk v. Kane, 1 Gallis. 371; Le Roy v. Crowninshield, 2 Mason, 151; British Linen Co. v. Drummond, 10 B. & C. 903; De la Vega v. Vianna, 1 B. & Ad. 284; De Couche v. Savetier, 3 Johns. Ch. (N. Y.) 190; Lincoln v. Battelle, 6 Wend. (N. Y.) 475; Gulick v. Loder, 2 Green (N. J.) 572; 3 Burge, Col. & For. Law, p. 883. The statute of Georgia is, "that actions of debt on judgments obtained in courts, other than the courts of this state, must be brought within five years after the judgment obtained." It would be strange if, in the now well understood rights of nations to organize their judicial tribunals according to their notions of policy, it should be conceded to them in every other respect than that of prescribing the time within which suits shall be litigated in their courts. Prescription is a thing of policy, growing out of the experience of its necessity; and the time after which suits or actions shall be barred has been, from a remote antiquity, fixed by every nation in virtue of that sovereignty by which it exercises its legislation for all persons and property within its jurisdiction. This being the foundation of the right to pass statutes of prescription or limitation, may not our states, under our system, exercise this right in virtue of their sovereignty? Or is it to be conceded to them in every other particular than that of barring the remedy upon judgments of other states by the lapse of time? The states use this right upon judgments rendered in their own courts; and the common law raises the presumption of the payment of a judgment after the lapse of twenty years. May they not then limit the time for remedies upon the judgments of other states, and alter the common law by statute, fixing a less or larger time for such presumption, and altogether barring suits upon such judgments, if they shall not be brought within the time stated in the statute? It certainly will not be contended that judgment creditors of other states shall be put upon a better footing in regard to a state's right to legislate in this particular, than the judgment creditors of the state in which the judgment was obtained. And if this right so exists, may it not be exercised by a state's restraining the remedy upon the judgment of another state, leaving those of its own courts unaffected by a statute of limitations, but subject to the common-law presumption of payment after the lapse of twenty years. In other words, may not the law of a state fix different times for barring the remedy in a suit upon a judgment of another state, and for those of its own tribunals? We use this mode of argument to show

(a) See Townsend v. Jemison, 9 How. 419.

582 *b. Distinction to be Observed.* — It may be important then carefully to distinguish between cases where the statute of limitations is strictly a mere bar to the remedy, and cases where it goes directly to the extinguishment of the debt, claim, or right. Where it professes to dispose of the latter, it would seem difficult to say that a mere removal to another country can revive an extinguished debt, claim, or right, or change the positive title of property acquired and perfected under the local law of the place where the parties and property are situated.[1] But where it professes to deny or control or extinguish the remedy only, other considerations may properly apply. It has indeed been decided upon a recent occasion in one of the American courts, that in cases falling within the latter predicament it will make no difference whether both parties have remained domiciled in the same country where the original cause of action arose, during the whole period required by the local statute of limitations to bar the remedy thereon, or whether they have changed their domicil after it has begun to run.[2] But the reasoning which thus repels any such distinction is not so clear or decisive as has been supposed. Every nation has a complete and exclusive sovereignty to enact laws which shall limit all rights of action to certain prescribed periods within its own tribunals, and to declare that after that period all rights of action shall be extinguished; and if the parties remain domiciled within the territorial jurisdiction during that whole period, the law ipso facto operates on the case, and the rights of action are completely extinguished there. But the same doctrine is not true, or rather may not be true, where before the prescribed period has arrived one or both of the parties have changed their national domicil; for by such change they

the unreasonableness of a contrary doctrine. But the point might have been shortly dismissed with this safe declaration, that there is no direct constitutional inhibition upon the states, nor any clause in the constitution, from which it can be even plausibly inferred that the states may not legislate upon the remedy in suits upon the judgments of other states, exclusive of all interference with their merits. It being settled that the statute of limitations may bar recoveries upon foreign judgments; that the effect intended to be given under our constitution to judgments is, that they are conclusive only as regards the merits; the common-law principle then applies to suits upon them, that they must be brought within the period prescribed by the local law, the lex fori, or the suit will be barred.'

[1] Don *v.* Lippmann, 5 Cl. & F. 1, 15-17.
[2] Bulger *v.* Roche, 11 Pick. (Mass.) 36.

have ceased to be under the exclusive dominion of the nation whose statute of limitations has begun to operate upon their rights of action, but has not as yet extinguished them. The laws thereof can no longer operate on those rights, at least not operate except within the territorial limits of the nation. Elsewhere they can be deemed as having only an inchoate and imperfect effect; and the change of domicil suspends their power to extinguish the rights of action in future, since they can have no binding extra-territorial force. It is no answer to say that when once the statute of limitations begins to run, no subsequent impediment stops it from continuing to run. That is true in the nation whose laws contain such provisions or inculcate such a doctrine. But no other nation is bound to give effect to such provisions or to such a doctrine. They are strictly intra-territorial regulations and interpretations of the lex fori, which other nations are not bound to observe or keep. While the parties were domiciled there, the statute of limitations continued to run against them, but it had not then extinguished any rights of action. When they changed their domicil, the statute, as to them or their rights of action, in respect to personal property or personal claims, was no longer operative or obligatory, but the statutes only of their new domicil. It would, or at least might, then require a very different consideration, where the local law had before the change of domicil actually extinguished all rights of action; for then to revive them is to create new rights, and not to enforce old rights subsisting at the time of the removal.[1]

---

[1] In Bulger v. Roche, 11 Pick. (Mass.) 36, the very case arose of a cause of action extinguished by the local law of the country (Nova Scotia) where both parties resided during the whole period of the running of the statute of limitations; and the supreme court of Massachusetts held that the right of action, after a change of domicil of the defendant by a removal to Massachusetts, was not thereby extinguished in the state tribunals, but might be pursued within the period prescribed by the statute of limitations of Massachusetts. On that occasion Mr. Chief Justice Shaw in delivering the opinion of the court said: 'The facts, so far as they are material, are these: that the cause of action accrued in 1821, more than six years before the commencement of this action; that the plaintiff and defendant were both domiciled at Halifax in Nova Scotia, and were subjects of the King of Great Britain; and that by the law of that country an action of assumpsit is barred in six years. It is stated in the replication, and admitted by the rejoinder, that the plaintiff came into this commonwealth for the first time in 1829, and that the action was commenced within six years from that time. That the law of limitations of a foreign country cannot of itself be pleaded as a bar to an action in this commonwealth

583. *Remarks of John Voet.* — What has been thus far stated on this head may be concluded by quoting a passage from John Voet, the correctness and force of which, in point of principle, are submitted to the consideration of the reader. ' Quod, si restitutio concedenda sit non ex causa, quæ ipsum negotium ab initio

seems conceded, and is indeed too well settled by authority to be drawn in question. Byrne *v.* Crowninshield, 17 Mass. 55. The authorities both from the civil and the common law concur in fixing the rule that the nature, validity, and construction of contracts are to be determined by the law of the place where the contract is made; and that all remedies for enforcing such contracts are regulated by the law of the place where such remedies are pursued. Whether the law of prescription, or statute of limitation, which takes away every legal mode of recovering a debt, shall be considered as affecting the contract like payment, release, or judgment, which in effect extinguish the contract, or whether they are to be considered as affecting the remedy only by determining the time within which a particular mode of enforcing it shall be pursued, were it an open question, might be one of some difficulty. It was ably discussed upon general principles in a late case (Le Roy *v.* Crowninshield, 2 Mason, 151) before the circuit court, in which however it was fully conceded by the learned judge, upon a full consideration and review of all the authorities, that it is now considered to be a settled question. A doubt was intimated in that case, whether, if the parties had remained subjects of the foreign country until the term of limitation had expired, so that the plaintiff's remedy would have been extinguished there, such a state of facts would not have presented a stronger case, and one of more serious difficulty. Such was the case in the present instance. But we think it sufficient to advert to a well-settled rule in the construction of the statute of limitations, to show that this circumstance can make no difference. The rule is this: that where the statute has begun to run, it will continue to run notwithstanding the intervention of any impediment which, if it had existed when the cause of action accrued, would have prevented the operation of the statute. For instance, if this action accrued in Nova Scotia in 1821, and the plaintiff or defendant had left that country in 1825, within six years, in 1828, after the lapse of six years, the action would be as effectually barred, and the remedy extinguished there, as if both had continued to reside in Halifax down to the same period. So that when the parties met here in 1829, so far as the laws of that country, by taking away all legal remedy, could affect it, the debt was extinguished, and that equally whether they had both remained under the jurisdiction of those laws till the time of limitation had elapsed, or whether either or both had previously, left it. The authorities referred to therefore must be held applicable to a case where both parties were subject to the jurisdiction of a foreign state when the bar arising from its statute of limitations attached. The same conclusion results from the reason upon which these cases proceed, which is, that statutes of limitation affect only the time within which a legal remedy must be pursued, and do not affect the nature, validity, or construction of the contract. This reason, whether well founded or not, applies equally to cases where the term of limitation has elapsed when the parties leave the foreign state, as to those where it has only begun to run before they have left the state, and elapses afterwards.' But see Don *v.* Lippmann, 5 Cl. & F. 1, 15–17.

comitabatur (uti comitatur metus, dolus, error), sed ex ea, quæ post supervenit (qualis est usucapio verum, aut præscriptio jurium et actionum, propter absentiam non interrupta), ita generaliter definiendum existimo, illius loci leges in restitutione facienda attendendas esse, secundum cujus loci leges impleta summo jure fuit per absentiam usucapio vel præscriptio. Quid enim, obsecro, aut justius aut æquius, quam ut ex eorundem legislatorum præscripto remedium adversus læsionem indulgeatur, ex quorum præscripto et summo jure primitus læsio nata fuit? Quibus cousequens est, ut si immobilium rerum usucapio impleta sit, serventur in restitutione facienda jura regionis, in qua immobiles res sitæ sunt: adeoque, ut in amittendo, sic et in recuperando dominio, regantur immobilia ex situs sui lege, juxta vulgatam regulam in materia statutaria. Sin mobilia usucapta fuerint, in restitutione magis erit, ut serventur leges domicilii ejus, qui per usucapionem dominium amiserat; ut ita mobilia, quæ censentur illic esse, ubi domicilium fovet dominus, ex lege domicilii redeant, uti fuerant amissa. Sed si actiones in personam temporis lapsu, per absentiam contingente, extinctæ sint; probabilius fuerit, in illis restituendis ob justam absentiæ causam spectandum esse jus loci, in quo debitor commoratur, contra quem restitutio petitur: cum etiam ex istius loci lege præscriptio implenda fuerit.' [1]

[1] J. Voet, ad Pand. 4, 1, 29, p. 241; Henry on Foreign Law, p. 56, 59.

CHAPTER XV.

FOREIGN JUDGMENTS.

584. *Subject of the Chapter.* We come in the next place to the consideration of foreign judgments, or of the force and effect of foreign sentences, exceptio rei judicatæ. As to the effect to be given to foreign judgments, there has been much diversity of practice, as well as of opinion, among jurists and nations. We do not speak here of cases where the point was, whether the court pronouncing the judgment had jurisdiction or not; but, assuming the jurisdiction to be unquestionable, what force and effect ought to be given to such judgment. Ought it to be held conclusive upon the parties? Or ought it to be open to impeachment by new evidence, or to be re-examined upon the original merits? The subject may be considered in two general aspects; first, in regard to judgments in rem; and secondly, in regard to judgments in personam.[1] The latter is again divisible into several heads: first, where the judgment is set up by way of defence to a suit in a foreign tribunal; and secondly, where the judgment is sought to be enforced in a foreign tribunal against the original defendant or his property; and thirdly, where the judgment is between subjects, or between foreigners, or between foreigners and subjects. These divisions will in some degree require a separate examination.[2]

[1] Burgundus divides judgments (sententiæ) into three classes: 1. In rem; 2. In personam; 3. Mixed, in rem et in personam. 'Omnium condemnationum summa divisio, pariter in tria genera deducitur. Aut enim in rem, aut in personam, aut in utramque concipiuntur. In rem, quoties alicui res asseritur, hoc est ejus esse dicitur, vel jure creditoris, aut alio modo possidenda datur. In personam, si condemnetur ad aliquid dandum aut patiendum, faciendum aut non faciendum, vel si personæ statum afficiat. In utramque, si et res et persona simul in condemnationem veniant.' Burgundus, tract. 3, n. 1, 2, p. 84, 85; 1 Boullenois, obs. 25, p. 602. See the learned opinion of Mr. Vice-Chancellor Bruce, in Barrs v. Jackson, 1 Y. & C. 585, as to what domestic judgments are conclusive or not.

[2] See, on this subject, 3 Burge, Col. & For. Law, pt. 2, c. 24, p. 1014-1080. See also 2 Sm. L. C. 436, note, 2d ed.

585. *Vattel.* — Vattel has said, with great force, that it is the province of every sovereignty to administer justice in all places within its own territory and under its own jurisdiction, to take cognizance of crimes committed there and of the controversies that arise within it. Other nations ought to respect this right; and, as the administration of justice necessarily requires that every definitive sentence, regularly pronounced, be esteemed just, and executed as such, when once a cause, in which foreigners are interested, has been decided in form, the sovereign of the defendants ought not to hear their complaints. To undertake to examine the justice of a definitive sentence is an attack upon the jurisdiction of the sovereign who has passed it.[1] Hence Vattel deduces the general rule that, in consequence of this right of jurisdiction, the decision made by the judge of the place within the extent of his authority ought to be respected, and to take effect even in foreign countries.[2]

586. *Jurisdiction of the Foreign Court.* — Reasonable as this doctrine seems to be, it is difficult to affirm that it has obtained the general assent of civilized nations in modern times in their intercourse with each other. The support which it has received from the common law is far more extensive and uniform than it has received in the jurisprudence of continental Europe. In order however to found a proper ground of recognition of any foreign judgment in another country, it is indispensable to establish that the court pronouncing judgment should have a lawful jurisdiction over the cause, over the thing, and over the parties.[3] (a) If the jurisdiction fails as to either, it is (as we have already seen) treated as a mere nullity, having no obligation, and entitled to no respect beyond the domestic tribunals.[4] And this is equally true, whether the proceedings be in rem or in personam, or in rem and also in personam.[5] (b)

---

[1] Vattel, b. 2, c. 7, s. 84.   [2] Id. s. 85.
[3] See 1 Boullenois, obs. 25, p. 618–620.
[4] Ante, s. 539, 546, 547; Buchanan *v.* Rucker, 9 East, 192; Bissell *v.* Briggs, 5 Mass. 462; Shumway *v.* Stillman, 6 Wend. (N. Y.) 447; Don *v.* Lippmann, 5 Cl. & F. 1, 20, 21; 4 Cowen (N. Y.) 524, n.; 1 Stark. Ev. pt. 2, s. 68, p. 214; Henry on Foreign Law, 18, n.; Id. 23, 73; Cavan *v.* Stewart, 1 Stark. 525; Hall *v.* Williams, 6 Pick. (Mass.) 232; Woodward *v.* Tremere, 6 Pick. 354; Ferguson *v.* Mahon, 11 A. & E. 179, 182, 183.
[5] Ibid.

(a) See Ferguson *v.* Mahon, 11 A. & E. 179, 182, 183.

(b) *Jurisdiction.* — In order that a judgment rendered in another state

587. *Rose* v. *Himely.* — This subject was a good deal considered in a celebrated case (a proceeding in rem) before the Su-

should have *full* force and effect elsewhere, it must have been rendered by virtue of jurisdiction acquired over the person of the defendant; unless indeed the defendant was a citizen of the state in which the judgment was rendered. In this latter case, if the proceeding for obtaining jurisdiction was according to the law of the forum, the defendant will be bound throughout the Union; for he is bound by the laws of his own state. Galpin *v.* Page, 18 Wall. 350; Bigelow, Estoppel, 149, note, 3d ed. See Don *v.* Lippmann, 5 Cl. & F. 1; Schibsby *v.* Westenholz, L. R. 6 Q. B. 155; Rousillon *v.* Rousillon, 14 Ch. D. 351; Douglas *v.* Forrest, 4 Bing. 686; Burlen *v.* Shannon, 99 Mass. 200, 207. In Rousillon *v.* Rousillon, and Schibsby *v.* Westenholz, supra, it is said that a judgment good by the local law will bind residents as well as citizens.

If jurisdiction was obtained against a non-resident by attachment of his property only, the judgment rendered thereon will have no extra-territorial effect further than to bind the property attached and disposed of. Galpin *v.* Page, supra; Cooper *v.* Reynolds, 10 Wall. 308. (Several cases to the contrary, under state insolvency laws, — Scribner *v.* Fisher, 2 Gray, 43; Smith *v.* Brown, 43 N. H. 44; Brown *v.* Collins, 41 N. H. 405, — have been overruled. Baldwin *v.* Hale, 1 Wall. 223; Gilman *v.* Lockwood, 4 Wall. 409; Stoddard *v.* Harrington, 100 Mass. 87; Newmarket Bank *v.* Butler, 45 N. H. 236. For certain peculiar cases, see Stoddard *v.* Harrington, supra; ante, s. 335, note.) Indeed the judgment is of no further avail even in the state in which it was rendered. No general execution can be issued for any balance unpaid after the attached property is exhausted; and no suit can be maintained on the judgment in the

same or in any other court. Cooper *v.* Reynolds, supra, Miller, J.; Pennoyer *v.* Neff, 95 U. S. 714, 725.

In England it appears to have been a question until very lately whether the existence of property in the country of the judgment might not give the court jurisdiction over the person of the defendant. See Schibsby *v.* Westenholz, L. R. 6 Q. B. 155, 163, criticising Douglas *v.* Forrest, 4 Bing. 703, and intimating that it would not; and so it has since been decided. The Mecca, 6 P. D. 106, reversing 5 P. D. 28. See London Ry. Co. *v.* Lindsay, 3 Macq. 99.

It was formerly a question of much doubt whether recitals of jurisdiction in the record of a judgment rendered in a sister state were conclusive. In many cases they were held indisputable. Wilcox *v.* Kassick, 2 Mich. 165; Lincoln *v.* Tower, 2 McLean, 473; Wilson *v.* Jackson, 10 Mo. 330; Bradstreet *v.* Neptune Ins. Co., 3 Sum. 600; Westcott *v.* Brown, 13 Ind. 88; Lawrence *v.* Jarvis, 32 Ill. 304; Lapham *v.* Briggs, 27 Vt. 26; Hall *v.* Williams, 6 Pick. 232; Shelton *v.* Tiffin, 6 How. 163. But this view was denied in other cases (Starbuck *v.* Murray, 5 Wend. 148; Kerr *v.* Kerr, 41 N. Y. 272; Carleton *v.* Bickford, 13 Gray, 591; Bodurtha *v.* Goodrich, 3 Gray, 508; Rape *v.* Heaton, 9 Wis. 328), and by recent decisions of the Supreme Court of the United States these latter cases have come to be the law. Thompson *v.* Whitman, 18 Wall. 457; Knowles *v.* Gaslight Co., 19 Wall. 58; Pennoyer *v.* Neff, 95 U. S. 714. See to the same effect, Wright *v.* Andrews, 130 Mass. 149; Kingsbury *v.* Yniestra, 59 Ala. 320; Napton *v.* Leaton, 71 Mo. 358; Ferguson *v.* Crawford, 70 N. Y. 253.

Appearance by a foreign defendant not notified, entered merely for the

preme Court of the United States, where the principal point was, whether there had been a change of the ownership of the property by the sentence of a foreign court in a suit there pending in rem. Upon that occasion Mr. Chief Justice Marshall, in delivering the opinion of the court, used the following language: ' The power of the [foreign] court then is of necessity examinable to a certain extent by that tribunal which is compelled to decide whether its sentence has changed the right of property. The power under which it acts must be looked into, and its authority to decide questions which it professes to decide must be considered.

588. ' But although the general power by which a court takes jurisdiction of causes must be inspected, in order to determine whether it may rightfully do what it professes to do, it is still a question of serious difficulty whether the situation of the particular thing on which the sentence has passed may be inquired into for the purpose of deciding whether that thing was in a state which subjected it to the jurisdiction of the court passing the sentence. For example, in every case of a foreign sentence condemning a vessel as prize of war, the authority of the tribunal to act as a prize court must be examinable. Is the question whether the vessel condemned was in a situation to subject her to the jurisdiction of that court, also examinable? This question, in the opinion of the court, must be answered in the affirmative.

589. ' Upon principle it would seem that the operation of every judgment must depend on the power of the court to render that judgment; or, in other words, on its jurisdiction over the subject-matter which it has determined. In some cases that jurisdiction unquestionably depends as well on the state of the thing as on the constitution of the court. If by any means whatever a prize court should be induced to condemn, as prize of war, a vessel which was never captured, it could not be contended that this condemnation operated a change of property. Upon principle then it would seem that, to a certain extent, the capacity of the court to act upon the thing condemned, arising from

purpose of contesting the jurisdiction of the court, will not, it seems, give the court entire jurisdiction over him. Walling v. Beers, 120 Mass. 548. See Wright v. Andrews, 130 Mass. 149; Bissell v. Briggs, 9 Mass. 462, 468, 469; Wright v. Boynton, 37 N. H. 9; Cunningham v. Goelet, 4 Denio, 71. And further, on the effect of partial appearance, see General Nav. Co. v. Guillou, 11 M. & W. 877, 894; Schibsby v. Westenholz, L. R. 6 Q. B. 155, 162.

its being within or without their jurisdiction, as well as the constitution of the court, may be considered by that tribunal which is to decide on the effect of the sentence.

590. 'Passing from principle to authority, we find that, in the courts of England, whose decisions are particularly mentioned, because we are best acquainted with them, and because, as is believed, they give to foreign sentences as full effect as are given to them in any part of the civilized world, the position that the sentence of a foreign court is conclusive with respect to what it professes to decide, is uniformly qualified with the limitation that it has, in the given case, jurisdiction of the subject-matter.'[1]

591. *Judgments in Rem. — Immovables.* — Let us now consider the operation of judgments in the different classes of cases which have been already adverted to. And first, in relation to judgments in rem. If the matter in controversy is land, or other immovable property, the judgment pronounced in the forum rei sitæ is held to be of universal obligation, as to all the matters of right and title which it professes to decide in relation thereto.[2] This results from the very nature of the case; for no other court can have a competent jurisdiction to inquire into or settle such right or title. By the general consent of nations therefore in cases of immovables, the judgment of the forum rei sitæ is held absolutely conclusive.[3] 'Immobilia ejus jurisdictionis esse reputantur, ubi sita sunt.'[4] On the other hand, a judgment in any foreign country, touching such immovables, will be held of no obligation. John Voet is explicit on this point: 'Licet autem regulariter judex requisitus non cognoscat de justitia sententiæ per alterum judicem latæ, nec eam ad examen penitius revocet, sed pro justitia ejus ac æquitate præsumat. Tamen si animadvertat, eam directo contra sui territorii statuta latam esse circa res immobiles, in suo territorio sitas, eandem non exsequitur; uti nec, si alias absque prolixa causæ cognitione constet, sententiam nullam esse.'[5] (a)

---

[1] Rose v. Himely, 4 Cranch, 269, 270.　　[2] Ante, s. 532, 545, 551.

[3] 1 Boullenois, obs. 25, p. 618, 619, 623.

[4] Id. p. 619; 1 Hertii Opera, de Collis. s. 4, n. 78, p. 153, 154, ed. 1737; Id. p. 216, ed. 1716. See also J. Voet, ad Pand. 1, 1, ps. 2, n. 11, p. 44, and ante, s. 362, note 3.

[5] J. Voet, ad Pand. 2, 42, 1, n. 41, p. 788.

(a) The case of Cammell v. Sewell, 5 H. & N. 728, illustrates this doctrine. There a cargo of deals consigned to an English firm was shipped

592. *Movables.* — The same principle is applied to all other cases of proceedings in rem against movable property within the

in a Russian port on board a Prussian vessel, which, on its way to England, was cast away upon the coast of Norway; but the cargo was safely landed. Steps were taken by the captain, without authority or the existence of any necessity, to sell the cargo; and for that purpose certain judicial proceedings took place, under which an auction was decreed, and the deals sold to a purchaser, under whom the defendant claimed, notwithstanding the protest of the agent of the plaintiffs, who were English underwriters, and who had become owners of the deals by having accepted an abandonment and paid as upon a total loss. The plaintiffs thereupon instituted a suit in the Superior Diocesan Court in Norway, praying that the public auction should be disallowed, and the purchaser compelled to deliver up the goods in specie. That court however affirmed the previous proceedings, and directed that the auction should be confirmed. The goods were afterwards consigned by the purchaser to the defendants in England, who refused to deliver them up to the plaintiffs. The Court of Exchequer held that the judgment of the Diocesan Court in Norway was in the nature of a judgment in rem, and that the plaintiffs were concluded by it as such, but seemed to think that, even if not a judgment in rem, it would still bind the plaintiffs, as being the judgment of a court of competent jurisdiction, to which the plaintiffs had themselves resorted, and accordingly gave judgment for the defendant. Upon appeal all the judges in the Exchequer Chamber were of opinion (without finding it necessary directly to decide the point) that the judgment in Norway was not a judgment in rem; but they held (Byles, J. dissenting) that, inasmuch as by the law of Norway an

innocent purchaser at the judicial sale would have a good title to the goods purchased, even though the master could not, as between himself and his owners, or the owners of the cargo, justify such sale, the law of Norway would prevail; and in terms proceeded to affirm the proposition that ' if personal property is disposed of in a manner binding according to the law of the country where it is, that disposition is binding everywhere; ' and the judgment of the Court of Exchequer was affirmed, but on that ground only.

And in a still later case a ship was, while in a port of an English colony, repaired and furnished with necessaries for the voyage. The captain drew on his owner for the amount due, but the bill was never accepted. The ship sailed on its prescribed voyage, and before reaching England entered a French port. The bill was indorsed to a French subject, who sued the captain on it in the Tribunal de Commerce, and obtained a judgment against him; but the judgment freed him from personal arrest, and declared the debt ' privileged on the ship,' that is, having a priority over others; and the ship was taken possession of by the French authorities under this judgment. While the ship was on its voyage, and before its arrival in the French port, the owner had executed a mortgage thereof to a creditor, and neither the original owner nor the mortgagee was in any way personally cited in the action on the bill. The ship could not be actually sold under the judgment of the Tribunal de Commerce until such judgment was approved by the Civil Tribunal of the district. It was confirmed after citing in the original owner and his assignee in bankruptcy (for he had in the meantime become bankrupt), and the

jurisdiction of the court pronouncing the judgment.[1] Whatever the court settles as to the right or title, or whatever disposition it makes of the property by sale, revendication, transfer, or other act, will be held valid in every other country, where the same question comes directly or indirectly in judgment before any other foreign tribunal. (a) This is very familiarly known in the cases of proceedings in rem in foreign courts of admiralty, whether they are causes of prize, or of bottomry, or of salvage, or of forfeiture, (b) or of any of the like nature, over which such courts have a rightful jurisdiction, founded on the actual or constructive possession of the subject-matter (res).[2] (c) The same rule is

[1] See Kames on Equity, b. 3, c. 8, s. 4; French v. Hall, 9 N. H. 137.
[2] Croudson v. Leonard, 4 Cranch, 434; Williams v. Armroyd, 7 Cranch, 423; Rose v. Himely, 4 Cranch, 241; Hudson v. Guestier, 4 Cranch, 293; The Mary, 9 Cranch, 126, 142-146; 1 Stark. Ev. pt. 2, s. 81, p. 238, &c.; Marshall, Insur. b. 1, c. 9, s. 6, p. 412, 435; Cases cited in 4 Cowen (N. Y.) 520, n. 3; Grant v. McLachlin, 4 Johns. (N. Y.) 34; Peters v. Warren Ins.

Civil Tribunal disregarded the opinion of an English lawyer as to the relative rights of the holder of a bill of exchange, and the holder of a bill of sale of the ship. The assignee of the mortgage afterwards instituted before the Civil Tribunal a process in the nature of a replevy of the ship, but failed in the suit, and the ship was sold. It was held by the House of Lords, after great deliberation, that there had been a judgment in rem in the French court, and that the title of the vendee of the ship, although an Englishman, could not be disturbed in that country. Castrique v. Imrie, Law Rep. 4 H. L. 414. And Lord Chelmsford declared the rule to be that a proceeding in a foreign court to enforce a maritime lien, which by the law of that foreign country, and of all foreign codes founded upon the civil law, is a proceeding in rem, though not so recognized by the law of England, must be so treated and held there. Comp. The Mecca, 6 P. D. 106.

(a) In Castrique v. Imrie, supra, it was said by Mr. Justice Blackburn: ' We may observe that the words as to an action being in rem or in personam, and the common statement that the one is binding on third persons and the other not, are apt to be used by English lawyers without attaching any very definite meaning to those phrases. We apprehend the true principle to be that indicated in the last few words quoted from Story. We think the inquiry is: first, whether the subject-matter was so situated as to be within the lawful control of the state under the authority of which the court sits; and secondly, whether the sovereign authority of that state has conferred on the court jurisdiction to decide as to the disposition of the thing, and the court has acted within its jurisdiction. If these conditions are all fulfilled, the adjudication is conclusive against all the world.'

(b) Or of damage by collision. Harmer v. Bell, 7 Moore, P. C. 267; 22 Eng. L. & Eq. 62.

(c) See Whitney v. Walsh, 1 Cush. (Mass.) 29; The Mary Anne. Ware, 103; Barrow v. West, 23 Pick. (Mass.) 270; Monroe v. Douglas, 4 Sandf. (N. Y.) Ch. 179.

applied to other courts proceeding in rem, such as the Court of Exchequer in England, and to other courts exercising a like jurisdiction in rem upon seizures.[1] And in cases of this sort it is wholly immaterial whether the judgment be of acquittal or of condemnation. In both cases it is equally conclusive.[2] But the doctrine however is always to be understood with this limitation, that the judgment has been obtained bona fide and without fraud; for if fraud has intervened, it will doubtless avoid the force and validity of the sentence.[3] So it must appear that there have been regular proceedings to found the judgment or decree; and that the parties in interest in rem have had notice or an opportunity to appear and defend their interests, either personally or by their proper representatives, before it was pronounced; for the common justice of all nations requires that no condemnation should be pronounced before the party has an opportunity to be heard.[4]

592 a. Garnishment. — Proceedings also by creditors against the personal property of their debtor in the hands of third persons, or against debts due to him by such third persons (commonly called the process of foreign attachment, or garnishment, or trustee process), are also treated as in some sense proceedings in rem, and are deemed entitled to the same consideration.[5] But in this last class of cases we are especially to bear in mind that to make any judgment effectual the court must possess and exercise a rightful jurisdiction over the res, and also over the person, at least so far as the res is concerned; otherwise it will be disregarded. And if the jurisdiction over the res be well founded,

Co., 3 Sumner, 389; Blad v. Bamfield, 3 Swanst. 604, 605; Bradstreet v. Neptune Ins. Co., 3 Sumner, 600; Magoun v. New England Ins. Co., 1 Story, 157.

[1] Ibid. And Stark. Ev. p. 2, s. 67, 80, 81, p. 336; Gelston v. Hoyt, 3 Wheat. 246; Williams v. Armroyd, 7 Cranch, 423.

[2] Ibid.

[3] See post, s. 597; Duchess of Kingston's Case, 11 State Trials, p. 261, 262; 20 Howell, State Trials, p. 355; Id. p. 538, the opinion of the judges; Bradstreet v. Neptune Ins. Co., 3 Sumner, 600; Magoun v. New England Ins. Co., 1 Story, 157.

[4] Sawyer v. Maine Ins. Co., 12 Mass. 291; Bradstreet v. Neptune Ins. Co. 3 Sumner, 600; Monroe v. Douglas, 4 Sandf. Ch. 180 (an important case on this subject); Magoun v. New England Ins. Co., 1 Story, 157.

[5] See cases cited in 4 Cowen (N. Y.) 520, 521, n.; ante, s. 549; Holmes v. Remsen, 20 Johns. (N. Y.) 229; Hull v. Blake, 13 Mass. 153; McDaniel v. Hughes, 3 East, 367; Phillips v. Hunter, 2 H. Bl. 402, 410.

but not over the person, except as to the res, the judgment will not be either conclusive or binding upon the party in personam, although it may be in rem.[1] (a)

<hr/>

[1] Ante, s. 549, and note; Bissell *v.* Briggs, 9 Mass. 468. See also 3 Burge, Col. & For. Law, pt. 2, c. 24, p. 1014–1019. Some very important questions may arise in cases of foreign attachment or garnishment. Suppose A., a creditor of B., should bring a suit by foreign attachment or garnishment in a foreign country against C. as garnishee of the property or credits of B., will a judgment rendered in that suit conclude D., who claims the same property or credit by a prior title in another suit therefor in the same country, or in another country? Will it make any difference that A., before obtaining his judgment, had notice of D.'s claim and right? Will it make any difference that D. might by the lex fori have intervened in the first suit to vindicate his title, and to support it, if he was not domiciled in the country at the time, although he had notice of the same suit? Another case may be put involving similar considerations. Suppose a suit is brought in a foreign country by A. against B. to recover property there situate, to which C., who is domiciled in a foreign country, also claims title; and by the law of the country where the suit is brought, C. might intervene for his title; but he does not, although he has notice of the suit. If A. obtains judgment in the suit for the property against B., will that judgment bind C. in the courts of that country in a subsequent suit brought there by C. against A. for the same property? If it will bind him there, will it bind him in a suit brought in the country of his own domicil, or in another foreign country? These questions are propounded for the consideration of the learned reader, without any attempt to discuss or solve them.

(a) See Ocean Ins. Co. *v.* Portsmouth Ry. Co., 8 Met. (Mass.) 420; Danforth *v.* Penny, Id. 564. The truth is that in the chief sense which distinguishes judgments in rem from judgments in personam, the sense, that is to say, in which the former proceed irrespective of individual rights, while the latter proceed wholly upon the rights of individuals, — in this sense judgments in cases of attachment, garnishment, and the like are not judgments in rem at all. They bind at most only the specific parties to the action, including of course their successors in right. It is very different with a true proceeding in rem, such as an action in admiralty against a vessel for violating the laws of neutrality. Judgment executed in such a case concludes all the world.

The nature of proceedings at common law in attachment has been most clearly stated by Sir John Jervis in The Bold Buccleugh, 7 Moore, P. C. 267, 282; where he says: 'The foreign attachment is founded upon a plaint against the principal debtor, and must be returned "nihil" before any step can be taken against the garnishee; the proceeding in rem, whether for wages, salvage, collision, or on bottomry, goes against the ship in the first instance. In the former case the proceedings are in personam; in the latter, they are in rem. The attachment, like a common-law distringas, is merely for the purpose of compelling an appearance.' See to the same effect Megee *v.* Beirne, 39 Penn. St. 50. And see further, Woodruff *v.* Taylor, 20 Vt. 65; Barber *v.* Hartford Bank, 9 Conn. 407; Myers *v.* Beeman, 9 Ired. (N. C.) 116; Ormond *v.* Moye, 11 Ired. (N. C.) 564; Kieffer *v.* Ehler, 18 Penn. St. 388. Nor are

593. *Conclusiveness of the Judgment.* — In all these cases the same principle prevails, that the judgment acting in rem shall be held conclusive upon the title and transfer and disposition of the property itself, in whatever place the same property may afterwards be found, and by whomsoever the latter may be questioned, and whether it be directly or incidentally brought in question. But it is not so universally settled that the judgment is conclusive of all the points which are incidentally disposed of by the judgment, or of the facts or allegations upon which it professes to be founded. In this respect different rules are adopted by different states both in Europe and in America. In England such judgments are held conclusive, not only in rem, but also as to all the points and facts which they professedly or incidentally decide.[1] In some of the American states the same doctrine prevails. While in other American states the judgments are held conclusive only in rem, and may be controverted as to all the incidental grounds and facts on which they profess to be founded.[2] (a)

[1] In Blad v. Bamfield, decided by Lord Nottingham, and reported in 3 Swanst. 604, a perpetual injunction was awarded to restrain certain suits of trespass and trover for seizing the goods of the defendant (Bamfield) for trading in Ireland contrary to certain privileges granted to the plaintiff and others. The property was seized and condemned in the Danish courts; Lord Nottingham held the sentence conclusive against the suits, and awarded the injunctions accordingly.

[2] See 4 Cowen (N. Y.) 522, n. and cases cited; Vandenheuvel v. U. Ins. Co., 2 Caines Cas. (N. Y.) 217; 2 Johns. Cas. (N. Y.) 451, 481; Robinson v. Jones, 8 Mass. 536; Maley v. Shattuck, 3 Cranch, 488; 2 Kent, Com. 120, 121, and cases there cited; Tarleton v. Tarleton, 4 M. & S. 20. See Peters v. Warren Ins. Co., 3 Sumner, 389; Gelston v. Hoyt, 3 Wheat. 246.

the statutory proceedings in replevin proceedings in rem in this proper sense. Megee v. Beirne, supra; Certain Logs of Mahogany, 2 Sum. 589; Dow v. Sanborn, 3 Allen (Mass.) 181.

(a) *Facts incidentally decided.* — It is not quite clear what is here meant by facts 'incidentally' decided; and the same term is sometimes loosely employed by the courts. If facts unnecessary to the decision are meant (and that is the sense to which the word as applied to judgments is commonly used), it is pretty clear that the judgment, whether in rem or in personam, has no binding effect thereon. The settled rule even with regard to domestic judgments is that a judgment or decree is conclusive only of facts without the existence and proof or admission of which it could not have been rendered; Burlen v. Shannon, 99 Mass. 200; Leonard v. Whitney, 109 Mass. 265; West v. Platt, 127 Mass. 367; Morse v. Elms, 131 Mass. 151; Porter v. Wagner, 86 Ohio St. 471; Marvin v. Dutcher, 26 Minn. 391; Dunham v. Bower, 77 N. Y. 76;

594. *Guardianship.* — A similar doctrine has been contended for, and in many cases successfully, in favor of sentences of a peculiar character ; such as those which touch the general capacity of persons, and those which concern marriage and divorce. Thus foreign jurists strongly contend that the decree of a foreign court, declaring the state (status) of a person, and placing him, as an idiot, or minor, or prodigal, under guardianship, ought to be deemed of universal authority and obligation.[1] And so it ought and doubtless would be deemed, in regard to all acts done

[1] 1 Boullenois, obs. 25, p. 663, Burgundus's opinion. Indeed Burgundus seems to have been of opinion that the only judgments which ought to have any force or operation extra-territorially are those which respect the state and condition of persons. ' Sed quoniam omnis propositi nostri summa eo spectat, ut sciatur, utrum suum sentenzia egrediatur territorium, executiamus itaque naturam singularum. Nam mihi sola,' says he, ' illa sentenzia quæ de statu personæ fertur, explicare vires extra territorii limites videtur.' Burgundus, tract. 3, n. 11, 12, p. 90; 1 Boullenois, obs. 25, p. 603.

Providence *v.* Adams, 11 R. I. 190; Supples *v.* Cannon, 44 Conn. 424. The term 'incidentally' however is probably used here in the less common sense of facts on which the judgment was founded when brought into the case by way of avoidance of other facts directly alleged on the one side or on the other. Whether the judgment would be conclusive upon such facts is a disputed question. In an ably reasoned case in New Hampshire it is held (of a domestic judgment) that the decision would not control such facts. King *v.* Chase, 15 N. H. 9, followed in Vaughan *v.* Morrison, 55 N. H. 580, 589. See also Western Ins. Co. *v.* Virginia Coal Co., 14 W. Va. 250; Lentz *v.* Wallace, 17 Penn. St. 412. So in New York it is held that a foreign decree of condemnation in admiralty, though conclusive of the change of property, is only prima facie evidence of the facts on which it purports to have been founded. Ocean Ins. Co. *v.* Francis, 2 Wend. 64; s. c. 6 Cow. 404; Radcliff *v.* United Ins. Co., 9 Johns. 277; Vandenheuvel *v.* United Ins. Co., 2 Johns. Cas. 451; Smith *v.* Williams, 2 Caines Cas. 110, 118. But the better rule in the case of domestic judgments, and a fortiori in the case of foreign judgments, appears to be that the judgment is conclusive of all facts which become under the pleadings or evidence necessary to it, whether presented by direct affirmation and denial or by avoidance. See Railroad Co. *v.* Schutte, 103 U. S. 118, 143; Bissell *v.* Kellogg, 60 Barb. 617; Wood *v.* Jackson, 8 Wend. 9; Bigelow, Estoppel, 110–113, 3d ed. Indeed courts in one or two cases have gone still further, and held foreign judgments in rem conclusive of facts not necessary to the decision where it appeared nevertheless that a clear and precise issue had been joined and decided upon them. Bernardi *v.* Motteux, 2 Doug. 574; Hughes *v.* Cornelius, 2 Show. 232, note.

On the other hand, it is perfectly clear that the judgment will have no effect in regard to facts that cannot be clearly shown to have been in issue. In cases of obscurity or ambiguity there can be no estoppel. Bradstreet *v.* Neptune Ins. Co., 3 Sum. 600; Christie *v.* Secretan, 8 T. R. 192; Robinson *v.* Jones, 8 Mass. 536.

and authority exercised within the jurisdiction of the sovereign whose tribunals have pronounced the sentence. But the necessity of giving it universal effect, so as to make the guardianship operative and effectual in all other countries, in regard to the person and his property in those countries, is not so obvious. But we have already had occasion to consider this subject in another place.[1] (a)

595. *Sentences concerning Marriage and Divorce.* — As to sentences confirming marriages or granting divorces, they may well stand upon a distinct ground. If they are pronounced by competent tribunals in regard to persons within the jurisdiction, there is great reason to say that they ought to be held of universal conclusiveness, force, and effect in all other countries. Lord Hardwicke is reported to have said in a case before him, in which the validity of a marriage in France was asserted to have been established by the sentence of a court in France having the proper jurisdiction thereof: ' It is true that, if so, it is conclusive whether in a foreign court or not, from the law of nations in such cases; otherwise the rights of mankind would be very precarious.'[2]

596. *Remarks of Lord Stowell.* — On the other hand, Lord Stowell, in a case before him in which the validity of a foreign sentence of divorce was set up as a bar to proceedings in the English ecclesiastical courts between the same parties, said: ' Something has been said on the doctrine of law regarding the respect due to foreign judgments; and undoubtedly a sentence of separation in a proper court for adultery would be entitled to credit and attention in this court. But I think the

[1] Ante, s. 495-594.

[2] Roach *v.* Garvan, 1 Ves. sen. 157. See also a case in the time of Charles II., cited by Lord Hardwicke in Boucher *v.* Lawson, Cas. t. Hard. 89; and also in Kennedy *v.* Cassillis, 2 Swanst. 326, note.

(a) It is held in Louisiana that a decree rendered in that state appointing a tutor to a minor cannot be impeached in any collateral action by a debtor of the minor. Succession of Gorrisson, 15 La. An. 27. This is much like the effect of a decree appointing a particular person administrator of an estate, which binds all the world. Lawrence *v.* Englesby, 24 Vt. 42; Farrar *v.* Olmstead, Id. 123; Steen *v.* Bennett, Id. 303; Loring *v.* Steineman, 1 Met. (Mass.) 204; Connolly *v.* Connolly, 32 Gratt. (Va.) 657. A foreign decree establishing a person's pedigree may also bind all persons. Ennis *v.* Smith, 14 How. 400.

conclusion is carried too far, when it is said that a sentence of nullity of marriage is necessarily and universally binding on other countries. Adultery and its proofs are nearly the same in all countries. The validity of marriage however must depend in a great degree on the local regulations of the country where it is celebrated. A sentence of nullity of marriage therefore in the country where it was solemnized would carry with it great authority in this country. But I am not prepared to say that a judgment of a third country on the validity of a marriage not within its territories, nor had between subjects of that country, would be universally binding. For instance, the marriage alleged by the husband is a French marriage; a French judgment on that marriage would have been of considerable weight; but it does not follow that the judgment of a court at Brussels on a marriage in France would have the same authority, much less on a marriage celebrated here in England. Had there been a sentence against the wife for adultery in Brabant, it might have prevented her from proceeding with any effect against her husband here; but no such sentence anywhere appears.'[1]

597. *Validity of such Sentences.* — This subject however has already been considered at large in the preceding discussions relative to divorces. The result of the doctrine therein stated is, that the English courts seem not to be disposed to admit that any valid sentence of divorce can be pronounced in any foreign country, which shall amount to the dissolution of a marriage celebrated in England between English subjects, at least so far as such a divorce is to have any force or operation in England. At the same time it may be remarked that the doctrine, so apparently held, has undergone very elaborate discussions at a very recent period; and the grounds upon which it rests have been greatly shaken.[2] (a) But in Scotland and in America a different doctrine is maintained; and it is firmly held that a sentence of divorce pronounced between parties actually domiciled in the country, whether natives or foreigners, by a competent tribunal

---

[1] Sinclair v. Sinclair, 1 Hagg. Cons. 297. See also Scrimshire v. Scrimshire, 2 Hagg. Cons. 397, 410.

[2] Ante, s. 215, 225-228.

(a) See Dolphin v. Robins, 7 H. L. Cas. 390; Shaw v. Gould, L. R. 3 H. L. 55; Harvey v. Farnie, 8 App. Cas. 43; *ante*, note (a) to s. 229 a.

having jurisdiction over the case, is valid, and ought to be held everywhere a complete dissolution of the marriage, in whatever country it may have been originally celebrated.[1] (a) Of course we are to understand that the sentence is obtained bona fide and without fraud; for fraud in this case, as in other cases, will vitiate any judgment, however well founded in point of jurisdiction.[2]

598. *Judgments in Personam.* — In the next place as to judgments in personam. And here a distinction is commonly taken between suits brought by a party to enforce a foreign judgment, and suits brought against a party who sets up a foreign judgment in bar of the suit by way of defence. In the former case it is often urged that no sovereign is bound jure gentium to execute any foreign judgment within his dominions; and therefore if execution of it is sought in his dominions, he is at liberty to examine into the merits of the judgment, and to refuse to give effect to it, if upon such examination it should appear unjust and unfounded. He acts in executing it upon the principles of comity, and has therefore a right to prescribe the terms and limits of that comity.[3] But it is otherwise (it is said) where the defendant sets up a foreign judgment as a bar to proceedings; for if it has been pronounced by a competent tribunal and carried into effect, the losing party has no right to institute a new suit elsewhere, and thus to bring the matter again into controversy; and the other party is not to lose the protection which the foreign judgment gave him. It is then res judicata, which ought to be received as conclusive evidence of right; and the exceptio rei judicatæ under such circumstances is entitled to universal conclusiveness and respect.[4] This distinction has been very

---

[1] See Ante, s. 212, 215–230.

[2] See Stark. Ev. pt. 2, s. 77, 79, 83; Duchess of Kingston's Case, 11 State Trials, 261, 262; s. c. 20 Howell, State Trials, 355, and the opinion of the judges; p. 538, note. See also Mr. Hargrave's learned argument in this case, as to the conclusiveness of res judicata, especially in cases of jactitation of marriage and divorce, and of the effect of fraud in procuring such sentences. Harg. Law Tracts, 449, 479, 483. See also Bowles v. Orr, 1 Y. & C. 464.

[3] 2 Kent, Com. 119, 120; and the cases there cited. See also 1 Boullenois, obs. 25, p. 601; post, s. 611–618.

[4] 2 Kent, Com. 119, 120, and cases there cited.

(a) See Burlen v. Shannon, 99 Mass. 200; Kerr v. Kerr, 41 N. Y. 272.

frequently recognized as having a just foundation in international justice.[1] (a)

599. *Remarks of Lord Chief Justice Eyre.* — Lord Chief Justice Eyre has stated it with his usual force in an elaborate judgment. 'If we had the means,' said he, 'we could not examine a judgment of a court in a foreign state brought before us in this manner (that is, by the defendant as a bar). It is in one way only that the sentence or judgment of the court of a foreign state is examinable in our courts, and that is when the party who claims the benefit of it applies to our courts to enforce it. When it is thus voluntarily submitted to our jurisdiction, we treat it, not as obligatory perhaps in the country in which it was pronounced, nor as obligatory to the extent to which by our law sentences and judgments are obligatory; not as conclusive, but as matter in pais; as a consideration prima facie sufficient to raise a promise. We examine it as we do all other considerations or promises; and for that purpose we receive evidence of what the law of the foreign state is, and whether the judgment is warranted by that law. In all other cases we give entire faith and credit to the sentences of foreign courts, and consider them as conclusive upon us.'[2] The same distinction is found applied in the same manner in the jurisprudence of Scotland.[3]

599 a. *Merger by Foreign Judgment.* — The view which was thus taken by Lord Chief Justice Eyre does not appear to have been acted upon to its full extent in subsequent times. It would seem a natural result from that view, that if a suit was brought for the same cause of action in an English court, which had already been decided in favor of either party in a foreign court of competent jurisdiction, and was final and conclusive there, that judgment might be well pleaded in bar of the new suit upon the original cause of action, and would, if bona fide, be conclusive. It may be doubted however whether the same doctrine is

[1] Id.; Burrows *v.* Jemino, 2 Str. 733; cited Cas. t. Hard. 87; Boucher *v.* Lawson, Cas. t. Hard. 80; 2 Swanst. 326, note; Tarleton *v.* Tarleton, 4 M. & S. 20; Taylor *v.* Phelps, 1 Har. & G. (Md.) 492; Griswold *v.* Pitcairn, 2 Conn. 85.

[2] Phillips *v.* Hunter, 2 H. Bl. 410.

[3] Erskine, Inst. b. 4, tit. 3, s. 4.

(a) See Burnham *v.* Webster, 1 Wood. & M. 174; Rangely *v.* Webster, 11 N. H. 299.

at present entertained in England. (*a*) In a recent case the court seem to have thought that, if a plaintiff has recovered judgment in a foreign country upon any original cause of action, he may, notwithstanding, sue in England upon that original cause of action, or may sue upon the judgment there obtained at his option; because the original cause of action is not merged in

(*a*) It is well settled in England now that judgment in a foreign court in favor of the plaintiff will not be treated as a merger of the cause of action, and the plaintiff may sue thereon again in the domestic forum. Bank of Australasia *v.* Harding, 9 C. B. 661; Bank of Australasia *v.* Nias, 16 Q. B. 717. See Wilson *v.* Tunstall, 6 Tex. 221; Frazier *v.* Moore, 11 Tex. 755; Wood *v.* Gamble, 11 Cush. (Mass.) 8. But the rule concerning judgments of the American states is different under the constitution and act of congress pertaining thereto, and the doctrine of merger prevails. Bank of United States *v.* Merchants' Bank, 7 Gill, 415; McGilvray *v.* Avery, 30 Vt. 538; Green *v.* Starr, 52 Vt. 426; Hatch *v.* Spofford, 22 Conn. 485; Walsh *v.* Durkin, 12 Johns. 100. See North Bank *v.* Brown, 50 Me. 214 ; Child *v.* Eureka Powder Works, 45 N. H. 547; Baxley *v.* Linah, 16 Penn. St. 241; Cleaves *v.* Lord, 43 Me. 290; Bank of North America *v.* Wheeler, 28 Conn. 433.

In some cases it has been held that a judgment recovered in one state upon a judgment rendered in another merges the first judgment, so as to destroy all rights, such as liens on land, created by it. Gould *v.* Hayden, 63 Ind. 443, citing Purdy *v.* Doyle, 1 Paige (N. Y.) 558, 561; Denegre *v.* Haun, 13 Iowa, 240; Whiting *v.* Beebe, 7 Eng. (Ark.) 421, 549; Chitty *v.* Glenn, 3 Mon. (Ky.) 424; Frazier *v.* McQueen, 20 Ark. 68; Neale *v.* Jeter, Id. 98; Bank of U. S. *v.* Patton, 5 How. (Miss.) 200; Brown *v.* Clarke, 4 How. (U. S.) 4. But the cases cited for this proposition are cases of domestic judgments; some others may be added to the same effect.

McNutt *v.* Wilcox, 3 How. (Miss.) 419; Phillips *v.* Wills, 14 Ark. 595; Dougherty *v.* McDonald, Id. 597; Smiser *v.* Robertson, 16 Ark. 599. The contrary view has been held in Weeks *v.* Pearson, 5 N. H. 324; Mumford *v.* Stocker, 1 Cow. (N. Y.) 178; Griswold *v.* Hill, 2 Paine, 492; Andrews *v.* Smith, 9 Wend. (N. Y.) 53. And see Bank of Old Dominion *v.* Allen, 13 Rep. (Va.) 509. The first and last of these (but the point was only alluded to in the last) were cases of judgments of other states; the rest were cases of domestic judgments rendered by other courts of the state. In most of these cases it was pointed out that the rule of merger applies only in favor of a higher obligation over a lower (while here we have only obligations of the same degree); and this irrespective of the court in which the judgment was rendered. See Gould *v.* Hayden, 63 Ind. 443.

It may be inconvenient that two judgments should subsist in the same state against the same person on the same demand; but no such inconvenience can exist in the case of judgments rendered in different states, and there is no sufficient reason for the application of the purely technical doctrine of merger, subversive of substantial justice as it would be in such cases. Indeed in view of the fact that one satisfaction would satisfy both judgments, there is little to be said in favor of the doctrine of merger, reasonable as that doctrine may be in ordinary cases, by a second judgment obtained upon the first even in the same state.

such a judgment.[1] Now if the original cause of action is not merged in a case where the judgment is in favor of the plaintiff, it seems difficult to assert that it is merged by a judgment in the foreign court in favor of the defendant.[2]

600. *Distinction stated by Lord Kames.* — Lord Kames has marked out and supported another distinction, between suits sustaining and suits dismissing a claim. 'In the last place,' says he, ' come foreign decrees; which are of two kinds, one sustaining the claim, and one dismissing it. A foreign decree sustaining the claim is not one of those universal titles which ought to be made effectual everywhere. It is a title that depends on the authority of the court whence it issued, and therefore has no coercive authority extra territorium. And yet, as it would be hard to oblige the person who claims on a decree to bring a new action against his party in every country to which he may retire, therefore common utility, as well as regard to a sister court, has established a rule among all civilized nations that a foreign decree shall be put in execution, unless some good exception be opposed to it in law or in equity; which is making no wider step in favor of the decree than to presume it just till the contrary be proved. But this includes not a decree decerning for a penalty; because no court reckons itself bound to punish or to concur in punishing any delict committed extra territorium.'

601. ' A foreign decree which, by dismissing the claim, affords an exceptio rei judicatæ against it, enjoys a more extensive privilege. We not only presume it to be just, but will not admit any evidence of its being unjust. The reasons follow. A decreet-arbitral is final by mutual consent. A judgment-condemnator ought not to be final against the defendant, because he gave no consent. But a decreet-absolvitor ought to be final against the plaintiff, because the judge was chosen by himself; with respect to him, at least, it is equivalent to a decreet-arbitral. Public utility affords another argument extremely cogent. There is nothing

---

[1] Smith *v.* Nicolls, 5 Bing. N. C. 208, 221-224. There were peculiar circumstances in the case, and therefore the point was not positively decided. The same doctrine seems to have been asserted in Hall *v.* Odber, 11 East, 118; but there also it was not directly decided. But see Plummer *v.* Woodburne, 4 B. & C. 625; ante, s. 547, note; Becquet *v.* McCarthy, 2 B. & Ad. 951; ante, s. 548 a.

[2] A foreign judgment for costs may be enforced in England. Russell *v.* Smyth, 9 M. & W. 810.

more hurtful to society than that lawsuits be perpetual. In every lawsuit there ought to be a ne plus ultra; some step ought to be ultimate; and a decree dismissing a claim is in its nature ultimate. Add a consideration that regards the nature and constitution of a court of justice. A decree dismissing a claim may, it is true, be unjust, as well as a decree sustaining it. But they differ widely in one capital point; in declining to give redress against a decree dismissing a claim, the court is not guilty of authorizing injustice, even supposing the decree to be unjust; the utmost that can be said is, that the court forbears to interpose in behalf of justice. But such forbearance, instead of being faulty, is highly meritorious in every case where private justice clashes with public utility. The case is very different with respect to a decree of the other kind; for to award execution upon a foreign decree, without admitting any objection against it, would be, for aught the court can know, to support and promote injustice. A court, as well as an individual, may in certain circumstances have reason to forbear acting, or executing their office; but the doing injustice, or the supporting it, cannot be justified in any circumstances.'[1]

602. *Remarks upon this Distinction.* — It does not appear that this distinction of Lord Kames, between judgments sustaining suits and judgments dismissing them, has been recognized in the common law.[2] And there seems quite as much reason that a defendant should be protected against a new litigation, after there has been a final sentence in his favor, as there is that a plaintiff should be protected in the enjoyment of any right which is established by a sentence in his favor. The sentence for the defendant may, in its legal operation, as completely establish a right in him, or as completely establish the non-existence of any right in the plaintiff, as the contrary sentence would establish an adverse right in the plaintiff, and the non-existence of any repugnant right in the defendant.

603. *Enforcing Judgments.* — In the next place as to judgments in personam, which are sought to be enforced by a suit in a foreign tribunal. There has certainly been no inconsiderable fluctuation of opinion in the English courts upon this subject. It

[1] 2 Kames on Equity, p. 365, 3d ed. 1778.
[2] See the cases cited in Stark. Ev. pt. 2, s. 80; Hoyt v. Gelston, 13 Johns. (N. Y.) 561; 3 Wheat. 246; The Bennet, 1 Dodson, 175, 180.

is admitted on all sides, that in such cases the foreign judgments are prima facie evidence to sustain the action, and are to be deemed right until the contrary is established ;[1] (a) and of course they may be avoided if they are founded in fraud, or are pronounced by a court not having any competent jurisdiction over the cause.[2] But the question is, whether they are to be deemed conclusive ; or whether the defendant is at liberty to go at large into the original merits, to show that the judgment ought to have been different upon the merits, although obtained bona fide. If the latter course be the correct one, then a still more embarrassing consideration is, to what extent, and in what manner, the original merits can be properly inquired into.

604. *Different Opinions.* — Lord Nottingham, in a case where an attempt was made to examine a foreign sentence of divorce in Savoy, in the reign of Charles the Second, held that it was conclusive, and its merits not examinable. ' We know not,' said he, ' the laws of Savoy. So, if we did, we have no power to judge by them. And therefore it is against the law of nations not to give credit to the sentences of foreign countries till they are reversed by the law, and according to the form, of those countries wherein they were given. For what right hath one kingdom to reverse the judgment of another? And how can we refuse to let a sentence take place until it be reversed? And what confusion would follow in Christendom, if they should serve us so abroad, and give no credit to our sentences.'[3] Lord Hardwicke manifestly held the same opinion, saying, ' That where any court, foreign or domestic, that has the proper jurisdiction of the cases, makes the determination, it is conclusive to all other courts.'[4]

605. On the other hand, Lord Mansfield thought that foreign

[1] See Walker *v.* Witter, Doug. 1, and cases there cited; Arnott *v.* Redfern, 3 Bing. 353 ; Sinclair *v.* Fraser, cited Doug. 4, 5, note; Houlditch *v.* Donegall. 2 Cl. & F. 470; 8 Bligh, 301; Don *v.* Lippmann, 5 Cl. & F. 1, 19, 20; Price *v.* Dewhurst, 8 Sim. 279; Alivon *v.* Furnival, 1 C. M. & R. 277; Hall *v.* Odber, 11 East, 118; Ripple *v.* Ripple, 1 Rawle (Pa.) 386.

[2] See Bowles *v.* Orr, 1 Y. & C. 464; ante, s. 544, 545-550; Ferguson *v.* Mahon, 3 P. & D. 143; Price *v.* Dewhurst, 8 Sim. 279, 302; Don *v.* Lippmann, 5 Cl. & F. 1, 19-21; Ferguson *v.* Mahon, 11 A. & E. 179, 182.

[3] Kennedy *v.* Cassillis, 2 Swanst. note, 326, 327.

[4] Boucher *v.* Lawson, Cas. t. Hard. 89. See also Roach *v.* Garvan, 1 Ves. 157.

(a) See Monroe *v.* Douglas, 4 Sandf. Ch. (N. Y.) 126.

judgments gave a ground of action, but that they were examinable.[1] The same doctrine was held by Lord Chief Baron Eyre[2] and Mr. Justice Buller,[3] the latter relying upon a decision of the House of Lords as giving the true line of distinction between foreign and domestic judgments. In that case the House of Lords reversed a decision of the Court of Session of Scotland, in which the latter court held the plaintiff bound, in a suit upon a foreign judgment, to prove before the court the general nature and extent of the demand on which the judgment had been obtained. The reversal expressly declared that the judgment ought to be received as evidence, prima facie, of the debt; and that it lay upon the defendant to impeach the justice thereof, or to show the same to have been irregularly or wrongfully obtained.[4] But it may be remarked of this last decision, that it does not go to the extent of establishing the doctrine that the merits of the judgment ab origine are re-examinable de novo; but only that its justice may be impeached, or its irregularity or fraud shown.[5]

606. *Present English Doctrine.* — Lord Kenyon seems clearly to have been of a different opinion, and expressed serious doubts whether foreign judgments were not binding upon the parties here.[6] And Lord Ellenborough, upon an occasion in which the argument was pressed before him that a foreign judgment was re-examinable, and that the defendant might impeach the justice of it, pithily remarked that he thought he did not sit at nisi prius to try a writ of error upon the proceedings of the court abroad.[7] In a more recent case Sir L. Shadwell, the Vice-Chancellor, upon

[1] Walker v. Witter, Doug. 1, 6, note 3; Herbert v. Cook, Willes, 36, note; Hall v. Odber, 11 East, 118; Bayley v. Edwards, 3 Swanst. 703, 711, 712.

[2] Phillips v. Hunter, 2 H. Bl. 410; ante, s. 2.

[3] Galbraith v. Neville, cited Doug. 6, note 3.

[4] Sinclair v. Fraser, Doug. 4, 5, note 1.

[5] Ante, s. 544–550, 603. In Alivon v. Furnival, 1 C. M. & R. 277, it seems to have been held, although not expressly so laid down by the court, that the proceedings of foreign courts must be presumed to be consistent with the foreign law, until the contrary is distinctly shown; and that therefore the principle adopted by a foreign court in assessing damages cannot be impugned, unless contrary to natural justice, or proved not to be conformable to the foreign law. The same point was adjudged in Martin v. Nicolls, 3 Sim. 458, and Becquet v. McCarthy, 2 B. & Ad. 951; Ferguson v. Mahon, 11 A. & E. 179, 182.

[6] Galbraith v. Neville, Doug. 5, note 3. See also Guinness v. Carroll, 1 B. & Ad. 459.

[7] Tarleton v. Tarleton, 4 M. & S. 21. But see Hall v. Odber, 11 East, 118.

a full examination of the authorities, held the opinion that the true doctrine was that foreign judgments were conclusive evidence, and not re-examinable; that this was the true result of the old authorities; and therefore, in a suit brought in England to enforce a foreign judgment, he held the judgment to be conclusive.[1] The present inclination of the English courts seems to be to sustain the conclusiveness of foreign judgments;[2] although certainly there yet remains no inconsiderable diversity of opinion among the learned judges of the different tribunals.[3] (a)

607. *Objections to a Different Doctrine.* — It is indeed very difficult to perceive what could be done if a different doctrine were maintainable to the full extent of opening all the evidence and merits of the cause anew on a suit upon the foreign judgment. Some of the witnesses may be since dead; some of the vouchers may be lost or destroyed. The merits of the cause, as formerly before the court upon the whole evidence, may have been decidedly in favor of the judgment; upon a partial possession of the original evidence, they may now appear otherwise. Suppose a case purely sounding in damages, such as an action for an assault, for slander, for conversion of property, for a malicious prosecution, or for a criminal conversation; is the defendant to be at liberty to retry the whole merits, and to make out, if he can, a new case upon new evidence?[4] Or is the court to review the former decision, like a court of appeal, upon the old evidence? In a case of covenant, or of debt, or of a breach of contract, are all the circumstances to be re-examined anew? If they are, by what laws and rules of evidence and principles of justice is the

[1] Martin v. Nicolls, 3 Sim. 458.

[2] See Guinness v. Carroll, 1 B. & Ad. 459; Becquet v. McCarthy, 2 B. & Ad. 951.

[3] In Houlditch v. Donegall, 8 Bligh, 301, 337–340, Lord Brougham held a foreign judgment to be only prima facie evidence, and gave his reasons at large for that opinion. On the other hand, Sir L. Shadwell, in Martin v. Nicolls, held the contrary opinion, that it was conclusive; and also gave a very elaborate judgment on the point, in which he reviewed the principal authorities. Of course the learned judge meant to except, and did except in a later case (Price v. Dewhurst, 8 Sim. 279, 302), judgments which were produced by fraud. See also Don v. Lippmann, 5 Cl. & F. 1, 20, 21; ante, s. 545–605; Alivon v. Furnival, 1 C. M. & R. 277, 284. See also Ferguson v. Mahon, 11 A. & E. 179, 182; Henderson v. Henderson, 3 Hare, 100, 113–115.

[4] See Alivon v. Furnival, 1 C. M. & R. 277.

(a) See note to s. 608.

validity of the original judgment to be tried? Is the court to open the judgment, and to proceed ex æquo et bono? Or is it to administer strict law, and stand to the doctrines of the local administration of justice? Is it to act upon the rules of evidence acknowledged in its own jurisprudence, or upon those of the foreign jurisprudence? These and many more questions might be put to show the intrinsic difficulties of the subject. Indeed the rule that the judgment is to be prima facie evidence for the plaintiff would be a mere delusion, if the defendant might still question it by opening all or any of the original merits on his side ; for under such circumstances it would be equivalent to granting a new trial. It is easy to understand that the defendant may be at liberty to impeach the original justice of the judgment by showing that the court had no jurisdiction, or that he never had any notice of the suit;[1] or that it was procured by fraud ; or that upon its face it is founded in mistake; or that it is irregular and bad by the local law, fori rei judicatæ. To such an extent the doctrine is intelligible and practicable. Beyond this, the right to impugn the judgment is in legal effect the right to retry the merits of the original cause at large, and to put the defendant upon proving those merits.[2]

608. *American Doctrine.* — The general doctrine maintained in the American courts in relation to foreign judgments certainly is that they are prima facie evidence, but that they are impeachble.[3] (a) But how far and to what extent this doctrine is to be

[1] Ferguson v. Mahon, 11 A. & E. 179, 182.

[2] See Arnott v. Redfern, 2 C. & P. 88; 3 Bing. 353; Novelli v. Rossi, 2 B. & Ad. 757; Douglass v. Forrest, 4 Bing. 686; Obicini v. Bligh, 8 Bing. 335; Martin v. Nicolls, 3 Sim. 458; Alivon v. Furnival, 1 C. M. & R. 277. See also Stark. Ev. pt. 2, s. 67; Phillips & Amos on Evidence (8th ed.), p. 537, 538 (1838); Buttrick v. Allen, 8 Mass. 273; Huberus, tom. 2, lib. 1, tit. 3, de Conflictu, s. 6.

[3] Many of the cases are collected; 2 Kent, Com. 118, &c.; in 4 Cowen, 520, note 3; and in Mr. Metcalf's notes to his valuable edition of Starkie on Evidence, pt. 2, s. 67, 68, ed. 1830, p. 214–216. See also Bissell v. Briggs, 9 Mass. 462; Borden v. Fitch, 15 Johns. (N. Y.) 121; Green v. Sarmiento, 1 Pet. C. C. 74; Field v. Gibbs, 1 Pet. C. C. 155; Aldrich v. Kinney, 4 Conn. 380; Shumway v. Stillman, 6 Wend. (N. Y.) 447 ; Hall v. Williams, 6 Pick. (Mass.)

(a) The cases cited for this proposition are founded upon dicta of early English cases now overruled. The true view of the effect of a judgment rendered in another country by a court of competent jurisdiction is that of the recent English decisions, to wit, that they are conclusive of the merits

carried does not seem to be definitely settled. It has been declared that the jurisdiction of the court, and its power over the parties and the things in controversy, may be inquired into; and that the judgment may be impeached for fraud. (a) Beyond this no definite lines have as yet been drawn.

247; Starbuck v. Murray, 5 Wend. (N. Y.) 148; Davis v. Packard, 6 Wend. (N. Y.) 327; Buttrick v. Allen, 8 Mass. 273; Pawling v. Bird, 13 Johns. (N. Y.) 192; Hitchcock v. Aicken, 1 Caines (N. Y.) 460; Wharton's Dig. Judgment, I.; Bigelow's Dig. Judgment, H.; Johnson's Dig. Debt, H.; Coxe's Dig. Judgment; Hoxie v. Wright, 2 Vt. 263; Bellows v. Ingham, 2 Vt. 575; Barney v. Patterson, 6 Har. & J. (Md.) 182.

of the cause of action, and of all facts doubtless of which a domestic judgment would be conclusive. Godard v. Gray, L. R. 6 Q. B. 139; Bank of Australasia v. Nias, 16 Q. B. 717; Bank of Australasia v. Harding, 9 C. B. 661; De Cosse Brissac v. Rathbone, 6 H. & N. 301; Castrique v. Imrie, L. R. 4 H. L. 445; Scott v. Pilkington, 2 Best & S. 11; Vanquelin v. Bouard, 15 C. B. N.S. 341; Ricardo v. Garcias, 12 Cl. & F. 368; Doglioni v. Crispin, L. R. 1 H. L. 301. (But see Simpson v. Fogo, 1 Hem. & M. 195, of the case of a perverse disregard, by the foreign court, of the law which ought to govern. And see Liverpool Credit Co v. Hunter, L. R. 3 Ch. 479, 484.) And the cases make no distinction between judgments in rem and judgments in personam, though the former came to be treated as conclusive long before the settled rule of conclusiveness obtained in regard to judgments in personam. Bernardi v. Motteux, 2 Doug. 574; Hughes v. Cornelius, 2 Show. 232; Carth. 32; 2 Ld. Raym. 893, 935; The Helena, 4 Ch. Rob. 3. So in this country. Grant v. McLachlin, 4 Johns. (N. Y.) 34; Croudson v. Leonard, 4 Cranch, 434; Dempsey v. Ins. Co. of Penn., 1 Binn. (Penn.) 299, note; Baxter v. New England Ins. Co., 6 Mass. 277.

It cannot as yet be said on *authority* that the effect of a judgment in personam rendered in a foreign country is settled in this country; but it is apprehended that the tendency of the courts is with the later English cases above cited. The view of conclusiveness was upheld in Lazier v. Westcott, 26 N. Y. 146. Contra Rankin v. Goddard, 54 Me. 28. See also Cummings v. Banks, 2 Barb. (N. Y.) 602; Monroe v. Douglas, 4 Sandf. Ch. (N. Y.) 126; Noyes v. Butler, 6 Barb. (N. Y.) 613; Middlesex Bank v. Butman, 29 Me. 19; Taylor v. Barron, 30 N. H. 78; Burnham v. Webster, 1 Woodb. & M. 172; Benton v. Burgot, 10 Serg. & R. (Penn.) 240.

A foreign judgment for the plaintiff, as Mr. Baron Parke said in Williams v. Jones, 13 Mees. & W. 628, 633, raises a binding obligation to pay; binding because the proper authorities have fixed its effect. See Godard v. Gray, L. R. 6 Q. B. 139, 148; Schibsby v. Westenholz, Id. 155. The effect of a valid judgment, like the effect of a valid contract, should depend upon the law of the land in which it was rendered. It is true that just as a foreign contract may be impeached for want of consideration or for fraud, a judgment rendered in a foreign nation may be impeached for want of jurisdiction or for fraud; but if it be admitted that the judgment would be binding where rendered, then like a contract binding where made or performable, no question should be permitted whether a correct view was taken either of the law or of the facts on which it was founded.

(a) Wood v. Watkinson, 17 Conn.

609. *Effect of the Constitution.* — By the constitution of the United States it is declared that full faith and credit shall be given in each state to the public acts, records, and judicial proceedings of every other state. And congress, in pursuance of the power given them by the constitution in a succeeding clause, have declared that the judgments of state courts shall have the same faith and credit in other states as they have in the state where they are rendered.[1] (*a*) They are therefore put upon the same footing as domestic judgments. (*b*) But this does not prevent an inquiry into the jurisdiction of the court in which the original judgment was rendered to pronounce the judgment, nor an inquiry into the right of the state to exercise authority over the parties or the subject-matter, nor an inquiry whether the judgment is founded in and impeachable for a manifest fraud. (*c*) The constitution did not mean to confer any new power upon the states, but simply to regulate the effect of their

[1] Constitution, art. 3, s. 4; Act of Congress of 26th May, 1790, c. 11; 3 Story, Constit. c. 29, s. 1297–1307.

500; Welch *v.* Sykes, 3 Gilm. (Ill.) 197. The prevailing opinion concerning the plea of fraud to a judgment rendered in another state appears to be that it cannot be pleaded unless it could be pleaded in the sister state itself. Christmas *v.* Russell, 5 Wall. 290; Bicknell *v.* Field, 8 Paige (N. Y.) 440; Anderson *v.* Anderson, 8 Ohio, 108; McRae *v.* Mattoon, 13 Pick. (Mass.) 53; Sanford *v.* Sanford, 28 Conn. 6, 28. But see Pearce *v.* Olney, 20 Conn. 544; Engel *v.* Scheuerman, 40 Ga. 206; Rogers *v.* Gwinn, 21 Iowa, 58. And see further Luckenbach *v.* Anderson, 47 Penn. St. 123; Dobson *v.* Pearce, 12 N. Y. 156; Granger *v.* Clark, 22 Me. 130; Boston & W. R. Co. *v.* Sparhawk, 1 Allen (Mass.) 448; Atkinson *v.* Allen, 12 Vt. 624; Hammond *v.* Wilder, 25 Vt. 342; Embury *v.* Conner, 3 Comst. (N. Y.) 522.

In Ochsenbein *v.* Papelier, L. R. 8 Ch. 695, it is held that a plea of fraud in obtaining a judgment is good at law, and hence that equity will not interfere with regard to such a case.

(*a*) Phillips *v.* Godfrey, 7 Bosw. (N. Y.) 150; McFarland *v.* White, 13 La. Ann. 394; Rogers *v.* Rogers, 15 B. Mon. (Ky.) 354. This applies to judgments of the United States courts when relied upon in the state courts. Niblett *v.* Scott, 4 La. Ann. 246; Barney *v.* Patterson, 6 H. & J. 182.

(*b*) Without this act the judgments of each state would be regarded as foreign judgments in the courts of every other state. Dorsey *v.* Maury, 10 Smedes & M. (Miss.) 298; Seevers *v.* Clement, 28 Md. 426; Buckner *v.* Finley, 2 Pet. 586; Smith *v.* Lathrop, 44 Penn. St. 326.

(*c*) Taylor *v.* Bryden, 8 Johns. (N. Y.) 173. See Cummings *v.* Banks, 2 Barb. (N. Y.) 602; Davis *v.* Smith, 5 Ga. 274; Gleason *v.* Dodd, 4 Met. (Mass.) 333; Ewer *v.* Coffin, 1 Cush. (Mass.) 23; D'Arcy *v.* Ketchum, 11 How. 165; Carleton *v.* Bickford, 13 Gray (Mass.) 591; Folger *v.* Columbian Ins. Co., 99 Mass. 273.

acknowledged jurisdiction over persons and things within their territory.[1] It did not make the judgments of other states domestic judgments to all intents and purposes, (a) but only gave a general validity, faith, and credit to them as evidence. No execution can issue upon such judgments without a new suit in the tribunals of other states. (b) And they enjoy not the right of priority, or privilege, or lien which they have in the state where they are pronounced, but that only which the lex fori gives to them by its own laws in their character of foreign judgments.[2] (c)

[1] See Story, Constit. c. 29, s. 1297–1307, and cases there cited; Hall v. Williams, 6 Pick. (Mass.) 237; Bissell v. Briggs, 9 Mass. 462; Shumway v. Stillman, 6 Wend. (N. Y.) 447; Evans v. Tatem, 9 Serg. & R. (Pa.) 260; Benton v. Burgot, 10 Serg. & R. (Pa.) 240; Harrod v. Barretto, 1 Hall (N. Y.) 155; 2 Hall, 302; Wilson v. Niles, 2 Hall (N. Y.) 358; Hoxie v. Wright, 2 Vt. 263; Bellows v. Ingham, 2 Vt. 575; Aldrich v. Kinney, 4 Conn. 380.

[2] McElmoyle v. Cohen, 13 Pet. 312, 328, 329; ante, s. 582 a, note.

(a) See D'Arcy v. Ketchum, 11 How. 165.

(b) Ante, note to s. 586.

(c) See Wood v. Watkinson, 17 Conn. 500. So if, by the laws and practice of one state, a discharge in bankruptcy is a good defence there to a judgment recovered after such discharge was obtained, but founded on a claim existing prior to the commencement of the bankruptcy proceedings, such discharge is a good defence to an action on such judgment in another state, although the rule in the latter state upon judgments recovered in that state might be different. Haggerty v. Amory, 7 Allen (Mass.) 458. On the other hand, such discharge would not be a defence, if the rule is the same in the state where the judgment was recovered as it is in the state where it is sought to be enforced; viz., that such a discharge is no bar. Bradford v. Rice, 102 Mass. 472.

The clause in the constitution before cited is held to prohibit a state from passing a law that an action shall not be maintained on a judgment recovered in another state, where the original cause of action was then barred by the statute of limitations of the state in which the judgment was sought to be enforced. Such an act would be unconstitutional and void. Christmas v. Russell, 5 Wall. 290. (For an analogous reason the judgment of one state in favor of a defendant, though rendered upon a plea of the statute of limitations, is conclusive in another. Sweet v. Brackley, 53 Me. 346.) It also prevents a defendant from showing that the judgment was founded in a mistake either of law or fact. Rocco v. Hackett, 2 Bosw. (N. Y.) 579; Hassell v. Hamilton, 33 Ala. 280; Milne v. Van Buskirk, 9 Iowa, 558. (And this is now the English rule as to judgments strictly foreign. A mistake of the law of its own country is no ground for impeaching a foreign judgment. Scott v. Pilkington, 2 B. & S. 11; Godard v. Gray, Law Rep. 6 Q. B. 139; Castrique v. Imrie, Law Rep. 4 H. L. 445.) So, too, such judgments are binding, although proceedings are pending in the state where they were rendered to annul or set aside the same. See Indiana v. Helmer, 21 Iowa, 370; Grover v. Grover, 30 Mo. 400; Gunn v. Howell, 35 Ala. 144; Barringer v. Boyd, 27 Miss. 473;

610. *Citizenship of Parties to Foreign Judgments.* — In the next place as to judgments in personam in suits between citizens, in suits between foreigners, and in suits between citizens and foreigners. The common law recognizes no distinction whatever as to the effect of foreign judgments, whether they are between citizens, or between foreigners, or between citizens and foreigners. In all cases they are deemed of equal obligation, whoever are the parties. The cases which have been already cited refer to no such distinction; but the same rules are indiscriminately applied to all persons.

Merchants' Ins. Co. v. De Wolf, 33 Penn. St. 45. And the like rule prevails in England as to suits on foreign judgments. Scott v. Pilkington, 2 B. & S. 11.

It is proper here to notice the effect of the pendency of another suit in a foreign tribunal, upon the same cause of action, and between the same parties. The weight of authority is in favor of the doctrine that the pendency of such suit in a tribunal strictly foreign is clearly no cause of abatement to a subsequent suit. Russell v. Field, Stuart's Canada, 558; Maule v. Murray, 7 T. R. 470; Bayley v. Edwards, 3 Swanst. 703; Ostell v. Lepage, 10 Eng. Law. & Eq. 255; 5 De Gex & Smale, 95; Cox v. Mitchell, 7 C. B. N.S. 55; Scott v. Seymour, 1 H. & C. 219. So, too, many cases hold that, in this respect, the different American states are so far foreign to each other that the pendency of a prior suit for the same cause in one state is no cause of abatement of a second suit in another. Bowne v. Joy, 9 Johns. (N. Y.) 221; Salmon v. Wootton, 9 Dana (Ky.) 423; McJilton v. Love, 13 Ill. 486; Drake v. Brander, 8 Texas, 352. And the Supreme Court of the United States have decided that the separate states are foreign to each other, except so far as united for national purposes under the constitution. Buckner v. Van Lear, 2 Pet. 586. This, also, may be considered the settled law on the subject. See Seevers v. Clement, 28 Md. 434; Smith v. Lathrop, 44 Penn. St. 326; Hatch v. Spofford, 22 Conn. 485; Goodall v. Marshall, 11 N. H. 99; Cook v. Litchfield, 5 Sandf. (N. Y.) 330. The same has also been held where the prior suit was pending in a court of the United States for a *different* district than one of the state where the second cause is instituted (Walsh v. Durkin, 12 Johns. (N. Y.) 99; Cook v. Litchfield, 5 Sandf. (N. Y.) 330), and vice versa. White v. Whitman, 1 Curtis, C. C. 494; Lyman v. Brown, 2 Id. 559. On the other hand, if the prior suit is pending in a circuit court for a district situated in the state where the second action is instituted, and that court has jurisdiction of the cause, this has been thought good cause of abatement of the second suit. Smith v. Atlantic Mut. Fire Ins. Co., 2 Foster (N. H.) 21. But whatever may be the rule where both actions are actions at law, it is uniformly agreed that if one is at law and the other in equity, neither is cause of abatement to the other. Colt v. Partridge, 7 Met. (Mass.) 570; Hatch v. Spofford, 22 Conn. 485. And so if the parties are reversed, although both actions are at law. Wadleigh v. Veazie, 3 Sumner, 165. In like manner a proceeding in one tribunal in personam, in which property is attached as collateral security to satisfy the judgment, is no bar to a subsequent proceeding in rem against the same

611. *Foreign Jurists.* — We have hitherto been principally considering the doctrines of the common law. But it cannot be affirmed that the same doctrines are generally maintained either by foreign courts or by foreign jurists. Many foreign jurists contend for the doctrine of Vattel, that the judgments of a foreign competent tribunal are to be held of equal validity in every other country.[1] Thus Huberus lays down the rule: 'Cuncta negotia et acta, tam in judicio quam extra judicium, sive mortis causa, sive inter vivos, secundum jus certi loci rite celebrata, valent, etiam ubi diversa juris observatio viget, ac ubi sic inita, quemadmodum facta sunt, non valerunt.'[2] And again : 'Simi-

[1] Henry on Foreign Law, 75, 76.
[2] Huberus, tom. 2, lib. 1, tit. 3, de Conflict. Leg. s. 3.

property in a foreign tribunal for the same cause of action. Harmer *v.* Bell, 7 Moore, P. C. 268; and see Certain Logs of Mahogany, 2 Sumner, 589. See however Taylor *v.* The Royal Saxon, 1 Wall. jun. 311. The courts also hold that a suit pending in one state by A. against B. is a bar to a suit in another state by a creditor of A. against B., in which B. is summoned as his trustee; so far, at least, that B. will not be charged as A.'s trustee, if he is liable on a prior suit pending against him by A. in another state. See American Bank *v.* Rollins, 99 Mass. 313. For a payment on such a trustee process would be no bar to the prior suit in another state. Whipple *v.* Robbins, 97 Mass. 107. See Merrill *v.* New England Ins. Co., 103 Mass. 249. But where a state court and the United States court both have jurisdiction in rem, the right to maintain the jurisdiction attaches to that tribunal which first exercises it, and takes possession of the thing. The Robert Fulton, 1 Paine, C. C. 621.

For a like reason if an officer of the United States court has attached personal property on mesne process issuing from a United States court having jurisdiction of the parties and the subject-matter, no officer of a state court can retake the property, on a replevin suit issuing from a state court on behalf of the rightful owner of such property. Freeman *v.* Howe, 24 How. 450, reversing the same case in 14 Gray, 566. For in America the state and national courts being independent of each other, neither can impede or arrest any action the other may take, within the limits of its jurisdiction, for the satisfaction of its judgments and decrees. Where either is in possession of the res sought to be · reached, the process of the other must pause until that possession is terminated. Amy *v.* The Supervisors, 11 Wall. 136; and see Riggs *v.* Johnson County, 6 Wall. 166. Further as to the relation of state and federal courts within the same state, see Pennoyer *v.* Neff, 95 U. S. 714.

Of course a domestic receiver will take choses in action in preference to a plaintiff under a foreign garnishment made after the receiver's appointment, the property being in the state of the receiver. Osgood *v.* Maguire, 61 N. Y. 524. But if the garnishment was before the receiver's appointment, the case would perhaps in some jurisdictions be different. Baltimore R. Co. *v.* May, 25 Ohio St. 347. See ante, s. 400, and note.

lem usum habet hæc observatio in rebus judicatis. Sententia in aliquo loco pronunciata, vel delicti venia, ab eo, qui jurisdictionem illam habet, data ubique habet effectum; nec fas est alterius reipublicæ magistratibus, reum alibi absolutum veniave donatum, licet absque justa causa persequi, aut iterum permittere recusandum, etc. Idem obtinet in sententiis rerum civilium.'[1] The same doctrine seems equally well founded in the expressive language of the Roman law. 'Res judicata pro veritate accipitur.'[2]

612. D'Argentré holds the like opinion. 'Nam de omni personali negotio, judicis ejus cognitionem esse, cui persona subsit, sic, ut quocunque persona abeat, id jus sit, quod ille statuerit.'[3] Gaill asserts that any other rule would involve absurdity. 'Absurdum enim fore, si post sententiam definitivam alia esset ferenda sententia, et processum in infinitum extrahi litemque ex lite oriri debere.'[4] John Voet maintains a similar opinion in all suits except those respecting immovables. 'Licet autem regulariter judex requisitus non cognoscat de justitia sententiæ per alterum judicem latæ, nec eam ad examen penitius revocet; sed pro justitia ejus ex æquitate præsumat; tamen, si animadvertat, eam directo contra sui territorii statuta latam esse circa res immobiles in suo territorio sitas, eandem non exsequetur.'[5]

613. There are however other foreign jurists who maintain a very different opinion.[6] We have already had occasion to take notice of the doctrines of Boullenois upon the right of jurisdiction,[7] and he applies them in an especial manner to the authority of foreign judgments. In regard to judgments in rem, or partly in rem and partly in personam, he deems the jurisdiction to belong exclusively to the tribunals of the place rei sitæ, and consequently that the judgment rendered there ought to

[1] Id. s. 6.   [2] Dig. 1, 5, 25.

[3] D'Argentr. Com. ad Leg. Briton. art. 218; gloss. 6, n. 47, p 665, ed. 1640; Henry on Foreign Law, p. 74; 1 Boullenois, obs. 25, p. 605.

[4] Henry on Foreign Law, p. 74, 75; Gaill, Pract. Obs. lib. 1, obs. 113, n. 11, p. 201; 1 Boullenois, obs. 25, p. 605, 606. There is an error in the reference of Boullenois to Gaill. It should be to obs. 113 instead of 123.

[5] J. Voet, ad Pand. 2, 42, 1, n. 41, p. 788.

[6] See 1 Boullenois, obs. 25, p. 601–650; 3 Burge, Col. & For. Law, pt. 2, c. 24, p. 1050–1060, 1062–1076.

[7] Ante, s. 552.

be of universal obligation.[1] But in regard to judgments in personal actions he makes the following distinctions. If the foreign judgment is in a suit between natives of the same country in which it is pronounced, and it is rendered by a competent tribunal, in such a case it ought to be executed in every other country without any new inquiry into the merits.[2] The reason assigned is, that the judgment has emanated from a lawful authority, and has been rendered between persons who are subject to that authority; and consequently the judgment ought not to be submitted to examination or discussion in any other tribunal, which for such purposes must be wholly incompetent. If the foreign judgment is rendered in a suit between mere strangers, who are foreigners found within the territorial authority of the court rendering it, and the jurisdiction is rightfully exercised over the parties, in such a case the judgment is equally conclusive, and not examinable by any other tribunal.[3] But he thinks that the jurisdiction cannot be rightfully exercised, merely because the foreigners are there, unless they are domiciled and have made themselves subject to the laws, or have made some contract there, or some contract to be executed there, which is the subject-matter of the suit.[4] Lastly, if the judgment is rendered in a suit between a native of the country where the judgment is pronounced and a foreigner, in such a case, if the foreigner be the plaintiff, then the judgment ought to be conclusive and not examinable, whether the foreigner has been successful or unsuccessful in his claim; for in such a case the suit is brought before the proper forum, according to the maxim, *actor sequitur forum rei*, and then standum est in judicio; and the execution of the judgment ought to be everywhere held perfect and entire without any new examination.[5] But if the foreigner be the defendant, and he has not entered into any contract in the place where the suit is brought, or into any contract which is to be performed there, and which is the subject-matter of the suit, in such a case the judgment is not conclusive against the defendant.[6]

614. Boullenois concludes his remarks upon this subject in the

[1] 1 Boullenois, obs. 25, p. 618–624, 635, 636.
[2] Id. p. 603, 605.   [3] 1 Boullenois, obs. 25, p. 607, 609.
[4] Id. p. 606–610.   [5] Id. p. 609.
[6] Id. p. 610, 617.

following manner: 'When then some of our authors say that foreign judgments are not to be executed in France, and that it is necessary to commence a new action, that is true without any exception in all matters touching the realty. It is also true in personal matters when the defendant is a Frenchman who has not contracted in the foreign country, nor promised to pay there, nor submitted himself voluntarily to the foreign jurisdiction; for in such a case a new action should be brought, saving the right to demand a provisional execution of the foreign judgment. But in the other cases above mentioned the judgment ought to be executed without a new action.'[1]

615. *Ancient French Law.* — There was in France an ancient ordinance, in 1629, one article of which expressly declared that judgments rendered in foreign countries, for any cause whatever, should not be executed within the realm, and that subjects against whom they were rendered might contest their rights anew throughout France.[2]

616. Emerigon says that judgments rendered in foreign countries against Frenchmen are not of the slightest weight in France, and that the causes must be there litigated anew. In support of this statement he quotes the remark of D'Aguesseau, that it is an inviolable maxim that a Frenchman can never be transferred to a foreign court. 'C'est une maxime inviolable, qu'un Français ne peut jamais être traduit devant un juge étranger.'[3] Immediately afterwards Emerigon adds that it is the same as to foreign judgments rendered in favor of a foreigner against a foreigner domiciled in France. He then proceeds to remark that it is only in suits between foreigners not domiciled in France that a foreign judgment will be executed in France. The rule equally applies, whether the Frenchman be plaintiff or be defendant in the cause. But, on the other hand, a Frenchman may sustain a suit in the French courts against a foreigner, and the judgment rendered by such foreigner may be executed against his property in France. Emerigon however admits that the rule is not exempt from doubt,

---

[1] Id. p. 646. Toullier has commented upon and denied the distinctions of Boullenois, as not being well founded in French jurisprudence. 10 Toullier, Droit Civ. Franç. c. 6, s. 3, p. 83.

[2] 1 Boullenois, obs. 25, p. 646; 2 Kent, Com. 121, 122, note. See 10 Toullier, Droit Civ. Franç. in c. 6, s. 3, n. 82, 83.

[3] D'Aguesseau, Œuvres, tom. 5, p. 87, 4to ed.

and has been much controverted; for the maxim, *actor sequitur forum rei*, belongs to the law of nations.[1] Vattel affirms the same maxim in explicit. terms.[2]

617. *Modern French Law.* — The doctrine thus promulgated by Emerigon has continued down to a very recent period.[3] But by the present Code of France the Ordinance of 1629 seems to be abolished, and foreign judgments are now deemed capable of execution in that country.[4] But the merits of the judgment are examinable; and no distinction seems to be made whether the judgment is in a suit between foreigners, or between Frenchmen, or between a foreigner and a Frenchman; or whether it is in favor of one party or of the other; or whether it is rendered upon default or upon confession, or upon a full trial and contestation of the merits.[5] Toullier considers it as now the established jurisprudence of France, that no foreign judgment can be rendered executory in France, but upon a full cognizance of the cause before the French tribunals, in which all the original grounds of the action are to be debated and considered anew.[6] And he adds that the same principle is applied to cases where foreign judgments are set up by the defendant by way of bar to a new action. The judgments are equally re-examinable upon the merits.[7]

618. *Rule in other Foreign Countries.* — It is difficult to ascertain what the prevailing rule is in regard to foreign judgments in some of the other nations of continental Europe; whether they are deemed conclusive evidence, or only prima facie evidence. Holland seems at all times, upon the general principle of reci-

---

[1] Emerigon, Traité des Ass. tom. 1, c. 4, s. 8, n. 2, p. 122, 123; 2 Kent, Com. 121, 122, note. The same doctrine is explicitly avowed to be the law of France in many other authorities. See Henry on Foreign Law, Appx. 209.

[2] Vattel, b. 2, c. 8, s. 103.

[3] Merlin, Répertoire, Jugement, s. 6; Id. Étranger, s. 2–5; Merlin, Questions de Droit, Jugement, s. 14; 2 Kent, Com. 121, 122, note; 10 Toullier, Droit Civ. Franç. c. 6, s. 3, p. 76, 81, 82, 86.

[4] Code de Procédure Civile, art. 546; Code Civil, art. 2123, 2128; 10 Toullier, Droit Civ. Franç. c. 6, s. 3, n. 76–78, 84–86.

[5] 10 Toullier, Droit Civ. Franç. c. 6, s. 3, n. 76–78, 80, 81, 84–86; Pardessus, Droit Com. tom. 5, art. 1488; 3 Burge, Col. & For. Law, pt. 2, c. 24, p. 1048, 1049.

[6] Id. n. 85, 86; 2 Kent, Com. 121, 122, note; Pardessus, Droit Com. tom. 5, art. 1488.

[7] 10 Toullier, Droit Civ. Franç. c. 6, s. 8, n. 76–86; Merlin, Répertoire, Jugement, s. 6; Merlin, Questions de Droit, Jugement, s. 14; Pardessus, Droit Com. tom. 5, art. 1488; 2 Kent, Com. 118–121.

procity, to have given great weight to foreign judgments, and in many cases, if not in all cases, to have given to them a weight equal to that given to domestic judgments, wherever the like rule of reciprocity with regard to Dutch judgments has been adopted by the foreign country whose judgment is brought under review. This is certainly a very reasonable rule, and may perhaps hereafter work itself firmly into the structure of international jurisprudence.[1]

[1] Henry on Foreign Law, c. 10, s. 2, p. 75, 76; Id. Appx. p. 209–214.

CHAPTER XVI.

PENAL LAWS AND OFFENCES.

619. *General Remarks.* — We are next led to the consideration of the operation of foreign laws in regard to penalties and offences. And this will not require any expanded examination, as the topics are few, and the doctrines maintained by foreign jurists, and by tribunals acting under the common law, involve no intricate inquiries into the peculiar jurisprudence of different nations.

620. *Locality of Crimes.* — The common law considers crimes as altogether local, and cognizable and punishable exclusively in the country where they are committed.[1] No other nation therefore has any right to punish them, or is under any obligation to take notice of or to enforce any judgment rendered in such cases by the tribunals having authority to hold jurisdiction within the territory where they are committed.[2] Hence it is that a criminal sentence of attainder in the courts of one sovereign, although it there creates a personal disability to sue, does not carry the same disability with the person into other countries. Foreign jurists indeed maintain on this particular point a different opinion, holding that the state or condition of a person in the place of his domicil accompanies him everywhere.[3] Lord Lough-

---

[1] 'Crimes,' said Lord Chief Justice de Grey, in Rafael *v.* Verelst, 2 W. Bl. 1058, 'are in their nature local, and the jurisdiction of crimes is local.'

[2] Rutherf. Inst. b. 2, c. 9, s. 12; Martens, Law of Nations, b. 3, c. 3, s. 22-25; Merlin, Répertoire, Souveraineté, s. 5, n. 5, 6, p. 379-382; Commonwealth *v.* Green, 17 Mass. 515, 545-548.

[3] Ante, s. 91, 92; 1 Hertii Opera, de Collis. Leg. s. 4, n. 8, p. 124, ed. 1737; Id. p. 175, ed. 1716; 1 Boullenois, obs. 4, p. 64, 65. Boullenois states this doctrine in strong terms. 'A l'égard des statuts qui prononcent une morte civile pour crimes, ou une note d'infamie, l'état de ces misérables se porte partout, indépendamment de tout domicile; et cela par un concert et un concours général des nations, ces sortes de peines étant une tache, une plaie incurable, dont le condamné est affligé, et qui l'accompagne en tous lieux. C'est ce que dit D'Argentré.' 1 Boullenois, obs. 4, p. 64, 65.

borough, in declaring the opinion of the court on one occasion, said: 'Penal laws of foreign countries are strictly local, and affect nothing more than they can reach, and can be seized by virtue of their authority. A fugitive, who passes hither, comes with all his transitory rights. He may recover money held for his use, and stock, obligations, and the like; and cannot be affected in this country by proceedings against him in that which he has left, beyond the limits of which such proceedings do not extend.'[1] Mr. Justice Buller in the same case, on a writ of error, said: ' It is a general principle that the penal laws of one country cannot be taken notice of in another.'[2] The same doctrine was affirmed by Lord Ellenborough in a subsequent case.[3] And it has been recently promulgated by Lord Brougham in very clear and authoritative terms. 'The lex loci,' says he, 'must needs govern all criminal jurisdiction, from the nature of the thing and the purpose of the jurisdiction.'[4]

621. *Judicial Opinions.* — The same doctrine has been frequently recognized in America. On one occasion, where the subject underwent a good deal of discussion, Mr. Chief Justice Marshall, in delivering the opinion of the Supreme Court, said: 'The courts of no country execute the penal laws of another.'[5] On another occasion, in New York, Mr. Chief Justice Spencer said: ' We are required to give effect to a law (of Connecticut) which inflicts a penalty for acquiring a right to a chose in action. The defendant cannot take advantage of, nor expect the court to enforce, the criminal laws of another state. The penal acts of one state can have no operation in another state. They are strictly local, and affect nothing more than they can reach.'[6] (a)

---

[1] Folliott v. Ogden, 1 H. Bl. 135.
[2] Ogden v. Folliott, 3 T. R. 733, 734.   [3] Wolff v. Oxholm, 6 M. & S. 99.
[4] Warrender v. Warrender, 9 Bligh, 119, 120.
[5] The Antelope, 10 Wheat. 66, 123.
[6] Scoville v. Canfield, 14 Johns. (N. Y.) 338, 340. See also State v. Knight, Taylor (N. C.) 65.

(a) See Western Transp. Co. v. Kilderhouse, 87 N. Y. 430; Lemmon v. People, 20 N. Y. 562; Henry v. Sargeant, 13 N. H. 321. But this doctrine is not to be carried too far. Courts will not enforce penalties imposed by foreign laws, but an illegal act done in a foreign jurisdiction in the execution of a penal statute may be redressed elsewhere. A citizen of New Hampshire brought an action of trespass in that state against a citizen of Vermont to recover damages for assessing an illegal tax upon the plain-

criminal is arrested in another country, he is to be punished according to the law of his domicil, or according to the law of the place where the offence was committed.[1] If any nation should suffer its own courts to entertain jurisdiction of offences committed by foreigners in foreign countries, the rule of Bartolus would seem to furnish the true answer. 'Delicta puniuntur juxta mores loci commissi delicti, et non loci, ubi de crimine cognoscitur.'[2] (a)

[1] See 1 Hertii Opera, de Collis. Leg. s. 4, n. 19-21, p. 131, 132, ed. 1737; Id. p. 185-188, ed. 1716; P. Voet, de Stat. s. 11, c. 1, s. 1, 4, 5, p. 291-297, ed. 1715; Id. p. 335-360, ed. 1661.

[2] Henry on Foreign Law, p. 47. I quote the passage as I find it in Henry. Upon examining Bartolus in the place apparently intended to be cited by Mr. Henry (Bartolus, Com. ad Cod. 1, 1, 1, n. 20, 21; Id. n. 44; Id. n. 47, tom. 7, p. 4, ed. 1602), I have not been able to find any such language used by Bartolus. Martens deems it clear that a sovereign in whose dominions a criminal has sought refuge may, if he chooses, punish him for the offence, though committed in a foreign country; though he admits that the more common usage in modern times is to remand the criminal to the country where the crime was committed. Martens, Law of Nations, b. 3, c. 3, s. 22, 23. See also Vattel. b. 2, c. 2, s. 76; Grotius, de Jure Belli et Pac. b. 2, c. 21, s. 2-5; Burlemaqui, pt. 4, c. 3, s. 24-26. See Lord Brougham's opinion in Warrender v. Warrender, 9 Bligh, 118-120.

(a) It is well settled that common-law torts, and probably statutory torts not in derogation of any settled rule of the common law, may be redressed as well in the courts of other states as in those of the state in which the wrong was committed. Le Forest v. Tolman, 117 Mass. 109; Needham v. Grand Trunk Ry. Co., 38 Vt. 294; Stout v. Wood, 1 Blackf. (Ind.) 71; General Steam Nav. Co. v. Guillou, 11 Mees. & W. 877; Phillips v. Eyre, L. R. 4 Q. B. 225, 239; L. R. 6 Q. B. 1. See Pittsburgh Ry. Co. v. Lewis, 33 Ohio St. 196; Selma R. Co. v. Lacey, 49 Ga. 106; The Halley, L. R. 2 P. C. 193 (reversing L. R. 2 Adm. 3).

Recent decisions, proceeding upon a supposed distinction between statutory rights in derogation of the common law and general common-law rights, have refused to go further and to recognize rights growing out of foreign statutory law where that is inconsistent with the unwritten law. Richardson v. New York Cent. R. Co., 98 Mass. 85; Buckles v. Ellers, 72 Ind. 221; Anderson v. Milwaukee Ry. Co., 37 Wis. 321; Bettys v. Milwaukee Ry. Co., Id. 323 (a case of penalty); Woodard v. Michigan Southern R. Co., 10 Ohio St. 121; McCarthy v. Chicago R. Co., 18 Kans. 46; Pickering v. Fisk, 6 Vt. 102; Probate Court v. Hibbard, 44 Vt. 597. And see The Halley, L. R. 2 P. C. 193. Three of these cases, Richardson v. New York Cent. R. Co., Woodard v. Michigan Southern R. Co., and McCarthy v. Chicago R. Co., might have been decided on the ground that the suit had been instituted by the wrong party. The suits were brought for the death of the plaintiff's intestate, and the plaintiff was administrator under the law of the forum alone. It would seem doubtful in principle if any administrator not qualified under the law of the state in which the wrong was committed could sue. But this technical objection has not been allowed to prevail in other cases. Leonard *v.* Columbia Nav. Co., 84 N. Y. 48; Dennick *v.* Central R. Co., 103 U. S. 11. The Vermont cases cited were actions upon official bonds, which it was held would not be enforced out of the state in which they were executed.

The distinction between statutory and common-law rights above alluded to (see particularly Richardson *v.* New York Cent. R. Co., referring to language of Mr. Justice Denio in Whitford *v.* Panama R. Co., 23 N. Y. 465) has little to commend it, and the Supreme Court of the United States in Dennick *v.* Central R. Co., supra, disregarded and exploded it. In the absence of some plainly prohibitory law the case can hardly be rested upon the ground that the existence of such rights is so opposed to the policy or law of a state that it ought to be repudiated. The New York courts, after much discussion of the subject, have lately fallen in with the better view, so far at least as to permit an action based upon the foreign law (for death caused by negligence in another state) where the foreign statute is like the domestic. Leonard *v.* Columbia Nav. Co., 84 N. Y. 48. See also McDonald *v.* Mallory, 77 N. Y. 546. The Vermont courts also give redress. Needham *v.* Grand Trunk R. Co., 38 Vt. 294. See also Boyd *v.* Clark, 13 Rep. 40.

The true doctrine, as declared by the Supreme Court of the United States, proceeds upon the broad ground of the right of action given by the law of the foreign state; whether the domestic law provides for redress in like cases should in principle be immaterial, so long as the right is a reasonable one and not opposed to the interests of the state.

How immaterial is the existence of a law of the forum like that of the foreign state is seen in the rule everywhere laid down in this country, that the plaintiff's case must stand, if at all, upon the existence of the supposed foreign law. The mere fact that a statute exists in the state of the forum which would entitle him to redress if the offence had been committed there, will not justify an action. Le Forest *v.* Tolman, 117 Mass. 109; Crowley *v.* Panama R. Co., 80 Barb. 99; Beach *v.* Bay State Co., Id. 433; Whitford *v.* Panama R. Co., 3 Bosw. 67; 23 N.Y. 465; Needham *v.* Grand Trunk Ry.Co., 38 Vt. 294 ; Carpenter *v.* Grand Trunk Ry. Co., 72 Me. 388. See Hall *v.* De Cuir, 95 U. S. 485. But see Scott *v.* Seymour, 1 Hurl. & C. 219, infra.

In Le Forest *v.* Tolman, supra, this doctrine was applied to the case of one suing in Massachusetts for an injury received in New Hampshire by the bite of a dog owned and kept by the defendant in Massachusetts. It was held, in accordance with the common-law rule, that, in the absence of evidence that the dog was kept scienter of a disposition to bite people, the plaintiff could not recover; Popplewell *v.* Pierce, 10 Cush. (Mass.) 509, and Pressey *v.* Wirth, 8 Allen (Mass.) 191, being cited as common-law authority. The court declined to apply a domestic statute providing that the owner or keeper of a dog should forfeit to any one injured by it double the amount of the damage sustained.

In Hahnemannian Ins. Co. *v.* Beebe, 48 Ill. 87, it was left a question whether a foreign corporation could sue in the domestic courts for libel.

If the foreign law has for its object the imposition of punishment, then only the courts of the injured sovereignty should inflict the punishment. Bettys *v.* Milwaukee Ry. Co., 37 Wis. 323; First National Bank *v.* Price, 33 Md. 487. And see The Halley, L. R.

whether a nation is bound to surrender up fugitives from justice who escape into its territories and seek there an asylum from punishment. The practice has, beyond question, prevailed as a matter of comity, and sometimes of treaty, between some neighboring states, and sometimes also between distant states having much intercourse with each other.[1] Paul Voet remarks that under the Roman Empire this right of having a criminal remitted for trial to the proper forum criminis was unquestionable. It resulted from the very nature of the universal dominion of the Roman laws. 'Jure tamen civili notandum, remissionibus locum fuisse de necessitate, ut reus ad locum, ubi deliquit, sic petente judice, fuerit mittendus, quod omnes judices uni subessent imperatori. Et omnes provinciæ Romanæ unitæ essent accessorie, non principaliter.'[2] But he remarks that, according to the customs of almost all Christendom, except Saxony, the remitter of criminals, except in cases of humanity, is not admitted; and, when done, it is to be upon letters rogatory, so that there may be no prejudice to the local jurisdiction. 'Moribus nihilominus (non tamen Saxonicis) totius fere Christianismi, nisi ex humanitate, non sunt admissæ remissiones. Quo casu, remittenti magistratui cavendum per litteras reversoriales, ne actus jurisdictioni remittentis ullum pariat præjudicium. Id quod etiam in nostris Provinciis Unitis est receptum.'[3] And he adds, 'neque enim Provinciæ Fœderatæ uni supremo parent;'[4] a remark strictly applicable to the Ameri-

[1] See Vattel, b. 2, c. 6, s. 76.
[2] P. Voet, de Stat. s. 11, c. 1, n. 6, p. 297, ed. 1715; Id. p. 358, ed. 1661.
[3] Ibid.
[4] Ibid. See also Matthæi Com. de Criminibus, Dig. 48, 14, 1, s. 3.

2 P. C. 193, where it was held that liability imposed by foreign law upon the owners of a vessel for misconduct of a pilot they were compelled to employ would not be enforced in England. 'The English court,' said Selwyn, L.J., in this case, 'admits the proof of the foreign law as part of the circumstances attending the execution of the contract, or as one of the facts upon which the existence of the tort or the right to damages may depend, and it then applies and enforces its own law so far as it is applicable to the case thus established.' But an English court will not give a remedy in damages 'in respect of an act which according to its own principles imposes no liability on the person from whom the damages are claimed.' See Phillips v. Eyre, L. R. 6 Q. B. 1, 28, 29.

On the other hand, it has been intimated that if an action would lie by the English law for a particular wrong, the English courts will give redress for it, though it was committed in a country by the laws of which no redress would be granted, supposing the parties were both British sub-

can states. It is manifest that he treats it purely as a matter of comity, and not of national duty.

627. It has however been treated by other distinguished jurists as a strict right, and as constituting a part of the law and usage of nations, that offenders charged with a high crime, who have fled from the country in which the crime has been committed, should be delivered up and sent back for trial by the sovereign of the country where they are found. Vattel manifestly contemplates the subject in this latter view, contending that it is the duty of the government where the criminal is, to deliver him up, or to punish him; and if it refuses so to do, then it becomes responsible as in some measure an accomplice in the crime.[1] This opinion is also maintained with great vigor by Grotius, by Heineccius, by Burlemaqui, and by Rutherforth.[2] There is no inconsiderable weight of common-law authority on the same side; and Mr. Chancellor Kent has adopted the doctrine in a case which called directly for its decision.[3]

628. On the other hand, Puffendorf explicitly denies it as a matter of right.[4] Martens is manifestly of the same opinion, contending that, with respect to crimes committed out of his territo-

[1] Vattel, b. 2, c. 6, s. 76.

[2] Grotius de Jure Belli et Pacis, c. 21, s. 2–5; Heineccii Prælect. in Grot. h. t.; Burlemaqui, pt. 4, c. 3, s. 23–29, p. 258, 259, ed. 1763; Rutherf. Inst. b. 2, c. 9, s. 12.

[3] In re Washburn, 4 Johns. Ch. (N. Y.) 106; 1 Kent, Com. 36; Rex v. Hutchinson, 3 Keble, 785; Rex v. Kimberley, 2 Str. 848; East India Co. v. Campbell, 1 Ves. sen. 246; Mure v. Kaye, 4 Taunt. 34, per Heath, J.; Wynne's Eunomus, dialog. 3, 67; Lundy's Case, 2 Vent. 314; Rex v. Ball, 1 Amer. Jurist, 287.

[4] For this reference to Puffendorf's opinion, I must rely on Burlemaqui (pt. 4, c. 3, s. 23, 24), not having been able to find it in his treatise on the Law of Nations. The only reference to the point which I have met with in that work is in b. 8, c. 3, s. 23, 24.

jects. Scott v. Seymour, 1 Hurl. & C. 219, Wightman, J. speaking for himself only. See Phillips v. Eyre, L. R. 4 Q. B. 225, 240; L. R. 6 Q. B. 1, 28, 29.

It may be added that if the statutes of one state create, contrary to the common law, a personal liability on the part of a stockholder in a corporation for the debts of the company, and prescribe a remedy, as by bill in equity, the courts of another state will not give a different remedy, even if the very remedy itself could be enforced beyond the state which created it. Erickson v. Nesmith, 15 Gray (Mass.) 221; s. c. 4 Allen (Mass.) 233; 46 N. H. 371.

A provision of this sort may or may not be penal; if it is to be deemed penal, then it will not be enforced in other states. First National Bank v.

ries, no sovereign is obliged to punish the criminal who seeks shelter in his dominions, or to execute a sentence pronounced against his person or his property.[1] Lord Coke expressly maintains that the sovereign is not bound to surrender up fugitive criminals from other countries who have sought a shelter in his dominions.[2] Mr. Chief Justice Tilghman has adhered to the same doctrine in a very elaborate judgment.[3] The reasoning of Mr. Chief Justice Parker, in a leading case,[4] leads to a similar conclusion ; and it stands indirectly confirmed by the opinion of a majority of the judges of the Supreme Court of the United States in a very recent case of the deepest interest.[5] (a)

---

[1] Martens, Law of Nations, b. 3, c. 3, s. 23.   [2] 3 Co. Inst. 180.

[3] Commonwealth v. Deacon, 10 Serg. & R. (Pa.) 125; 3 Story, Const. s. 1802. See also Merlin, Répertoire, Souveraineté, s. 5, n. 5, 6, p. 379–382.

[4] Commonwealth v. Green, 17 Mass. 515, 540, 541, 546–548.

[5] Holmes v. Jennison, 14 Pet. 540. Mr. Justice Barbour maintained the same opinion in the case of Jose Ferreira dos Santos, 2 Brock. C. C. 493. Most of the reasoning on each side will be found very fully collected in the case of In re Washburn, 4 Johns. Ch. (N. Y.) 106; that of Commonwealth v. Deacon, 10 Serg. & R. (Pa.) 125; Holmes v. Jennison, 14 Pet. 540–598; and that of Rex v. Ball, 1 Amer. Jurist, 297. The latter case is the decision of Mr. Chief Justice Reid of Canada. See also 1 Amer. State Papers, 175; Commonwealth v. De Longchamps, 1 Dall. 111, 115; United States v. Davis, 2 Sumner, 482, 486. The subject respecting the restitution by our government or extradition of fugitives from justice from a foreign country has been brought at various times before our government. The various cases, and the opinions of the law officers, will be found collected in the executive documents, House of Rep. No. 199, 26th Congress, 1st Session, 1840; Report of Secretary of State, of May, 1840. Mr. Wirt, in his able opinions as Attorney-General, denies the right and duty.

Price, 33 Md. 487. The great difficulty is in determining whether the statute is of a penal nature. See the case just cited, which contains a review of the authorities.

(a) The question of surrendering fugitives from justice from the provinces bordering upon the different American states is one that for many years, while no treaty powers existed upon the subject, became of the greatest importance. It was at first attempted to induce the national government to act in the matter. But this it uniformly declined to do. It therefore became matter of mere discretion between the executives of the conterminous states, to be settled in each particular instance according to circumstances. It was never supposed, until the decision in the case of Holmes, that the general government, while declining to act of itself, and while no legislative provisions upon the subject existed whereby it was required to act, or could afford any adequate redress, would presume to interpose any obstacle in the way of the states disposing of such escaped offenders in any way they might deem proper. But while all this was conceded by the Supreme Court at Washington, and while it was conceded that it was entirely competent for the states, under their general powers, to regulate their own police, to ' remove from their territory every description of offenders who in the judgment of the legislature are dangerous to the peace of the state,' — it seemed to the government that the fact of expelling a murderer or robber, in such a direction and in such a manner as to secure his apprehension and punishment in the province from which he escaped, and where he had been guilty of the offence, amounted to ' entering into an agreement or compact with a foreign power.' It is certain that this practice, which existed for many years by a kind of courtesy between the governors of the conterminous provinces and states, was never supposed to infringe upon this or any other provision of the United States constitution, or to interfere in any degree with the international relations of the two countries, until after the decisions in the case of Holmes. Since that the question has been regarded as one exclusively under the control of the national sovereignty.

CHAPTER XVII.

EVIDENCE AND PROOFS.

629. *Competency of Witnesses.* — *Proof of Writings.* — We come, in the last place, to the consideration of the operation of foreign laws in relation to evidence and proofs. And here, independently of other more complicated questions, two of a very general nature may arise. In the first place, what rule is to prevail as to the competency or incompetency of witnesses? Is the rule of the law of the country where the transaction, to which the suit relates, had its origin, to govern, or the law of the country where the suit is brought? In the next place, what is the rule which is to prevail in the proof of written instruments? In other words, in what manner are contracts, instruments, or other acts made or done in other countries to be proved? Is it sufficient to prove them in the manner and by the solemnities and proofs which are deemed sufficient by the law of the place where the contracts, instruments, or other acts were executed? Or it is necessary to prove them in the manner and according to the law of the place where the action or other judicial proceeding is instituted?

630. *Instances.* — Various cases may be put to illustrate these questions. A contract or other instrument is executed and recorded before a notary public in a foreign country, in which by law a copy of the contract or other instrument certified by him is sufficient to establish its existence and genuineness; would that certificate be admissible in the courts of common law of England or America to establish the same facts?[1] Again, persons who are interested, and even parties in the very suit, are in some foreign countries admissible witnesses to prove contracts, instruments, and other acts, material to the merits of the suit; would they be admissible as witnesses in suits brought in the

---

[1] See Mascardus, de Probat. vol. 2, conclus. 927, n. 4–8, p. 336 (455. ed. 1781).

courts of common law in England and America to prove the like facts in relation to contracts, instruments, or other acts, made or done in such foreign countries, material to the suit? These are questions more easily put than satisfactorily answered upon principles of international jurisprudence.

630 *a. Presumptions.* — Similar considerations may arise in respect to the rules as to presumptions de facto and de jure, which may be different in different countries. Thus for example the title to movable property may depend upon the question of survivorship of one of two persons, who both died under the like circumstances; as for example on board a ship which foundered at sea, or was totally lost with all her crew by shipwreck. Now different countries may, and probably do, adopt different presumptions as to the survivorship in such calamitous circumstances, founded upon considerations of the age, or sex, or other natural or even artificial grounds of belief or presumption.[1] What rule, then, is to be adopted? The law of the place of domicil of the parties, or the law of the forum where the suit is instituted? On one occasion, when a question of this very nature was before him, a late learned judge, Sir William Grant, said: 'There are many instances in which principles of law have been adopted from the civilians by our English courts of justice; but none, that I know of, in which they have adopted presumptions of fact from the rules of the civil law.'[2]

630 *b. Immovables. — Testaments of Movables.* — There are certain rules of evidence which may be affirmed to be generally, if not universally, recognized. Thus in relation to immovable property, inasmuch as the rights and titles thereto are generally admitted to be governed by the law of the situs, and as suits and controversies touching the same ex directo properly belong to the forum of the situs, and not elsewhere, it would seem a just and natural, if not an irresistible, conclusion, that the law of evidence of the situs touching such rights, titles, suits, and controversies must and ought exclusively to govern in all such cases.[3] So in cases relating to the due execution of wills and testaments

---

[1] See Fearne's Posthum. Works, 38; The Case of Gen. Stanwix and Daughter; Code Civil of France, art. 720–722; 4 Burge, Col. & For. Law, pt. 1, c. 3, s. 5, p. 152, 153.

[2] Mason v. Mason, 1 Meriv. 308, 312.

[3] See Tulloch v. Hartley, 1 Y. & C. Ch. 114, 115.

of immovables, the proofs must and ought to be according to the law of the situs. So in respect to the due execution of wills and testaments of movables, as they are governed by the law of the domicil of the testator, the proofs must and ought to be according to the law of his domicil. By the present law of England, a will or testament of movable property, in order to be valid, must be executed in the presence of two witnesses. If, then, an Englishman, domiciled in England, should make his will in England, in the presence of one witness only, that will could not be admitted to proof in Scotland to govern movable property situate there.[1] The like rule would apply to a case where the will was executed in the presence of two witnesses, both or either of whom were incompetent by the law of England, although competent by the law of Scotland.

631. *Essentials of Contracts.* — Similar principles may well be applied to many other cases. There are certain formalities of proof which are required by the laws of foreign countries in regard to contracts, instruments, and other acts, which are indispensable to their validity there; and these are therefore held to be of universal obligation, and must be duly proved in every foreign tribunal in which they are in litigation, before any right can be founded on them.[2] An illustration of this doctrine may be drawn from the known rule of the common law, that a bill of exchange upon its dishonor must be protested before a notary; and if not proved to be so protested, no remedy can be had against the drawer or indorsers.[3] Another illustration may be drawn from the registration of deeds and other instruments which cannot be given in evidence unless proved to be duly registered according to the lex loci rei sitæ. Another illustration may be drawn from cases of contract under the statute of frauds, which must be in writing, and must state a good consideration, in order to be valid in point of legal obligation or evidence.[4] Another illustration may be drawn from the known doctrine as to stamps, by which it is held that no instrument can be given in evidence unless it is properly stamped.[5] In all these cases the proper proofs must

---

[1] Yates v. Thomson, 3 Cl. & F. 544, 576, 577.

[2] See Trasher v. Everhart, 3 Gill & J. (Md.) 234, 242; ante, s. 260–263.

[3] See Bryden v. Taylor, 2 Harr. & J. (Md.) 396; ante, s. 260 a, 360, 361; Wilcox v. Hunt, 13 Pet. 878.

[4] Ante, s. 262, 262 a.   [5] Ante, s. 260.

doubtless be given in conformity with the local law.[1] And if the proofs are given in the mode which the local law requires, there is some difficulty in asserting that such proofs ought not to be deemed everywhere a full authentication of the instrument.[2]

632. *Foreign Jurists.* — Boullenois divides the formalities of acts into several classes : those which are required before the act (quæ requiruntur ante factum) ; those which are required at the time of the act (quæ requiruntur in facto) ; and those which are required afterwards (quæ requiruntur ex post facto).[3] But a more important distinction in his distribution is of the formalities at the time of the act, which he denominates the formalities of proof (formalités probantes), and those which are substantial and intrinsic formalities.[4] Among the former he includes those which respect the number of witnesses who are to witness the execution of the act, their age and quality and residence, and the date and place of the act. And here he holds that, as to the formalities of proof, the maxim applies : ' Solemnitates testimoniales non sunt in potestate contrahentium, sed in potestate juris.[5] Solemnitates sumendæ sunt ex consuetudine loci, in quo res et actus geritur.'[6]

632 a. Mascardus holds a similar opinion ; and says that an act executed before a notary in any place, if duly executed according to the law of that place, and valid as a notarial act, ought to be held of the same obligation and validity in every other place. ' Unde jus probationis, ortum a principio, non tollitur mutatione loci.'[7] Paul Voet appears to entertain a different opinion ; and he puts the case, whether, if an instrument were executed in one place before a notary, who by the lex loci is competent for that purpose, the validity or force of that instrument would extend to another place where the notary would be deemed incompetent, so that he could not there give public authenticity to the instrument. ' Quid si tamen in uno loco factum sit instrumentum coram notario, qui ibidem est habilis, an extendetur vis illius instrumenti ad alium locum, ubi censetur inhabilis, sic ut

---

[1] Ante, s. 260, 260 a, 360, 361, 363–373.
[2] See Ersk. Inst. b. 3, tit. 2, s. 39, 40.   [3] 1 Boullenois, obs. 23, p. 491.
[4] Id. p. 492, 498, 506, &c.   [5] Id. p. 492, 493; ante, s. 260.
[6] Ibid.
[7] Mascard. de Probat. Conclus. 927, tom. 2, p. 336, 337 (454, 455, ed. 1731), n. 4–14; ante, s. 260 a.

publicum ibidem nequeat facere instrumentum.'[1]   After giving
the opinions of several jurists in the affirmative, he proceeds to
give his own to this effect; that it is not so much a question of
solemnities as of the efficacy of proof, which, although it may
be sufficient in one place, may not be so everywhere; and that
the tribunal of one country cannot give such validity and force
to any instrument as that it shall have operation elsewhere.[2]

633. Paul Voet also in another place, speaking upon the subject of the operation of the lex fori, as to the modes of proceeding in suits, uses the following language.   ' Si de probationibus,
et quidem testibus; sic eas adhibebit, sic examinabit hosce,
prout exigit forum judicis, ubi producuntur.   Si de instrumentis;
sic exhibenda, sic edenda, ut fert loci statutum, ubi exhibentur,
vel eduntur.'[3]   The generality of these expressions must lead
us to the conclusion that he was of opinion that the modes of
proof and the law of evidence of the lex fori ought to regulate the proceedings in all suits, whether these suits arose from
foreign contracts, or instruments, or other acts, or not.   But perhaps he may have intended to give them a more limited application.[4]

[1] P. Voet, de Stat. s. 10, c. 1, n. 11, p. 287, 288, ed. 1715; Id. p. 347, ed.
1661.

[2] Ibid.   His language is: Quid si tamen in uno loco factum sit instrumentum coram notario, qui ibidem est habilis, an extendetur vis illius instrumenti,
ad alium locum, ubi censetur inhabilis, sic ut publicum ibidem nequeat facere
instrumentum?   Sunt qui id adfirmant.   Quasi loci consuetudo, dans robur
scripturæ, etiam obtineat extra territorium.   Sunt qui id ideo adfirmant, quod
non tam de habilitate et inhabilitate notarii laboremus, quam de solemnibus.
Quod si verum foret, res extra dubitationis aleam esset collocata.   Verum, ut
quod res est dicam existumem hic agi, non tam de solemnibus, quam probandi
efficacia; quæ licet in uno loco sufficiens, non tamen ubique locorum; quod
judex unius territorii nequeat vires tribuere instrumento, ut alibi quid operetur.   Hinc etiam mandatum ad lites, coram notario et testibus hic sufficienter
factum, non tamen erit validum in Geldriæ partibus, ubi notarii non admittun-
tur, ut coram lege loci, hic confectum esse oporteat, quo in Geldria sortiatur
effectum.   Quemadmodum enim personam non subditam, non potest quis alibi
inhabilitare; ita nec personam subditam potest alibi facere habilem.

[3] P. Voet, de Stat. s. 10, c. 1, n. 9, 10, p. 287, ed. 1715; Id. p. 347, ed. 1661.

[4] Erskine, in his Institutes, says that in suits in Scotland with foreigners
upon obligations made in a foreign country, they may prove payment or extinguishment lege loci.   If for instance the law of the foreign country allows
the payment of a debt constituted by writing to be proved by witnesses, that
manner of proof will also be allowed by the Scottish courts as sufficient for
extinguishing such debt, although by the Scottish law obligations formed
by writing are not extinguishable by parol evidence.   Ersk. Inst. c. 3, tit. 5,

634. Bouhier states a case where a suit was brought in France by an Englishman against another person for money supposed to be lent by him to the latter; and he offered proof thereof by witnesses. It was objected that, by the Ordinance of Moulins (art. 54), such parol proof was inadmissible. But the court admitted it upon the ground that the law of England, where the contract was made, admitted such parol proof, and therefore it was admissible in a controversy on the contract in France. Bouhier holds the decision to be correct, if the contract was made, as he supposes it to have been, in England.[1]

634 *a. General Principles.* — Upon this subject it is not perhaps possible to lay down any rules which ought to be, or even which can be, applied to all cases of evidence. Generally speaking, it seems true that neither the lex loci contractus nor the lex loci domicilii is applicable to the course of procedure; but the course of procedure ought to be according to the law of the forum where the suit is instituted.[2] (*a*) And perhaps it may

---

s. 7. This seems a mixed case of the law of the place governing as to the discharge of contracts, and also of the mode of proof of the discharge.

[1] 1 Bouhier, Cout. de Bourg. c. 21, s. 205, p. 415. See also Strykius, tom. 2, diss. 1, c. 3, s. 18–25, p. 21, 27.

[2] See Yates *v.* Thomson, 3 Cl. & F. 577, 580; Don *v.* Lippmann, 5 Cl. & F. 1, 14–16.

(*a*) See Bain *v.* Whitehaven R. Co., 3 H. L. C. 1, 19; Downer *v.* Chesebrough, 36 Conn. 39; Fant *v.* Miller, 17 Gratt. (Va.) 47; Bristow *v.* Sequeville, 5 Ex. 275. The courts of one country are not bound to pursue the laws of another country having sole reference to the mode of giving a remedy in a particular case. Gott *v.* Dinsmore, 111 Mass. 45. Thus a foreign statute authorized the formation of joint-stock companies without conferring the immunities of corporations upon them, and provided that suits against them should be prosecuted in the first instance against the company, and that only after judgment and return of execution unsatisfied against the same should suits be brought against the members. But this was treated as a matter of local law only; and the court refused to be bound by it. Gott *v.* Dinsmore, supra.

The important distinction between facts and the evidence by which facts are proved is enforced in a recent English case. The Gaetano, 7 P. D. 137. This was an action on a bottomry bond, in which the question arose whether the master of an Italian ship, who had borrowed money in Fayal on the credit of the ship and cargo to make repairs, ought first to have communicated with the English owners of the cargo. Brett, L.J., said: 'Now it is alleged that this rule [the English rule exempting the owners from liability because of the master's failure to communicate with them] must bind the plaintiffs, although the ship is an Italian ship, because it was said that the matter to be proved was whether there was a necessity which gave the

be stated, as a general truth, that the admission of evidence and the rules of evidence are rather matters of procedure than matters attaching to the rights and titles of parties under contracts, deeds, and other instruments; and therefore they are to be governed by the law of the country where the court sits. But, then (as has been well observed by an eminent judge), in all questions of international jurisprudence it is easy to say how things are here and there, when there is very great difference be-

captain a right to hypothecate the cargo in this way, and that, inasmuch as that is a matter of procedure, it is to be governed according to the law of the forum. That raises the question whether this is a matter of procedure. It is said it is, because it is a matter of evidence. Now the manner of proving the facts is matter of evidence, and, to my mind, is matter of procedure; but facts to be proved are not matters of procedure; they are the matter with which procedure has to deal.'

An illustration may be seen in the case of Hoadley v. Northern Transp. Co., 115 Mass. 304. A contract for the shipment of goods had been made in Illinois with the defendants as common carriers, who gave the plaintiff shipper a bill of lading containing an exemption clause, within which the loss occurred. By the law of Illinois the clause referred to was without force unless there was express evidence of the shipper's assent to it; but the suit was brought in Massachusetts, where the acceptance of the bill of lading is itself sufficient evidence of assent. The real question was whether the plaintiff had assented; and the mode of proof was of course to be determined by the lex fori. The result was to receive the bill of lading, without requiring the express evidence prescribed by the law of Illinois. On the other hand, an incorrect decision appears to have been made, though the result was not affected, in the similar case of Michigan Cent. R. Co. v. Boyd, 91 Ill. 268.

In this connection should be noticed the language of Lord Brougham, in Bain v. Whitehaven Ry. Co., 3 H. L. C. 1, 19, where he says: 'Whether a witness is competent or not, whether a certain matter requires to be proved by writing or not, whether certain evidence proves a certain fact or not, that is to be determined by the law of the country where the question arises.' See also Yates v. Thompson, 3 Cl. & F. 544. Taking this to be correct, the case of Koster v. Merritt, 32 Conn. 246, appears to have been wrongly decided. There the law of New York was applied to a sale made in that State, to wit, that retention of possession by the vendor, with certain other facts, was not conclusive of fraud, as it would have been by the lex fori. The case of Dunn v. Welsh, 62 Ga. 241, must also be considered as wrong. In that case parol evidence to explain a blank indorsement was excluded, on the ground that it would not have been admissible where the indorsement was made, though such evidence was admissible lege fori.

If a foreign document would be void in the country in which it was executed for a want of certain formalities, as for the want of a stamp, it will be void everywhere else; but if it be only declared inadmissible in evidence, it may still be received in other countries if proper according to the lex fori. Fant v. Miller, 17 Gratt. (Va.) 47; Bristow v. Sequeville, 5 Ex. 275; Alves v. Hodgson, 7 T. R. 241.

tween the points; but when we come to the confines, and when
one province runs into the other, then arises the difficulty, and
then we get inter apices juris.[1] There may be cases which at

[1] Lord Brougham, in Yates v. Thomson, 3 Cl. & F. 577, 580. Lord
Brougham on this occasion said (it being a case where a question arose in
Scotland upon the interpretation of a will made in England): 'It is on all
hands admitted that the whole distribution of Mr. Yates's personal estate
must be governed by the law of England, where he had his domicil through life,
and at the time of his decease, and at the dates of all the instruments executed by him. Had he died intestate, the English statute of distributions,
and not the Scotch law of succession in movables, would have regulated the
whole course of the administration. His written declarations must therefore
be taken with respect to the English law. I think it follows from hence, that
those declarations of intention touching that property must be construed as
we should construe them here by our principles of legal interpretation. Great
embarrassment may no doubt arise from calling upon a Scotch court to apply
the principles of English law to such questions, many of those principles being
among the most nice and difficult known in our jurisprudence. The Court of Session may for example be required to decide whether an executory devise is void
as being too remote, and to apply, for the purpose of ascertaining that question,
the criterion of the gift passing or not passing what would be an estate in the
realty, although in the language of Scotch law there is no such expression as
executory devise, and within the knowledge of Scotch lawyers no such thing
as an executory estate tail. Nevertheless this is a difficulty which must of
necessity be grappled with, because in no other way can the English law be
applied to personal property situated locally within the jurisdiction of the
Scottish forum; and the rule which requires the law of the domicil to govern
succession to such property could in no other way be applied and followed out.
Nor am I aware that any distinction in this respect has ever been taken between testamentary succession and succession ab intestato, or that it has been
held, either here or in Scotland, that the court's right to regard the foreign
law was excluded, wherever a foreign instrument had been executed. It is
therefore my opinion that in this, as in other cases of the like description, the
Scotch court must inquire of the foreign law as a matter of fact, and examine
such evidence as will show how in England such instruments would be dealt
with as to construction. I give this as my opinion upon principle, for
I am not aware of the question ever having received judicial determination
in either country. But here I think the importing of the foreign code
(sometimes incorrectly called the comitas) must stop. What evidence the
courts of another country would receive, and what reject, is a question into
which I cannot at all see the necessity of the courts of any one country entering.
Those principles which regulate the admission of evidence are the rules
by which the courts of every country guide themselves in all their inquiries.
The truth with respect to men's actions, which form the subject-matter
of their inquiry, is to be ascertained according to a certain definite course
of proceeding, and certain rules have established that in pursuing this investigation some things shall be heard from witnesses, others not listened to; some
instruments shall be inspected by the judge, others kept from his eye. This
must evidently be the same course, and governed by the same rules, whatever
be the subject-matter of investigation. Nor can it make any difference

once partake of the nature of the law of evidence and also of the substance of the weightier matters of international jurisprudence.[1] (a)

whether the facts concerning which the discussion arises happened at home or abroad; whether they related to a foreigner domiciled abroad, or a native living and dying at home. As well might it be contended that another mode of trial should be adopted, as that another law of evidence should be admitted in such cases. Who would argue that in a question like the present the Court of Session should try the point of fact by a jury according to the English procedure, or should follow the course of our depositions or interrogatories in courts of equity, because the testator was a domiciled Englishman, and because those methods of trial would be applied to his case were the question raised here? The answer is, that the question arises in the Court of Session, and must be dealt with by the rules which regulate inquiry there. Now the law of evidence is among the chief of these rules; nor let it be said that there is any inconsistency in applying the English rules of construction and the Scotch ones of evidence to the same matter, in investigating facts by one law and intention by another. The difference is manifest between the two inquiries; for a person's meaning can only be gathered from assuming that he intended to use words in the sense affixed to them by the law of the country he belonged to at the time of framing his instrument. Accordingly, where the question is, what a person intended by an instrument relating to the conveyance of real estate situated in a foreign country, and where the lex loci rei sitæ must govern, we decide upon his meaning by that law, and not by the law of the country where the deed was executed, because we consider him to have had that foreign law in his contemplation. The will of April, 1828, has not been admitted to probate here; it has not even been offered for proof, so that there is no sentence of any court of competent jurisdiction upon it either way. But in England it would never be received in evidence nor seen by any court; neither would it have been seen if it had been proved ever so formally. Our law holds the probate as the only evidence of a will of personalty, or of the appointment of executors, in short, of any disposition which a testator may make, unless it regards his real estate. Can it be said that the Scotch court is bound by this rule of evidence, which though founded upon views of convenience, and, for anything I know, well devised, is yet one which must be allowed to be exceedingly technical, and which would exclude from the view of the court a subsequent will clearly revoking the one admitted to probate? The English courts would never look at this will, although proof might be tendered that it had come to the knowledge of the party on the eve of the trial. A delay might be granted to enable him to obtain a revocation of the probate of the former will. It is absurd to contend that the Court of Session shall admit all this technicality of procedure into its course of judicature as often as a question arises upon the succession of a person domiciled in England. Again, there are certain rules just as strict, and many of them not less technical, governing the admission of parol evidence with us. Can it be contended that, as often as an English succession comes in question before the Scotch court, witnesses are to be admitted or rejected upon the practice of the English

---

[1] Yates v. Thomson, 3 Cl. & F. 577, 580.

(a) And see Pickering v. Fisk, 6 Vt. 108, Phelps, J.

685. *Competency of Witnesses.* — There are very few traces to be found in the reports of the common law, of any established doctrines on this subject. We have already seen, in regard to witnesses generally, that their competency is governed in common cases by the lex fori.[1] But suppose the only witness to a contract, written or verbal, was incompetent on account of inte-

courts; nay, that examination and cross-examination are to proceed upon those rules of our practice, supposing them to be (as they may possibly be) quite different from the Scotch rules? This would be manifestly a source of such inconvenience as no court ever could get over. Among other embarrassments equally inextricable there would be this, that a host of English lawyers must always be in attendance on the Scotch courts, ready to give evidence, at a moment's notice, of what the English rules of practice are touching the reception or refusal of testimony, and the manner of obtaining it; for those questions which, by the supposition, are questions of mere fact in the Scotch courts, must arise unexpectedly during each trial, and must be disposed of on the spot in order that the trial may proceed. The case which I should however put as quite decisive of this matter comes nearer than any other to the one at bar, and it may with equal advantage to the elucidation of the argument be put as arising both in an English and in a Scotch court. By our English rules of evidence no instrument proves itself unless it be thirty years old or is an office copy, authorized by law to be given by the proper officer, or is the London Gazette, or is by some special act made evidence, or is an original record of a court under its seal, or an exemplification under seal, which is quasi a record. By the Scotch law all instruments prepared and witnessed according to the provisions of the act of 1681 are probative writs, and may be given in evidence without any proof. Now suppose a will of personalty, or any other instrument relating to personal property, attested by two witnesses and executed in England according to the provisions of the Scotch act, as tendered in evidence before the Court of Session; it surely never will be contended that the learned judges, on being satisfied that the question relates to English personal succession, ought straightway to examine what is the English law of evidence, and to require the attendance of one or other of the subscribing witnesses where the instrument is admissible by the Scotch law as probative. Of this I can have no doubt. But suppose the question to arise in England, and that a deed is executed in Scotland according to the act of 1681 by one domiciled here, would any court here receive it as proving itself, being only a year old, without calling the attesting witnesses; it would have a strange effect to hear the circumstance of there being two subscribing witnesses to the instrument, which makes it prove itself in the Parliament House of Edinburgh, urged in Westminster Hall as the ground of its admission without any parol testimony. The court would inevitably answer, "two witnesses, — then because there are witnesses it cannot be admitted, but they must one or other of them be called to prove it." The very thing that makes the instrument prove itself in Scotland, makes it in England necessary to be proved by witnesses. I have therefore no doubt whatever that the rules of evidence form no part of the foreign law, according to which you are to proceed in disposing of English questions arising in Scotch courts.'

[1] Ante, s. 621–623.

rest by the common law, but competent by the law of the place of the contract; in a suit in a tribunal of the common law on the contract, ought his testimony to be rejected? Again, suppose that the books of account of merchants, which (as is well know)[1] are by the laws of some states admissible, and by those of other states inadmissible, as evidence, are offered in the forum of the latter to establish debts contracted in the former; ought they to be rejected?[2]

635 a. Cases, vice versa, may easily be put which will present questions quite as embarrassing. Thus for example let us suppose the case of a crime committed on board an American ship on the high seas by a white man, or upon a white man, and the principal witnesses of the offence are black men, either free or slaves; and suppose (as is or may be the fact) that in the slaveholding states black men are competent witnesses only in cases in which black men are parties, and not in cases where white men are parties; and that in the non-slaveholding states black men are in all cases competent witnesses. If the offender is apprehended and tried for that offence before a court of the United States in a slave-holding state, would the black men be witnesses or not? If not there, would they be witnesses in the case if the trial were in a non-slaveholding state? In other words, will the rules of evidence in such a case, in the courts of the United States, depend upon the rules of evidence in the state where the trial is had? If not, then what rules of evidence are to prevail? The answer in the present state of our law cannot be given with entire confidence as to its accuracy and universality of adoption.

635 b. *Remarks of Lord Brougham.* — Lord Brougham, in a recent case where the question was much considered, both as to the law of procedure and the rules of evidence on foreign contracts, sued in another country, used the following language: 'No one will contend, in terms, that the foreign rules of evidence should

---

[1] See Pothier on Oblig. pt. 4, c. 1, art, 2, s. 4, n. 719; Cogswell v. Dolliver, 2 Mass. 217; 1 Stark. Ev. pt. 2, s. 130, 131; Strykius, tom. 7, diss. 1, c. 4, s. 5.

[2] Upon this very point foreign jurists have delivered opposite opinions as appears from Hertius, who however abstains from giving any opinion on the subject. 1 Hertii Opera, de Collis. Leg. s. 4, n. 68, p. 152, ed. 1737; Id. p. 214, ed. 1716; 4 Burge, Col. & For. Law, pt. 2, c. 8, s. 5, p. 153. Paul Voet thinks they are to be deemed prima facie evidence, but not conclusive. P. Voet, de Stat. s. 5, c. 2, n. 9, p. 160, ed. 1715; Id. p. 183, ed. 1661.

guide us in such cases; and yet it is not so easy to avoid that principle in practice, if you once admit that, though the remedy is to be enforced in one country, it is to be enforced according to the laws which govern another country. Look to the rules of evidence, for example. In Scotland some instruments are probative; in England, until after the lapse of thirty years, they do not prove themselves. In some countries forty years are required for such a purpose; in others thirty are sufficient. How, then, is the law to be ascertained which is to govern the particular case? In one court there must be a previous issue of fact; in another there need be no such issue. In the latter, then, the case must be given up as a question of evidence. Then come to the law. The question whether a parol agreement is to be given up, or can be enforced, must be tried by the law of the country in which the law is set in motion to enforce the agreement. Again, whether payment is to be presumed or not must depend on the law of that country, and so must all questions of the admissibility of evidence, and that clearly brings us home to the question on the statute of limitations. Until the act of Lord Tenterden, a parol agreement or promise was sufficient to take the case out of the statute of limitations; but that has never been the case in Scotland. It is not contended here that the practice of England is applicable to Scotland, but these are illustrations of the inconvenience of applying one set of rules of law to an instrument which is to be enforced by a law of a different kind.' [1]

635 *c. Notarial Instruments.* — In many foreign countries original contracts, deeds, conveyances, and other solemn instruments are often written in the public books of notaries public, and executed and registered and kept there, and are not allowed to be given out to the parties; but certified copies only thereof are delivered to the parties, and these copies are deemed in such countries admissible evidence in all suits to establish and prove such original papers and documents. The question has arisen in England whether such copies, so certified, are admissible, either as original or as secondary evidence in suits pending in the English courts. It has been held that they are not, at least not without proof that they were made at the time of entering and registering the original paper, and in the presence of the parties, although

[1] Don *v.* Lippmann, 5 Cl. & F. 15, 17.

they were admissible in the country where the originals were executed. The ground of this decision seems to have been, that the rules of evidence of the foreign country were not to be followed, but the rules of evidence of England; and by the law of England copies of original documents were not admissible under such circumstances, unless proved by some witness who had compared them with the original as in common cases.[1] So upon the like ground it has been held that copies of a judgment of the Supreme Court of Jamaica, signed by the clerk thereof, are not admissible evidence in a suit in England, although such copies would be admissible in Jamaica.[2]

635 d. *Case in Louisiana.* — By the old law of Louisiana, in case the party formally disavowed his signature to an instrument, proof thereof was required to be made by experts.[3] In a case where a written paper or receipt was executed in the state of Mississippi, and a suit brought thereon in Louisiana, and the signature was disavowed, the question arose whether the proof of the signature in such a case was to be made by experts, or might be made by witnesses, as was the law of Mississippi. The court on that occasion said: ' In treating of the third and last question,' that is, the question now under consideration, ' it is proper to observe that we believe it to be admitted as a principle in all tribunals, that the lex loci, or law of the country where the contract is made, ought to govern in suits commenced in any other country on such contracts; and it does appear by a law of the partidas, that this principle extends even to the proof of the contract expressed in general terms, which might perhaps be applied to the mode of proving facts as well as to the amount of evidence necessary to their verification. But it is unnecessary to determine this point absolutely in the present case, because there is sufficient found in the determination of the first and second questions on which to decide against the opinion of the judge of the

---

[1] Brown v. Thornton, 6 A. & E. 185.

[2] Appleton v. Lord Braybrook, 6 M. & S. 34; Black v. Lord Braybrook, 6 M. & S. 39. In a recent case Vice-Chancellor Bruce held that a copy of a deed of real estate in Jamaica, taken from the registry in Jamaica, in which it is required to be recorded, was good evidence in chancery in England, in a suit where it was pertinent, although it was a copy of a copy, i.e., of the registered deed, because it would be admissible in evidence in Jamaica. Tulloch v. Hartley, 1 Y. & C. Ch. 114, 115.

[3] Code of Louisiana, 1809, art. 226.

District Court.'¹ From this language it would seem to have been the inclination of the court to admit the evidence.

636. *Testaments of Movables.* — In regard to wills of personal property made in a foreign country, it would seem to be almost a matter of necessity to admit the same evidence to establish their validity and authenticity abroad as would establish them in the domicil of the testator; for otherwise the general rule, that personal property shall pass everywhere by a will made according to the law of the place of the testator's domicil, might be sapped to its very foundation if the law of evidence in any country where such property was situate was not precisely the same as in the place of his domicil. And therefore parol evidence has been admitted in courts of common law to prove the manner in which the will is made and proved in the place of the testator's domicil in order to lay a suitable foundation to establish the will elsewhere.²

637. *Foreign Liens.* — Passing from this most embarrassing, and as yet in a great measure unsettled class of questions, let us consider in what manner courts of justice arrive at the knowledge of foreign laws. Are they to be judicially taken notice of? Or are they to be proved as matters of fact? The established doctrine now is, that no court takes judicial notice of the laws of a foreign country, but they must be proved as facts.³ (a)

¹ Clark v. Cochran, 8 Mart. (La.) 353, 361, 362. See also Wilcox v. Hunt, 13 Pet. 378.

² De Sobry v. De Laistre, 2 Harr. & J. (Md.) 191, 195. See Yates v. Thomson, 3 Cl. & F. 544, 574.

³ See Mostyn v. Fabrigas, Cowp. 175; Male v. Roberts, 3 Esp. 163; Douglas v. Brown, 2 Dow & C. 171; De Sobry v. De Laistre, 2 Harr. & J. (Md.) 193; Trasher v. Everhart, 3 Gill & J. (Md.) 234; Brackett v. Norton, 4 Conn. 517; Talbot v. Seeman, 1 Cranch, 38; Church v. Hubbart, 2 Cranch, 187, 236, 237; Andrews v. Herriott, 4 Cowen (N. Y.) 515, 516, note; Stark. Ev. pt. 2, s. 33; Id. s. 92; Id. pt. 4, p. 569; Consequa v. Willings. Pet. C. C. 229; Legg v. Legg, 8 Mass. 99; Hosford v. Nichols, 1 Paige (N. Y.) 220.

(a) *Presumption concerning Foreign Law.* — No principle in the law is more frequently affirmed than that stated in the text, that foreign laws are to be proved as facts. Whelan v. Kinsley, 26 Ohio St. 131; Evans v. Reynolds, 32 Ohio St. 163; Railway Co. v. Lewis, 33 Ohio St. 196; Niagara Bank v. Baker, 15 Ohio St. 68; Stanglein v. State, 17 Ohio St. 453; Smith v. Bartram, 11 Ohio St. 690; Champion v. Wilson, 64 Ga. 184; Roots v. Merriwether, 8 Bush (Ky.) 397; Syme v. Stewart, 17 La. An. 73; Pecquet v. Pecquet, Id. 204; Leake v. Bergen, 27 N. J. Eq. 360; Hull v. Augustine, 23 Wis. 383; Kline v. Baker, 99 Mass. 253; Murphy v. Collins, 121 Mass. 6; Meyer

638. *Function of Court and Jury.* — But it may be asked whether they are to be proved as facts to the jury, if the case is

v. McCabe, 73 Mo. 236; Charlotte *v.* Chouteau, 25 Mo. 405; Cubbedge *v.* Napier, 62 Ala. 518; Baltimore R. Co. *v.* Glenn, 28 Md. 287. The principle is a thoroughly sound one, and ought to have been applied in many cases where it was disregarded or overlooked. It should not of course be strictly applied in all cases. Presumption has a proper place within limits in regard to foreign laws. Thus it could not be necessary to give evidence that in a foreign country breach of contract, battery, conversion, or damage caused by fraud or negligence would give a right of action. See for example Whitford *v.* Panama R. Co., 23 N. Y. 465; Langdon *v.* Young, 33 Vt. 136; McDonald *v.* Mallory, 77 N. Y. 546; Leonard *v.* Columbia Nav. Co., 84 N. Y. 48; Smith *v.* Bull, 17 Wend. (N. Y.) 323; Lewis *v.* Woodfolk, 2 Baxter (Tenn.) 25. It could not be necessary to give evidence to support the right of recovery in England or in any of the states of the Union by the holder of a negotiable promissory note against an indorser who had been notified of the dishonor of the paper by the maker at its maturity, or on the other hand that there could be no recovery against the indorser without notice of such dishonor. So also between immediate parties to a promissory note, it may well be presumed that the foreign law would allow the defence of failure of consideration. Roots *v.* Merriwether, 8 Bush (Ky.) 397. So again it would be a reasonable presumption that protest of a promissory note would be unnecessary. Dunn *v.* Adams, 1 Ala. 527.

The presumption arises on grounds of probability, growing out of the fact that the law is known to be widespread and uniform. Nothing short of this should be sufficient to turn the burden of proof upon him who would deny the existence of such law. There is no ground in principle for raising presumption upon a single fact, declaring for instance that because a law exists in the state of the forum it will be presumed in the absence of proof to exist in another state or country, or (what is the same thing) that if evidence of the foreign law is not shown, the domestic law will be applied. And yet language to this effect is constantly used in the books. Monroe *v.* Douglass, 5 N. Y. 447; Savage *v.* O'Neil, 44 N.Y. 298; Chapin *v.* Dobson, 78 N. Y. 74; Harris *v.* White, 81 N. Y. 532; Hynes *v.* McDermott, 82 N. Y. 41; Chase *v.* Alliance Ins. Co., 9 Allen (Mass.) 311; Ely *v.* James, 123 Mass. 36; Rau *v.* Von Zedlitz, 132 Mass. 164, 170; Pauska *v.* Daus, 31 Tex. 67; Bonds *v.* Foster, 36 Tex. 68; Johnson *v.* Johnson, 30 Mo. 72; Desnoyer *v.* McDonald, 4 Minn. 515; Leake *v.* Bergen, 27 N. J. Eq. 360; Haden *v.* Ivey, 51 Ala. 381; Robinson *v.* Dauchy, 3 Barb. (N. Y.) 20; Syme *v.* Stewart, 17 La. An. 73; Smoot *v.* Russell, 1 Mart. N.S. (La.) 523; Allen *v.* Watson, 2 Hill (S. Car.) 319; Carpenter *v.* Grand Trunk Ry. Co., 72 Me. 388; Roots *v.* Merriwether, 8 Bush, 397; Hickman *v.* Alpaugh, 21 Cal. 225; Hill *v.* Grigsby, 32 Cal. 55; Norris *v.* Harris, 15 Cal. 226, 252; Bemis *v.* McKenzie, 13 Fla. 553; Flato *v.* Mulhall, 72 Mo. 522; Morrissey *v.* Wiggins Ferry Co., 47 Mo. 521; Lewis *v.* Woodfolk, 2 Baxter (Tenn.) 25; Shaw *v.* Wood, 8 Ind. 518; Blystone *v.* Burgett, 10 Ind. 28. The last two cases are overruled by Smith *v.* Muncie Bank, 29 Ind. 158. Many of these cases may have been correctly decided (some of them clearly were not), notwithstanding the form in which the rule of presumption is stated, for the law in question may have been uniform and general in other states or countries; but the presumption should have been

a trial at the common law, or as facts to the court? It would seem as facts to the latter; for all matters of law are properly

based on that fact, and not on the fact of its existence in the state of the forum. That alone could create no probability of its existence elsewhere. For a court to say that merely because a law prevails in New York (and not generally) it probably prevails in England, is to say what is not true; if it be not widespread and uniform, it is quite as probable that it does not prevail there.

This criticism will apply to cases (among others) in which it has been held on a question of interest growing out of a foreign contract that, in the absence of agreement or of evidence concerning the rate in the country of the contract, it will be presumed that the rate there is the same as that allowed in the country of the forum; for though allowance of interest is general enough, nothing is less uniform than rates thereof. The existence of such a presumption as that referred to has however often been declared. Leavenworth v. Brockway, 2 Hill (N. Y.) 201; Forsyth v. Baxter, 2 Scam. (Ill.) 9; Pauska v. Daus, 31 Tex. 67 (statute); Desnoyer v. McDonald, 4 Minn. 515; Cooper v. Reaney, Id. 528; Brown v. Gracey, Dowl. & R. N. P. 41, note. See Hall v. Kimball, 58 Ill. 58. But in none of these cases is there any satisfactory consideration of the subject. A contrary, and, it is conceived, correct, decision was rendered in Peacock v. Banks, Minor (Ala.) 387. Nothing was there said on the subject of presumption. The true rule also appears in Smith v. Muncie Bank, 29 Ind. 158; Engler v. Ellis, 16 Ind. 475; Buckinghouse v. Gregg, 19 Ind. 401; Greenwade v. Greenwade, 3 Dana (Ky.) 495. It may have been proper in the nisi prius case of Brown v. Gracey, supra, to declare that the law of Scotland as to interest would be treated as the same as that of England in the

absence of evidence; that rule may have been in keeping with the principle of presumption. (See however Male v. Roberts, 3 Esp. 163, where Lord Eldon refused to presume that the law of Scotland was the same as that of England in respect of a defence of infancy to an action for money paid to the defendant's use to obtain his release from imprisonment for debt.) But it is quite another thing to say that rates of interest in a sister state of the Union will be considered the same as at home unless evidence is adduced to the contrary. The difference between rates of interest in the eastern and the western states, for instance, is well known; and the rates in states near each other often vary.

It is no justification of presumption in favor of the domestic law in such cases that the domestic law must be applied because the court has no other on which to act, as was said in Allen v. Watson, 2 Hill, S. Car. 319; and see Harris v. Allnutt, 12 La. 465; Norris v. Harris, 15 Cal. 226; for that assumes that the court must act at all events. It is no more required of the court to act upon failure of proof of a fact of that kind than of any other. If the party on whom rests the burden of proof fails to produce satisfactory evidence concerning the rate of interest, he should not be allowed interest. The court cannot know what to award him, and it has no right to act in the dark more than in other cases. It is enough that judgment for the principal sum can be rendered; so far the plaintiff comes within proper presumption.

With regard to damages for breach of contract, the same principle should prevail; the plaintiff, in the absence of evidence of any rule of law upon the subject, may well call upon the jury or judge to give him reasonable damages,

referable to the court, and the object of the proof of foreign laws is to enable the court to instruct the jury what, in point of law,

not so much because that would be the rule in a case arising in the jurisdiction of the forum as because in all probability that would be the rule in the foreign state.

Indeed if the fact is not improbable in the particular case, it may safely be presumed that the common law prevails in another state, excepting states that were adopted into the Union with another system of law already in existence, as in the case of Florida, Louisiana, and Texas. Norris v. Harris, 15 Cal. 226, 252; Roethke v. Philip Best Brewing Co., 33 Mich. 340; Webber v. Donnelly, Id. 469; Winslow v. Brown, 7 R. I. 95; Stout v. Wood, 1 Blackf. 71; Titus v. Scantling, 4 Blackf. 89; Smith v. Peterson, 63 Ind. 243; Lichtenberger v. Graham, 50 Ind. 288; Trimble v. Trimble, 2 Ind. 76; Smith v. Muncie Bank, 29 Ind. 158; Johnson v. Chambers, 12 Ind. 102; Crake v. Crake, 18 Ind. 156; Southwestern R. Co. v. Webb, 48 Ala. 585; Brown v. Camden R. Co., 83 Penn. St. 316; Klinck v. Price, 4 W. Va. 4; McDougald v. Carey, 38 Ala. 320; Cubbedge v. Napier, 62 Ala. 518; Meyer v. McCabe, 73 Mo. 236; Carpenter v. Grand Trunk Ry. Co., 72 Me. 388. See Du Val v. Marshall, 30 Ark. 230.

Thus with regard to defamatory language it is presumed that the common law prevails in a sister state. Stout v. Ward, supra. So with regard to the validity of submitting differences to arbitration, whether oral or written, sealed or not sealed. Titus v. Scantling, supra. So also it is presumed, in absence of evidence, that the succession to a trust estate upon the death of the trustee of an express trust is governed in another state by the common-law rule. McDougald v. Cary, 38 Ala. 320. Also the like presumption concerning the liability of a common carrier for failing to deliver goods. Southwestern R. Co. v. Webb, 48 Ala. 585; Brown v. Camden R. Co., 83 Penn. St. 316. So of the effect of part payment by one joint debtor for his personal discharge merely. Winslow v. Brown, 7 R. I. 95. So of the right at common law to sell liquor. Roethke v. Philip Best Brewing Co., 33 Mich. 340; Webber v. Donnelly, Id. 469. And the law merchant is presumed to exist in another state. Dunn v. Adams, 1 Ala. 527. And this even in Louisiana, in a suit upon a foreign bill of exchange with regard to demand and protest. Donegan v. Wood, 49 Ala. 242. The law applied in these cases, it will be observed, is not the lex fori, but the general and uniform rule of the common law or the law merchant, presumably the true law because of probability.

But the presumption of the existence of the common law even in states where it has always had an existence should be taken within limits, as has already been intimated. It should be applied only when based on probability; it should never, it is conceived, be applied as it was in Alford v. Baker, 53 Ind. 279, where it was held that it must be presumed that the common law as it existed before the stat. of Anne, rather than the law merchant, prevailed in a sister state in a question of liability on a promissory note. Nor should it be applied where it is probable that it has been abolished, or rather where the presumption of its existence is not strong, as in the case of the common-law rule that a wife's personalty vests on marriage in her husband. Proof of the existence of that rule should clearly be required, though there is authority to the contrary. Smith v. Peterson, 63 Ind. 243; Lichtenberger v. Graham, 50 Ind. 288; Meyer v. McCabe, 73 Mo. 236. Pre-

is the result of the foreign law to be applied to the matters in controversy before them. The court are therefore to decide

sumption of the existence of the common law is not, it is conceived, an arbitrary rule of law, but like presumption in other cases; it should be raised if the facts make it reasonable, otherwise not.

It would seem doubtful also in principle whether a court could act where the common law to be applied was itself unsettled. But courts have in such cases assumed to determine the law to be applied. Crake v. Crake, 18 Ind. 156. And see Chase v. Alliance Ins. Co., 9 Allen, 311, where the doctrine of the English courts upon a question of a Scotch contract was rejected, though there was no clear evidence of the Scotch law. See also National Bank v. Green, 33 Iowa, 140.

In some cases the courts have gone a great length in refusing to yield to presumption. Thus in Thompson v. Ketcham, 8 Johns. (N .Y.) 189, Kent, C.J., speaking for the court in a suit upon a promissory note governed by the law of Jamaica, refused to presume that infancy would be a good defence to the action by that law; following Male v. Roberts, 3 Esp. 163, already referred to, where Lord Eldon refused to entertain a like presumption concerning the law of Scotland. It is not to be supposed that these cases would be followed on a question of the common law of England; though it should not be overlooked that the defence of infancy in some of its particulars is by no means agreed. In Gilbreath v. Bunce, 65 Mo. 349, it may be noticed, the court refused to receive evidence of a foreign law giving majority to one who by the lex fori would be an infant, — a doubtful decision.

On the other hand presumption has sometimes been raised that statutory law prevails in another state like that of the forum, or (what is much the same thing) that in the absence of evidence of the foreign law a domestic statute may be applied to the question in hand. Norris v. Harris, 15 Cal. 226, 252; Hickman v. Alpaugh, 21 Cal. 225; Hill v. Wilker, 41 Ga. 449. And see the doubts in McCulloch v. Norwood, 58 N. Y. 562; Harris v. White, 81 N. Y. 532; Wilcox Co. v. Green, 72 N. Y. 17. This view of presumption has however generally been repudiated. Thus no presumption is raised from the lex fori of the existence, in another state, of law authorizing actions for damage for the death of near kindred caused by negligence. McDonald v. Mallory, 77 N. Y. 546; Whitford v. Panama R. Co., 23 N. Y. 465; Leonard v. Columbia Nav. Co., 84 N. Y. 48. Nor will any presumption be raised of the existence in another state of usury or penal laws. Cutler v. Wright, 22 N. Y. 472; Leake v. Bergen, 27 N. J. Eq. 360; Campion v. Kille, 15 N. J. Eq. 476; Stark Bank v. Pottery Co., 34 Vt. 144; Flanagan v. Packard, 41 Vt. 561; Hull v. Augustine, 23 Wis. 383. Nor of the existence of statute making wagers on horse-racing illegal. Harris v. White, 81 N. Y. 532. And generally that presumption is not raised concerning the existence of statute law abroad, see Doe d. Holman v. Collins, 1 Ind. 24; Johnson v. Chambers, 12 Ind. 102; Ellis v. Maxson, 19 Mich. 186; Great Western Ry. Co. v. Miller, Id. 305; Kling v. Fries, 33 Mich. 275; Flato v. Mulhall, 72 Mo. 522; Murphy v. Collins, 121 Mass. 6; Abell v. Douglass, 4 Denio (N. Y.) 305.

But it appears to be too sweeping to deny presumption altogether in regard to foreign statutory law. The existence of the Sunday law may well be presumed in the various states. Hill v. Wilker, 41 Ga. 449. So it may properly be presumed that registration laws exist in all the states, that con-

what is the proper evidence of the laws of a foreign country; and, when evidence is given of those laws, the court are to judge of their applicability, when proved, to the case in hand.[1] (a)

[1] De Sobry *v.* De Laistre, 2 Harr. & J. (Md.) 193, 219. But see Brackett *v.* Norton, 4 Conn. 517. In Trasher *v.* Everhart, 3 Gill & J. (Md.) 234, 242, the court said: 'It is in general true that foreign laws are facts which are to be found by the jury. But this general rule is not applicable to a case in which foreign laws are introduced for the purpose of enabling the court to determine whether a written instrument is evidence. In such the evidence

veyances of land must be in writing, and that verbal leases of land for a period exceeding three years will not be enforced. And so of such other statutes and parts of statutes as are known to be sufficiently uniform and general; such perhaps as some of the fundamental principles of the statutes making void conveyances in fraud of debtors. See Hickman *v.* Alpaugh, 21 Cal. 225.

An exception in regard to the necessity of proving the foreign law is said to exist where that law was once the law of the forum, as in the case of a question arising in Louisiana of the law of Spain. Pecquet *v.* Pecquet, 17 La. An. 204, 227; Malpica *v.* McKown, 1 La. 254; Arayo *v.* Currell, Id. 532. In the two cases from 1 La. 'the law of the place of the contract (Mexico), which was the Spanish law, had been the prevailing law of Louisiana, and the court therefore had judicial knowledge of the law of Spain.' In Berluchaux *v.* Berluchaux, 7 La. 539, the court say: 'Although the Spanish law has no longer any force in the state of Louisiana since the repealing act of 1828, yet having been considered previously the law of this country, so far as it was not abrogated or altered by statutory enactments, we may still, without violation of the rule which requires foreign laws to be proved as facts, assume some knowledge of it.' According to this doctrine it would for example be proper to assume in West Virginia, in the absence of proof, that a statute re-enacted in that state from Virginia still prevailed in Virginia.

The same presumption indeed would probably arise with regard to a statute enacted in Michigan from the laws of New York. Perhaps it might also be presumed that a rule of the common law in West Virginia derived from Virginia still prevailed in the latter state. So too it may be presumed that a law of Massachusetts which prevailed before the separation of the state of Maine prevails still in Maine. See Ely *v.* James, 123 Mass. 36.

The objection to presumption arising from the domestic law has of course no application to the question of the construction to be put upon a foreign law actually proved. The best evidence of the meaning of such law is the construction put upon it by the courts of the foreign state. Niagara Bank *v.* Baker, 15 Ohio St. 68; Leonard *v.* Columbia Nav. Co., 84 N.Y. 48; Jessup *v.* Carnegie, 80 N. Y. 441; Hunt *v.* Hunt, 72 N. Y. 218; Grant *v.* Clay Coal Co., 80 Penn. St. 208; Stevenson *v.* Payne, 109 Mass. 378; Botanico Medical College *v.* Atchinson, 41 Miss. 188. See Ames *v.* McCamber, 124 Mass. 85. But see National Bank *v.* Green, 33 Iowa, 140. But if no such evidence is at hand, the domestic tribunal may well apply to it the construction which has already been applied in the state to the same language, unless indeed there was something special and peculiar in the circumstances of the domestic law. Smith *v.* Bartram, 11 Ohio St. 690; Niagara Bank *v.* Baker, supra; Hall *v.* Pillow, 31 Ark. 32.

(a) See Donegan *v.* Wood, 49 Ala.

689. *Proof of Foreign Laws.* — As to the manner of proof, this must vary according to circumstances. The general princi-

always goes in the first instance to the court, which, if the evidence be clear and uncontradicted, may and ought to decide what the foreign law is, and according to its determination on that subject admit or reject the instrument of writing as evidence to the jury. It is offered to the court to determine a question of law, — the admissibility or inadmissibility of certain evidence to the jury. It is true that if what the foreign law is be a matter of doubt, the court may decline deciding it, and may inform the jury that if they believe the foreign law, attempted to be proved, exists as alleged, then they ought to receive the instrument in evidence. On the contrary, if they should believe that such is not the foreign law, they should reject the instrument as evidence. Is not foreign law offered in all cases to instruct the court in matters of law material to the point in issue? Can the court properly leave it to the jury to find out what the law is, and apply it to the case? Lord Mansfield, in Mostyn v. Fabrigas, Cowp. 174, said: " The way of knowing foreign laws is by admitting them to be proved as facts; and the court must assist the jury in ascertaining what the law is. In the absence of other proof, the court will treat the foreign law as being like our law as to liabilities on contracts and interest." ' Leavenworth v. Brockway, 2 Hill (N. Y.) 201.

242; Cecil Bank v. Barry, 20 Md. 287; Kline v. Baker, 99 Mass. 253; Robinson v. Dauchy, 3 Barb. (N. Y.) 20. But when the evidence consists of the parol testimony of experts as to the existence or prevailing construction of a statute, or as to any point of unwritten law, the jury must determine what the foreign law is, as in the case of any controverted fact depending upon like testimony. Kline v. Baker, 99 Mass. 255; Holman v. King, 7 Met. (Mass.) 384; Dyer v. Smith, 12 Conn. 384; Moore v. Gwynn, 5 Ired. (N. C.) 187; Ingraham v. Hart, 11 Ohio, 255. But the qualification of the experts, and all questions of competency of evidence, must be passed upon by the court; and when the evidence admitted consists entirely of a written document, statute, or judicial opinion, the question of its construction and effect is for the court alone. Kline v. Baker, 99 Mass. 255; Church v. Hubbart, 2 Cranch, 187; Di Sora v. Phillipps, 10 H. L. C. 624; Bremer v. Freeman, 10 Moore, P. C. 306; People v. Lambert, 5 Mich. 349; State v. Jackson, 2 Dev. (N. C.) 563; Owen v. Boyle, 15 Me. 147. In a late English case (Di Sora v. Phillips 10 H. L. C. 624) before the House of Lords it was held that when a contract is made in a foreign country and in a foreign language, an English court, having to construe it, must first obtain a translation of the instrument; secondly, an explanation of the terms of art, if any, used in it; thirdly, evidence of the foreign law applicable to it; and fourthly, evidence of any peculiar rules of construction which may exist in that law; and must then itself interpret the instrument on ordinary principles of construction. And the construction must be a matter of judgment on the part of the judge; it is not a question of fact to be proved by the mouth of witnesses. United States v. McRae, L. R. 3 Ch. 79, 86. The construction of a contract is nothing more than the gathering of the intention of the parties to it from the words used. If the law applicable to the case has ascribed a peculiar meaning to particular words, the parties using them must be bound by that

ple is, that the best testimony or proof shall be produced which the nature of the thing admits of; or, in other words, that no testimony shall be received which presupposes better testimony behind, and attainable by the party who offers it. This rule applies to the proof of foreign laws, as well as of other facts. But to require proof of such laws by such a species of testimony as the institutions and usages of the foreign country do not admit of, would be unjust and unreasonable. In this, as in all other cases, no testimony is required, which can be shown to be unattainable.[1] (a)

640. *Written Laws.* — Generally speaking, authenticated copies of the written laws, or of other public instruments of a

---

[1] Church v. Hubbart, 2 Cranch, 237.

---

meaning; but if there is no established sense, the intention must be collected in the ordinary manner from the language employed; and therefore the meaning of a foreign instrument (cleared of the difficulty of technical terms) cannot be a fact to be proved; it is at the utmost merely a probable opinion of the witnesses as to the construction which would be likely to be put upon it by the foreign tribunal. And if a judge is implicitly to receive the opinion of the witnesses, or of the majority of them, they in fact perform his office, and construe the instrument for him. The office of construction of any written instrument, whether foreign or domestic, brought into controversy before an English tribunal, properly belongs to the judge. In the course of the trial in the Sussex Peerage Case, 11 Cl. & F. 115, Lord Brougham, speaking in the House of Lords to the question of the right of a particular witness (whose testimony concerning certain foreign law was offered) to look into a book of the law in testifying, said in approval that 'the House has not organs to know and to deal with the text of the foreign law, and therefore requires the assistance of a lawyer who knows how to interpret it.' It is not however to be inferred from this that the court has not the independent right to examine

the text of the foreign law itself, especially if skilled witnesses are not offered to speak to its terms or interpretation. See United States v. McRae, L. R. 3 Ch. 79, 86; Nelson v. Bridport, 8 Beav. 527; Lindo v. Belisario, 1 Hagg. Con. 216; Dalrymple v. Dalrymple, 2 Hagg. Con. 54; Bremer v. Freeman, 10 Moore, P. C. 306; Di Sora v. Phillipps, 10 H. L. Cas. 641. Lord Brougham's meaning simply is that upon a question of doubtful interpretation of foreign written law the testimony of skilled witnesses, when offered, should be received along with the text.

(a) See Isabella v. Pecot, 2 La. Ann. 391. The books of reports of another state are admissible evidence of the law. Ames v. McCamber, 124 Mass. 85. A witness appearing as an expert in foreign law may state the law without producing it in print. Or he may produce a copy of the statutes of the foreign state, referring to them to refresh his memory. Barrows v. Downs, 9 R.I. 446; Sussex Peerage Case, supra. The foreign law may be proved by any person, though not a lawyer or not having filled public office, who has been in a position to render it probable that he would make himself acquainted with it. American Ins. Co. v. Rosenagle, 77 Penn. St. 507.

foreign government, are expected to be produced. For it is not to be presumed that any civilized nation will refuse to give such copies, duly authenticated, which are usual and necessary for the purpose of administering justice in other countries. It cannot be presumed that an application to a foreign government to authenticate its own edict or law will be refused; but the fact of such a refusal must, if relied on, be proved. But if such refusal is proved, then inferior proofs may be admissible.[1] Where our own government has promulgated any foreign law or ordinance of a public nature as authentic, that may of itself be sufficient evidence of the actual existence and terms of such law or ordinance.[2]

641. *Usual Mode of Authentication.* — In general, foreign laws are required to be verified by the sanction of an oath, unless they can be verified by some other high authority, such as the law respects not less than it respects the oath of an individual.[3] The usual mode of authenticating foreign laws (as it is of authenticating foreign judgments) is by an exemplification of a copy under the great seal of a state; or by a copy proved to be a true copy by a witness, who has examined and compared it with the original; or by the certificate of an officer properly authorized by law to give the copy; which certificate must itself also be duly authenticated.[4] (a)

[1] Church v. Hubbart, 2 Cranch, 237, 238.
[2] Talbot v. Seeman, 1 Cranch, 39.
[3] Church v. Hubbart, 2 Cranch, 237; Brackett v. Norton, 4 Conn. 517; Hempstead v. Reed, 6 Conn. 480; Dyer v. Smith, 12 Conn. 384.
[4] Church v. Hubbart, 2 Cranch, 238; Packard v. Hill, 2 Wend. (N. Y.) 411; Lincoln v. Battelle, 6 Wend. (N. Y.) 475.

(a) In many American states, by express statutory enactment, printed copies of the statutes of any other state, purporting to be published by authority, are admitted as prima facie evidence of such laws. Maine Rev. Stat. c. 133, s. 47; Conn. Rev. Stat. c. 10, s. 131; Comparet v. Jernegan, 5 Blackf. (Ill.) 375. And in some states this practice prevails, even without the authority of a special statute (Emery v. Berry, 8 Foster (N. H.) 486, and cases cited; Barkman v. Hopkins, 6 English (Ark.) 157; Lord v. Staples, 3 Foster (N. H.) 449), while in others it has been held that, independent of such provision, foreign written laws can be proved only by an exemplification properly certified, and the printed statute-books of such state are not admissible. Packard v. Hill, 2 Wend. (N. Y.) 411; Chanoine v. Fowler, 3 Wend. (N. Y.) 173; Church v. Hubbart, 2 Cranch, 236; State v. Twitty, 2 Hawks (N. C.) 441; Bailey v. McDowell, 2 Harring. (Del.) 34; Van Buskirk v. Muloch, 3 Harrison (N. J.) 184; Brackett v. Norton, 4 Conn. 517;

·642. *Unwritten Laws.* — But foreign unwritten laws, customs, and usages may be proved, and indeed must ordinarily be proved, by parol evidence. The usual course is to make such proof by the testimony of competent witnesses, instructed in the laws, customs, and usages, under oath.[1] (*a*) Sometimes however certificates of persons in high authority have been allowed as evidence without other proof.[2] (*b*)

643. *Public Seal.* — It seems that the public seal of a foreign sovereign, affixed to a writing purporting to be a written edict or law or judgment, is of itself the highest evidence of its authority, and the courts of other countries will judicially take notice of such public seal, which is therefore considered as proving itself.[3] (*c*) But the seal of a foreign court does not prove

[1] Church *v.* Hubbart, 2 Cranch, 237; Dalrymple *v.* Dalrymple, 2 Hagg. Appx. p. 15-144; Brush *v.* Wilkins, 4 Johns. Ch. (N. Y.) 520; Mostyn *v.* Fabrigas, Cowp. 174.

[2] In re Dormoy, 3 Hagg. Ecc. 767, 769; Rex *v.* Picton, 30 Howell's State Trials, 515-573; The Diana, 1 Dods. 95, 101, 102.

[3] Lincoln *v.* Battelle, 6 Wend. (N. Y.) 475; Griswold *v.* Pitcairn, 2 Conn. 85; Church *v.* Hubbart, 2 Cranch, 238, 239; Anon., 7 Mod. 66; United States *v.* Johns, 4 Dall. 416; Appleton *v.* Lord Braybrook, 6 M. & S. 34; Black *v.* Lord Braybrook, 6 M. & S. 39.

Hempstead *v.* Reed, 6 Conn. 480. But in a case decided by the Supreme Court of the United States, a copy of the Civil Code of France, purporting to be printed at the royal press, Paris, and received in the course of our international exchange, with the indorsement 'Le Garde des Sceaux de France à la Cour Suprême des Etats Unis,' was held admissible as evidence of the law of France. Ennis *v.* Smith, 14 How. 400.

(*a*) See American Ins. Co. *v.* Rosenagle, 77 Penn. St. 507; Regina *v.* Povey, 14 Eng. Law & Eq. 549; Kenny *v.* Clarkson, 1 Johns. (N. Y.) 385, 394; Hosford *v.* Nichols, 1 Paige (N. Y.) 220; Isabella *v.* Pecot, 2 La. Ann. 391; De Bode's Case, 8 Q. B. 208. The knowledge required of the witness must, it seems, have been acquired by actual experience in the foreign country, and not by mere theoretical instruction in a foreign university. Bris-

tow *v.* Sequeville, 5 Exch. 275. But it is not indispensable, as we have seen (note (*a*) p. 870), that the witness himself should have been a practising lawyer, if he is possessed of sufficient information on the subject. American Ins. Co. *v.* Rosenagle, supra; Vander Donckt *v.* Thellusson, 8 C. B. 812; Hall *v.* Costello, 48 N. H. 176; Pickard *v.* Bailey, 26 N. H. 152.

(*b*) And it has been thought that the peculiar relation in which the American states stand to the common law of England might require some modification of the rule first above laid down. Carnegie *v.* Morrison, 2 Met. (Mass.) 404, Shaw, C.J. And in Louisiana it has been held that the courts of that state would not require proof of the common law, but would gather it from the most authentic books and treatises on that subject. Young *v.* Templeton, 4 La. Ann. 254.

(*c*) So in America the seal of one

itself, and therefore it must be established as such by competent testimony.[1] There is an exception to this rule in favor of courts of admiralty, which being courts of the law of nations, the courts of other countries will judicially take notice of their seal without positive proof of its authenticity.[2]

644. *Regulations in the United States as between the States.* — The mode by which the laws, records, and judgments of the different states composing the American Union are to be verified has been prescribed by congress, pursuant to an authority given in the constitution of the United States. It is therefore wholly unnecessary to dwell upon this subject, as these regulations are properly a part of our own municipal law, and do not strictly belong to a treatise on international law.[3] (a)

645. *Conclusion.* — And here these Commentaries on this interesting branch of public law are brought to a close. It will occur to the learned reader, upon a general survey of the subject, that many questions are still left in a distressing state of uncertainty as to the true principles which ought to regulate and decide them. Different nations entertain different doctrines and different usages in regard to them. The jurists of different countries hold opinions opposite to each other, as to some of the fundamental principles which ought to have a universal operation; and the jurists of the same nation are sometimes as ill

[1] Stark. Ev. pt. 2, s. 92; Delafield v. Hand, 3 Johns. (N. Y.) 310; De Sobry v. De Laistre, 2 Harr. & J. (Md.) 193; Henry v. Adey, 3 East, 221; Andrews v. Herriott, 4 Cowen (N. Y.) 526, note.

[2] See Yeaton v. Fry, 5 Cranch, 335; Thompson v. Stewart, 3 Conn. 171.

[3] See on this subject the act of congress of 26th of May, 1790, c. 11, and the act of congress of the 27th of March, 1804, c. 56; 3 Story Const. s. 1297–1307; Andrews v. Herriott, 4 Cowen (N. Y.) 526, 527, note.

state affixed to an act of the legislature proves itself, and imports absolute verity in the courts of another state; but such seal must be a seal valid at common law, and not merely an impression on paper, which in some states is made a valid seal for some purposes. Coit v. Millikin, 1 Denio (N. Y.) 376. And see Bank of Rochester v. Gray, 2 Hill (N. Y.) 227; Farmers' Bank v. Haight, 3 Hill (N. Y.) 493; Watson v. Walker, 3 Foster (N. H.) 471.

(a) But the acts of congress on this subject have been held not to apply to the United States courts; and therefore the records of a district court of the United States may be proved in a state court, simply by a copy under the seal of the court without further attestation. See Adams v. Way, 33 Conn. 419; Williams v. Wilkes, 14 Penn. St. 228.

agreed among themselves. Still however with all these deductions, it is manifest that many approximations have been already made towards the establishment of a general system of international jurisprudence, which shall elevate the policy, subserve the interests, and promote the common convenience of all nations. We may thus indulge the hope that at no distant period the comity of nations will be but another name for the justice of nations, and that the noble boast of the great Roman orator may be in some measure realized: 'Non erit alia lex Romæ, alia Athenis, alia nunc, alia posthac; sed et omnes gentes et omni tempore una lex, et sempiterna, et immortalis, continebit.'[1]

[1] Cicero, Fragm. de Repub.

www.ingramcontent.com/pod-product-compliance
Lightning Source LLC
Chambersburg PA
CBHW082138210326
41599CB00031B/6022